The *Sams Teach Yourself in 24 Hours* Series

Sams Teach Yourself in 24 Hours books provide quick and easy answers in a proven step-by-step approach that works for you. In just 24 ? hour or less, you will tackle every task you need to get the r? Let our experienced authors present the most accurate infor? get you reliable answers—fast!

G000128340

Windows Network Troubleshooting Cheat Sheet

TCP/IP Troubleshooting

COMMAND-LINE TOOLS

COMMAND	FLAG(S)	DESCRIPTION
arp	-a	Shows ARP entries in station's cache
	-d *IP*	Deletes *IP* address from ARP cache
ipconfig *flag*	/all	Shows Windows NT TCP/IP configuration
	/?	Displays help
	/release	Releases the IP address for the specified adapter
	/renew	Renews the IP address for the specified adapter
nbtstat *flag*		Displays protocol statistics and TCP/IP connections
	-a	Lists the remote machine's name table given its name
	-A	Lists the remote machine's name table given its IP address
	-c	Lists the remote name cache including the IP address
	-n	Lists the local NetBIOS names
	-r	Lists names resolved by broadcast and via WINS
	-R	Purges and reloads the remote cache name table
	-S	Lists sessions table with the destination IP address
	-s	Lists sessions table converting destination IP addresses to host names via the HOSTS file
netstat	-r	Shows routing table for this station
	-n	Shows output numerically (no host names or DNS)
	-a	Shows socket table for this station
	-e	Shows Ethernet statistics (Windows)

continued

CONTINUED

COMMAND	FLAG(S)	DESCRIPTION
ping flags host or IP		"Are you there?"
	-n	Number of times to Ping
	-l	Size of data in Ping packet
	-f	"Don't fragment" (useful for ruling out fragmentation problems)
route flag		Displays and manipulates the route table
	route print	Displays the route table
	route add	Adds a route
	route delete	Deletes a route
	route change	Modifies an existing route
telnet hostname socket number		Checks a TCP service to see if it's available (see the socket number table on this card to determine which socket represents which service)
tracert host or IP		Shows each router that a packet passes through to get to a destination
	-d	Don't resolve addresses to host names
	-h maximum_hops	Specifies the maximum number of hops to search for target
	-j host-list	Specifies loose source route along the host list
	-w timeout	Waits the number of milliseconds specified by timeout for each reply
winipcfg flag	/all	Shows Windows 9x TCP/IP configuration

COMMON TCP/IP SOCKET NUMBERS

SERVICE NAME	NUMBER	COMMENT
FTP	21	File Transfer Protocol
Telnet	23	Login service for UNIX, sometimes NT or Novell
SMTP	25	Internet-style server-to-server email
domain	53	DNS services (UDP and TCP)
gopher	70	Internet Gopher
http	80	Hypertext Transfer Protocol (the Web!)
pop2	109	Post Office Protocol version 2 (user email)
pop3	110	Post Office Protocol version 3 (user email)
nntp	119	Usenet news
netbios-ns	137	NetBIOS Name Service
netbios-dgm	138	NetBIOS "datagram" service
netbios-ssn	139	NetBIOS "session" service
imap	143	Interactive Mail Access Protocol(user email)
shell	514	"Rlogin" socket—UNIX or NT
printer	515	Line Printer Daemon—Network printing for UNIX
socks	1080	Socks proxy server (Socks 4 and Socks 5)

SAMS

Peter Kuo, PH.D.
John Pence

SAMS
Teach Yourself
Windows Networking
in 24 Hours

SAMS

A Division of Macmillan Computer Publishing
201 West 103rd St., Indianapolis, Indiana, 46290 USA

Trademarks

Warning and Disclaimer

EXECUTIVE EDITOR:
Christopher Will

DEVELOPMENT EDITOR:
Kate Shoup Welsh

MANAGING EDITOR:
Brice Gosnell

PROJECT EDITOR:
Lisa M. Lord

INDEXER:
Tina Trettin

TECHNICAL EDITORS:
Kackie Charles
Scott Humphries
Bill Bruns

PROOFREADERS:
Andrew Beaster
Louise Martin, BooksCraft, Inc.

LAYOUT TECHNICIANS:
Brian Borders
Marcia Deboy
Susan Geiselman

Overview

		Introduction	1
PART I		COVERING YOUR BASICS	**3**
Hour 1		Learning the Lingo	5
	2	Networking Basics	15
	3	Protocols	35
PART II		WINDOWS 98 NETWORKS	55
Hour 4		Direct Cable Connection Network	57
	5	Installing a Two-Node Peer-to-Peer Windows 98 Network	75
	6	Sharing Windows 98 Resources	91
	7	Installing a Multi-Node Windows 98 Network	105
	8	Accessing NetWare Resources from Windows 98	115
	9	Backing Up and Restoring Data on Windows 98	135
PART III		NT NETWORKS	147
Hour 10		NT Server Basics	149
	11	Sharing NT Resources	161
	12	NT Remote Access Service (RAS)	183
	13	Accessing NetWare Resources from NT	197
	14	Installing a Windows NT Server	213
	15	Managing NT Servers	223
	16	Backing Up and Restoring Data on NT	247
	17	Advanced NT Server Management	263
PART IV		BEYOND THE BASICS	**297**
Hour 18		DHCP	299
	19	Troubleshooting	311
	20	Connecting Your Windows 98 Desktop to the Internet	335
	21	Surfing Tools	373
	22	Connecting Your Network to the Internet	409

| 23 | Support Resources | 431 |
| 24 | Online Resources | 441 |

APPENDIXES

A	Glossary	447
B	Answers to Quiz Questions	469
	Index	477

Contents

NTRODUCTION   1

PART I COVERING YOUR BASICS   3

HOUR 1 LEARNING THE LINGO   5

What Is a Network? 6
    Peer-to-Peer Networking 6
    Client/Server Networking 6
LANs and WANs 8
Why Have a Network? 9
The Internet: A Really, Really, Big Network! 9
    Web Servers and Web Browsers 10
    Telnet 11
    FTP: File Transfer Protocol...12
Summary...13
Workshop 14
    Q&A 14
    Quiz 14

HOUR 2 NETWORKING BASICS   15

Network Architectures 15
    Ethernet 16
    Token Ring 17
Network Hardware 19
    NICs..19
    Cabling..20
    Hubs..24
    Repeaters 25
    Bridges..25
    Switches..27
    Routers..30
    MSAUs 31
Summary...32
Workshop 32
    Q&A 32
    Quiz 33

HOUR 3 PROTOCOLS   35

The OSI Model 36
NetBEUI 39

IPX/SPX 40

TCP/IP 41

    IP Addressing...42

    Default Gateway 46

    ARP: Address Resolution Protocol 47

    DHCP: Dynamic Host Configuration Protocol...............................48

    IP Utilities 50

Summary 52

Workshop 53

    Q&A 53

    Quiz 54

PART II WINDOWS 98 NETWORKS   **55**

    HOUR 4 DIRECT CABLE CONNECTION NETWORK   **57**

    Selecting Ports and Cables 58

        Different Types of Serial Ports 59

        Different Types of Parallel Ports 60

        Speed Comparison...61

        Null-Modem Serial Cable 62

        Parallel Cable..64

        Using Infrared Ports 65

    Common Configurations for Both Computers 65

    Configuring the Host Computer 68

    Configuring the Guest Computer 70

    Establishing a Connection 70

    Summary 72

    Workshop 72

        Q&A 72

        Quiz 73

    HOUR 5 INSTALLING A TWO-NODE PEER-TO-PEER WINDOWS 98 NETWORK   **75**

    Installing Network Hardware 76

        10Base2 Coaxial Cable 76

        Cross-Over 10BaseT Ethernet Cable 77

        Configuring the Network Adapter...78

    Installing and Configuring Client Software 79

    Adding a Protocol..80

        Protocol Configuration 82

    Selecting Your Primary Network Logon...87

    Identifying Your Computer 88

    Summary 89

    Workshop 89

Q&A 89
Quiz 89

HOUR 6 SHARING WINDOWS 98 RESOURCES   91

Sharing Resources...92
  Setting Up File and Print Sharing 92
  Setting Up Access Control 93
  Sharing Drives and Folders 94
  Sharing Printers 96
Accessing Shared Resources 97
  Logging on to the Network 97
  Using the Network Neighborhood 98
  Using the Universal Naming Convention Format..99
  Mapping a Network Drive...99
Troubleshooting Connectivity..101
  When in Doubt, Restart...101
  Is It Plugged In? 101
  Protocol Settings 101
  IP Protocol Configuration 102
Summary 103
Workshop 103
  Q&A 103
  Quiz 104

HOUR 7 INSTALLING A MULTI-NODE WINDOWS 98 NETWORK   105

Physical Topologies 106
  Bus Topology..106
  Star Topology 106
  Ring Topology 107
Ethernet Network Topology 107
  10Base2 107
  10Base5 108
  10BaseT 109
  The 3-4-5 Rule...109
Token Ring Network Topology 110
Let's Do the Twist! 111
Troubleshooting Common Issues 112
Summary..113
Workshop 113
  Q&A 113
  Quiz 113

HOUR 8 ACCESSING NETWARE RESOURCES FROM WINDOWS 98   115

Microsoft Client for NetWare Networks 116
  Configuring the Client..116
  Adding Novell Directory Services 117
Novell Client for Windows 95/98...117
  Installing the Novell Client 118
  Configuring the Novell Client...122
Accessing NetWare Resources 126
  Connecting to a NetWare Server...126
  Browsing a NetWare Network...128
  Mapping a Network Drive...129
  Network Printing 130
Summary 133
Workshop 133
  Q&A 133
  Quiz 134

HOUR 9 BACKING UP AND RESTORING DATA ON WINDOWS 98   135

Backup Strategy 136
  Full Backup 136
  Differential Backup 136
  Incremental Backup...137
  Implementing a Strategy 137
Selecting Appropriate Backup Devices 137
  Tape Drives 137
  Other Media...138
Using Microsoft Backup...138
  Using the Backup Wizard 139
  Using the Restore Wizard 142
Scheduling Backups 143
Other Backup Tools 144
Summary 145
Workshop 145
  Q&A 145
  Quiz 146

PART III NT NETWORKS   147

HOUR 10 NT SERVER BASICS   149

Workgroups...149
Domains 150
  Single Domain Model 152
  Single Master Domain Model 152
  Multiple Master Domain Model 153

Users and Groups 154
    User Accounts 154
    Groups 156
File Systems 156
Security 159
Summary 159
Workshop 160
    Q&A 160
    Quiz 160

HOUR 11 SHARING NT RESOURCES   **161**

Sharing Files and Folders 161
    Creating Shares 162
    Assigning Permissions to Shared Folders 164
    Assigning Permissions to NTFS Volumes..............................167
    Combining Shared Folder Permissions and NTFS Permissions 171
    Accessing Shared Folders 171
Network Printing..173
    Setting Up a Network Printer 174
    Printer Permissions 175
    Managing Network Printers 176
    Print Server Properties..177
    Printer Pooling..178
    Scheduling 179
Summary 180
Workshop 180
    Q&A 180
    Quiz 181

HOUR 12 NT REMOTE ACCESS SERVICE (RAS)   **183**

The Protocols 184
Installation..184
Configuration 187
Administration 189
Troubleshooting 191
The Other End: Dial-Up Networking 193
Summary..193
Workshop 194
    Q&A 194
    Quiz 195

HOUR 13 ACCESSING NETWARE RESOURCES FROM WINDOWS NT   **197**

    Microsoft's Client Service for NetWare 198
        Accessing Novell Directory Services 199
        Configuring the Client...199
    Novell Client for Windows NT...200
        Installing the Novell Client 201
        Configuring the Novell Client 205
    Accessing NetWare Resources 207
        Connecting to a NetWare Server..207
        Working with NetWare Volumes 209
        Using Windows Point and Print 211
    Summary 211
    Workshop 211
        Q&A 211
        Quiz 212

HOUR 14 INSTALLING A WINDOWS NT SERVER   **213**

    Hardware Requirements 214
        The HCL 215
    File System and Partitioning...215
    Installing NT Server 216
        Licensing Modes 217
        Server Types 218
    Installing Networking 218
        Alternative Installation Methods 219
    Removing NT 220
    Summary 220
    Workshop 221
        Q&A 221
        Quiz 222

HOUR 15 MANAGING NT SERVERS   **223**

    Service Packs 223
        Installing SP3..224
        Uninstalling SP3 226
    User Manager 227
        Defining the Account Policy 227
        Creating Accounts 229
        Managing Accounts 233
    Server Manager..234
    Event Viewer...236
        The Find Function 237
        The Filter View 238

The Network Dialog Box 239
Services..242
Promoting a BDC to PDC 243
Planned Changes to PDC Status 244
Unplanned Changes to PDC Status..244
Summary 245
Workshop 246
Q&A 246
Quiz 246

HOUR 16 BACKING UP AND RESTORING DATA ON WINDOWS NT   247

Windows NT Server Fault Tolerance 248
Disk Mirroring and Duplexing 248
RAID 5 248
Using Microsoft Windows NT Backup 249
Backing Up Files 250
Restoring Files..252
Automating Windows NT Backup 253
Backing Up and Restoring Windows NT Registry....................................254
Using Windows NT Backup 254
Using Registry Editor 255
Using Last Known Good Configuration 257
General Windows NT Backup Notes 257
Make Sure Registry Is Backed Up 257
Permissions and Rights Required 257
Backing Up Remote Windows NT Registry and Shares................................258
Disconnecting Users 258
LFN Support 258
NTFS Support 259
Third-Party Backup Tools for Windows NT...259
Summary 260
Workshop 260
Q&A 260
Quiz 261

HOUR 17 ADVANCED NT SERVER MANAGEMENT   263

Trust Relationships 263
Groups and Trust Relationships 264
Establishing One-Way Trust 265
Establishing Two-Way Trust 267
Trust Management...268

Auditing 270

  Setting the Audit Policy..270

  Auditing Files and Directories 271

  Auditing Printers 273

  Viewing the Log Files 274

  Managing the Log Files...276

Windows Internet Name Service (WINS) 277

  Installing WINS...279

  WINS Manager 280

  Backing Up the WINS Database...283

Disk Administration 283

  Partitions 284

  Stripe Sets 287

  Volume Sets 288

  Mirroring 288

  Stripe Set with Parity..290

  The Fault Tolerance Menu..291

  Boot.ini and ARC Paths 291

  Partition Numbering 293

  NT Boot Disk 294

Summary..294

Workshop 295

  Q&A 295

  Quiz 296

PART IV BEYOND THE BASICS   297

HOUR 18 DHCP   299

Installation and Configuration 300

Creating the Scope 301

  Scope Options 303

Client Reservations...306

Managing the DHCP Server...306

Summary..308

Workshop 309

  Q&A 309

  Quiz 310

HOUR 19 TROUBLESHOOTING   311

Browsing and Network Neighborhood.......................................311

  The Browse List 312

  Browsing Network Neighborhood 312

Utilities That Can Help..313
   The winipcfg Tool..314
   The ipconfig /all Command 315
   The ping Command...316
   NT Diagnostics 318
   Server Manager 319
   The nbtstat Command..320
   The tracert Command 321
   The route Command..322
   The arp Command 323
   Performance Monitor...324
   Task Manager 327
   Event Viewer and the Event Logs 328
Name Resolution...328
   The lmhosts File 330
   The hosts File 330
Network Monitor 330
Summary 332
Workshop 333
   Q&A 333
   Quiz 334

HOUR 20 CONNECTING YOUR WINDOWS 98 DESKTOP TO THE INTERNET   335

Overview...335
Selecting and Installing a Modem 336
   Modem Basics 337
   Modem Standards 337
   Installing a Modem 339
Choosing an Internet Service Provider....................................341
   What Is an ISP?...342
   ISP Features...342
   Alternatives to Dial-Up Connections 344
   Comparing ISPs...345
Dial-Up Networking 347
   Setting Up DUN 347
   Turning Off File and Print Sharing 355
   Connecting to the Internet..356
   Using the Internet Connection Wizard 358
   Troubleshooting DUN 365
Troubleshooting the ISP Connection 366
   Using a Different Dialer 367
   Using PING 367

Using Tracert 368
Using winipcfg 369
Summary 370
Workshop 370
Q&A 370
Quiz 371

HOUR 21 SURFING TOOLS   **373**

Browsers 374
Internet Explorer 374
Netscape Communicator 379
Others 381
Surfing the Net 382
Browsing the World Wide Web 382
Downloading Files with FTP 384
Accessing Remote Hosts with Telnet 387
Sending and Receiving Email 389
Email Protocols 389
Using Outlook Express 390
Other Email Clients 392
Newsgroups 393
Usenet Basics 394
Newsreaders 395
Configuring Your Newsreader 396
Reading, Replying, and Posting Messages to a Newsgroup 398
Net Security 401
Want a Cookie? 401
What's SSL? 402
Shopping on the Internet 403
Is Java Safe? 404
Is JavaScript Safe? 405
Summary 405
Workshop 406
Q&A 406
Quiz 407

HOUR 22 CONNECTING YOUR NETWORK TO THE INTERNET   **409**

What Do You Need? 410
Do You Need a Router? 410
Additional Equipment Required 411
IP Address Considerations 411
Internet Domain Name 413

    Other Required Services 416
    Desktop Configuration 417
  Security Concerns 419
    What's a Proxy Server? 419
    What's a Firewall? 420
    Virus Threats 422
  Usage Policy 423
  Speeding Up Web Access 424
    Proxy Caching 425
    Proxy Cache Hierarchies 427
    Web Server Acceleration 427
  Summary 429
  Workshop 429
    Q&A 429
    Quiz 430

HOUR 23 SUPPORT RESOURCES   431

  TechNet 432
    Purchasing TechNet 432
    Installing and Using TechNet 433
  The Resource Kit 436
  Summary 439
  Workshop 439
    Q&A 439
    Quiz 440

HOUR 24 ONLINE RESOURCES   441

  The World Wide Web 441
  Microsoft Newsgroups 443
  Mailing Lists 445
  Summary 446
  Workshop 446
    Q&A 446
    Quiz 446

APPENDIXES

APPENDIX A GLOSSARY   447

APPENDIX B ANSWERS TO QUIZ QUESTIONS   469

  Hour 1 469
  Hour 2 469
  Hour 3 470

Hour 4 470
Hour 5 470
Hour 6 471
Hour 7 471
Hour 8 471
Hour 9 471
Hour 10 472
Hour 11 472
Hour 12 472
Hour 13 473
Hour 14 473
Hour 15 473
Hour 16 474
Hour 17 474
Hour 18 474
Hour 19 475
Hour 20 475
Hour 21 475
Hour 22 476
Hour 23 476
Hour 24 476

INDEX   **477**

About the Authors

Peter Kuo, Ph.D., is president of DreamLAN Network Consulting Ltd., a Toronto-based firm. Peter's first introduction to networking was with DEC PDP machines while working on his M.Sc. His extensive networking experience stemmed from working with UNIX, the Internet, and LAN operating systems. Peter is the first Canadian Enterprise CNE (Certified Novell Engineer), one of the world's first Master CNEs and Master CNIs, and is the first Novell Certified Internet Professional (CIP) in the world. Furthermore, he is a Certified Network Expert (CNX Ethernet and Token Ring). In addition to presenting seminars at conferences, such as NetWorld+InterOp and NetWare Users International (NUI), Peter has authored, co-authored, and contributed to many computer books from Macmillan Publishing. When not working on books and articles, Peter is a volunteer Novell Support Connection SysOp on Novell's NSC Web Forum, helping Novell provide support to a worldwide audience on many advanced subject areas, such as connectivity, network management, NetWare 4 and NetWare 5, and Novell Directory Services. You can reach him at peter@dreamlan.com.

John Pence is President of MagicNet Network Consulting and the Network Engineer/Analyst at a major regional newspaper. He has over a decade of experience networking computers and has worked with numerous operating systems. Before becoming involved with networking computers, John was a cryptographics technician in the United States Coast Guard, which led him into electronics and ultimately networks. John is a CNE and former Novell Support Connection SysOp. His specialty is using protocol analyzers to troubleshoot the really tough ones by looking at what's happening on the wire. John can be reached via email at jpence@jpence.com.

Dedication

I dedicate this book to my grandparents.

—Peter Kuo

I dedicate this book to my friend and partner, Peter Kuo, from whom I have garnered an immense amount of knowledge, motivation, and inspiration. And to George and Grace, the two reasons I do anything at all.

—John Pence

Acknowledgments

This book was written and developed in a remarkably short time. We acknowledge with great pleasure the confidence of our Executive Editor Chris Will, who gave us this *Mission: Impossible*. A great deal of thanks goes to Kate Welsh, our Development Editor. Without her hounding, nagging, and hard work, we'd never have met the schedule to bring this book to you. Special thanks also go to our Tech Editors, Kackie Charles, Scott Humphries, and Bill Bruns, for a wonderful job.

Peter would like to thank SAS for calling him a "glutton for punishment" and for not telling him "Just Say No" until after the book was done! What Peter appreciated most during this particular project was his parents' stocking the fridge with brain food and keeping the coffeepot filled! Peter also thanks John for not telling him how short the time frame was when John struck the deal with Chris.

John would like to thank Peter for not telling him in advance what it takes to write a book, especially when doing the writing in a remarkably short time! It must be true that fools rush in where angels fear to tread. Tom and Becky, thanks for your patience!

Tell Us What You Think!

As the reader of this book, *you* are our most important critic and commentator. We value your opinion and want to know what we're doing right, what we could do better, what areas you'd like to see us publish in, and any other words of wisdom you're willing to pass our way.

As the Executive Editor for the Operating Systems team at Macmillan Computer Publishing, I welcome your comments. You can fax, email, or write me directly to let me know what you did or didn't like about this book—as well as what we can do to make our books stronger.

Please note that I cannot help you with technical problems related to the topic of this book, and that because of the high volume of mail I receive, I might not be able to reply to every message.

When you write, please be sure to include this book's title and authors, as well as your name and phone or fax number. I will carefully review your comments and share them with the authors and editors who worked on the book.

Fax: 317-817-7070

Email: opsys@mcp.com

Mail: Executive Editor
          Operating Systems
          Macmillan Computer Publishing
          201 West 103rd Street
          Indianapolis, IN 46290 USA

Introduction

Why a book on Windows networking? Simple. Within the past several years, there has been an explosion of NT servers. And on the desktop, Windows 95 and Windows 98 have taken over. Where there was once only UNIX and Novell, the advent of NT Server changed the playing field. Interoperability is what we're all after now, as well as the need to access all the corporate resources, no matter what platform they're on.

Windows is ideally suited for this. A Windows client can easily connect to several operating systems. It's not at all uncommon to simultaneously connect to both NT and Novell servers. On the server side, NT can do the same thing, supporting multiple operating systems and protocols.

In this book, we're going to show you how. But don't think it has to be read sequentially. Depending on your needs, don't hesitate to jump around! For example, suppose you've gotten another home computer, and your son keeps wanting to hook them together so that he and his buddies can play multiplayer DOOM. Skip on over to Hour 4 and quickly learn how to put together a direct cable connection network. That will get him playing network-aware games, and you can get back to the ballgame.

Or how about you arrive at work, and the first thing you learn is that you're now in charge of the network because the administrator just quit? Don't laugh—it's happened to more people than you might think! Your priorities at that time won't be learning about the different types of Ethernet; right then, you need to learn how to add, create, and delete users, so head for Hour 15 and start there.

If you already have a networking background, but no experience with NT, you don't need the first few chapters. You already know how a network is put together. You just want to learn about NT, so start with Hour 10.

There is something for everyone here, so have fun, and good luck with the networking!

PART I
Covering Your Basics

Hour

1 Learning the Lingo

2 Networking Basics

3 Protocols

HOUR 1

Learning the Lingo

Just like carpentry, medicine, plumbing, or any other specialized field, networking has its own terminology. In this Hour, you begin with a high-level look at networking, and then delve into some of the jargon. This Hour covers the very basics, so if you already have a background working with networks, just take a quick look at the Q&A and Quiz sections. If you're brand new to networking, read on; you'll take a quick look at the following topics:

- What is a network?
- Peer-to-peer networking
- Client/server networking
- LANs and WANs
- Why have a network?
- The Internet
- Web servers and Web browsers
- Telnet
- FTP

What Is a Network?

Today, computers and networks are fundamental to almost any business, regardless of the size of the company or the product being sold or manufactured. In the most basic terms, a network consists of the following:

- A cabling scheme, used to physically connect the computers
- A common *protocol*, or *language*, that the computers use to communicate with each other

There are basically two types of networks:

- Peer-to-peer networks
- Client/server networks

Peer-to-Peer Networking

In a peer-to-peer network, all computers are equal. Peer-to-peer networks are ideal for the home or small office. In this type of environment, it isn't practical or economical to dedicate a machine to specific tasks. Each computer not only is used as a workstation, but also shares its resources, such as the files on the hard disk or the printer. For example, I can use my PC to do word processing, and at the same time, I can share my printer with other computers. Figure 1.1 shows a sample peer-to-peer network.

FIGURE 1.1

In a peer-to-peer net-work, all machines are equal and can share resources among them-selves.

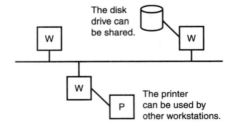

W = Work station
P = Printer
D = Disk Drive

Client/Server Networking

In a client/server network, at least one machine (and possibly more) is a *dedicated server*. No one uses these machines for a workstation—they are dedicated to a specific task. Client/server networks are more common in larger environments, where it is feasible to invest in a large, powerful server with lots of memory and disk space, and then spread this cost across a large number of users. Figure 1.2 shows a sample client/server network.

FIGURE 1.2

In a client/server net-work, at least one machine is dedicated to acting as a server.

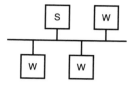

S = Server
W = Workstation

There are three basic types of servers:

- **File server**—File servers are used to share files and printers.
- **Print server**—A print server is dedicated to receiving print jobs into a print queue and then spooling them to the printer.
- **Application server**—Instead of just sharing files and printers, an application server shares applications. A Web server is a simple example of this type.

Why wouldn't you want someone using a server as a workstation? One reason is security. With file servers, for example, many users are storing their documents on the server, so you have to be very careful about who has access. Another reason you don't want to use your server as a workstation is to protect yourself against user error. If your NT server provides file and print services, and for some reason a user locks it up or shuts it down without meaning to, it's going to affect everyone using it at the time, not just the one user. An abend or shutdown causes everyone to lose access to their shares and printers, which can make for irate users.

An *abend*, short for ABnormal ENDing, can ruin your day. When you walk into the computer room and see the infamous cryptic blue screen instead of what you normally expect to see, it's time to reboot and hope that all comes up as expected.

For the jokers among you, there are "blue screen" screen savers that you can download from the Internet. Sneak one onto your buddy's system and watch his reaction!

A *share* is a directory that has been identified as a mount point (available for local access). In other words, the fact that c:\users\pence exists does not mean I have access to it across the network. The administrator must "share" this directory before it can then be accessed across the network.

A server might perform only one task, or it might perform several. You can use a machine only as a file server, or that same machine can act as a file server, print server, and application server, all at the same time.

LANs and WANs

I would be remiss if I didn't touch on some of the most fundamental networking acronyms:

- A LAN, or local area network, is a network in one location, such as the corporate office.

A LAN can be either a client/server network or a peer-to-peer network.

- A WAN, or wide area network, is formed by connecting two or more LANs with a router. Figure 1.3 shows a sample WAN.

FIGURE 1.3

In a wide area network, or WAN, two networks are connected with a router.

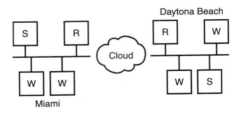

R = Router
S = Server
W = Workstation

Routers are covered in more detail in Hour 2, "Networking Basics." For now, just realize that a router is used to connect networks.

Why Have a Network?

There are many reasons to have a network, not the least of which is that a network allows you to share resources, such as files, printers, and data. This reaps savings in time, money, and efficiency.

Imagine, for example, that you work at a small office, with 10 or so personal computers. Suppose that Diane has been working on a document for the boss, and this document needs to be revised. The only problem is that Diane is on vacation this week, so Danny must make the revisions. Without a network, Danny has no choice but to get up and physically sit at Diane's station—inconvenient to say the least. Or Danny could do the "sneakernet" routine, where he copies the document to a floppy and carries it to his workstation. But this isn't such a good solution because now there are two copies of the document floating around, and they don't match! If all the documents could be saved on a central computer (or *file server*) that everyone could access, Danny could work on the document for Diane's boss from his own computer.

And consider this: If your data is spread out over 10 computers, that means you, the system administrator, have to perform 10 separate backups (or take a chance, decide not to back up, and hope you don't lose data). With a file server, you need to perform only one backup.

And how does a network save you money? A printer is an excellent example. Generally speaking, printers are idle more often than they are being used. Without a network, you would need to purchase 10 printers—one for each computer—for your hypothetical office. But if you could connect a printer to a network, everyone could share it; this means you need to buy only one printer. Because the cost of the printer is spread across 10 users, you can probably afford to buy one with more features than you could have otherwise.

The Internet: A Really, Really, Big Network!

You can think of the Internet as a really, really, big network that spans the globe, but in truth, it's really a lot of small networks hooked together. With the advent of Web browsers and the World Wide Web, which gave us a user-friendly interface, using the Internet is now very common (perhaps too common—my mother sends me email!). The rest of this hour covers some terms and applications that you might have heard about already, such as

- Web browsers
- Web servers
- FTP
- Telnet

Web Servers and Web Browsers

A *Web server* is a file server that stores HTML documents. *HTML*, short for *Hypertext Markup Language*, is the "code" used to create Web pages. A Web browser, such as Netscape or Microsoft Internet Explorer, is the program you must use to correctly display the HTML pages held on Web servers.

For example, somewhere, attached to the Internet, is a machine acting as a Web server for Microsoft. When you want to see the content at this site, you point your Web browser to www.microsoft.com. The browser gets in touch with the Web server at this address and requests the index.html page, which it then downloads and displays on your PC. Figure 1.4 shows Microsoft's home page displayed on the Netscape browser.

When you *upload* a file, you send it from your workstation to a remote computer. A *download* is just the reverse: You copy the file to your computer from a remote host.

FIGURE 1.4

A browser—in this case, Netscape Navigator—displays Web pages that it downloads from Web servers.

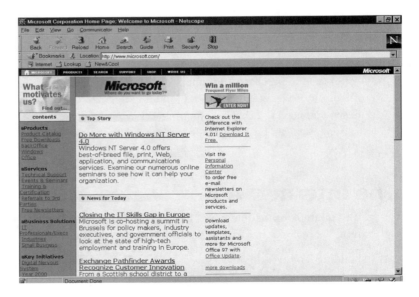

The server looks for default files named index.html, index.htm, home.html, and welcome.html, in that order. If none of these files is found, a directory listing is returned (see Figure 1.5). You can load the HTML documents that show up in the listing by double-clicking them, or they can be specified by URL.

FIGURE 1.5

*If no index or home
page is found, the
browser displays a
directory listing.*

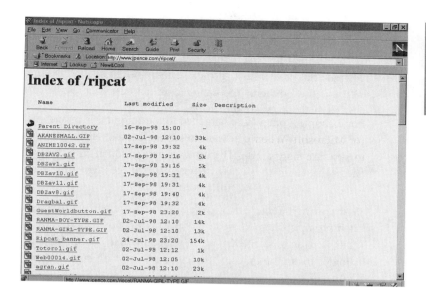

1

A *uniform resource locator*, or *URL*, is the "street address" of the Web page. If people ask you for a URL, they want to know what to put in the address field of their Web browser. For example, the URL for Microsoft's home page is www.microsoft.com. *HTTP*, short for *Hypertext Transfer Protocol*, is the protocol, or language, used by Web servers and browsers. Many times, you see the URLs written not as www.jpence.com, but as http://www.jpence.com.

Most browsers use HTTP by default, so people seldom type the http://
when they are browsing.

Telnet

Because the physical machine acting as the Web server might not be in the same building—or even in the same city—as you, the ability to establish a remote session is very important. Telnet is an application that does just that. When you establish a Telnet session with a remote host, it's just as though you are sitting there at the host computer issuing commands.

Unless you have physical access to all machines, Telnet is something you can't do without. (Even if all the machines you need to administer are in the same building, you might still have to go down several floors just to issue a command—inconvenient, at best!)

If, for example, you have a server that you allow users to upload files to, you need to have control over where the files are going. This control keeps things organized and lets you check the files first. Otherwise, you wind up with files all over the place and have no idea who put what where. Typically, there might be an "incoming" directory, and uploads are only allowed there. You can then Telnet into your server, check the files, and move them to the appropriate directory.

> Both Windows 98 and Windows NT come with Telnet.

After you start Telnet and enter a valid account name and password, you receive a command prompt, where you can run any command-line program. Figure 1.6 shows a brief Telnet session to a UNIX host, in which the `dir` command has been entered to get a listing of files in the present directory (the session is then terminated with the `exit` command).

FIGURE 1.6

A Telnet session between a Windows workstation and a UNIX host.

```
Telnet - jpence.com
Connect  Edit  Terminal  Help
jpence@or%
jpence@or%
jpence@or% dir
total 56
drwxr-xr-x    3 jpence  users      512 Sep 16 18:43 .
drwxr-xr-x  249 root    wheel     4096 Aug 24 22:12 ..
-rw-r--r--    1 jpence  users     1009 Nov 15  1997 .cshrc
-rw-r--r--    1 jpence  users      277 Nov 15  1997 .login
-rw-r--r--    1 jpence  users      254 Nov 15  1997 .mailrc
-rw-r--r--    1 jpence  users      435 Nov 15  1997 .profile
-rw-r--r--    1 jpence  users       41 Feb 18  1998 passwd
lrwxr-xr-x    1 jpence  users       22 Sep 16 18:43 public_ftp -> /usr/public_ftp/
jpence
lrwxr-xr-x    1 jpence  users       21 Sep 16 18:43 public_html -> /usr/www/users/
jpence
-rw-r--r--    1 jpence  users    17288 Sep 16 18:43 ripcat
drwx------    2 jpence  users      512 Sep 27 11:11 www_logs
jpence@or%
jpence@or% exit
```

FTP: File Transfer Protocol

FTP, short for *File Transfer Protocol*, is the language used to move files between hosts. You can use either the command-line version of FTP or your Web browser (which most people find easier).

When using the Web browser, instead of typing `http://www.`*something*`.com` at the address line, enter `ftp://ftp.`*something*`.com`. You then use your browser to upload and download files. Figure 1.7 shows Microsoft's FTP site.

FIGURE 1.7

Notice that in the address field, `ftp://ftp` *is used instead of* `http://www`, *which kicks the browser into FTP mode.*

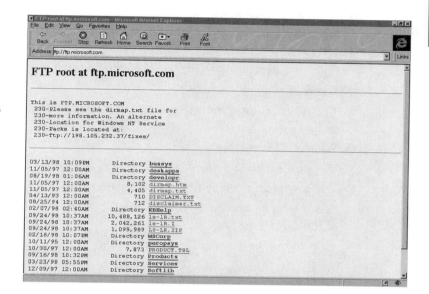

For those of us from the old school, Windows 9x and NT have a command-line FTP program that can also be used. Simply drop to a command prompt and enter the following command:

ftp

When you get an `ftp>` prompt, type **help** for a list of commands.

Summary

Well, you got off to a good start, touched on some terminology, and learned about a few utilities, such as Telnet and FTP. Next hour, you'll take on more of the network hardware.

Workshop

Q&A

Q What is the relationship between a URL, HTTP, a Web server, and a Web browser?

A The URL, or uniform resource locator, is the complete address of the Web page. HTTP is the protocol used by the Web server and the Web browser.

Q When should you use Telnet?

A To establish a session with a remote host so you can run command-line programs on it.

Q What is FTP used for?

A FTP, or file transfer protocol, is used to send and receive files between hosts.

Q When would implementing a peer-to-peer network be appropriate?

A Peer-to-peer networking is most suitable for small environments, such as a home office or small business.

Quiz

1. True or False: In a peer-to-peer network, one or more machines is dedicated to acting as a file server, and is normally not used as a workstation.

2. True or False: FTP is used to establish a command-line session with a remote host.

3. A WAN is

    A. A standalone network.

    B. Two or more isolated networks.

    C. A router.

    D. Two or more networks connected via a router.

HOUR 2

Networking Basics

In this Hour, you take a look at the difference between network architectures (Ethernet, Token Ring, and hybrid), along with the actual networking infrastructure. This infrastructure consists of the following hardware:

- NICs
- Cabling
- Hubs
- Repeaters
- Bridges
- Switches
- Routers

Network Architectures

The two major players in networking at the desktop are Ethernet and Token Ring.

Another type of network is Fiber Distributed Data Interface, or FDDI, which uses fiber-optics. Because this type of network is used more for backbones than for the desktop, I won't go into FDDI technology in this Hour.

NEW TERM A *backbone* is a high-speed connection between the more important building blocks of the network. For example, you might have your file servers connected with a high-speed backbone feeding a switch, which would then branch out to the individual workstations.

NEW TERM *Fiber-optics* use light for signaling instead of the electrical signals used by Ethernet and Token Ring. Naturally, this requires a special fiber-optic cable.

Ethernet

Ethernet is prevalent; because it's cheap and easy to install, you'll find that it's more common than Token Ring. Ethernet comes in several flavors, including

- 10 megabit (Mb) Ethernet.
- Fast Ethernet, which runs at 100Mb.
- Gigabit Ethernet. This technology is just now emerging, so it could be some time before it makes its way onto your desktop.

The *10* and *100* refer to the speed at which the network interface card can place data onto the wire.

But Ethernet is not without its flaws. For one, Ethernet is contention based, which means it works exactly like a party line. When only two people are talking on the line, they can hear each other perfectly well without any interference. But when 25 people are talking on the line, having a conversation starts to become impossible. Just when the line goes quiet and you open your mouth for your chance to talk, guess what? So do the other 24 people! The end result is chaos—no one can hear anything meaningful because they are all trying to talk at once.

Because Ethernet is contention based, it is possible to degrade the performance of the network by adding too many users to the same segment.

In the Ethernet world, this situation is called a *collision*. When two or more computers try to talk at the same time, the signal on the wire is naturally garbled. When a machine trying to transmit via Ethernet experiences a collision, its response is to back up and try the transmission again (and again, and again) until the transmission is successful. The technical name for this access method is a mouthful of letters: *CSMA/CD*, short for *Carrier Sense, Multiple Access, Collision Detection*.

2

> Are collisions bad? Yes! You would expect to see some collisions on a shared Ethernet segment, but too many is a sign that you have a problem—probably that you have too many users on that network.

NEW TERM   A *segment* is a physical division of the network. Any traffic generated by any computer on a network segment is seen by all the other computers attached to that particular piece of wire. An Ethernet segment can also be defined as a *collision domain*, a fancy way to talk about all the computers on a network that are vying with each other for opportunities to transmit data. If, for example, you have 100 computers on a segment, or collision domain, then your NIC potentially has 99 others to fight with for time on the wire.

> When collisions become a problem, it is time to break the network into multiple segments. This method reduces the size of the collision domain and speeds things up.

Token Ring

Token Ring is completely different from Ethernet. As opposed to being contention based, Token Ring is deterministic, using an electronic "token" to decide which machine can transmit when. This means that workstations aren't competing for time on the wire; they simply have to wait for the token to be passed to them. This "token" is a packet that contains special data, giving the machine holding the token permission to transmit.

> With Ethernet, it is possible to bring the network to its knees with enough workstations fighting for time on the wire. With Token Ring, however, a network might begin to slow down as you add more and more stations, but it never stops.

Although Token Ring networks are in many ways more efficient than Ethernet networks, Token Ring is less prevalent because it is more difficult and more expensive to implement. The access method for Token Ring is far more complex than CSMA/CD, which is used for Ethernet.

Historically, Token Ring was wired with shielded twisted pair (STP) wiring, which is heavy and bulky compared to unshielded twisted pair (UTP) wiring (see the "Cabling" section in this Hour for more information about STP and UTP).

 Newer implementations of Token Ring allow you to use UTP wiring, so if you are considering Token Ring, that is definitely the path to take.

In simple terms, Token Ring networks act like this (refer to Figure 2.1 while you read these steps):

1. When a workstation receives the token (1), it can send a frame to the next station (2).

2. After the frame has made it completely around the ring and back to the transmitting station (3), the frame is removed from the wire.

3. To check for errors, the information in the frame that was removed is compared to the information in the frame that was initially transmitted.

4. As soon as the sending station is done, it then generates a new token (4) and sends it to the next station.

FIGURE 2.1

Token passing.

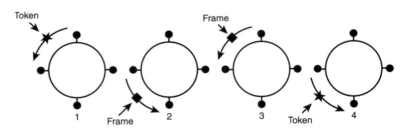

● = Computers

Of course, the preceding steps are a bit simplistic; there are all sorts of magic going on behind the scenes. For example, in a Token Ring network, one machine acts as the *active monitor*, the referee for the ring. The active monitor might provide timing, remove continuously circulating frames, and so on.

Network Hardware

2

Your network consists of two fundamental building blocks:

- **Hardware**   The computers themselves, the network interface cards, the cabling, and other equipment used to tie the network together
- **Software**   The operating systems running on the servers and workstations

In this section, you'll take a look at the hardware.

If you think of data as water, then think of hardware as the plumbing. Your house might be plumbed with cast-iron pipe, and your neighbor's house might be plumbed with copper pipe. Each of these types of plumbing has its strengths and weaknesses; network hardware is no different. In either case, the water (data) still flows, which is what you're after.

NICs

The *network interface card*, or *NIC*, is a card installed on the PC or workstation. It's the job of the NIC to take the information passed to it from the higher levels of the protocol stack and physically put it out onto the wire. The NIC doesn't just start spraying out data; instead, it forms it into nice neat packets. A *packet* contains information in a certain format, such as a source address, a destination address, and data.

How packets are formed is dictated by what type of NIC is used. An Ethernet NIC puts out a packet of a certain length in a certain format, which differs from a Token Ring packet. When choosing a NIC, it's important that you get the correct type. Don't come back with a Token Ring NIC when you have an Ethernet network!

Whether your network is Ethernet or Token Ring is not the only factor to consider when choosing a NIC for a certain computer; the type of bus used within that computer is equally important. A complete discussion of buses is beyond the scope of this book, but the different bus types you might encounter include ISA, EISA, PCI, and possibly Microchannel. So if, for example, you have PCI slots in your machine, you need to get a PCI NIC. You can probably determine which type of bus your machine uses by checking that machine's documentation.

Also, keep in mind the cabling implementation used on your network when purchasing a NIC. If the network is wired for UTP wiring and you bring back a NIC with only a 10Base2 connector, then expect connectivity problems!

Cabling

Cabling is another important part of networking. Don't stint on cabling—the cost of the cable is negligible. (It's having it installed that costs the money!) The cabling scheme of choice today is unshielded twisted pair (UTP) wiring, which can be used by Ethernet, Token Ring, and fiber networks. UTP cabling consists of four twisted pairs of wire, which are then enclosed in the outer sheath.

Shielded twisted pair (STP) wiring is used for older versions of Token Ring. Unlike UTP, each twisted pair in STP had a foil wrapper, or *shield*, around it. Then, both shielded pairs were again wrapped in yet another shield, a wire mesh, and then finally in the outer sheath. Naturally, this cabling is more expensive than UTP, more bulky, and harder to install.

Ethernet Cabling

Older implementations of Ethernet were wired in a bus topology using thick heavy cable. Both this type of cabling and the bus topology have fallen from grace, and any modern implementation is wired using UTP.

10Base5   Ethernet networks originally consisted of using huge, thick, 10Base5 cabling wired in a bus topology, the type of wiring scheme used for both 10Base5 and 10Base2 (which is discussed shortly). Figure 2.2 shows a sample bus network.

The *10* in *10Base5* means 10 megabits (that is, information can travel the wire at 10 megabits/second, or *Mbps*), the *Base* means baseband, and the *5* means that the cable is good for 500 meters. *Baseband* means that the entire capacity of the wire is used for the signal, as opposed to *broadband*, which describes the cable going to your television. There are many signals (channels) on broadband cable, but only one signal on baseband cable.

FIGURE 2.2

See how the cable goes from computer to computer in a straight line? This straight line is called a bus topology, and it forms one network segment.

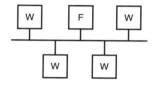

F = File Server
W = Workstation

This setup had a few problems:

- 10Base5 cabling is big, thick, and hard to work with.

- A bus topology goes from machine to machine in a straight line; very few locations lend themselves to wiring in this fashion.

- Bus topologies are wired in much the same way as Christmas lights: A problem anywhere in the line shuts the whole thing down. In addition to making for an inefficient network, this setup makes troubleshooting a chore because the problem could be anywhere on the network segment.

Each end of the line on a bus topology has a terminator on it, which is actually a resistor. Without the terminator, things won't work. So to troubleshoot a scenario like the one just described, you move the terminator halfway down the wire and see if things work. Keep moving it halfway until you narrow down to the problem. This is called *half stepping*; after enough tries, you find the culprit.

For more information on troubleshooting your network, pick up a copy of *Sams Teach Yourself Network Troubleshooting in 24 Hours* by Jonathan Feldman.

10Base2 The next iteration of Ethernet was 10Base2, which is similar to 10Base5, but on a length of cable good for 200 meters (actually, it's 185 meters, but what's a few meters between friends?). This shorter distance is the result of using a smaller cable. However, compared to 10Base5, 10Base2 cable was much thinner, cheaper, and easier to work with. Instead of being as thick as your thumb, it was about the thickness of a pencil. Nevertheless, a real problem remained: 10Base2 still used a bus topology, wired just like the network shown in Figure 2.2.

10BaseT As mentioned, the bus topology used by 10Base5 and 10Base2 caused some problems:

- Problems on the network affected everyone on the line.
- The setup of most office environments made it difficult to wire everyone in a straight line.

Enter 10BaseT. With 10BaseT, you still have cabling that is 10Mb and baseband, but this time it's with cheap, easy to work with, twisted pair wiring known as UTP. Here's the best part, however: With 10BaseT cabling, networks can be wired in a star topology instead of a bus topology (see Figure 2.3). This new mode of wiring is made possible with a new piece of equipment—a 10BaseT hub. The workstations are plugged into the hub, and when the hub receives a signal on one of its ports, it sends it out to all its ports. This makes the star logically like a bus, in that the signal placed on the wire is seen by all the workstations. Physically, however, the wiring goes from a central point and out in different directions, hence the idea of a star.

FIGURE 2.3

A star topology has a central point that things spread out from. Instead of wiring from A to B to C, you wire in a "star," from the hub to each workstation.

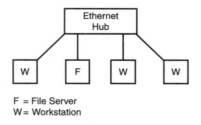

The specifications for 10BaseT cabling call for a maximum cable length of 100 meters. So the key is to centrally locate the hub, which would give you a range of up to 200 meters for your network (100 meters in each direction).

A hub can be connected to another hub, so you can actually achieve a network range of more than 200 meters by using multiple hubs. But be careful here; you can't just keep on daisy chaining, or cascading, hubs forever.

2

UPGRADING LEGACY NETWORKS

What if you have a thin-wire Ethernet network laid out in a bus topology, and it is time to expand? Is the solution to rip out everything and rewire? That would work, but it's not always feasible. Simply get a hub with 10BaseT ports as well as a port that can hook up to your existing network. Figure 2.4 shows how you can expand your network using 10BaseT, while keeping your legacy network in place. This same strategy can be used to migrate from a bus to a star network, and it can be done one machine at a time, which makes it very easy on the administrator!

FIGURE 2.4

The hybrid layout shown here lets you keep your legacy network in place while expanding by using 10BaseT.

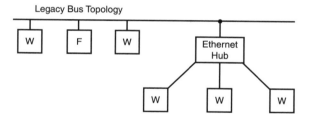

F = File Server
W = Workstation

100BaseT If you have grasped the concept of 10BaseT, then congratulations—you now know about *100*BaseT, or Fast Ethernet. It works the same way as 10BaseT, only faster (data can travel the wire at a rate of 100Mbps instead of 10Mbps).

Of course, to use 100BaseT, you need a hub capable of handling Fast Ethernet: a 10/100 hub. (If you are going to be purchasing any Ethernet NICs, make sure they are also 10/100.)

Each port on a 10/100 hub is capable of autosensing the speed at which the NIC plugged into it is communicating and adjusting its communication speed accordingly. This automatic adjustment lets you migrate over to Fast Ethernet as you buy new equipment or NICs.

You might not be able to reach the speeds advertised by Fast Ethernet if you're running it on older existing wiring. Fast Ethernet requires CAT5 100BaseT cable. (The UTP cable used for networking comes in several categories; CAT3, or category 3, works with 10BaseT, but would be unsuitable for Fast Ethernet.) If you're installing new cable, make sure it is category 5.

Token Ring Cabling

Token Ring networks have in the past been wired with STP. This type of wiring, although still prevalent, is seldom used in modern implementations. Newer advances in Token Ring technology allow Token Ring to run over UTP cabling, the same type of cabling used to wire 10BaseT networks.

Hubs

You can think of a *hub* as a splitter (that's a bit simplified, but it works for our purposes); a hub *splits* a signal, sending it out through all its ports. Hubs are used only in 10BaseT Ethernet networks, not Token Ring.

This doesn't reduce your collision domain any; traffic generated by workstation A is seen by all the other machines plugged into the hub. The term *collision domain* refers to the number of workstations you have to compete with for free time on the wire. If you have a 10BaseT hub with 24 ports, and your workstation is plugged into one of them, you would be competing with 23 other machines for a chance to talk.

So what's the point? Well, one major advantage is that each machine has its own piece of wire! This makes troubleshooting very simple: The problem is with the NIC, the wire, the hub port, or the connectors. In addition, when a network problem occurs, it might affect only one user instead of everyone on the wire.

Imagine, for example, that the cable going from Suzie's workstation to the hub accidentally gets cut while the building is being remodeled. Instead of bringing down the entire network, only one user—Suzie—is affected. As an administrator, it's much better to have only one irate user breathing down your back instead of 100!

There are smart hubs and dumb hubs. Dumb hubs are cheaper, and just move the signal along. Smart hubs—also called *manageable hubs*—cost more because you can use the vendor's management software to monitor the hub from your management console. (This is important in a large environment—such as a campus—where things are spread out.) You can, for example, monitor the status of the hub's power supply, the collision rate, or the status of a particular port without having to physically go to the hub itself.

2

Repeaters

A *repeater* is something you seldom see, except perhaps on a legacy Ethernet network. A repeater accepts the packet, rebuilds it, and then sends it on, as shown in Figure 2.5. This allows you to extend the range of your network. This rebuilding is important; if you simply amplified the signal, you would be amplifying any noise or other problems in addition to the signal you want to send.

FIGURE 2.5

The repeater strips the pertinent information out and rebuilds the packet before sending it to the other segment.

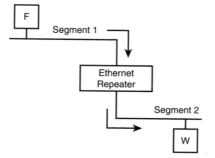

F = File Server
W = Workstation

Bridges

Suppose you have an Ethernet segment with two file servers (a production file server and a business file server) and 100 workstations on it (not that I am recommending these numbers!), as shown in Figure 2.6. The load is fairly evenly divided—with about 50 users accessing the production server and about 50 accessing the business server—but you do have staff who require access to both servers.

FIGURE 2.6

One network segment with two file servers and multiple users. About half the users access the production server, and the other half generally access the business server.

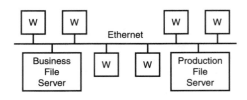

This works, so what's the problem? Contention. To put it another way, the collision domain has 102 machines in it, all fighting for time on the wire. Even if I access the business server, used by only 50 or so other people, I am competing with the entire group (all 100 of them) for time on the wire! Why should the production users trying to reach their server have to get in my way?

This problem should be simple enough to solve: Why not make two separate networks, one for business and one for production? Remember, though, that you do have staff who need to access both servers. You surely don't want them to have to get up and walk over to another workstation!

A *bridge* helps you solve your network configuration problem. You can break the network into two segments—one with the production file server, the other with the business file server—but use a bridge to join these segments, as shown in Figure 2.7. The bridge then forwards any packets that need to reach the server on the other segment, while blocking packets whose destination is on the same segment. This means your staff can use both servers without getting up. It also eases the contention problem.

FIGURE 2.7

The bridge listens to the traffic on each of its adjoining network segments and builds a table of where each workstation lives.

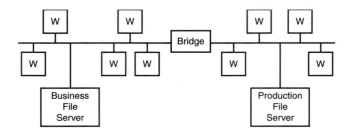

A bridge determines whether a packet should be forwarded or blocked by examining the packet's destination address. If the destination of the packet is on the same side of the bridge as the source of the packet, the bridge ignores it. If the destination is on the other segment, the packet is forwarded (see Figure 2.8).

FIGURE 2.8

A packet from machine A has a destination address of server A; the bridge ignores this packet. A packet from machine A destined for server B gets forwarded. The decision to ignore or forward is based on the packet's destination address.

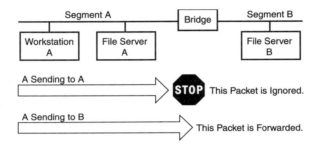

Can you just break the network right in the middle and put in your bridge, or do you need to consider the placement of the resources your users are accessing? Not surprisingly, you have to pay attention to the placement of your users and the resources they normally access. It's best to put the business file server on the business segment along with the business users, and the production server across the bridge on the production segment with the production users. That way, you halve the collision domain; instead of competing with all 100 machines for time on the wire, users compete with only 50.

With the advent of switch technologies, covered in the next section, bridges are no longer as prevalent as they once were.

Switches

As you've seen, using a bridge to segment your network reduces the size of your collision domain, resulting in a faster network. But segmenting comes with its own share of problems. First, there is IP addressing, which is covered in Hour 3, "Protocols." IP addressing, and specifically subnet masks, can make even the heartiest of networking professionals run for the hills! Second, and of even greater importance, is the complexity that continued segmenting adds.

As the network administrator, you have worked hard to make sure your resources and users are located correctly to help minimize traffic. But suppose your company decides to add another server to the network—this one for the engineering department. They are going to be moving huge CAD (computer assisted design) files around on the network, so you'll need yet another network segment to isolate their traffic; however, they also need to have access to the servers you already have. To top it off, the new segment has to run on fiber, even though all the rest of the network is 10BaseT!

> Fiber Distributed Data Interface, or FDDI, is simply another type of plumbing. It runs at 100Mbps, and can be implemented over either true fiber-optic cable or UTP. Fiber over UTP is referred to as *CDDI*, or Copper Distributed Data Interface.

The idea behind a switch is to feed several small hoses from one large hose. Imagine, for example, what would happen if you attached some T connectors to your garden hose so that you could tap off 10 other garden hoses. (Hmmmm, this is starting to sound like a gardening manual, not a book about networking!) When you turn on the water, each of the 10 hoses gets only a trickle. Even though each hose is the same size as the hose that's feeding it, the feed is getting split 10 times. Now imagine that the hose doing the feeding is a firehose—it's much bigger and has much more capacity than the little garden hose you were originally using. Now when you turn on the water, you have more than enough pressure at each of your 10 feeds.

Figure 2.9 shows a network that looks a lot like that mess you created with the garden hose. Think of the wires extending from the Ethernet switch to the workstations as the garden hoses, and of the Fast Ethernet wire between the file server and the Ethernet switch as the fire hose.

FIGURE 2.9

This switch has three Ethernet (10BaseT) ports and one Fast Ethernet (100BaseT) port. The slower ports have workstations plugged into them, and the faster port connects to the server.

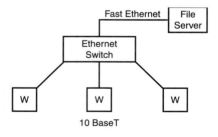

With this configuration, your collision domain is reduced to nothing; each workstation is the only workstation on the wire. When a packet needs to be transferred, the source workstation's 10BaseT port "switches" the packet to the correct destination—one of the other 10BaseT ports or the file server on the Fast Ethernet line.

> With such a fast pipe leading to it, quick access to your file server is virtually guaranteed.

> You don't have to connect only one workstation to a switch port; you could attach a hub and connect multiple workstations to that hub. Your collision domain would then be determined by the number of workstations plugged into the hub.

In larger corporate environments, a switch is used to achieve what's called a *collapsed backbone*. In such a configuration, the actual network is the *backplane* of a large switch. These large switches are generally empty, but have slots for inserting modules from the manufacturer. The backplane has connectors on it that tie together all the modules, or cards, that you insert. Hence the idea of a collapsed backbone—all the switch cards are tied together via the backplane. The backplane acts as a special network segment, or backbone, that ties it all together. For example, you might take three 36-port Ethernet switch cards and plug them into the backplane. These switch cards can communicate with each other because they are all plugged into a common network—in this case, the backplane of the switch.

These large enterprise (not to be confused with the starship) switches accept numerous cards; what makes them especially attractive is that the cards do not have to be the same type. In other words, you can plug in some Fast Ethernet cards, some fiber cards, and some 10BaseT cards. Each of these switches will, as in the previous example, switch the packet to another of its own ports (the data never hits the backplane), or the card will switch the packet onto the backplane.

So, you can plug anything you need in, and it can see any of the other boxes. Your new headache with the fiber addition is solved. You put in a fiber card, and relax. The network becomes the backplane (hence, collapsed backbone), and the only question becomes, "How fast do you want to access the backplane?" You might put in a fiber card and plug your file servers into it, while workstations get either a dedicated or shared 10BaseT port. A workstation accessing the server sends out a packet, the switch moves it onto the backplane, and then the fiber switch module picks it up from the backplane and sends it on to the server.

If the network is the backplane, then it stands to reason that it must be capable of handling very high amounts of traffic without degrading performance. In these enterprise switches, the vendors use a proprietary method to move data across the backplane and achieve speeds of 2GB or better. The backplane is the fire hose, and the switch modules are the garden hoses. Needless to say, an enterprise solution like this is expensive, and it needs management tools provided by the vendor. Figure 2.10 shows the Spectrum Element Manager software from Cabletron looking at an Mmac+, one of Cabletron's more powerful switches.

FIGURE 2.10

Spectrum Element Manager from Cabletron, looking at an enterprise switching solution.

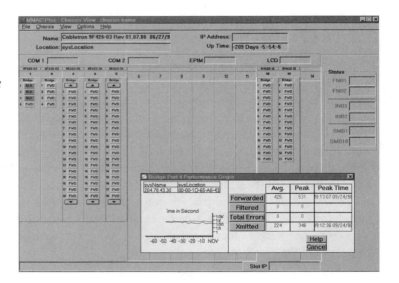

Routers

So far, the bridges and switches you have used to segment your network have worked at a very low level. (Stay tuned for the discussion of the OSI model, which discusses networks in terms of layers, or levels, in Hour 3.) You have focused only on splitting up one segment into multiple segments. Even though you have split it up, however, there's still only one network.

But now the corporate office is going to roll out a new application, and you have been charged with getting your LAN connected to the corporate office LAN, forming a wide area network. Some charge, eh? You have to form a WAN, and a router does just that. After you have your WAN, you can access resources on the corporate LAN, such as a file or application server.

As I have said, every packet contains both a source and destination address. Well, each packet also contains a source network address and a destination network address. Like a bridge, a router examines a packet and makes a decision based on the destination address, except the router looks at the network address field to make this decision. The router then either ignores the packet or forwards it across the link to the other router, which in turn places the packet onto the remote LAN. The bottom line? A bridge knows where the workstations and servers on a network live; a router knows where the networks on a WAN live. Figure 2.11 shows a sample WAN, which uses routers to connect the LAN in Miami with the LAN in Daytona Beach.

FIGURE 2.11

Two networks connected with routers. A router has at least two interfaces: one for your network and one for the link to the other router.

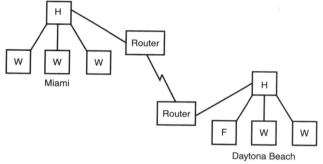

H = 10 BaseT Hubs
F = File Server
W = Workstation

MSAUs

That isn't a hub; it's a Multistation Access Unit, or MSAU (see Figure 2.12). Many people refer to them as MAUs (pronounced *mows*), even though MSAU is technically correct. Token Ring networks are wired like 10BaseT networks. In both, the wiring goes from a central point and then out to the workstations. On a 10BaseT network, this central point is the hub. On a Token Ring network, this central point is the MSAU. You should note that an MSAU has connectors for attaching the workstations, and also two special connectors labeled "Ring In" and "Ring Out." These Ring In and Ring Out ports are used to connect more than one MSAU.

FIGURE 2.12

Token Ring networks use MAUs.

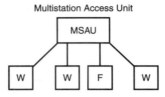

Multistation Access Unit

F = File Server
W= Workstation

Summary

This has been a huge hour! You have learned about Ethernet of different kinds, Token Rings, hubs, repeaters, bridges, switches, routers, and MSAUs...whew! You learned to segment your networks using bridges and switches to reduce the collision domains. To connect separate networks, you use a router.

Don't stint on buying quality cabling. As I said, it's the installation cost that hurts, not the cost of the wire. If you are wiring a network, then by all means put in Category 5 UTP cabling. CAT5 UTP works for 10BaseT, Token Ring, or fiber networks.

Workshop

Q&A

Q What is the advantage of a star topology over a bus topology?

A In the star configuration, each machine has its own wire, which makes the network more robust. A failure affects only the one workstation. In the case of the bus, a cable failure affects the entire network. Also, the star configuration is easier to wire.

Q What is a collision domain?

A Each network segment defines a collision domain; all the workstations on that segment must contend with each other for time on the wire.

Q What level of cabling is required to implement Fast Ethernet?

A CAT5.

Q What is the difference between a bridge and a router?

A A bridge is used to connect segments within the same network. A router is used to connect networks.

Quiz

1. True or False: Ethernet uses a token-passing scheme to determine when a machine can place packets onto the wire.

2. How many yards are there in 100 meters? (Hint: A football field is 100 yards.)

    A. 147 yards

    B. 112 yards

    C. I couldn't care less

    D. 109.36 yards

3. True or False: If a legacy network, such as 10Base5, is already in place and you want to move to Fast Ethernet, the entire network needs to be rewired at the same time.

4. The first version of Ethernet to enable using a star topology was

    A. 10Base5

    B. 10BaseT

    C. Token Ring

    D. Fast Ethernet

5. True or False: A bridge is used to connect two separate networks.

2

HOUR 3

Protocols

In the preceding Hour, you took a look at the hardware used to build your network; now you have to get the machines talking to each other. If you're trying to access a machine that understands only IP, then your machine must also be able to communicate using IP; the language, or protocol, must be understood by both parties.

All the protocols discussed—NetBEUI, IPX, and IP—have their strengths and weaknesses. Even so, many people champion one over the other with absolute religious fervor! If you've ever monitored a networking forum (something covered in Hour 24, "Online Resources"), you know what I'm talking about. But the reality is that in a network of any size, there's more than one protocol running. This means TCP/IP, IPX/SPX, AppleTalk—you name it.

What comes in the door isn't always up to the network administrator! That's why multiple protocols running on both the server and workstations are the norm rather than the exception.

Just think of protocols as tools, and pick the right one for the job. An understanding of each one is the key. This Hour focuses on IP because it has become the universal language; it's the protocol used on the Internet. Also, you take the obligatory tour through the OSI (Open Systems Interconnect) model, something no book on networking would be complete without, as well as touch on NetBEUI and IPX. Don't worry about the alphabet soup I just tossed out—that's what this Hour is for!

Keep in mind that your look at these protocols is at a basic level—a view from 40,000 feet, as it were. There's no breaking down of frame formats and seeing where the bits and bytes fall. There are entire tomes devoted to just that, and such a detailed look would leave no room for Windows networking!

The OSI Model

In 1978, the International Standards Organization (ISO) introduced a seven-layer model in an attempt to standardize networking communication. The ISO's efforts were largely unsuccessful because hardly anyone runs OSI protocols, but the model has stayed with us nonetheless. These are the seven layers:

- **Layer 7: Application**   The application level, at the top of the stack, is your window; the applications you are familiar with are running here.

- **Layer 6: Presentation**   The presentation level formats the data to pass it up to the final level, the application layer.

- **Layer 5: Session**   The session level is for establishing sessions between processes.

- **Layer 4: Transport**   The transport level is for sequenced and acknowledged exchange of data.

- **Layer 3: Network**   The network level is concerned with routing frames among networks. A frame, or packet, is what is actually placed on the wire by a network interface.

- **Layer 2: Data Link**   The data link level provides error-free transmission, thus freeing the layers above from worrying about errors in transmission.
- **Layer 1: Physical**   The physical level, at layer 1, is concerned only with placing a raw bit stream (packet) from the NIC on the physical medium, your network cable.

As a networking professional, you're mainly concerned with the physical, network, and transport levels.

There are many mnemonics floating around to help you remember the order for the seven layers, but the one that has always stuck in my head is "All People Seem To Need Data Processing."

The idea behind the model is that each layer is an independent module and needs to know how to communicate only with the layers immediately above and below itself. The post office is the best analogy for explaining the idea behind the OSI model, so here goes. Suppose you want to send a letter to Bill Gates expressing your views on bloated code. There are just a few simple rules you need to follow:

- You need to use an envelope (packet or frame). Just putting the letter (data) into the mailbox (network port) isn't enough.
- The return address (source address) must be in the upper-left corner of the front of the envelope.
- Bill Gates's address (destination address) must be in the middle of the front of the envelope.

If you follow these simple rules, your envelope (packet) is ready to be handed off to the next level—the mailbox in front of your house. After you've put the envelope in the mailbox, you've done your job; the actual path the envelope takes isn't really your concern. You hope that the postal service uses trucks and planes, but it really wouldn't matter if they used a 20-mule team, as long as the letter reaches Bill Gates.

Notice in Figures 3.1 and 3.2 that your data (the letter) travels down the model:

1. From your mailbox, it winds up in a mailbag.
2. Information (a header) is put on the mailbag—in this case, a destination address for the mailbag.

3. The mailbag is then placed on a truck, and another header is appended: the destination of the truck.

4. The next hop of the mailbag is an airplane; once again, a header is added to tell the pilot the plane's destination.

5. At the other end of the connection, the process is reversed.

After the mailbag is taken off the plane and put on a truck, the plane information is discarded. When the truck reaches the post office, the truck information can be discarded, and so on.

FIGURE 3.1

All you need to know about using the system is a few simple rules, and then you pass off your packet (envelope) to the next layer. The odds are pretty good that the other computer you are accessing isn't on your network segment. There's no physical connection between the layers, yet each layer communicates with its counterpart on the other computer; there's a "logical connection" between each layer.

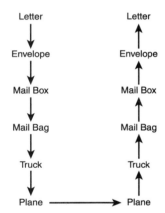

FIGURE 3.2

The OSI model. Data flows down the stack, across the physical medium, and then the process is reversed on the other side.

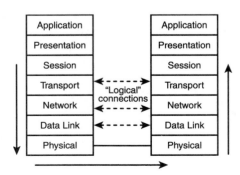

NetBEUI

I just want to touch on *NetBEUI*, short for *NetBIOS Extended User Interface*. NetBEUI is the simplest of the three protocols discussed in this Hour. Originally invented by IBM in 1985, NetBEUI was designed for use on small, department-sized LANs to work with programs that used the Network Basic Input/Output System (NetBIOS).

Take a moment to consider that description: small, department-sized LANs. That means if you have a home office or small business and you're not worried about the Internet or anyone else's network, then, by all means, choose NetBEUI and forget about it. The most important thing to keep in mind about NetBEUI is this: It's not a routable protocol. (Remember, even though you have only one network, you might have multiple segments on that single network.)

3

The protocol was designed for small independent LANs, so why should it have the capability of routing to another network? It's not a flaw; NetBEUI was simply designed that way.

If NetBEUI is not routable, what effect does this have on the design of your network? If you're using NetBIOS over a WAN, where routing is a requirement, then the packets need to be encapsulated. *Encapsulation* is taking the packet from one protocol and then using another protocol to get it where it needs to go, such as NetBIOS over IPX or IP.

NetBEUI is very simple to implement, but in a large environment, this simplicity is its downfall. (Of course, this begs the question of why someone would implement NetBEUI in a large, complex environment, when it was designed for a small one.) How is this simplicity achieved? Through using broadcasts for many functions, such as name resolution and discovery. This heavy dependence on broadcasting gives NetBEUI the reputation of being a "chatty" protocol.

A *broadcast packet* is one with a destination address of "anybody and everybody." Not only do broadcast packets eat up network bandwidth, they also slow you down for another reason: Because the packet is broadcast, your NIC is going to pick it up and begin handing it up the protocol stack until it's either dealt with or ignored, meaning that each machine spends resources paying some degree of attention to the broadcast packet. It's also possible for networks to experience broadcast storms, which will get your attention in a hurry! In a broadcast storm, you have so many broadcast packets bouncing around on the wire that everything either stops or slows to a crawl.

The bottom line on NetBEUI: Use it if you have a small, standalone network. For anything more, you need to think about using IPX, which is covered next, or IP, which is discussed in detail later this Hour.

IPX/SPX

IPX is a network-level protocol, fitting in the third layer of the OSI model. As mentioned, the network level is concerned with routing frames among networks. This means that, unlike NetBEUI, IPX understands how to get a frame from one network to another. With IPX, you can have multiple networks and connect them with an IPX router.

When routers were covered in Hour 2, "Networking Basics," I didn't bring protocols into the equation. The router does the same thing with IPX that it does with IP: makes a decision about forwarding a packet based on the packet's destination address.

At the network level, you haven't gotten to the point of having sequenced and acknowledged exchange of data, which is the function of the transport level (layer 4). Your IPX packets are merely *sent*. IPX is unsequenced and unacknowledged—very much like the postal service. You put the letter in the mailbox, and that's the extent of your responsibility. You don't expect any confirmation that your letter was delivered (okay, unless you're sending something by certified mail).

You can't think of IPX without thinking of Novell; in fact, Novell's release of NetWare 5 will be the first NetWare version capable of using pure IP, without IPX. (This version of NetWare will provide a gradual migration path from IPX to IP.) But IPX is a protocol that can be run just fine by Windows machines, too, so you can't think only in terms of NetWare when dealing with IPX.

To establish a transport-level session, SPX (Sequenced Packet Exchange) comes into play. Operating at layer 4 of the OSI model, packets sent by SPX are both sequenced and acknowledged. The machines at both end agree on some session parameters, and then they keep track of the packets they pass off to IPX (see Figure 3.3). You see how the model is coming into play? SPX is keeping up with who should have each packet. This SPX packet is then handed down to layer 3, IPX. IPX doesn't care one iota about what it just received; to IPX, the entire SPX packet is only data, so IPX just moves it on to the appropriate network. That means the application doesn't have to worry about keeping up with packets. You're assured of good data; even if an SPX packet gets lost, SPX detects this and rectifies the situation, and you get the data you expected.

> Note that SPX "rides" on top of IPX.

FIGURE 3.3

IPX, a network-level protocol, fits in the OSI model at layer 3. SPX, a transport-level protocol, fits in at layer 4.

Transport	SPX is a transport-level protocol.
Network	IPX is a network-level protocol.
Data Link	
Physical	

3

> One benefit of IPX is that you don't have to worry about addressing, which, as you will see, is a big concern when it comes to IP!

TCP/IP

IP, or *Internet Protocol*, requires more care and feeding than either NetBEUI or IPX, but with the explosion of interest in getting connected to the Internet, your understanding of IP is critical.

IP, like IPX, is a network-level protocol. As such, it maps to the OSI model at layer 3. *TCP*, short for *Transmission Control Protocol*, is a transport-level protocol, like SPX. That means IP is unsequenced and unacknowledged and that TCP, which rides on top of IP, is used for reliable transfers (see Figure 3.4).

FIGURE 3.4

IP is a layer 3 network-level protocol. TCP rides on top of IP at layer 4. Again, even though data flows up and down the model, you should think of each layer as communicating with its corresponding layer on the other computer.

Transport	TCP is a transport-level protocol.
Network	IP is a network-level protocol.
Data Link	
Physical	

IP Addressing

Each IP address on the network must be unique. IPX handled this requirement for you automatically by using a combination of the IPX network address plus the burned-in address of the NIC. Each NIC has a unique address physically hard-coded, or *burned-in*, often referred to as a MAC (Media Access Control) address.

With IP, you must assign the addresses. This can be done automatically through DHCP (Dynamic Host Configuration Protocol; more on DHCP later this hour), or it can be done manually.

An IP address is 32 bits, or four octets. You can write an address in one of two ways: in binary or in dotted decimal notation. Binary works well for the computer, but for us human life-forms, the dotted decimal notation is the preferred method.

> 11001100 01001110 00110100 00101011 is a four-octet IP address written in binary form. It is easier for me (and, I would think, everyone else) to use the much simpler dotted decimal notation of 204.78.52.43!

Of the 32 bits in an IP address, some are used to designate the network number. *Some* isn't very specific, is it? Well, it varies. The *subnet mask* is what determines how many bits are used for the network portion of the address, as you will see shortly. The bits left after the subnet mask are used for the *host*, or workstation address. Both the network address and the host ID are contained in the 32 bits, and the subnet mask determines what is what.

Notice that Figure 3.5 specifies a subnet mask of 11111111 11111111 11111111 00000000—or, using the more friendly dotted decimal notation, 255.255.255.0. This means that three octets (24 bits) have been given to the network address portion of the number. This leaves the last octet, or 8 bits, for the host ID. Using a sample address of 204.78.52.43, you know you're located on IP network 204.78.52.0 and that your host ID on the network is 43.

FIGURE 3.5

Specifying, or hard-wiring, the IP address and giving both an IP address and a subnet mask. The default gateway field is discussed later this Hour.

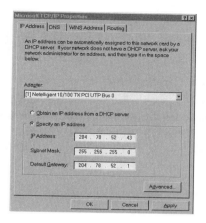

IP Address Classes

The subject of subnet masks leads into a discussion of IP address classes because there are certain default subnet masks for each address class, as you can see in Table 3.1. Address classes range from A to E, but because Class D and Class E are reserved, I'm going to focus only on Classes A, B, and C.

TABLE 3.1   IP ADDRESS CLASSES.

Address Class	First Octet Range	Number of Networks	Number of Hosts/ Network	Default Subnet Mask
Class A	1–126	126	16,777,214	255.0.0.0
Class B	128–191	16,384	65,534	255.255.0.0
Class C	192–223	2,097,152	254	255.255.255.0

Because this table looks a bit imposing, pick a row, go through the columns, and do the math to see where these numbers come from. Try using the Class B row of the table to look deeper into things.

Range of the First Octet   A Class B network ranges in the first octet from 128–191. By looking at an address of 142.x.y.z, you can immediately tell that it's a Class B address because 142 falls in between 128 and 191.

Number of Networks   Sneaking a peek over to the Default Subnet Mask column, you see that the default subnet mask for a Class B network is 255.255.0.0. Don't forget that an IP address is 32 bits long, or four octets. An octet is 8 bits long. If the first two octets are used to specify the network portion of the address, then that's 16 bits. How many networks can you get out of 16 bits? Raising 2 to the 16th power should do the trick: 65,536.

> Why jump right in and say "raise 2 to the 16th power"? Keep it simple, and work with only 3 bits. Using 3 bits, you can count from 000–111 or from 0–7. You get a total of eight numbers, which is 2 raised to the 3rd power, or 2 raised to the number of bits you have to work with.

So if 2 to the 16th power is 16,536, why does the table show only 16,384 networks? You have to look at the first octet for the reason. The high-order bits, the ones at the left—or the front of the address—are always 10xx xxxx for a Class B address. In other words, they are stuck, fixed; you can't change them. The fact that they are fixed is what specifies the range for a Class B address as between 128 and 191.

This means you can only raise 2 to the 14th power because you can't work with the first 2 bits, and 2 raised to the 14th power is—you guessed it—16,384.

> Keep this in mind when working with Class C; of high-order bits there are 110x xxxx.

Number of Hosts per Network   From looking at the number of networks and the default Class B subnet mask, you know you're using two octets to identify the network, which leaves two octets, or 16 bits, for assigning host IDs. So again, 2 raised to the 16th power is 65,536 (hosts); why does the chart show only 65,534?

You're probably starting to think that something is wrong with this chart, but the chart is right. This is because it's illegal for the host portion to be all ones (as in 11111111 11111111) or all zeros (as in 00000000 00000000).

The zero address is invalid because it's used to specify a network without specifying a host. The 255 address (in binary notation, a host address of all ones) is used to broadcast a message to every host on a network. Just remember that you can never use the first (all zeros) and last numbers (all ones) in the range when assigning host addresses. This means you can't give out 00000000 00000000 as a host address, nor can you assign 11111111 11111111 as a host address. Out of the 65,536 host addresses available, two of them can't be used, so you are left with 65,536 – 2 for a total of 65,534.

Divide and Conquer: Subnetting

Things have been going great. You've put in a Token Ring network and have been given a Class C address to use. For a bit more resilient network design, you've decided to put another Token Ring card in the server so that you have two rings and, therefore, aren't putting all your eggs in one basket. But how are you going to handle the IP addressing on the new ring?

It's time to subnet. Because the subnet mask is something you assign, you don't necessarily have to take the default. If you can steal some of the bits from the host portion and add them to the network portion, you could provide for multiple IP networks from the same address class. How's that? It makes my head ache, too, if it's any consolation!

Take the sample Class C address and see if you can break it up. Originally, you had an address of 204.78.52.43, with a subnet mask of 255.255.255.0. Take 2 bits away from the host portion and give them to the network portion of the address. Your mask then becomes 11111111 11111111 11111111 11000000, or 255.255.255.192. With these 2 bits, you can get four possible combinations, as shown in Table 3.2.

TABLE 3.2   255.255.255.192 SUBNETS.

Binary Value	Decimal Value	Subnet Range
00xx xxxx	0	0–63
01xx xxxx	64	64–127
10xx xxxx	128	128–191
11xx xxxx	192	192–255

Because you can't have a network address—or in this case, a subnetwork address—of all zeros, as in row one of Table 3.2, or of all ones, as in row four of Table 3.2, you have to discard them. This leaves you with a network address range of 65–126 and 193–254. What? That means the previous address is now invalid! Sadly, subnetting costs you some addresses.

If you're still a bit confused, check out Figure 3.6. Both Token Rings are online, and the server itself acts as a router between the two subnetworks. You effectively have two networks: 204.78.52.(Subnet)64 and 204.78.52.(Subnet)192.

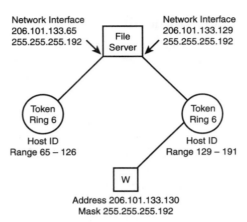

FIGURE 3.6

By changing your subnet mask, you can add to the network portion of the IP address and split your address range over multiple network segments.

If you've caught on to subnetting, you should consider yourself one of the few and the proud. Without a doubt, it's the one aspect of IP addressing that gives people the most trouble. I'll make sure there's a subnetting question on the quiz, though!

Default Gateway

If you refer back to Figure 3.5, the IP configuration screen, you can see that you need to give your host a default gateway, too. To sum up, if a host is sending packets destined for a remote network, the packets are sent to the default gateway. If the default gateway is not set correctly, the host can communicate only with other hosts on its own IP network. Being able to communicate only with people on your own network sort of takes the stuffing out of the word *Internet* in *Internet Protocol*, so make sure your default gateway is set correctly!

The term *default gateway* probably isn't the best choice of words; *default router* would be better because the term *gateway* has another meaning. Your default gateway is actually a router, which, as you know, takes packets destined for another network and routes them there. The term *gateway* has another meaning in the computer world, generally referring to a device that does protocol translation, such as an IPX/SNA gateway. It really is a router you're sending the packets to if they are destined for another network, but Microsoft has chosen to call it a *default gateway*.

In Figure 3.7, host 204.78.52.6 (Jim) with a subnet mask of 255.255.255.0 is ready to send data to host 204.78.52.91 (Bob). Using his subnet mask, Jim determines that he is on IP network 204.78.52.0. Jim then applies his subnet mask to the destination address (Bob), 204.78.52.91, and determines that he and Bob are on the same subnet. Because both workstations are on the same IP network, there is, of course, no need for the router, or default gateway.

FIGURE 3.7

When two hosts on the same subnet communicate, they do it directly, with no need for the router.

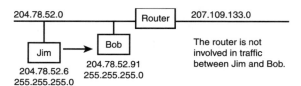

 All Jim needs now is the hardware address of Bob's NIC. He can get it by using the Address Resolution Procotol (ARP), which is covered in the next section.

Suppose, however, that Jim wants to send data to Jill. Once again, Jim applies his subnet mask to Jill's destination address and realizes that he and Jill aren't on the same network. As a result, the packet is sent to Jim's default gateway, or router (see Figure 3.8). (Remember from Hour 2 that the function of a router is to get packets from one network to another.) After the remote router receives the packet, it delivers it to Jill.

FIGURE 3.8

Because Jill resides on another network, Jim sends the packet to his default gateway.

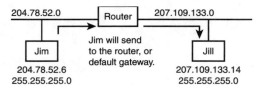

ARP: Address Resolution Protocol

All this talk about IP addressing is great, but with IP, you're up at the network level, layer 3 of the OSI model. On the other hand, the NIC—the guy that actually has to put the packet on the wire—is way down at the physical level, layer 1. At that level, no one knows anything about IP addresses. So how is this dealt with? By using *ARP*, short for *Address Resolution Protocol*.

When you know the destination IP address, be it another host on your network or the interface of the default gateway, you need to find the physical address of the destination. ARP does exactly that. What happens is this:

1. The workstation is ready to send to an address, such as 204.78.52.19. An ARP packet, a broadcast, is sent asking everyone "I want the physical (MAC) address of 204.78.52.19; anyone know what it is?"

2. 204.78.52.19 gets this broadcast packet, thinks to itself, "Hey! That's me," and responds. The response is not a broadcast; 204.78.52.19 knows who asked for the information in the first place and can respond directly.

ARP has the advantage of *caching* this information, meaning that it stores it in memory. So before the broadcast is sent, the workstation first takes a look at the ARP cache. If the physical address associated with the requested IP address is in the cache, then it's used.

Without caching, the sending host would have to repeat the question/answer scenario for every packet! You can view the ARP cache on NT Workstation and Server (see Figure 3.9), both of which include ARP.EXE, by dropping to a command prompt and entering the following command:

```
arp -a
```

FIGURE 3.9

To view the ARP cache, use the command arp -a. *By default, entries are valid for 10 minutes.*

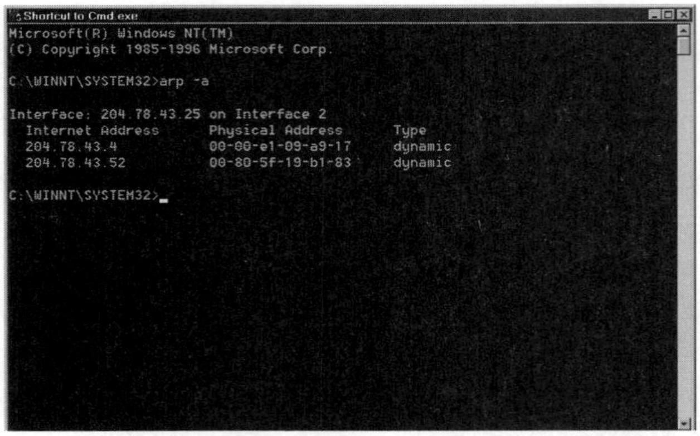

DHCP: Dynamic Host Configuration Protocol

Hard-wiring the machine by manually entering the IP address can be troublesome to administer:

- A spreadsheet or database must be kept, detailing which machine has been given which IP address—and as you know, it's not uncommon for documentation to fall by the wayside.

- If you move one of your hard-wired machines to another subnet, the machine won't function correctly. Among other things, the default gateway would be wrong, and you would have one lonely machine on your hands.

- If changes occur on the network, each machine needs to be updated by hand.

Say, for example, that the address of the default gateway changes. If, in the IP Properties dialog box (refer back to Figure 3.5), you have specified the default gateway, then every one of the machines you have hard-wired needs to be updated. That means you must trek around the building and, on each machine, navigate to the IP Properties dialog box, make the change, and then—of course—reboot!

If you delve deeper into the IP Properties dialog box, you see that quite a bit of information can be specified there, such as the WINS server (Windows Internet Naming Service) and the DNS (Domain Name Server). Again, any changes made to these addresses have to be made on every machine.

A much cleaner and simpler method is to use DHCP. You simply implement the DHCP service on your NT server. Then, as workstations come online, you can automatically hand out not only IP addresses, but also all kinds of other information, such as the address of the default gateway, the address of the WINS server, and the address of the DNS. With DHCP, if you have to make a change to your network configuration, you have to make the change in only one place: at the DHCP Manager's server configuration screen, shown in Figure 3.10.

FIGURE 3.10

Notice that in addition to the IP address, you can also hand out other information using DHCP, such as the default gateway (router) and WINS server.

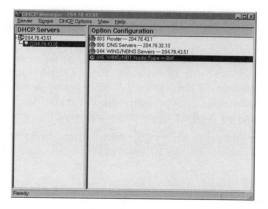

You *lease* your addresses from the DHCP server, much as you lease a house. A house lease lets you use the house for a fixed period, and then you have to renew (perhaps at a different rate) or move out. The same is true here: Your lease allows you to use the IP address you're given for a fixed period and then you have to renegotiate.

When a workstation begins to initialize and wants to get an IP address from the DHCP server, there are five steps:

1. **Lease request**   Your poor client doesn't know anything—it doesn't even know its own address, let alone the address of anyone else, so it's forced to broadcast.

2. **Lease offer**   When the DHCP servers see the request, all of them respond with offers. Each offer includes the following:

   - The IP address for the workstation to use
   - The correct subnet mask
   - How long the lease is good for
   - The responding server's address

3. **Lease acceptance**   The client takes the first offer it gets, regardless of how many offers it receives from the DHCP servers. The client then sends a broadcast packet accepting the lease. The other DHCP servers learn from this broadcast that their offer wasn't accepted, so they keep the address they offered available for other requests.

4. **Lease acknowledgement**   The server then reserves that address and sends an acknowledgement to the client.

5. **Lease renewal**   The lease is good for some number of hours, which can be configured at the DHCP server. A machine tries to renew its lease every time it's powered up. If the server knows of no reason the workstation shouldn't have the same address, it renews the lease and resets the renewal time.

A workstation tries to renew its lease when 50 percent of the lease time has expired. This conversation is with the DHCP server that originally handed out the address. If the client gets no response (or gets a negative response) from the server, the client tries again after 87.5 percent of the lease period has expired. At the 87.5 percent mark, any DHCP server can jump right in.

IP Utilities

Utilities are covered in more depth later on, so for now, take a quick look at `winipcfg`, `ipconfig`, and `ping`. These utilities enable you to get information about your current IP address status. To start `winipcfg` on Windows 9*x*, click the Start button, choose Run, and type `winipcfg` in the Run dialog box. Figure 3.11 shows the IP Configuration window that appears.

FIGURE 3.11

*You can get
information on the
status of your IP
configuration by
running* winipcfg.

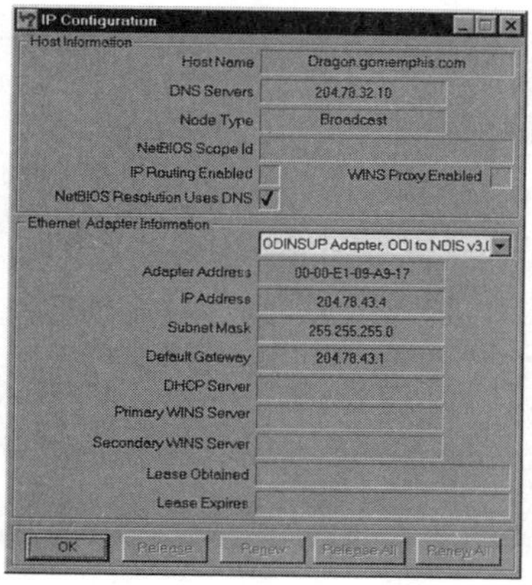

To start ipconfig for NT Server or NT Workstation, simply go to a command prompt
and enter the following command (Figure 3.12 shows the resulting window):

ipconfig /all

FIGURE 3.12

*On the NT platform,
you use the command
prompt to run*
ipconfig /all.

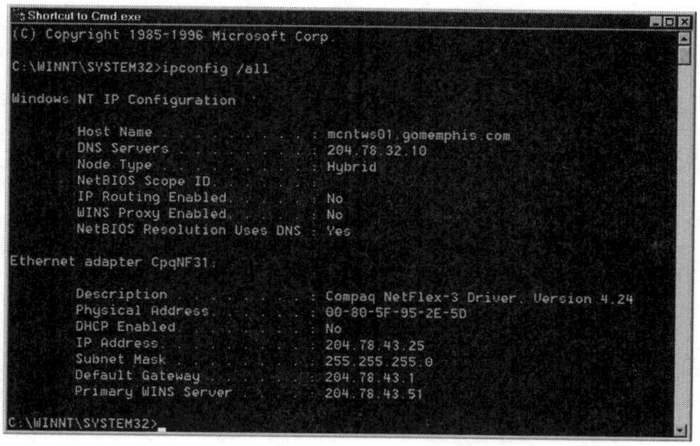

Of course, there's no way you can leave IP without discussing ping, the IP handyman's
choice of tools. It works exactly like sonar worked in those old World War II movies.
When you Ping a workstation, you send it a echo packet that asks "Are you there?" If the
other host is alive, you get back an echo response, along with the time it took for the
answer to return (see Figure 3.13). The ping command is your first line of defense when
troubleshooting IP configuration problems, as you will see in Hour 19,
"Troubleshooting."

FIGURE **3.13**

Drop to a command prompt and Ping another host.

```
Shortcut to Cmd.exe                                                  _ □ ×
Microsoft(R) Windows NT(TM)
(C) Copyright 1985-1996 Microsoft Corp.

C:\WINNT\SYSTEM32>ping 204.78.43.1

Pinging 204.78.43.1 with 32 bytes of data:

Reply from 204.78.43.1: bytes=32 time<10ms TTL=255
Reply from 204.78.43.1: bytes=32 time<10ms TTL=255
Reply from 204.78.43.1: bytes=32 time<10ms TTL=255
Reply from 204.78.43.1: bytes=32 time<10ms TTL=255

C:\WINNT\SYSTEM32>_
```

You can Ping another host by IP address, as in ping 204.78.43.1, or you can Ping by name, as in ping Elvis. For you to be able to Ping by name, the name must first be resolved (name resolution is discussed in Hour 19).

A neat thing about a UNIX host is that if you Ping one, it answers with *"name"* is alive; "name" is the name given to the host. So if you set up one of your UNIX boxes to respond to the name Elvis, you can type ping elvis and get back the answer Elvis is alive. Just remember, you heard it here first!

Summary

You have covered an enormous amount of ground this Hour. You began with protocols, the computer equivalent of human languages. It's not uncommon for servers or workstations to have multiple protocols running, allowing you to connect to a variety of operating systems. Next, you learned about the OSI model. Each layer of this model needs to be able to speak only to the layers above and below it. Data flows down the model, going from the complex to the simple, and then the process is reversed on the other side. Even though you think in terms of data flowing up and down, each level communicates only with its corresponding level on the other side of the connection.

You learned about a few protocols: NetBEUI, IPX/SPX, and TCP/IP. NetBEUI, which is not routable, is simple, easy to implement, and excellent for small standalone networks; it's considered "chatty" because of its heavy reliance on broadcasts.

IPX/SPX is also easy to implement because workstation addresses are automatically assigned through a combination of the IPX network address plus the workstation's MAC, or burned-in, address. IPX is an extremely popular protocol because of the huge installed base of Novell networks.

TCP/IP, the language of the Internet, is the protocol you really want to learn. It's a bit more complex to implement because you have to assign addresses yourself. In addition to learning about the IP address classes, you took a look at subnet masks, which determine what portion of your 32-bit address is the network portion and what part is the host ID. You learned about the default gateway (the address you use for any packet whose destination address is on another network) and ARP (used to get the hardware address of a workstation you want to communicate with). Finally, you gave yourself a headache by looking at subnetting (you subnet to break up your IP address block into more than one network; you do this by stealing some of the bits normally used for the host portion of the address).

In addition, you took a look at some of the hassles associated with manually (or *statically*) assigning IP addresses. These static assignments are referred to as being *hard-wired*. You learned that by running the DHCP service on your NT server, you can automatically hand out information such as IP addresses, the address of the default gateway, the default router, and more.

Finally, you took a brief look at a few utilities that help you get a handle on your current IP configuration. For example, the `ping` command can help you troubleshoot *and* deliver cryptic messages from Elvis!

Workshop

Q&A

Q What is the network level of the OSI model concerned with?

A The network level (at layer 3) is concerned with getting packets from one network to another, or *routing*.

Q How do the workstation addresses get assigned when using IPX?

A One of the benefits of IPX is that the workstation addresses are generated automatically. The address is a combination of the IPX network number and the MAC address of the NIC.

Q What is the length of an IP address?

A An IP address is 32 bits, or four octets, long.

Q What is a subnet mask?

A Subnet masks tell how many bits of the address refer to the network number. The remaining bits are for the host IDs.

Q What is the default gateway used for?

A All packets destined for another network are sent to the default gateway. The router then routes the packet to the other network.

Q What is ARP?

A ARP (Address Resolution Protocol) is used to get the physical address of the network interface you're sending data to.

Q What happens when you use DHCP to get an IP address?

A There are five stages: lease request, lease offer, lease acceptance, lease acknowledgement, and lease renewal.

Quiz

1. IP addresses can be handed out in two ways: by hard-wiring or by _____.

2. To get information about your current IP configuration, you can use the following utilities: _____ for Windows 98 machines and _____ for Windows NT machines.

3. You're using IP on your network, which is connected by a router to the corporate network. You can access the local resources easily enough, but can't seem to access anything at the corporate network. You can't even get an answer when you Ping the corporate server. Where should you start looking?

4. When a client using DHCP initializes, it sends out a lease request. The destination address of this packet is a _____ address.

5. You need to subnet. You have a Class C address to work with. If you take 3 bits away from the host portion and add it to your subnet mask, how many networks does this give you and how many hosts per network?

PART II

Windows 98 Networks

Hour

4   Direct Cable Connection Network

5   Installing a Two-Node Peer-to-Peer Windows 98 Network

6   Sharing Windows 98 Resources

7   Installing a Multi-Node Windows 98 Network

8   Accessing NetWare Resources from Windows 98

9   Backing Up and Restoring Data on Windows 98

Hour 4

Direct Cable Connection Network

Do you often need to transfer files between two machines? If you simply want to share files between a desktop machine and your laptop, going through the hassle and expense of putting in network cards and cables and installing a full-blown network between the two seems crazy. On the other hand, "sneaker-netting" diskettes between two machines, even with the Windows Briefcase (file synchronization) feature, can be a tedious process.

Luckily, Windows 98 offers the *Direct Cable Connection* (*DCC*) feature, a simple file transfer solution that is far easier to implement than a network connection and much less cumbersome than the sneaker-net approach. In a DCC "network," one computer is designated as the *host*, which acts as a kind of server by sharing its resources. The other machine, known as the *guest*, connects to the host and can access its shared resources.

Under Windows NT, you can use the Remote Access Service (RAS) to accomplish the same goal (see Hour 12, "Remote Access Service"). DCC is also available in Windows 95.

During this hour, you learn a little about serial and parallel ports and how to set up a Direct Cable Connection network with Windows 98. The following topics are covered:

- Selecting the ports and cables to use
- Configuring the host computer
- Configuring the guest machine
- Establishing the connection

Selecting Ports and Cables

Direct Cable Connection doesn't require you to install any additional hardware, save what you already have in your workstations. The only extra hardware you need is a special cable to connect the two computers. You can make the connection by using either the serial or parallel (printer) ports on the machines.

Many of the currently available laptop and notebook computers have built-in infrared ports so you can connect two such systems without any cables.

The following hardware requirements are necessary for DCC. You need a special cable between the machines' ports (no cable is needed if you're using the infrared ports) plus *one* of the following:

- A free serial port on each computer
- A free parallel port on each computer
- An infrared port on each computer

The computers must use the *same* type of ports. You can't use, for example, a serial port on one machine and the infrared port on the other.

With the advent of today's hardware, there are several different types of serial and parallel ports. You don't need to know them to use DCC; however, having an understanding of the different serial and parallel ports helps you get the best performance out of your systems.

Different Types of Serial Ports

Each serial port has a chip known as the *Universal Asynchronous Receiver Transmitter*, or UART (pronounced "u-art"), which is an integrated circuit that handles asynchronous serial communication. Every computer has a UART to manage the serial ports, and all internal modems have their own UART. As the need for faster serial communication increases (because of high-speed modems, for instance), the UART has come under greater scrutiny as the cause of transmission bottlenecks. If you are buying a fast external modem, make sure the computer's UART can handle the modem's maximum transmission rate. Four models of UART are typically used:

- 8250 UART
- 16450 UART
- 16550 UART
- 16650 UART

The 8250 UART was the original UART chip shipped with the IBM personal computer. This chip was limited to a 9,600-baud maximum rate. It was replaced with the 16450 UART, which had the same architecture as the 8250, but a higher maximum baud specification. Both of the chips have only a 1-byte buffer. The 16550 and 16650 have 16- and 32-byte buffers, respectively. When operating under DOS at speeds below 9,600bps, the 16450 should provide satisfactory performance. When operating under Windows 98 and higher, a 16450 is limited to about 1,200 or 2,400 baud. The 28,800bps modems, however, require running a COM port at 38,400bps or higher. These rates almost guarantee overrun errors, even in a DOS system, if a 16550 or 16650 UART isn't present. Therefore, a 16550 UART is the minimum any modern modem user should have.

A new external bus standard known as *Universal Serial Bus* (USB) has become increasingly common in recent years. USB supports data transfer rates of 12Mbps (12 million bits per second). A single USB port can be used to connect up to 127 peripheral devices, such as mice, modems, and keyboards. USB also supports *plug-and-play* (PnP) installation and hot plugging. USB has become more common; it is expected to eventually replace serial and parallel ports completely.

4

Baud, pronounced "bawd," is the number of signaling elements that occur each second. The term is named after J. M. E. Baudot, the inventor of the Baudot telegraph code.

At slow speeds, only one bit of information (signaling element) is encoded in each electrical change. The baud, therefore, indicates the number of bits per second that are transmitted. For example, 300 baud means that 300 bits are transmitted each second (abbreviated 300bps).

Assuming asynchronous communication, which requires 10 bits per character, this translates to 30 characters per second (cps). For slow rates (below 1,200 baud), you can divide the baud by 10 to see how many characters per second are sent. .

At higher speeds, it is possible to encode more than one bit in each electrical change. For example, 4,800 baud may allow 9,600 bits to be sent each second. At high data transfer speeds, therefore, data transmission rates are usually expressed in bits per second (bps) rather than baud. For example, a 9,600bps modem may operate at only 2,400 baud.

NEW TERM   *Plug-and-play* is the ability of the operating system to automatically determine the type of hardware without user intervention.

Hot plugging is the ability to add or remove a device without having to first shut off the computer.

Different Types of Parallel Ports

On PCs (including laptops and notebook computers), the parallel port uses a 25-pin connector (type DB-25) and is used to connect printers, computers, and other devices that need relatively high bandwidth. The port is often called a *Centronics* interface, after the company that designed the original standard for parallel communication between a computer and printer. (The modern parallel interface, however, is based on a design by Epson Corporation.)

Standard parallel ports come in two varieties:

- **Unidirectional**—A *unidirectional* port is designed for one-way communication between a computer and a printer. Output uses the full 8 bits of the parallel port, but input uses only 4 bits.

- **Bi-directional**—A *bi-directional* port allows for two-way communications and uses all 8 bits for both input and output operations.

Almost all parallel ports conform to the Centronics standard. These are two new parallel port standards that are backward-compatible with Centronics, but offer faster transmission rates:

- The *Enhanced Parallel Port* (EPP) protocol—This protocol was originally developed by Intel, Xircom, and Zenith Data Systems as a means to provide a high-performance parallel port link that would still be compatible with the standard parallel port. The EPP protocol offers many advantages (such as two-way communications) to parallel port peripheral manufacturers and was quickly adopted by many as an optional data transfer method. EPP has been used in laptops since mid-1991 and is now available for desktop systems.

- The *Extended Capabilities Port* (ECP) protocol—This protocol was developed jointly by Microsoft and Hewlett-Packard to extend the speed of the humble parallel port and to provide two-way throughput. Like the supercharged EPP spec, ECP is fast and bi-directional, but it works a little better than EPP in a multitasking environment because of its use of direct memory access (DMA) and buffering. Windows 95 and later supports ECP, but as of the end of 1995, a lot of exotic parallel port hardware (such as scanners, CD-ROM drives, and the like) didn't like the way the specification used DMA, so they are incompatible.

Because both ECP and EPP are supported by the IEEE 1284 specification, many new parallel ports can run in either fashion.

Speed Comparison

Generally, you'll find two serial ports and one parallel port available on a machine, so the most common choice is using the serial port for your DCC's link. However, parallel ports generally offer higher data transfer speed (unless you have a USB port). Therefore, when deciding which type of port to use, think about how much data you'll be transferring and how often. Table 4.1 shows the maximum theoretical data throughput for the different port types.

If your machine doesn't have a free port you can use, you'll have to connect and disconnect the link every time you need to use it. If you plan to use the link often, it is worthwhile to have a second port installed. In any given PC, you can easily have up to four serial ports and three parallel ports installed. The cost of a standard serial or parallel port is around $15.

TABLE 4.1   MAXIMUM DATA THROUGHPUT COMPARISON CHART.

Port Type	Data Rate (bits per second)	Data Rate (kilobytes per second)
Serial port (8250 or 16450 UART)	57,600bps	7KBps
Serial port (16650 UART)	115,200bps	14KBps
Parallel port (unidirectional)	491,520bps	60KBps
Parallel port (bi-directional)	983,040bps	120KBps
IrDA (infrared port)	983,040bps	120KBps
EPP/ECP parallel port	9,830,400bps	1,200KBps
USB	12,582,912bps	1,536KBps

Time out! That's a lot of information! Need some java? While waiting for your coffee to brew, take a look at the back of your PC and see if you can determine how many serial and how many parallel ports you have.

Null-Modem Serial Cable

When you're using serial ports for DCC, you need to use a *null-modem*, or *cross-over*, cable for the connection. What is a null-modem cable, and how does it differ from the standard modem cable you use for the external modem?

In a 9-pin serial cable, pin 2 is defined as the Receive Data wire and pin 3 as the Transmit Data wire. When you use a standard modem cable (which is a straight-through), data transmitted from one computer (through pin 3) is received by the other computer on *its* pin 3, which is for data transmit! This is like having your telephone's mouthpiece wired to the mouthpiece of another telephone (instead of the ear piece)—no communication is possible.

To prevent this, a null-modem is necessary. It uses a different pin configuration than a regular serial cable, so it ensures that the bits transmitted through the Transmit Data (pin 3) on one side end up on the Receive Data (pin 2) on the other side. A null-modem cable also makes sure the correct wires are used on both ends for the proper handshaking signals. Tables 4.2 through 4.4 specify the pin configurations of different null-modem cables.

TABLE 4.2   PINOUTS FOR A 9-PIN-TO-9-PIN NULL-MODEM CABLE.

Pin	Signal Name	Pin	Signal Name
2	Receive Data	3	Transmit Data
3	Transmit Data	2	Receive Data
4	Data Terminal Ready	6	Data Set Ready
5	Signal Ground	5	Signal Ground
6	Data Set Ready	4	Data Terminal Ready
7	Request To Send	8	Clear To Send
8	Clear To Send	7	Request To Send

TABLE 4.3   PINOUTS FOR A 25-PIN-TO-25-PIN NULL-MODEM CABLE.

Pin	Signal Name	Pin	Signal Name
2	Transmit Data	3	Receive Data
3	Receive Data	2	Transmit Data
4	Request To Send	5	Clear To Send
5	Clear To Send	4	Request To Send
6	Data Set Ready	20	Data Terminal Ready
7	Signal Ground	7	Signal Ground
20	Clear To Send	6	Data Set Ready

TABLE 4.4   PINOUTS FOR A 9-PIN-TO-25-PIN NULL-MODEM CABLE.

Pin	Signal Name	Pin	Signal Name
2	Receive Data	2	Transmit Data
3	Transmit Data	3	Receive Data
4	Data Terminal Ready	8	Data Set Ready
5	Signal Ground	7	Signal Ground
6	Data Set Ready	20	Data Terminal Ready
7	Request To Send	5	Clear To Send
8	Clear To Send	4	Request To Send

4

Some systems need the Carrier Detect signal enabled; otherwise, a Cable not connected message appears in the connection window. In this case, the cable works only if pins 6 and 8 (25-pin connector) and pins 6 and 1 (9-pin connector) get wired together.

Parallel Cable

As with null-modem cables, you can't use a standard parallel printer cable to make your DCC connections. You need what are generally called *parallel LapLink cables*, or *parallel InterLink cables*. They can be purchased easily—just ask for a LapLink cable. If you want to make one yourself, Table 4.5 shows the pinouts.

TABLE 4.5   PINOUTS FOR A 25-PIN-TO-25-PIN PARALLEL LAPLINK CABLE.

Pin	Signal Name	Pin	Signal Name
2	Data Bit 0	15	-Error
3	Data Bit 1	13	Select Out
4	Data Bit 2	12	Paper End
5	Data Bit 3	10	-Ack
6	Data Bit 4	11	Busy
10	-Ack	5	Data Bit 3
11	Busy	6	Data Bit 4
12	Paper End	4	Data Bit 2
13	Select Out	3	Data Bit 1
15	-Error	2	Data Bit 0
25	Ground	25	Ground

You can use the LapLink parallel cables for EPP ports. For ECP ports, however, you should use what is known as a *Universal Cable Module* (UCM) cable. UCM is not a simple cable, but it includes an electronic circuit in one of the connectors, which performs auto-detection of the type of parallel port and adjusts accordingly.

The UCM cable is available from Parallel Technologies
(http://www.lpt.com/lpt/). To make things confusing, Parallel
Technologies calls the UCM cable a *DirectParallel Universal Cable*.

The ECP cable is available from Warp Nine Engineering
(http://www.fapo.com). The pinout of this cable is not readily available
without buying the whole original IEEE 1284 document set. (Hint: It is *a lot*
cheaper to buy the cable than the document set!)

Using Infrared Ports

There are a few things to keep in mind when using infrared ports:

- Infrared ports are shown as "virtual serial COM ports." For example, if your PC
  has two serial ports and an infrared port, you refer to the infrared port as COM3.

- Infrared ports are not initialized by DCC, so you need to enable the ports manually.
  To do this, open Control Panel and start the Infrared Monitor.

- Because of the low-power transmitter used, infrared's communication distance is
  limited. Typically, the two infrared ports should be placed no more than 10 feet
  apart and no closer than 6 inches, without any obstructions between the two ports.

Common Configurations for Both Computers

A number of things need to be installed and configured on both machines before you can
get DCC working. First, you need to verify that DCC is installed. If you don't have the
Direct Cable Connection menu option under Start|Programs|Accessories|
Communications, you need to install DCC from your Windows 98 CD-ROM (or
diskette). Use the following steps to install DCC on your machine:

1. Choose Start|Settings|Control Panel.
2. Click on Add/Remove Programs, and then select Communications.
3. Select the Direct Cable Connection check box, and then click OK.

If the Dial-Up Networking check box is not checked, Windows requires its
installation, too.

You also need to install a network protocol that is common between the host and the guest computers. The easiest one to install is NetBEUI. However, when connecting to a computer on a LAN using the NetBEUI protocol, Microsoft recommends that the IPX/SPX-compatible protocol for Microsoft also be present. (If you already have the Client for Microsoft Networks installed, IPX/SPX is automatically installed.)

 If you want the guest machine to be able to access shared resources in the Network Neighborhood, you need to make sure the network protocol installed on the guest is common with that used on the network.

You might already have some of the necessary network drivers installed. You need to have Client for Microsoft Networks, File and Printer Sharing for Microsoft Networks, and at least one protocol other than TCP/IP (NetBEUI or IPX/SPX). In the Control Panel, click Network, and then select the Configuration tab to examine your network components.

The following steps show you how to install IPX/SPX and associate it with a network client:

1. From the Network properties sheet, click Add to bring up the Select Network Component Type dialog box.

2. Highlight Protocol and click Add to bring up the Select Network Protocol dialog box.

3. Highlight Microsoft from the Manufacturers list, highlight IPX/SPX-compatible Protocol from the Network Protocols list, and then click OK.

To remove a protocol, simply highlight it in the list of installed network components in the Network properties sheet, and then click the Remove button.

For Windows 98 networking to function properly, you must associate a network client with a protocol, and a protocol with a network adapter driver. These associations are called *bindings*. Windows 98 usually does them for you automatically. In other words, each installed client is bound to each installed protocol, and each installed protocol is bound to each installed adapter. To work with the client bindings for a given protocol, do the following:

1. Double-click the Network icon in Control Panel, highlight the protocol in the list of installed network components, and then click Properties.

2. In the properties sheet that appears, select the Bindings tab.

3. The clients that are bound to the protocol have their check boxes activated, as shown in Figure 4.1. To remove a binding, uncheck its associated check box.

FIGURE 4.1

Use the Bindings tab of a protocol's properties sheet to choose which clients are bound to the protocol.

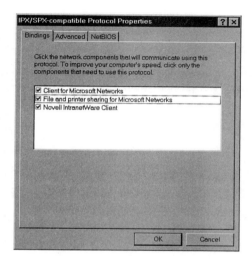

To work with protocol bindings for a network adapter, do the following:

1. Double-click the Network icon in Control Panel, highlight the adapter in the list of installed network components, and then click Properties.

2. In the properties sheet that appears, select the Bindings tab.

3. The protocols that are bound to the adapter have their check box selected. To remove a binding, uncheck its associated check box.

Now you must assign a unique name (up to 15 alphanumeric characters in length) to each of your Windows 98 computers by typing the appropriate name in the Computer Name text box in the Identification tab on the Network properties sheet. You need this name later in the DCC procedure.

If one of the computers is connected to a Microsoft networking LAN, enter your Workgroup name (you can find it by examining this panel on the LAN-connected computer).

Both computers must have a different computer name. If there are other computers, make sure each computer has a unique name.

Configuring the Host Computer

Keep in mind that in a DCC network, one computer is configured as the host (usually the desktop machine) and the other (usually the laptop) as the guest. The host machine should be set up first. To get started, choose Start|Programs|Accessories| Communications|Direct Cable Connection.

The DCC wizard checks the available ports on your system and displays a list of them, as illustrated in Figure 4.2. Highlight the port you want, and click Next to continue.

FIGURE 4.2

Select the port to be used for the DCC network.

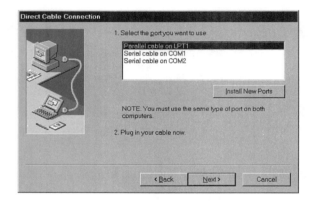

If the host machine isn't already on a network, it will not have file and print sharing set up—and you need to enable it for DCC to function, or the guest machine won't be able to access any resources on the host. The following steps show you how to enable the file and print sharing service (you might need to have your Windows 98 CD-ROM or disks handy):

1. Open the Network properties sheet and click the File and Print Sharing button.

2. If the File and Print Sharing button is enabled in the Network properties sheet, skip to step 5. Otherwise, click Add to bring up the Select Network Component Type dialog box.

3. Highlight Service and click Add to bring up the Select Network Service dialog box.

4. Highlight Microsoft from the Manufacturers list, highlight File and Printer Sharing for Microsoft Networks from the Network Services list (see Figure 4.3), and then click OK.

FIGURE 4.3

Use this dialog box to enable file and print sharing for Microsoft Networks.

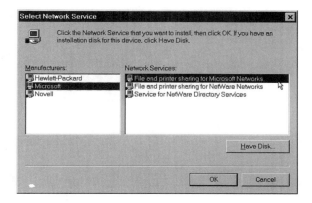

5. In the Network properties sheet, click the File and Print Sharing button.

6. In the File and Print Sharing dialog box, check the I Want to Be Able to Give Others Access to My Files check box. If you also want the guest machine to print over DCC, check the I Want to Be Able to Allow Others to Print to My Printer(s) check box. Click OK.

7. Click OK on the Network properties sheet. Click Yes to restart your computer for the new settings to take effect.

After Windows 98 is restarted, rerun the DCC wizard. After selecting the port, you are asked to share at least one folder (directory). For the guest computer to access folders and printers on the host, they need to be explicitly shared. By default, no host resources are shared. To share folders, follow these steps:

1. Click the folder you want to share.

2. Choose File|Sharing from the menu.

3. Check Share As, and then select the appropriate access type and security.

4. Click OK.

Hour 6, "Sharing Windows 98 Resources," has a detailed discussion about sharing. After setting up sharing for folders, drives, and printers, click Next to continue.

The last dialog box (see Figure 4.4) asks whether you want the guest computer to use a password when accessing the host. If you do, check the Use Password Protection check box and click the Set Password button. Enter the password (twice) and click OK. Click Finish to complete the host configuration.

FIGURE 4.4

*You can set up a pass-
word for DCC access.*

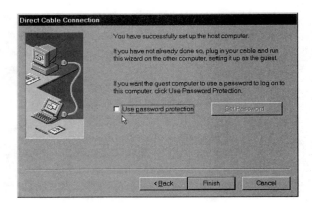

DCC then goes into a wait state waiting for the guest computer. You can close the dialog box if you don't want to connect right away. The next time you start DCC, click the Listen button to put the host into the wait mode.

Configuring the Guest Computer

As you did when setting up the host, you run the DCC wizard to configure the guest computer. However, the steps are much simpler:

1. Choose Start|Programs|Accessories|Communications|Direct Cable Connection.
2. In the first DCC dialog box, select the Guest option and click Next.
3. Highlight the port to use (make sure it's of the same type as that on the host), and click Next.
4. Click Finish.

Establishing a Connection

To establish a connection, you need to have DCC running on both the host and guest machines and the proper cable running between their ports.

On the host computer, choose Start|Programs|Accessories|Communications|Direct Cable Connection. Click the Listen button in the dialog box that appears. DCC initializes the port and then displays the dialog box shown in Figure 4.5.

FIGURE 4.5

The host computer is waiting for a connection request from the guest machine.

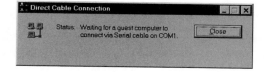

On the guest computer, also choose Start|Programs|Accessories|Communications|Direct Cable Connection. Click the Connect button in the dialog box that appears. You'll see some status messages on the two machines as they exchange information. You might be asked to enter the following information:

- If a host password was assigned, you have to enter that password.
- If you're connected to the network, such as an NT domain, you might be asked to enter a user name and password for authentication purposes.

When a DCC is established, the guest machine opens a folder window that shows all the shared resources on the host, as shown in Figure 4.6. If the host is attached to a network, the guest computer can use this window or Network Neighborhood to browse and access the network's shared resources.

FIGURE 4.6

The guest machine displays a folder window showing all shared resources available on the host.

4

Summary

During this hour, you have learned about the different types of serial and parallel ports available on your PC, as well as some information about using infrared ports. You also learned about Direct Cable Connection and how to configure the host and the guest machines so you can easily transfer files between them.

In the next hour, you find out how to install a two-node Windows 98 peer-to-peer network.

Workshop

Q&A

Q Should I make my own cable for Direct Cable Connection?

A Unless you're handy with electronics-related tasks, such as soldering, it is best to buy the necessary cable from a store—it's a lot less hassle. A null-modem serial cable costs no more than $10.

Q Can I surf the Net using a Dial-Up Networking connection on COM1 and at the same time transfer the downloaded files to my other machine over DCC?

A You can't have DCC and Dial-Up Networking (DUN) running at the same time because they both use the same driver, and only one instance of the driver can be loaded at a given time. You won't be able to establish a Direct Cable Connection until you close the DUN session.

Q My notebook computer has an IrDA port. What is that?

A The infrared port on a computer is generally referred to as an *IrDA* port. IrDA is short for Infrared Data Association, a group of device manufacturers that developed a standard for transmitting data via infrared light waves.

Q I added an extra parallel port to my machine so I can have a full-time DCC connection. Why doesn't the DCC wizard see the new port (LPT2)?

A If you have added ports to your machine since you installed DCC, rerun the DCC wizard. When you get to the dialog box shown in Figure 4.1, click Install New Ports to make the wizard aware of the new ports.

Q I'm having trouble making the Direct Cable Connection. The guest machine prompts me to enter the name of the host machine, but then says it can't find the host machine. I made sure the host machine name is entered correctly. What's wrong?

A When that happens, go to the IPX/SPX-compatible Protocol properties sheet, and activate the I Want to Enable NetBIOS Over IPX/SPX check box in the NetBIOS tab. Do this on both machines. You should now be able to connect.

Q I can't get my Windows 98 laptop to establish a Direct Cable Connection with my Windows 95 desktop machine, but it works just fine with another Windows 98 system. I even have NetBEUI enabled. Help!

A Look under the General tab of the System properties sheet and see if your Windows 95 desktop machine is running a non-English versions of Windows 95 OEM Service Release 2 (OSR2, A.K.A. Win95B) or OEM Service Release version 2.1 (OSR2.1). If you are, attempting to use Direct Cable Connection to connect two computers might not work at all.

Quiz

1. True or False: I can establish a Direct Cable Connection using the LPT1 port on the host and COM2 port on the guest.

2. Which type of port has the fastest throughput?

    A. USB port

    B. Serial port with 16650 UART

    C. Bi-directional parallel port

    D. Infrared port

3. To connect the ECP parallel ports between the host and the guest computer, a(n) _____ cable is needed.

4. To connect the serial ports between the host and the guest computers, a(n) _____ serial cable is needed.

4

Hour 5

Installing a Two-Node Peer-to-Peer Windows 98 Network

If you have installed and tried out the Direct Cable Connection discussed in the previous Hour, you're probably not very impressed with its speed. Keep in mind that DCC was meant to simply transfer files between two machines, not to be used as a "real" network. During this Hour, however, you learn how you can set up a a peer-to-peer network, using network interface cards and cables, between two Windows 98 machines.

The concepts and knowledge you gain during this Hour are not limited to just installing a two-node network. The same ideas apply to installing a network that consists of many nodes; the only change is in how you connect the machines.

The following topics are covered:

- Installing and cabling the NICs
- Installing and configuring client software
- Selecting and configuring a network protocol

Installing Network Hardware

When setting up a network, your first task is to install all the necessary hardware in each machine. This means adding the network cards, running cables, and tying everything together with whatever other components you need (such as a hub).

Ethernet is probably the predominant networking technology used today. Besides, Ethernet hardware is very inexpensive, so it's attractive to home and small-business networks. You can buy an Ethernet card for less than $50.

As you might recall from Hour 2, "Networking Basics," there are several different implementations for Ethernet networks. For home or small-sized networks, 10Base2 is quite suitable. On the other hand, 10BaseT can be used for networks of any size, including the two-node peer-to-peer network discussed here.

10Base2 Coaxial Cable

Because 10Base2 uses a bus topology, all you need to connect two machines is the following:

- One piece of RG-58/U coaxial cable
- Two T-connectors
- Two 50-ohm terminators
- Two 10Base2 Ethernet cards

Figure 5.1 illustrates how you connect two computers in a 10Base2 configuration.

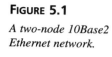

FIGURE 5.1

A two-node 10Base2 Ethernet network.

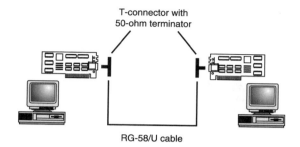

Cross-Over 10BaseT Ethernet Cable

There are two ways to connect two machines in a 10BaseT configuration. Because 10BaseT uses a star topology, the "conventional" method is to connect two machines with a hub and standard 10BaseT cables. However, you can also use what is called a *cross-over cable* instead of a hub.

The concept of a 10BaseT cross-over cable is exactly the same as that of a null-modem cable, discussed in the previous Hour—to transpose sending and receiving signals between the two computers. You can purchase 10BaseT cross-over cables for about $15, but just in case you want to build one yourself, Table 5.1 shows the pinouts for a 10BaseT cross-over cable.

TABLE 5.1 PINOUTS FOR A 10BASET CROSS-OVER CABLE.

Pin	Signal Name	Pin	Signal Name
1	Receive+	3	Transmit+
2	Receive-	6	Transmit-
3	Transmit+	1	Receive+
6	Transmit-	2	Receive-

5

Figure 5.2 shows how you connect two computers in a 10BaseT configuration using either standard 10BaseT cables and a hub or a cross-over 10BaseT cable.

FIGURE 5.2

A two-node 10BaseT Ethernet network.

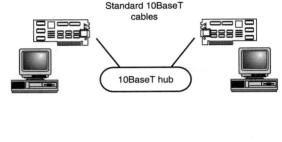

Standard 10BaseT cables

10BaseT hub

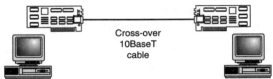

Cross-over 10BaseT cable

Configuring the Network Adapter

After the NIC is properly installed, you need to tell Windows 98 about it. Windows 98 usually does a pretty good job of detecting your network hardware, particularly if the NIC is plug-and-play (PnP) compliant. If you're installing Windows 98 from scratch, the Detection Manager should figure out your card and display it in the Network Configuration dialog box. If Windows 98 is already installed, the system should detect the new card the next time you restart.

In either case, Windows 98 installs the appropriate driver for the card (you may be asked to insert your Windows 98 CD-ROM or a diskette). Windows 98 comes with 32-bit protected mode drivers for many adapters, although you're free to use existing 16-bit drivers if Windows 98 doesn't have the driver for your card. (Most NICs come with a driver diskette that has a Windows 95/98/NT driver on it.)

If Windows 98 didn't detect your NIC, or if it detects the wrong type of card, you can easily change the adapter component. If the Network properties sheet shows the wrong adapter, you should first remove it by highlighting the adapter's name and then clicking Remove. When that's done, use the following steps to manually install your adapter:

1. Click Add to bring up the Select Network Component Type dialog box.

2. Highlight Adapter and then click Add to bring up the Select Network Adapters dialog box.

3. Scroll through the Manufacturers list and highlight the vendor of your NIC, and then highlight the specific model of your card in the Network Adapters list (see Figure 5.3).

If you don't see your particular NIC listed and the card came with a driver disk, click Have Disk and follow the prompts to choose the driver.

4. Click OK.

FIGURE 5.3

Select the make and model of your network card with this dialog box.

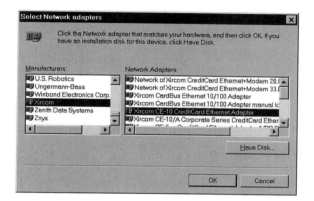

Installing and Configuring Client Software

After you have the network adapter defined, the next step is to install a network client. Windows 98 comes with several clients, but you can also add third-party clients (such as the ones from Novell). To set up a peer-to-peer network, you just need to install the Client for Microsoft Networks.

> If you need to access a NetWare server too, you need to install a NetWare client, which is discussed in Hour 8, "Accessing Novell Resources from Windows 98."

5

The following steps show you how to install the Client for Microsoft Networks (you might need to have your Windows 98 CD-ROM or diskettes handy):

1. Open the Network properties sheet.

2. Click Add to bring up the Select Network Component Type dialog box.

3. Highlight Client and click Add to bring up the Select Network Client dialog box.

4. Highlight Microsoft from the Manufacturers list, highlight Client for Microsoft Networks from the Network Clients list, and then click OK.

You should now see the Client for Microsoft Networks listed in the Network Components list.

In the next Hour, you'll see how you can "map" a drive letter to another computer's folder or drive so it appears to be part of your own system. If you have a lot of these mappings, it can take a while for them to be re-established each time you start Windows 98. To speed things up, you can configure the Network Logon options as follows:

1. From the Network properties sheet, highlight Client for Microsoft Networks and then click Properties.

2. Enable the Quick Logon option in the Network Logon Options section (see Figure 5.4).

3. Click OK.

FIGURE 5.4

This properties sheet allows you to set logon options for the Client for Microsoft Networks.

The Quick Logon option allows the logon process to finish without re-establishing the network drive mappings until you access them. If you have only a few network drive mappings, you can enable the Logon and Restore Network Connections option instead. This option logs you on to the network *and* re-establishes all network drive mappings automatically.

Adding a Protocol

Depending on the client installed, Windows 98 automatically installs some networking protocols. For example, when you install Client for Microsoft Networks, NetBEUI and IPX/SPX are added. You generally don't need TCP/IP in a two-node peer-to-peer environment. However, if you want to use IP between the machines, you can manually add it.

The following steps illustrate how to install another protocol (Microsoft TCP/IP):

1. Open the Network properties sheet.
2. Click Add to bring up the Select Network Component Type dialog box.
3. Highlight Protocol and click Add to bring up the Select Network Protocol dialog box.
4. Highlight Microsoft from the Manufacturers list, highlight TCP/IP from the Network Protocols list, and then click OK.

To remove a protocol you don't want, simply highlight it in the list of network components in the Network properties sheet and then click Remove.

As discussed in Hour 4, "Direct Cable Connection Network," for Windows 98 networking to function properly, you must *bind* a network client to a protocol and bind a protocol to a network adapter driver. Windows 98 does the bindings for you automatically. However, it binds every installed client to every installed protocol, and every installed protocol is bound to each installed network adapter. For performance reasons, you might want to remove some of the bindings. For example, you have installed both the Client for Microsoft Networks and Client for NetWare Networks, but because only Client for NetWare Networks uses the IPX/SPX protocol, you can unbind Client for Microsoft Networks from the IPX/SPX protocol. Table 5.2 lists the protocols used by the different networks.

TABLE 5.2   NETWORKING PROTOCOLS.

Network type	Protocol(s) used
Direct Cable Connection	NetBEUI, TCP/IP, or IPX/SPX
Dial-Up Networking (DUN)	NetBEUI, TCP/IP, or IPX/SPX
Microsoft (such as Windows NT)	NetBEUI, TCP/IP, or IPX/SPX
Internet	TCP/IP
NetWare 4 and below	IPX/SPX
NetWare 5 and above	IPX/SPX or TCP/IP

5

To work with the client bindings of a given protocol, take the following steps:

1. Open the Network properties sheet.
2. Highlight the protocol and click Properties.
3. Select the Bindings tab and uncheck any client(s) that you want to unbind.
4. Click OK.

Similarly, to work with the protocol bindings of a given network adapter, highlight the
adapter from the Network Components list and click Properties. Select the Bindings tab,
uncheck any protocol(s) that you want to unbind, and then click OK.

Protocol Configuration

With the exception of TCP/IP, you generally don't need to touch the protocol properties
at all. For the sake of completeness, however, you'll find a discussion of tunable settings
for TCP/IP as well as those for NetBEUI and IPX/SPX in the following sections.

NetBEUI Properties

NetBEUI is a "no-brainer" protocol—you install it and it works. When Windows 98 runs
in the Protected mode (default), it takes care of all the tunable NetBEUI settings, so you
don't have to worry about a thing. If, however, you start up Windows 98 in the Safe
mode with the network support option, there are two NetBEUI settings you can adjust if
needed. These two settings can be found under the Advanced tab in the NetBEUI
properties sheet:

- **Maximum Sessions**   This value specifies the maximum number of concurrent
  connections to remote computers that the redirector allows. The maximum allowed
  value is 117, the minimum allowed value is 3, and the default is 10.

NEW TERM   A *redirector* is a component of the networking software that redirects requests
for network resources, such as a shared printer, to the network instead of
allowing the local operating system (such as Windows 98) to service the request.

- **NCBS (NetBIOS Command Blocks)**   This value determines the maximum
  number of NetBIOS commands that can be used at any one time. The maximum
  allowed value is 255, the minimum allowed value is 7, and the default is 12.

IPX/SPX Properties

There are six changeable parameters for the Microsoft IPX/SPX-compatible protocol.
They can be found under the Advanced tab in the IPX/SPX-compatible protocol
properties sheet:

- **Force Even Length Packets**   Some network card drivers require the IPX packets
  to be an even number of bytes. This setting forces an IPX packet to contain an even
  number of bytes by adding a padding byte, if necessary.

- **Frame Type**   If you are using multiple frame types (such as Ethernet II and
  Ethernet 802.2), you can use this option to specify which specific frame type IPX
  should be bound to, instead of the first one detected by Windows 98.

- **Maximum Connections** This setting determines how many concurrent IPX/SPX connections the Windows 98 workstation can have with other devices. The maximum allowed value is 128; the minimum allowed value is 1 (which is also the default).

- **Maximum Sockets** This specifies the maximum number of sockets the workstation can allocate for IPX/SPX connections. Typically, an IPX/SPX application uses at least one socket. The maximum allowed value is 255; the minimum allowed value is 2, which is also the default.

NEW TERM A *socket* is a memory address used by networking software to send or receive data. It can be compared to the port address of a hardware device.

- **Network Address** This identifies the IPX network address. It should not be changed because the driver auto-detects the IPX number used on the wire.

- **Source Routing** In a Token Ring network, this parameter is used to control whether network traffic generated by the workstation can cross source route bridges. The default setting is off.

The IPX/SPX-compatible protocol properties sheet also has a NetBIOS tab, which allows you to specify whether NetBIOS applications are to use IPX/SPX as the transport/network protocol.

TCP/IP Properties

Unlike NetBEUI or IPX/SPX, TCP/IP is not a Plug-and-Play protocol. You need to configure some settings for it to function correctly. If you have installed multiple network adapters (say an Ethernet card and a Dial-Up Adapter), you need to configure each binding separately because Windows 98 supports the use of multiple TCP/IP configurations. If you see multiple entries for the TCP/IP protocol, highlight the appropriate binding and click Properties. You'll see the following tabs in the TCP/IP Properties dialog box:

- Bindings
- Advanced
- NetBIOS
- DNS Configuration
- Gateway
- WINS Configuration
- IP Address

Bindings As previously discussed, the Bindings tab is where you select which clients and services should use the TCP/IP protocol. For best performance, enable only the components that need to use TCP/IP.

5

It is worth mentioning that if your computer connects to the Internet, make sure file and printer sharing for Microsoft Networks is *unbound* from TCP/IP because it can create a huge security risk. (This risk is explained during Hour 20, "Connecting Your Windows 98 Desktop to the Internet.")

Advanced   The only configurable "advanced" setting under this tab is the Set This Protocol to be the Default Protocol setting. You should leave it off unless you're on a pure TCP/IP network.

NetBIOS   There is only one option under the NetBIOS tab: I Want to Enable NetBIOS over TCP/IP. It is enabled by default and can't be changed. As mentioned back in Hour 3, "Protocols," NetBIOS over TCP/IP is also known as *RFC NetBIOS.*

DNS Configuration   If you have a Domain Naming System (DNS) server on your network or if the workstation is accessing the Internet via a Dial-Up Networking connection, select Enable DNS on the DNS Configuration tab, and then fill in the following properties (see Figure 5.5):

- **Host**   The host name of your computer.
- **Domain**   The domain name of your network, or that of your Internet service provider (ISP).
- **DNS Server Search Order**   List, in order, the IP address(es) of the DNS server that your system will query for name resolution.
- **Domain Suffix Search Order**   Your Windows 98 machine can belong to multiple domains. List, in order, the domain suffix(es) that can be used to construct a fully qualified domain name when doing a DNS lookup.

For more about DNS, see Hour 19, "Troubleshooting a Microsoft Network." For more about ISPs, see Hour 20.

FIGURE 5.5

Use this dialog box to fill out your DNS configuration information.

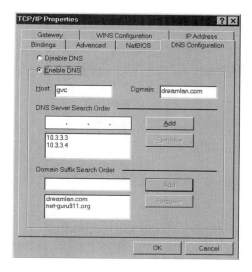

Gateway   If you have routers on your network, list the IP address of the router that's local to your segment. If there is more than one router on your segment, you generally list them in order of physical distance, with the one closest to your machine first. If you are connecting to the Internet via an ISP, it's the IP address of one of your ISP's routers (get this information from your ISP).

WINS Configuration   If your network uses WINS name resolution, you need to select the Enable WINS Resolution option in this tab (see Figure 5.6). If you don't have a DHCP server on your network, enter the IP addresses of your primary and secondary WINS server in the WINS Server Search Order property box. In most cases, you can leave the Scope ID property blank. You need to specify it only if your network runs NetBIOS over TCP/IP (for example, RFC NetBIOS) and you want to set a "scope" on a group of machines (only computers with the same scope ID can talk to each other). The scope ID can be any alphanumeric characters and the following symbols, and can be up to 234 characters in length:

```
~ ! @ # $ % ^ & ( ) _ - { } ' .
```

NEW TERM   A NetBIOS *scope* is a logical grouping of machines, so that only computers with the same scope ID (same workgroup) can communicate with each other.

FIGURE 5.6

Use this dialog box to specify your WINS name resolution configuration.

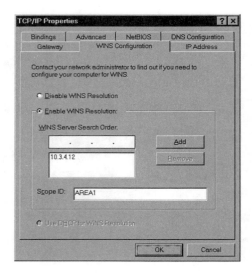

 It is not advisable to change your scope in a production environment, unless you're explicitly instructed to. If you do, you won't be able to see and talk to other machines not in your new scope.

If your machine is using DHCP to get its IP address, instead of filling in the IP addresses for the WINS servers, simply activate the Use DHCP for WINS Resolution option. This tells Windows 98 to use the DHCP server to get all the WINS information it needs.

 For more about WINS, see Hour 17, "Advanced NT Server Management."

IP Address   There are two ways in which you can assign an IP address to a Windows 98 workstation:

- If you have a DHCP server on your network, or if your ISP assigns you an IP address on-the-fly whenever you log on, select the Obtain an IP Address Automatically option in this tab.

- If the workstation has been assigned a permanent IP address, select the Specify an IP Address option in this tab, enter the supplied IP address in the IP Address text box, and enter its corresponding subnet mask in the Subnet Mask text box, as illustrated in Figure 5.7.

FIGURE 5.7

Use this dialog box to specify your IP address information.

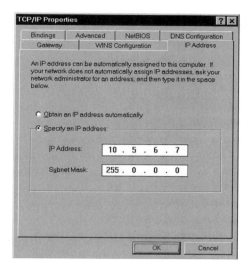

Selecting Your Primary Network Logon

To complete the Network Configuration dialog box (if you're doing a Windows 98 custom install from scratch) or the Configuration tab in the Network properties sheet, you need to select your primary network logon (see Figure 5.8). From the drop-down list, select Client for Microsoft Networks as the primary network logon.

FIGURE 5.8

The primary network logon determines the logon dialog box you see at startup.

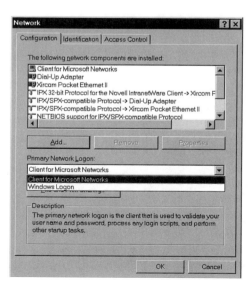

5

Identifying Your Computer

The last step is to set up the identity of your computer. If you're installing Windows 98 from scratch, the Setup wizard displays an Identification dialog box after you've clicked Next in the Network Configuration dialog box. Otherwise, access the Identification tab from the Network properties sheet. You need to enter three pieces of information (see Figure 5.9):

- **Computer Name**   Enter a name of up to 15 characters to identify your computer. This name *must* be unique on the network. The computer name is what other people see when they browse for network resources. You can use any of the alphanumeric characters (but spaces are not allowed) as well as any of the following symbols:

    ~ ! @ # $ % ^ & ( ) _ - { } ' .

- **Workgroup**   Enter a name of up to 15 characters to identify your workgroup. In a peer-to-peer network, computers are organized into workgroups by giving them the same name in their respective Workgroup text boxes. If you're logging onto an NT domain, enter the domain name here. The same naming rule for the computer name applies here.

- **Computer Description**   Enter up to 48 characters (spaces are permitted, but commas are not) to supply a detailed description of your computer.

FIGURE 5.9

Identify your computer to the network in this dialog box.

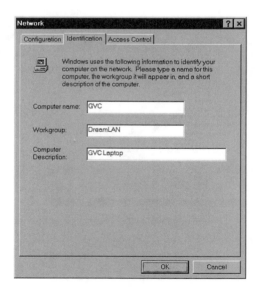

Summary

This Hour has given you the basics for installing a "real" network, in which networking cards and cables are used. You have learned how to install and configure network adapters, clients, and protocols, how to establish your primary network logon, and so on.

In the next Hour, you find out how to share and access resources in a peer-to-peer environment, as well as some troubleshooting tips.

Workshop

Q&A

Q I'm not sure which driver to use for my network card. What can I do?

A You can try using the Add New Hardware wizard to have Windows 98 detect your card automatically; with luck, the wizard will pick the correct driver for you. Otherwise, you should ask someone who knows about network cards for some assistance.

Q I have TCP/IP bound to both my Client for Microsoft Networks and Client for NetWare networks. Do I really need that?

A No, you don't. You can unbind TCP/IP from the Client for NetWare Networks because it uses IPX/SPX.

Quiz

1. The association of a network client to a protocol is known as _____.
2. What protocol(s) is(are) installed when Client for Microsoft Networks is installed?
3. True or False: Each computer on the network must have the same computer and workgroup names.

5

HOUR **6**

Sharing Windows 98 Resources

You just spent the past hour reading about how to set up a two-node Windows 98 network; now you must be anxious to know how you can share files and printers between those two machines! Great—because that's exactly what you'll be doing during this hour. The following topics are covered:

- How to set up Windows file and print sharing service
- How to share drives and folders
- How to share printers
- How to access shared resources
- What to do if one machine can't see the shared resource on the other machine

Sharing Resources

In a peer-to-peer network, each computer can act as both a client and a server. To set up a Windows 98 machine as a peer server, you need to enable the file and print sharing service as you did for the host machine in the Direct Cable Connection network (see Hour 4, "Direct Cable Connection Network"). After the file and print sharing service is running, you can then share individual drives, folders, and printers with the network.

When sharing resources in a Windows network, there are two things to keep in mind:

- Each shared resource (generally referred to as a *share*) on a given machine must be given a unique name.
- Proper configuration of access control is important.

 The term *access control* is used here in reference to security restrictions.

For a server resource to be referenced uniquely, each shared resource must have a different name. However, shared resources on different servers can have the same name because the "complete name" (UNC; Universal Naming Convention) includes the computer name. Therefore, you can have a shared folder called BOOK on a computer named DESKTOP and a shared folder also called BOOK on a computer named LAPTOP, but you can't have two shares called BOOK on the same computer.

Setting Up File and Print Sharing

If you have set up a Direct Cable Connection as discussed in Hour 4, the following is nothing new and you can skip ahead to the next section; otherwise, read on. If the server machine isn't already on a network, it will not have File and Print Sharing set up. The following steps show you how to enable the file and print sharing service (you might need to have your Windows 98 CD-ROM or disks handy):

1. Double-click the Network icon in Control Panel to open the Network properties sheet.
2. If the File and Print Sharing button is enabled in the Network properties sheet, skip to step 5. Otherwise, click Add to bring up the Select Network Component Type dialog box.
3. Highlight Service and click Add to bring up the Select Network Service dialog box.
4. Highlight Microsoft from the Manufacturers list, highlight File and Print Sharing for Microsoft Networks from the Network Services list, and then click OK.
5. In the Network properties sheet, click the File and Print Sharing button.

6. In the File and Print Sharing dialog box (see Figure 6.1), check the I Want to Be Able to Give Others Access to My Files check box. If you want other machines to be able to print with your printer, check the I Want to Be Able to Allow Others to Print to My Printer(s) check box. Click OK.

7. Click OK on the Network properties sheet. Click Yes to restart your computer for the new settings to take effect.

FIGURE 6.1

This dialog box turns your Windows 98 workstation into a peer server.

Setting Up Access Control

In a networking environment where many users can access your shared resources, it is important to impose some kind of access control security. You might choose to leave your machine wide open so that anyone can read and delete files from your workstation, but you might want others to only read (not delete) files from your machine.

Windows networking allows you to set up a *share-level* security in which security is assigned on a resource-by-resource basis, and any user with the correct password can access the share. If, however, you have a Windows NT or NetWare server on your network, you can implement a more flexible security measure, known as *user-level* or *pass-through* security. In this configuration, share access is controlled on a user-by-user basis, instead of a share-by-share basis. In other words, when you share a resource, you specify the users or groups who are allowed to use the resource. This security information is stored on a security provider server (a NetWare or Windows NT server). When a user tries to access one of the shared resources, Windows 98 asks the server to authenticate the request. The server checks the requester's user name and password, and then checks whether the user is on your list of authorized users. If so, the server grants access; otherwise, access is denied.

The Access Control tab in the Network properties sheet controls the security model to be used (see Figure 6.2). When setting up user-level security, enter in the text box the name of the NT domain where you will get the list of users and groups. Windows 98 queries the server designated as the primary domain controller for that domain to get the information.

6

FIGURE 6.2

Use this dialog box to switch between share-level and user-level security.

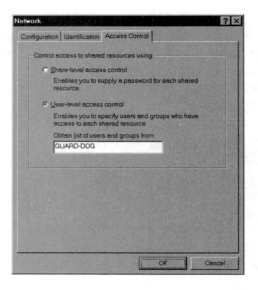

You'll learn about Windows NT lingo in Hour 10, "NT Server Basics."

Be aware that when you switch security modes, any shares you have configured will be "forgotten," so you'll need to reconfigure them.

The rest of this Hour concentrates on dealing with share-level security; user-level security is discussed in the NT Server section of this book.

Sharing Drives and Folders

With the file sharing service activated, you can share any file-related devices, such as your hard drive and CD-ROM drives, attached to your computer. To set up any of these devices as a share, use any one of the following techniques:

- Select the device or folder, and then choose File|Sharing from the menu.
- Right-click the device or folder, and select Sharing from the context menu.
- Open the properties sheet for the device or folder, and select the Sharing tab.

When using share-level security, a Sharing tab similar to the one in Figure 6.3 is displayed. The tab contains the following settings:

- **Not Shared**—Turns off the sharing for the selected resource.
- **Shared As**—Enables sharing for the selected resource.
- **Share Name**—In this text box, you enter a name of up to 12 characters to identify the shared resource. This name must be unique among the shares on *this* computer and is displayed in the Names column (if View|Details is enabled) when others browse your computer with Explorer. The name is also used as part of the shared resource's UNC path.

  You can use any of the alphanumeric characters as well as any of the following symbols:

  ~ ! @ # $ % ^ & ( ) _ - { } ' .

- **Comment**—(Optional) Use this field to enter text, up to 48 characters in length, to supply a short description of the share. This text appears in the Comments column when others browse your computer with Explorer.
- **Access Type**—Select one of three possible access levels to grant to remote users:
    - **Read-Only**—A user can view the contents of a file and copy it, but can't modify the resource in any way.
    - **Full**—Users have complete access to all the contents within the shared resource.
    - **Depends on Password**—The level of access is determined by the password provided by the remote user when the share is accessed.
- **Passwords**—Use these fields to specify the passwords remote users need to enter to access the share.

FIGURE 6.3

Use the Sharing tab to establish access security for a shared resource.

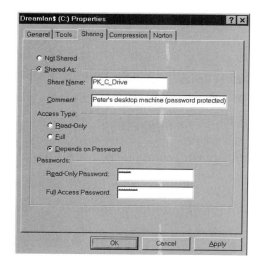

6

Click OK to put the settings into effect. If any passwords were assigned, you'll be asked to confirm them.

As shown in Figure 6.4, Windows 98 adds a hand icon underneath the resource's existing icon to indicate that the resource is shared.

FIGURE 6.4

Windows 98 adds a hand icon to denote a shared drive or folder resource; a shared printer is denoted with a check mark.

Shared printer

Shared drive

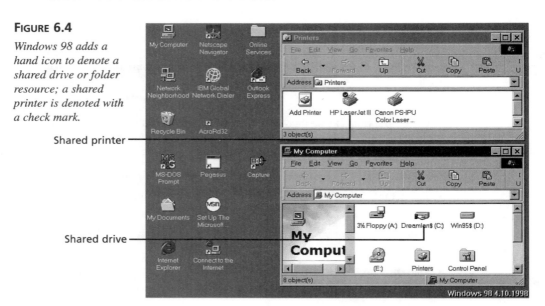

Sharing Printers

The procedure for sharing a printer is very similar to that for sharing drives and folders. You can do any of the following:

- Select the printer, and then choose File|Sharing from the menu.
- Right-click the printer and select Sharing from the context menu.
- Open the properties sheet for the printer and select the Sharing tab.

As before, you select the Share As option and then fill in the share name, comment, and, optionally, the password fields. You'll notice that there is no Access Type (see Figure 6.5) because that doesn't apply to a printer. You can, however, restrict access to the printer by requiring a password.

FIGURE 6.5

The Sharing tab for a printer is simpler than that for a folder.

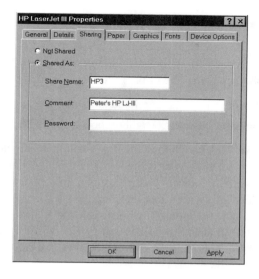

As shown in Figure 6.4, Windows 98 adds a check mark above the printer icon to indicate that the printer is shared.

Accessing Shared Resources

If everything has gone well up to this point, you're ready for some action! Your new network is up and running, and you have configured at least one of your Windows 98 machines as a peer server and made some of its resources shared. Time to log on to the network and nose around.

Logging on to the Network

Just about every network requires you to log on with a user name and password as part of the basic security measures, and Windows 98 is no different. With networking enabled, Windows 98 gives you a logon prompt each time you restart the system. One of the nice features of Windows 98 is a single logon for all your networks (including Windows 98 itself). The very first time you start Windows 98, however, you might have to fight through multiple logon dialog boxes. The trick for a single logon is to assign the same password for all your networks. At this point, you should have only the Windows 98 logon dialog box.

Single logon refers to the ability to enter your user name and password only *once* and be logged on to all networks you want to be attached to.

Using the Network Neighborhood

Network Neighborhood is a special folder that appears as part of your desktop when Windows networking is enabled; otherwise, you wouldn't see it. You can view the Network Neighborhood by using one of the following two methods:

- Double-click the Network Neighborhood icon on the desktop.
- In Explorer, highlight Network Neighborhood in the Folders pane.

The top level of the Network Neighborhood shows you the computers that share your workgroup or domain, including your computer. You'll notice an icon called Entire Network. It shows you the Windows workgroups and domains and other network resources (such as NetWare servers) that make up the network. For example, Figure 6.6 shows one workgroup (Dreamlan) and a workstation that is also part of a Novell network (as there is a folder for IntranetWare servers and for the Novell Directory Services trees). Each icon in Network Neighborhood acts as a folder, so you can open each one and "drill down" to display more information.

FIGURE 6.6

The Entire Network icon displays all the workgroups and domains and other shared network resources (NetWare servers and NDS trees in this example).

At the computer level, Network Neighborhood shows you which resources each computer is sharing with the network. You can access any drives and folders shared just as though they were part of your computer. If, however, a password was assigned to protect the shared resource, you'll see a Network Password dialog box like the one shown in Figure 6.7. Without knowing the correct password, you're not permitted to access a password-protected resource.

FIGURE 6.7

A password is needed to access a protected resource.

Using the Universal Naming Convention Format

Microsoft networks support using the UNC format for accessing resources. Here is the syntax:

`\\COMPUTER_NAME\SHARE_NAME`

`COMPUTER_NAME` is the name of the computer (as defined in the Identification tab of the Network properties sheet), and `SHARE_NAME` is the name given to the shared resource.

You can access shared network resources by using any one of the following methods:

- In a 32-bit application's Open or Save As dialog box, you can use a UNC name in the File Name text box (see Figure 6.8).
- You can open a shared resource by entering the UNC into a Run dialog box, or by using the `start` command at a DOS prompt (for example, `start \\dlan98\desktop_c`).
- You can use a UNC name as part of a DOS command, such as `dir \\dlan98\desktop_c\*.dat`.

FIGURE 6.8

You can specify a UNC name in a 32-bit application, such as Netscape Communicator.

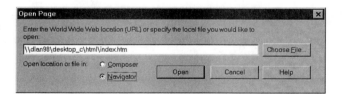

Mapping a Network Drive

UNC names are convenient, but if you access the same share often, you can easily get tried of typing them. To circumvent that, you can map a shared network drive or folder to your own computer. *Mapping* assigns a drive letter to the share so that it appears to be just another disk drive on your machine.

6

To establish a network drive, use either of the following methods:

- In Explorer or Network Neighborhood, highlight the resource and choose File|Map Network Drive.
- In Explorer or Network Neighborhood, right-click the resource and select Map Network Drive from the context menu.

Regardless of which method you use, you'll see the Map Network Drive dialog box, shown in Figure 6.9. By default, the Drive drop-down list displays the first unused drive letter on your system, but you can use the drop-down list to select any other unused letter.

FIGURE **6.9**

Use the Map Network Drive dialog box to map a drive letter to a share.

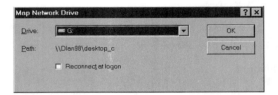

If you want Windows 98 to map the resource each time you log on to the network, make sure the Reconnect at Logon check box is checked. Click OK, and Windows 98 adds the new drive letter to your system. The new drive letter can be seen listed in My Computer, as shown in Figure 6.10. (If the share is password protected, you might have to enter a password at this point.)

FIGURE **6.10**

All network drives are shown in My Computer.

You should disconnect the mapped drive when you no longer need it. To disconnect a mapped drive, use one of the following methods:

- In My Computer or Explorer, right-click the mapped resource and select Disconnect from the context menu.

- In My Computer, highlight the mapped resource and choose File|Disconnect.

 Don't disconnect a mapped drive when one of your applications is using files from it because you might lose your work. Windows 98 displays a warning if you do, but it is better to get in the habit of closing the files on a mapped drive before disconnecting the drive.

Troubleshooting Connectivity

There could be any number of reasons why you don't see or can't access the shares from the peer server. The following are a few things that can be easily overlooked.

When in Doubt, Restart

Windows 98 and NT often require you to restart for new settings to take effect. If you didn't restart your machine when prompted during the addition of new services and protocols, your changes will not have taken effect.

Also, sometimes changes to a share on the peer server are not immediately seen by the clients. The client might simply need to wait for a few minutes, or need to close down Network Neighborhood and reopen it.

Is It Plugged In?

Make sure your network cable is properly plugged in. If you are testing your two-node Ethernet network without using a 10BaseT hub, ensure that the cable between the two machines is a cross-over cable. If you are using a 10BaseT hub, confirm that its power supply is plugged in.

If you are using 10Base2 or 10Base5 Ethernet, check that each end of the cable segment is terminated correctly with a 50-ohm terminator. If a grounding wire is attached to the terminator, make sure only one of the wires is used.

Protocol Settings

For the workstations to communicate with each other, they must use a common protocol. Therefore, check in the Network properties sheet of all machines to make sure there's at least one protocol (such as NetBEUI) common to all machines.

6

IP Protocol Configuration

If you are using TCP/IP between the systems, you can use the PING utility to confirm TCP/IP connectivity. Also, you need to make sure the IP addresses and subnet masks used on all machines are consistent.

Using PING

Similar to the sonar "pings" used by naval vessels to locate submarines, the PING utility checks whether other machines on the network can be located (that is, are reachable). To see if your machine can "see" another machine, simply run PING from a DOS prompt as follows:

```
D:\>ping 10.1.1.1

Pinging 10.1.1.1 with 32 bytes of data:

Reply from 10.1.1.1: bytes=32 time=5ms TTL=128
Reply from 10.1.1.1: bytes=32 time=3ms TTL=128
Reply from 10.1.1.1: bytes=32 time=2ms TTL=128
Reply from 10.1.1.1: bytes=32 time=3ms TTL=128

Ping statistics for 10.1.1.1:
    Packets: Sent = 4, Received = 4, Lost = 0 (0% loss),
Approximate round-trip times in milliseconds:
    Minimum = 2ms, Maximum = 5ms, Average = 3ms
```

This example shows that a communication path exists between your workstation and the IP host 10.1.1.1. If the remote host can't be reached or if the path between your system and the remote host is down, you'll see the following response from PING:

```
D:\>ping 10.1.1.1

Pinging 10.1.1.1 with 32 bytes of data:

Request timed out.
Request timed out.
Request timed out.
Request timed out.

Ping statistics for 10.1.1.1:
    Packets: Sent = 4, Received = 0, Lost = 4 (100% loss),
Approximate round-trip times in milliseconds:
    Minimum = 0ms, Maximum = 0ms, Average = 0ms
```

IP Network Address

When dealing with TCP/IP networks, it is important to keep the IP network addressing straight. Unless you have routers in your network, the IP network addresses on all the machines must be the same. For example, if you are using a Class B address, such as 123.10.0.0, then all IP hosts on the network must have an IP address starting with 123.10.

If necessary, review the IP address section in Hour 3, "Protocols."

IP Subnet Masks

Unless you're familiar with IP addressing and subnetting, it is best to use the default subnet masks as follows:

- Class A subnet mask: 255.0.0.0
- Class B subnet mask: 255.255.0.0
- Class C subnet mask: 255.255.255.0

Make sure that all workstations are using the same subnet mask.

Summary

During this past hour, you learned how to set up file and print sharing and how to turn your Windows 98 machine into a peer server. You also found out how to share drives, folders, and printers and to access them using various techniques.

In the next hour, you'll learn how to expand your two-node network into a network with multiple workstations.

Workshop

Q&A

Q Can I share my Windows 98 resources with machines that are not Windows 98 systems?

A If you are using the Client for Microsoft Networks, you can share resources with machines running Windows NT, Windows for Workgroup, LAN Manager, and any other networks that use the Server Message Block (SMB) file-sharing protocol.

6

Q Do I need to install TCP/IP to have my network running?

A No—as long as the machines are running the same protocol. You can use NetBEUI, IPX/SPX, or TCP/IP.

Q Can I access Network Neighborhood from within an application?

A Yes! If you are using a 32-bit application, you can access the Network Neighborhood through the Save As and Open dialog boxes. In the Save As dialog box, open the Save In drop-down list and select Network Neighborhood; in the Open dialog box, use the Look In drop-down list instead.

Q I tried to access a share using UNC names at the DOS prompt, but I get a sharing violation error. What's wrong?

A Is that share password protected? If so, you need to first access it from the desktop using Network Neighborhood where the password is entered.

Q What does PING stand for?

A You really want to know? Ping stands for *Packet Internet Groper*.

Quiz

1. True or False: You can only share a folder as read-only.

2. How do you establish single logon?

3. What does UNC stand for?

4. What is the UNC syntax for accessing WP.EXE from the WordPro share located on a computer named DESKTOP?

Hour 7

Installing a Multi-Node Windows 98 Network

As your network requirements grow, you'll need to add more machines to your existing network. Two network card types commonly used today are Ethernet and Token Ring. Ethernet is by far the most popular, and is easier and much less expensive to install than Token Ring.

The software configuration procedure (discussed in Hour 5, "Installing a Two-Node Peer-to-Peer Windows 98 Network") is the same, regardless of how many machines you have on the network. What's different is how you cable the machines together. You'll spend this hour finding out what you need to know to implement a multi-node (more than two nodes) network. The concepts here apply equally to Windows 98 and Windows NT systems. The following topics are covered:

- Physical topologies
- Ethernet 10Base2 topology
- Ethernet 10Base5 topology
- Ethernet 10BaseT topology

- Token Ring topology
- Troubleshooting common issues in Ethernet and Token Ring networks

Physical Topologies

Physical topology is the actual way the wiring is strung between network nodes. Three common LAN topologies are used today:

- Bus
- Star
- Ring

You have already read about them briefly during Hour 2, "Networking Basics"; a quick review here can help you make an informed decision when you're ready to expand your network.

> When talking about topologies, you often hear references to physical topology versus logical topology. Physical topology is the actual way cables are strung between networked computers; logical topology refers to how signals travel within the network.

Bus Topology

The bus topology is the simplest form of multi-node network. In a bus topology, all network nodes are connected directly to the same piece of cable. Network nodes in a bus topology can be compared to bus stops along a bus route. A segment of a network that uses a bus topology is a length of wire that does not wrap back on itself. Each end of this cable *must* be capped with a "terminator"—a resistor of a certain impedance matching that of the cable's.

A bus network is easy to cable because you simply run the cable to each workstation and attach the network card in the workstation to the cable with either a T-connector or a tapping device known as an *external transceiver*. The major drawback of a bus network is that a single cable break or a malfunctioning node can bring down the whole LAN.

Star Topology

In a star cabling topology, a central system, which can be a server or a wiring hub, connects your workstations. Each node is connected to the central system by its own dedicated cable. Because each network node requires its own cable, the star topology generally uses much more cable than bus or ring topologies. On the positive side, because each node has its own cable, a cable break affects only the node connected by that cable.

Depending on the implementation, unused ports on the central system may or may not need to be "terminated." If you put a terminator on the open port when one is not called for, you could create communication problems. If you're unsure whether an unused port should be terminated, consult your hub's documentation.

Ring Topology

As the name implies, the foundation of a ring network is a closed loop of cable. The signal within a ring network is passed, in a single direction, from one node to the node that is its nearest neighbor. Each node is connected to two other nodes in the network, and each connection uses a dedicated cable. Because the nodes are linked in a circular manner, however, a single cable break can disrupt the whole network, as is the case with a bus topology.

Most ring networks provide fault tolerance by implementing a backup signal path. If a break affects one of the ring segments, the signal can often be routed back through the ring's backup path within the hub. When a cable break occurs in a network, it causes the network to reroute the signals through the backup path, which usually runs in the direction opposite the main path. This doubles the ring distance and, thus, slows the network somewhat—but it does keep the network functioning until a repair can be made.

> Grab some coffee, sit back, and consider this: Given what you have just reviewed, which of the three topologies would be best for your new network?

Ethernet Network Topology

As you might recall from Hour 2, Ethernet networks can be implemented with several different types of cables. Depending on your choice of cable, your Ethernet's network topology will look like a bus or a star.

10Base2

A 10Base2 Ethernet network is a bus network that uses either RG-58/U or RG-58 A/U "thin cable." As a result, 10Base2 networks are also referred to as *thinnets* (sometimes known as *cheapernets* because of the cable's low cost). RG-58 coaxial cables are 0.2

7

inches in diameter, and you can easily determine whether you have the correct cable by looking closely at it, because it's generally labeled.

A few things to keep in mind when cabling a 10Base2 network:

- Each segment can have no more than 30 nodes (a repeater counts as one of the nodes).
- Minimum distance between two nodes is 1.6 feet (0.5 meters).
- Maximum distance for a segment is 607 feet (185 meters).
- Each end of the cable run must be terminated by a 50-ohm terminator.
- A T-connector is used to attach each node to the cable.

10Base5

A 10Base5 Ethernet network is a bus network and uses RG-11 "thick cable." As a result, 10Base5 networks are also referred to as *thicknets* because of the size of the coaxial cable (0.4 inches in diameter). You can determine whether you have the correct cable by examining it because it's usually labeled.

Unlike 10Base2 networks, you need some additional hardware to connect a node to a 10Base5 bus. The node's network card is first connected to a device known as a *transceiver*, and this (external) transceiver is attached to the thick Ethernet cable; in a way, the transceiver acts as the T-connector used in 10Base2 networks.

Here are a few things to keep in mind when cabling a 10Base5 network:

- Each segment can have no more than 100 nodes (a repeater counts as one of the nodes).
- Minimum distance between two nodes is 8 feet (2.5 meters).
- Maximum distance for a segment is 1,640 feet (500 meters).
- Each end of the cable run must be terminated by a 50-ohm terminator.
- A transceiver plus transceiver cable is used to attach each node to the cable.
- Maximum transceiver cable length is 165 feet (50 meters).

Because 10Base2 and 10Base5 nodes both transmit and receive through the same connector, they are a logical as well as a physical bus.

10BaseT

A 10BaseT network is cabled by using wiring hubs. Each node is connected to the hub with an individual twisted pair cable (UTP), which makes a 10BaseT network take on a physical star topology. Within the hub, however, the individual signals are combined into a bus (on the "backplane"). Therefore, 10BaseT is a physical star but a logical bus.

10BaseT networks can be cabled using Category 3, 4, or 5 UTP cables. However, if you have plans for upgrading to 100BaseT, it is worth your while to install CAT5 cables right from the get-go. As with the coaxial cables used in 10Base2 and 10Base5 networks, you can verify the grade of your UTP cables by looking for the marking on them.

You should keep these things in mind when cabling a 10BaseT network:

- Each segment can have only one node (the node is cabled directly to the hub).
- Maximum distance for a segment is 328 feet (100 meters).
- 10BaseT cables use RJ-45 (6-pin) connectors.

The 3-4-5 Rule

Ethernet has a cabling rule known as the "3-4-5 rule," which limits the number of cabling segments and repeaters configured in series. Figure 7.1 illustrates the rules for limiting serial segments. Under the 3-4-5 rule, you can have no more than five segments in series (connected by four repeaters), of which only three can be *populated* (that is, can have more than two repeaters—one at each end). The two "empty" segments are used for extending distance only, or in the case of 10BaseT, each cabling segment contains only two connections (the node and the port on the hub) and is therefore "unpopulated."

FIGURE 7.1

This figure illustrates Ethernet's 3-4-5 cabling rule.

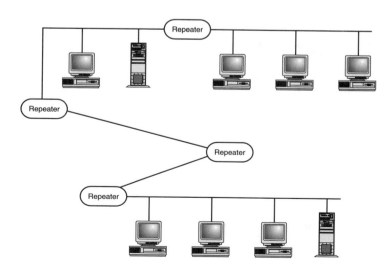

7

Because each port in a hub acts like a repeater, no two nodes in a 10BaseT configuration can be separated by more than four hubs. Consequently, when you are designing your 10BaseT network, you need to be sure no user workstation needs to cross more than four hubs to reach any shared resources it needs, as shown in Figure 7.2. If, however, the location of the server FS is switched with workstation WS, then workstation WS2 can't access the server because it needs to cross *five* hubs to reach the server. A good guideline is to place the server in the "center" of your 10BaseT network.

FIGURE 7.2

Ethernet's 3-4-5 cabling rule is also applicable to 10BaseT networks.

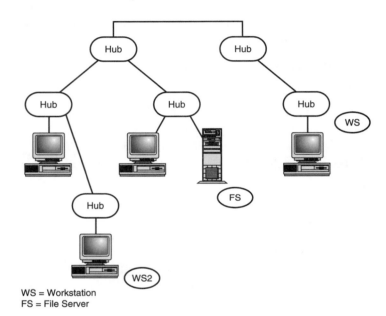

WS = Workstation
FS = File Server

Token Ring Network Topology

If you look closely at the wiring of a Token Ring network, you'll find that it has all the characteristics of a star. Token Ring uses central wiring hubs (as in the case of 10BaseT Ethernet), and each node is wired to the hub with an individual cable. If you look inside the hubs and wires, however, you'll find that the signals are passed around in a circuitous path. Therefore, Token Ring is a physical star but a logical ring topology.

Token Ring can use either shielded twisted pair (STP) cable or unshielded twisted pair (UTP) cable:

- 4Mbps Token Ring uses IBM Type 3 STP cable.
- 16Mbps Token Ring uses IBM Type 1 STP or CAT5 UTP.

You can use Type 1 STP or CAT5 UTP cables for 4Mbps Token Ring networks, but you must *not* use Type 3 cable for 16Mbps Token Ring networks.

Here are a few things to keep in mind when cabling a Token Ring network using IBM equipment:

- No more than 96 nodes should be on a given ring when using IBM's 8228 MSAU.
- No more than 12 IBM 8228 MSAUs can be connected together.
- Maximum adapter cable distance is 8 feet (2.5 meters).
- Maximum patch cable distance between an 8228 unit and a workstation node (not including the adapter cable) is 150 feet (45 meters).
- Maximum patch cable distance connecting *all* 8228 units is 400 feet (120 meters).
- To form a ring with 8228 units, a patch cable is connected from the Ring Out (RO) receptacle of an 8228 unit to the Ring In (RI) receptacle of the next 8228 unit. This continues until a patch cord has been connected to the RI receptacle of the first 8228 unit. (If a network has only one 8228 unit, its RO and RI receptacles *don't* need to be connected with a patch cable.)
- Use IBM Type 6 cables for patch cables.
- UTP cables use RJ-45 (6-pin) connectors.

Let's Do the Twist!

After reading over the differences between 10Base2, 10Base5, 10BaseT, and Token Ring, does it seem to you that 10BaseT is the easiest to implement and the most fault-tolerant of the four? If that is what's on your mind right now, you're absolutely right!

The cost of installing a 10BaseT network today is comparable to that of a 10Base2 cheapernet. The only extra piece of hardware you need for 10BaseT is a hub, which you can get for less than $100 (depending on the number of ports and feature sets). That extra $100 investment will pay you back many times over when someone cuts one of your cables by accident—only one user is affected instead of the *whole* network, as would be the case for 10Base2.

Also, if you install 10BaseT today using CAT5 cables, you're ready to move on to 100BaseT tomorrow without any rewiring! All you need are 100BaseT network cards. *That* is smart planning—you can't do that if you put in 10Base2 or 10Base5. I wouldn't even mention Token Ring in this discussion—you can buy as many as three 10BaseT cards for the price of one Token Ring card, and then there is the cost of the Token Ring hub—which is a lot more than $100!

7

Troubleshooting Common Issues

From experience, I have found that over 75 percent of the network problems encountered are cable related. Therefore, here are some commonly used cable troubleshooting tips:

- **Signal attenuation**   Any electromagnetic signal loses strength as it moves away from its source, and LAN signals are no exception. If the distance is too great, the signal could be severely attenuated, resulting in poor LAN performance. Ensure that your cables are within distance specifications. For example, on a 10Base2 network, make sure no one segment is more than 608 feet (185 meters) long. A good rule of thumb is to keep the maximum segment length to about 80 percent of the specification's maximum.

- **Mismatched cables**   Don't mix different types of cable on the same segment. For example, thin Ethernet uses RG-58/U (50-ohm) cables. You must not substitute TV coaxial cable (RG-59/U) or ARCnet cable (RG-62/U). If you do, you might be able to access the network, but there will be extensive LAN errors and poor performance issues.

- **Good connectors**   If you're the handyman type, you might decide to make your own cables to save some money. There's nothing wrong with that. However, when making coaxial cables, don't use twist-on connectors; use the crimp-on ones instead. Twist-ons have a tendency to come loose over time or if the cable is connected and disconnected often. A poor connection means intermittent connection problems.

- **Data-grade UTP cables and connectors**   UTP cables come in different colors as well as different "grades." Make sure the cables and connectors, as well as any wall-plates, are rated for data instead of voice.

- **Missing termination**   Often, when you add a new node to the end of a bus topology, you need to remove the terminator and add a new piece of cable. Be sure to put that terminator back on the end of the new cable!

- **Built-in diagnostics**   Very often, your 10BaseT or Token Ring hub has a set of LEDs for each port. Their color, or the presence or absence of a certain LED light, can indicate certain types of problems. For example, if the LINK STATUS light on the port isn't on (when the node and the hub are powered on), chances are you have a faulty cable between the hub and the node. If the LINK STATUS light is on, but you don't see a blinking DATA light when the workstation is trying to connect to the network, you could have a faulty cable, a dead port on the hub, or a bad NIC in the workstation. The LEDs are there for a reason, so make use of them during troubleshooting.

Summary

During this Hour, you reviewed the basics of Ethernet and Token Ring networks and gained some knowledge of what to look out for when implementing and troubleshooting a multi-node network. You will find your choice of 10BaseT to be a wise choice because it's ready for easy growth to 100BaseT when you have the need.

In the next Hour, you find out how you can access shared resources on a NetWare server from your Windows 98 workstation.

Workshop

Q&A

Q What is the impedance of an RG-58 cable?

A 50 ohms.

Q Can I connect two Ethernet nodes using an RG-58 cable but without using T-connectors and terminators?

A No, you can't. You must terminate both ends of a bus network with terminators.

Q Why is Token Ring hardware so much more expensive compared with, say, Ethernet?

A As of this writing, IBM still holds the patent to Token Ring, so there's the issue of royalty cost.

Quiz

1. What is the physical network topology of a Token Ring network?
2. What type of cable(s) can be used for 16Mbps Token Ring networks?
3. What is the Ethernet 3-4-5 rule?
4. True or False: The Ethernet 3-4-5 rule applies equally to 10Base2, 10Base5, and 10BaseT?

7

HOUR **8**

Accessing NetWare Resources from Windows 98

Novell's NetWare is the world's most popular client/server-based network operating system. Therefore, chances are good you'll need to access resources located on a NetWare server from a Windows 98 workstation. You need to load a NetWare client on your Windows 98 machine to gain access to a NetWare server. Windows 98 comes with Microsoft's 32-bit NetWare client, called Client for NetWare Networks. You can get, at no charge, Novell's 32-bit NetWare client for Windows 98 (called Novell Client for Windows 98/95) from Novell; this client software is included with NetWare 5.

During this hour, the following topics are covered:

- Installing and configuring Microsoft's NetWare client
- Installing Microsoft's Novell Directory Services service
- Installing and configuring Novell's NetWare client
- Using the clients to access NetWare resources

Microsoft Client for NetWare Networks

The steps for installing the Microsoft Client for NetWare Networks are very similar to those for the Client for Microsoft Networks described during Hour 5, "Installing a Two-Node Peer-to-Peer Windows 98 Network." The only difference is that when you get to the Select Network Client dialog box, you highlight Microsoft in the Manufacturers list, and Client for NetWare Networks in the Network Clients list.

> You might find that the Microsoft Client for NetWare Networks is already installed. Windows 98 automatically installs this client if it detects the presence of a NetWare network while you're installing its networking components.

Don't forget to select the Microsoft Client for NetWare Networks in the Primary Network Logon drop-down list to make it the primary network logon.

Configuring the Client

The Microsoft Client for NetWare Networks has only two properties tabs:

- **General**   Under the General tab (see Figure 8.1), you can select a preferred server, choose the driver letter to be used for the first network drive, and specify whether a login script should be executed at logon.

- **Advanced**   Under the Advanced tab, there is only one property: Preserve Case. Unless you have good reason to change it, leave it at the default of Yes.

FIGURE 8.1

Configure your gen eral logon properties using this dialog box.

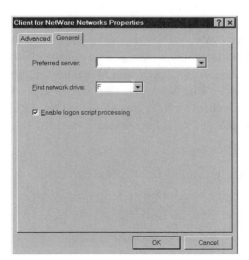

Adding Novell Directory Services

If you're connecting to a NetWare 4 or NetWare 5 server using the Microsoft client, you should also install the Microsoft Service for NDS (Novell Directory Services). This allows you to take advantage of the features offered by NDS. The installation steps are very similar to those for file and printer sharing for Microsoft networks. To install the NDS service, do the following:

1. From the Network properties sheet, click Add to bring up the Select Network Component Type dialog box.

2. Highlight Service and then click Add to bring up the Select Network Service dialog box.

3. Highlight Microsoft from the Manufacturers list, and then highlight Service for NetWare Directory Services from the Network Services list.

4. Click OK. Windows 98 adds the service to the list of network components.

No additional configuration is necessary.

NNDS is the directory service for Novell NetWare networks. It complies with the X.500 standard and provides a logical tree–structure view of all resources on the network so that users can access them without knowing where they're physically located. NDS also works with other types of networks. (X.500, referred to as *X-dot-500*, is an international standard that defines how global directories should be structured. X.500 directories are hierarchical, with different levels for each category of information, such as country, state, and city.)

Novell Client for Windows 95/98

Novell took an approach in installing its client that's different from the traditional Windows method. Novell's procedure is, in some respects, easier than Microsoft's.

If you have the Microsoft Client for NetWare Networks installed on your Windows 98 machine, Novell's installation program removes it before installing the Novell Client for Windows 95/98.

> If you don't have NetWare 5, you can download the latest Novell Client for
> Windows 95/98 from the Internet, free of charge, at http://www.nov-
> ell.com/download. Be aware that it's a sizable download. If you have a
> slow link to the Internet, it would be best to order the CD-ROM from Novell
> (http://www.novell.com/products/clientscd) for about $35.

Installing the Novell Client

Unlike previous versions of the client, the current version can be installed only from a
CD-ROM, server, or local hard drive because of its size. The following steps assume you
have the client on a CD-ROM (have your Windows 98 CD-ROM or diskettes nearby):

1. A language selection screen is displayed when you insert the CD-ROM into the
   drive. Click the language you want. (At the time of this writing, the client is available only in English.)

2. Select Windows 95/98 Client from the Clients and Z.E.N. Works (*Z.E.N.* is short
   for Zero Effort Networking) Starter Pack screen, and then click Install Novell
   Client.

3. The License Agreement dialog box appears. Click Yes to continue.

4. You have a choice of doing a typical install or a custom install. The typical install
   sets up the workstation for logging on to the server using either IPX or IP under
   NDS mode, and the Novell Distributed Print Services (NDPS) component is added.
   If you select the Typical Installation option, click Install to continue, and skip to
   step 7.

   The custom install allows you to choose your protocol preferences (see Figure 8.2).
   If you're connecting to a NetWare 4 or lower server, you can click the Custom
   option and select IPX as the protocol preference. If you're connecting to a NetWare
   5 server, depending on whether it's configured for IP, IPX, or IP with IPX compatibility, select the protocol accordingly. Click Next to continue.

> Click the Help button in this dialog box for a detailed explanation of the
> protocol choices.

FIGURE 8.2

Protocol preferences available under the Custom Installation option.

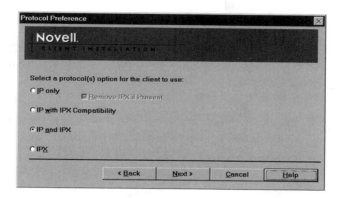

5. If you selected the Custom Installation option, you then need to specify whether you're logging into an NDS or a bindery server (see Figure 8.3). Select the appropriate option and then click Next.

FIGURE 8.3

Use this dialog box to specify if you're going to log on the NetWare server using NDS or bindery mode.

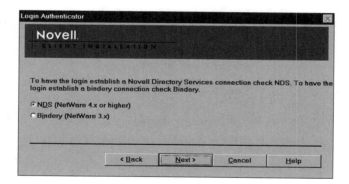

6. If you choose the Custom option in step 4, you see a dialog box for installing the following optional services (see Figure 8.4):

   • **Novell Workstation Manager**   This component allows you to manage all user account and Windows 98 desktop information (such as policy) from within NDS.

   • **Novell Distributed Print Services**   This component (NDPS) enables two-way communication in real time between your workstation and your network printer.

- **Novell NetWare/IP Protocol**   This protocol sends and receives IPX information inside IP packets. NetWare/IP enables network applications that use only IPX to communicate over TCP/IP networks. It also provides a way for separate IPX networks to communicate across IP-based internetwork connections.

- **Novell SNMP Agent**   This component enables you to monitor, from a Simple Network Management Protocol (SNMP) console, remote connections to computers running Windows 98. This agent supports multiple transport protocols.

- **Host Resources MIB for the Novell Client**   This component allows the SNMP agent to communicate with an SNMP console to provide workstation-specific information, such as the size of local drives and amount of RAM.

- **Network Management Responder for the Novell Client**   This component is a service that returns general workstation information to an SNMP console beyond what is normally available.

- **Novell Target Service Agent for Windows 95/98**   This component allows a server-based backup software to back up files from the Windows workstation.

- **Novell Remote Access Dialer**   This component installs software that enables the workstation to connect to a NetWare server that offers remote dial-in services.

- **Novell NDS Provider—ADSI**   This component enables an ADSI (Microsoft Active Directory Service Interface) application to communicate with NDS.

If you selected the Typical Installation option in step 4, only the NDPS component is installed.

Select the component(s) you want and then click Install to continue.

7. The setup program copies the necessary files to the workstation's hard drive.

8. At the end of the install process, a dialog box appears with a recommendation that you set some properties for the client. You can click Yes to perform this operation now (see next section on how to customize the client) or click No to continue.

9. Click Reboot on the resulting dialog box to make the new settings take effect.

FIGURE 8.4

Optional components for the Novell Client.

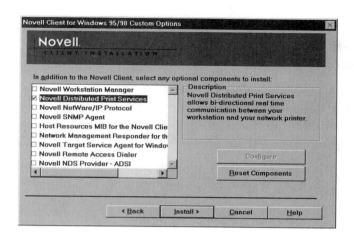

The following changes are made by the install program to your system:

- A new command is added to your Start menu for logging on to the network: Start | Programs | Novell | NetWare Login.

- New commands or submenus are added to the Start | Programs | Novell menu for any optional NetWare Client services installed.

- A system tray icon (called NetWare Services) that links to a number of NetWare commands is added to the taskbar (see Figure 8.5). The icon is a red letter *N*.

- Additional system tray icons might be installed if you have optional NetWare Client services (such as Workstation Manager) installed.

- Two new network components are added to the Network properties sheet: Novell NetWare Client and IPX 32-bit Protocol for the Novell NetWare Client.

- The Novell Client is automatically made the primary network logon.

FIGURE 8.5

The NetWare Services context menu.

Don't remove the IPX/SPX-compatible protocol because it's required by the Novell NetWare Client.

Configuring the Novell Client

Unlike the Microsoft Client for NetWare Networks, the Novell NetWare Client has many configuration tabs (see Figure 8.6). You can access these tabs as follows:

- When the Novell NetWare Client installation program asks whether you want to customize the client (as described in step 8 in the previous section), click Yes.
- In the Network properties sheet, highlight the Novell NetWare Client component and then click Properties.
- From the system tray, click the red N icon and then select Novell Client32 Properties from the context menu.

FIGURE 8.6

The Client configuration tab of the Novell NetWare Client for Windows 95/98.

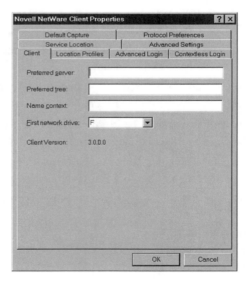

A detailed discussion of each of the settings is beyond the scope of this book. However, the more important settings are discussed in this Hour.

Advanced Login Properties

The check boxes in this tab control where the Windows 98 policy information is located, as well as what settings are displayed on the NetWare logon dialog box (see Figure 8.7).

FIGURE 8.7

The GUI logon dialog box for the Novell NetWare Client.

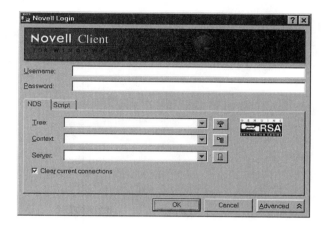

Advanced Settings Properties

Use the Advanced Settings tab (see Figure 8.8) to change the settings that might affect how the Novell NetWare client functions and its performance. For example, you can turn the Packet Burst function on or off. If you're familiar with the NET.CFG settings, you'll find that this sheet contains similar parameters.

Traditionally, NetWare Core Protocol (NCP) calls respond to *every* request with an acknowledgement. This makes it a very "chatty" protocol that is especially inefficient across WAN links. *Packet burst* allows a single acknowledgement for multiple file reads and writes (which are the most common NCP calls), thus making more efficient use of the network's bandwidth.

FIGURE **8.8**

Use this dialog box to set advanced options for the Novell NetWare Client.

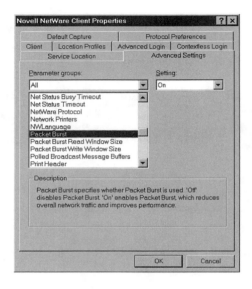

Client Properties

The Client tab (refer back to Figure 8.6) is where you specify your workstation's preferred server, preferred tree (if using NDS and you have multiple NDS trees on the network), name context (used with NDS mode only), and the drive letter to be assigned to the first network drive (default is F). This tab also displays the client version.

Contextless Login Properties

In previous versions of NetWare, when you logged into an NDS tree, you needed to know the location in the tree (name context) where your user name exists. However, starting with this version of the client, there's a contextless login feature (in other words, you don't need to know the name context anymore). The client software can search a catalog file (see Figure 8.9) containing user names and locations, so all you need to supply during logon is just the user name; the location is looked up from the catalog file.

This contextless login feature requires the installation of Catalog Services on the NetWare servers and is available only for NetWare 5.

FIGURE 8.9

Use this dialog box to configure the context-less login parameters.

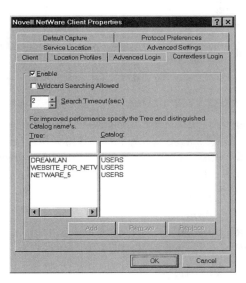

Default Capture Properties

The Default Capture tab (see Figure 8.10) sets up the print capture defaults for your workstation. For example, this is where you configure whether a banner page should be included and whether tab characters should be expanded to be spaces.

FIGURE 8.10

Use this dialog box to configure your printer capture settings.

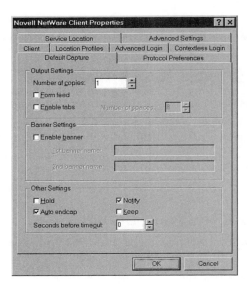

Location Profiles Properties

The Location Profiles tab allows you to create logon profile information, such as user name, name context, and login script execution preferences, so that you don't have to enter this information during login. You can define multiple profiles.

Protocol Preferences Properties

Use the Protocol Preferences tab to configure protocol-specific settings to be used by the Novell NetWare client. For example, if you installed the client with IPX and IP support, you can use the Protocol Order option to determine the sequence of protocols the client uses when trying to connect to a server. For example, if the order is IPX, then IP, the client first tries to connect using IPX; if an IPX connection can't be made, the client tries again using IP.

Also use this page to select the order in which protocols (such as NDS, DNS, and DHCP) are used for name resolution.

Service Location Properties

You can use the Service Location tab to configure the scope list and the directory agent list to be used by SLP (Service Location Protocol) applications running on the workstation. You can manually enter the scope names in the order they should be used. Scopes can also be configured through DHCP or discovered dynamically from directory agents.

The directory agent list shows the fully qualified domain names or the IP addresses of directory agents on the network; the agents can also be configured through DHCP or discovered dynamically.

Accessing NetWare Resources

Both the Microsoft NetWare client and the Novell NetWare client are tightly integrated with Windows 98 My Computer, Windows Explorer, and Network Neighborhood operations. However, the Novell NetWare client adds some nice extensions that aren't available in the Microsoft version. Therefore, the discussions in the following sections are Novell NetWare client specific (unless otherwise noted). The overall concepts, however, apply to both clients.

Connecting to a NetWare Server

To access any resources on a NetWare server, you must first authenticate to the server (in a NetWare 3.x environment) or to the NDS tree (in a NetWare 4 or NetWare 5 environment). If you're using the Microsoft NetWare client, the logon screen looks similar to the one shown in Figure 8.11. If you're using a bindery connection, simply enter your user name and password; if you're using an NDS connection, enter your fully qualified user name if a name context isn't set.

FIGURE 8.11

The logon screen for the Microsoft Client for NetWare Networks, without the NDS service installed.

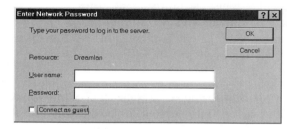

If you're using the Novell NetWare client, its logon screen looks like the one shown in Figure 8.12. If you haven't configured your NDS tree and name context preferences (or want to change them), click Advanced to make the selections.

FIGURE 8.12

The logon screen for the Novell NetWare client.

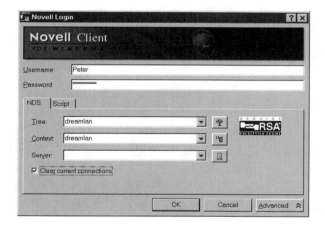

> You might notice that some options are not available. You'll need to enable them through the Advanced Login properties settings of the Novell NetWare client (see the previous "Configuring the Novell Client" section for details).

If you didn't log on to the NetWare server or network during Windows 98 bootup, you're greeted with a logon prompt when you try to access its resources.

Browsing a NetWare Network

You can easily browse for NetWare resources by using My Computer, Explorer, or
Network Neighborhood, just like browsing for shares on a Microsoft network as
described in Hour 6, "Sharing Windows 98 Resources." The easiest way is to use
Network Neighborhood because it also shows you NDS printers; My Computer does not.
The following steps illustrate how to browse your NetWare 4 resources using Network
Neighborhood:

1. Open Network Neighborhood. The number of icons you see depends on whether
   you're authenticated to the network. If you are, you'll see the icons for Entire
   Network, available NDS trees, and your current name context (see Figure 8.13); if
   you're not authenticated to the network, all you see is just the Entire Network icon.

FIGURE 8.13

*Network
Neighborhood showing
resources on a
NetWare 4 network.*

NDS tree

Current name context

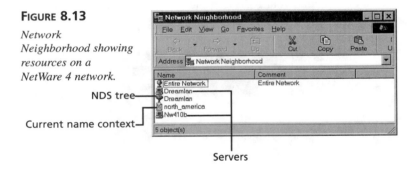

Servers

2. Double-click the Entire Network icon, and you'll see two folders: Novell Directory
   Services and NetWare Servers. (You see a third folder, NDPS Public Access
   Printers, if the NDPS component of the Novell NetWare Client is installed.)

3. Double-click the Novell Directory Services folder, and you see a list of NDS tree
   names.

4. Double-click a tree name. If you're authenticated to that tree, you see a list of containers and objects, located in the current name context. As you go through the
   tree, you see other containers, volumes, and printer objects in a given context; you
   wouldn't see other NDS object types, such as users.

   If you double-click a volume object, you see a list of directories and files, starting
   at the root of the volume. You can go through the directory tree on the volume by
   double-clicking the folder icons.

Mapping a Network Drive

You can map a drive to the NetWare volume in two ways. One is the traditional method of using the MAP.EXE command from a DOS prompt. Because Windows 98 is GUI-based, however, why not use Network Neighborhood or Explorer? Here are the steps:

1. Use either Network Neighborhood or Explorer to locate the volume and directory of interest.

2. Highlight the directory folder and then right-click. Select Novell Map Network Drive from the context menu to bring up the Map Drive dialog box (see Figure 8.14).

FIGURE 8.14

Use this dialog box to capture a network drive.

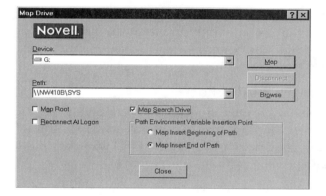

3. Use the Device drop-down list to select the drive letter you want to use.

4. If you want the drive to be reconnected at logon, enable the Reconnect At Logon check box.

5. If you want the drive to be map-rooted, enable the Map Root check box.

6. If you want the drive mapping to be a search map, enable the Map Search Drive check box and select the Path Environment Variable Insertion Point option you want.

7. Click Map, and the mapped drive shows up as a networked drive icon (a disk drive attached to a network cable).

Or, you can use the NetWare Services icon from the system tray. Right-click the red N symbol in the system tray, and click the Novell Map Network Drive option on the context menu to bring up the Map Drive dialog box. You can then use the Browse button to locate the directory you want to map to, and follow step 3 in the preceding list.

Releasing a Mapped Network Drive

When you no longer need a network drive, you should release it. There are several ways to do this; here are two of them:

- Open My Computer, right-click the network drive icon, and then select Disconnect from the context menu.
- Right-click the red N symbol in the system tray, and click the Disconnect Network Drive option on the context menu. Highlight the drive you want to release, and then click OK.

Network Printing

One of the reasons for installing a network is to share peripherals, such as printers. Any printer attached to a networked computer can be shared with the network. That means any users on the network can print to the shared printer as though it were directly attached to their own machines.

Capturing a Printer Port

In the same way you can map a shared network drive or folder and have it appear as though it were a physical drive on your system, you can map a shared network printer and have it appear as though it were a physical printer port on your system. This is called *capturing* a printer port. You can do it in one of three ways:

- Open the properties of any shared printer in your Printer folder, display the Details tab, and click Capture Printer Port. (The procedures for installing remote printers on your Windows 98 machine are explained in the next section.)
- Use the NetWare Services icon from the system tray. Right-click the red N symbol in the system tray, and click the Novell Capture Printer Port option on the context menu to bring up the Capture Printer Port dialog box.
- Using Explorer or Network Neighborhood, highlight a shared printer and choose File | Capture Printer Port, or right-click the shared printer and select Novell Capture Printer Port from the context menu.

Then, in the Capture Printer Port dialog box (see Figure 8.15), use the Device drop-down list to select a logical printer port. If you're using the printer's Details tab, you can use the Path text box and the Browse button to enter a network path to the shared printer. If you want the port to be recaptured at logon, enable the Reconnect At Logon check box. Click Capture to map the printer. Then click Close to close the dialog box.

FIGURE 8.15

Use the Capture Printer Port dialog box to map a shared network printer to a logical printer port on your local machine.

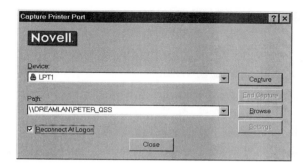

Releasing a Captured Printer Port

When you no longer want to redirect a print job for a particular port to a network printer, you should release it, or you might send your print job elsewhere without knowing it. Use the following steps to un-capture a printer port:

1. Open the properties for the shared printer.
2. Display the Details tab.
3. Click the End Capture button.
4. In the End Capture dialog box, highlight the port you want to release.
5. Click OK.

You can also use the NetWare Services icon from the system tray. Right-click the red N symbol in the system tray, and click the Novell End Capture option on the context menu to bring up the End Printer Capture dialog box. Highlight the port you want to release, and then click OK.

Using Point and Print

Using the Windows *point and print* feature, you don't need to capture a printer port to a specific printer before printing to it. With point and print, the printer driver and any other associated files can be stored on the NetWare server. That way, users can install or reinstall printers (to update drivers) easily without needing access to the Windows CD-ROM or diskettes. All you have to do is the following:

1. Log on to the NetWare server where the printer driver will be stored as the Admin/Supervisor or equivalent user.
2. In the Network Neighborhood, browse the network until you find the NetWare printer or print queue you want to associate a printer to. Right-click the queue and select Properties in the context menu.

3. Select the Setup Point and Print tab from the properties sheet. You don't see this tab if you're not logged in with the appropriate rights.

4. Make sure the Driver Platform setting is set correctly (see Figure 8.16).

5. Click the Select Printer Model button.

6. Select the manufacturer and model from the Driver Selection dialog box for your printer.

7. Click OK to copy the print driver files to the server.

8. After the drivers are copied, click OK to close the printer's properties sheet.

9. Make sure the users have at least read and file scan rights to the directory in which the printer files were copied.

FIGURE 8.16

The Setup Point and Print dialog box of a NetWare print queue.

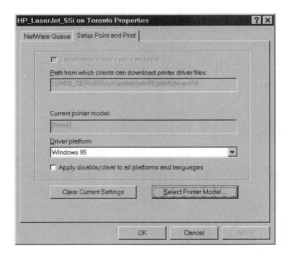

Before you can access this print queue, you need to add the queue to your Printers folder by using the Add Printer wizard, as follows:

1. Locate the print queue with Explorer or Network Neighborhood.

2. Drag the print queue icon into the Printers folder.

3. Follow the Add Printer wizard as it prompts you to set up printing. When you're done, the print driver is automatically copied to your workstation from the server, and the Printers folder is updated to show the new printer.

To use this printer, simply drag and drop a document onto the printer icon or select it from the list of available printers from within your application; no previous printer port capture is necessary.

8

Summary

During this Hour, you have learned the basics of installing the Microsoft and Novell clients for NetWare networks and how to access resources on a NetWare network. As you've probably noticed, accessing resources from a NetWare network is very similar to accessing resources from a Microsoft peer-to-peer network. If you also work with other brands of networks, you'll find all of them are very similar.

In the next Hour, you find out how to perform backup and restore operations on your Windows 98 system.

Workshop

Q&A

Q **I have a copy of IntranetWare Client for Windows 95 v2.2. Would it work with my Windows 98 machine, or must I get a new client?**

A Although not sanctioned by Novell Technical Support, you can use that version (or any version later than that one) with Windows 98. Seems to work just fine.

Q **I can't find the Novell client for Windows 95/98 on the Novell Web site. Where else can I look?**

A It is available from `http://www.novell.com/download`. You might have missed it because the client includes the Z.E.N. Works Starter Pack.

Q **My workstation hangs on bootup after the Novell NetWare Client is installed. What should I do?**

A This can happen if the install was not fully completed. Start the workstation in Safe mode, and then run `UNC32.EXE` from the `\PRODUCTS\WIN95\IBM_ENU\ADMIN` directory on the Novell Client CD-ROM. This completely removes the Novell NetWare client. Then do a reinstall of the client.

Q **I can't seem to get the Novell client for Windows 95/98 to work correctly on my Windows 95 machine. Help!**

A Which version of Windows 95 is that? There are three versions: the original Windows 95, Win95a, and Win95b. The Novell Client for Windows 95/98 does not support the original version of Windows 95.

Q **Why can't I save a file with long names on the NetWare server?**

A NetWare does support long names. However, the server's administrator must first enable long name support for the volume on which you want save the file.

Quiz

1. True or False: Microsoft Client for NetWare Networks supports NDS in NetWare 5.

2. Which client should you install if you need to access an IP-only NetWare 5 server?

3. Which client should you install if you need to access a NetWare 3 server?

HOUR 9

Backing Up and Restoring Data on Windows 98

Murphy's Law says "Disaster strikes when you have the least backup," and to err is simply human nature. A computer system, especially a network, generally contains very important data. That means coming up with a reliable backup and recovery strategy is a fundamental responsibility of the system owner.

During this Hour, you get information that helps you do the following:

- Develop an effective backup and recovery procedure
- Select an appropriate backup device
- Choose backup tools
- Automate backups

Backup Strategy

The purpose of performing backups is to be able to restore individual files or complete systems after a failure. How often to perform backups, what data should be backed up, and how to rotate backup media are issues that can be quite confusing.

Exactly how often you should back up which files depends on your system hardware configuration and particular needs. The criterion is, "If the system crashes, how much work are you willing to lose?" Ideally, you would want to back up all files every few minutes so that you would never lose more than a few minutes of work. Unfortunately, this approach is not practical.

To examine the problem another way, ask yourself "How often should I back up the files?" In a networked environment, the more users you have on the network, the more often you should back up the server where most of the data is stored. A common schedule is performing a full backup once or twice a week and partial backups daily.

Full Backup

A *full* backup is when every single file on every disk is backed up, regardless of their creation or modification time. This way, should you need to restore a single file or the whole system, you need to access only the latest backup and go from there. The drawback of doing full backups is the amount of time it takes. Depending on the backup media (such as tape) and the hardware you use, to fully back up 2GB of data could take anywhere from a few minutes to a few hours.

Another problem of performing daily full backups is the amount of backup media you need. Say you're using tapes as the backup media. A daily full backup would require 365 tapes—or more, if you require more than one tape or do more than one full backup per day. You could easily be faced with the storage problem of hundreds of tapes.

Differential Backup

A partial, or *differential*, backup is when only files that have been created or modified since the last full backup was done are backed up. This way, if your data is relatively static, then the incremental backups take very little time to process and only small amounts of backup media are needed.

The main drawback of doing differential backups is when you need to restore. You need to first restore the last full backup, and then apply *all* the differential backups from that point on. Therefore, you save some time during the backup process, but the restore phase takes longer.

Incremental Backup

An *incremental* backup is a variation of the differential backup. An incremental backup is when only files that have been created or modified since the last full *or* differential backup are backed up. This method has the same advantages and drawbacks as the differential method.

Implementing a Strategy

In a small to medium network, you can use the following backup strategy:

- Perform a full backup of your system once every six months and any time you're about to make any major changes to the system, such as upgrading software.
- Perform a monthly full backup of your data files (such as documents and spreadsheets) on, say, the last day of each month.
- Perform a weekly differential backup of your modified data files (every Friday, for example).
- Perform a daily incremental backup of your modified data files (at the end of each work day, for example).

Selecting Appropriate Backup Devices

With the first PCs, floppy diskettes were the norm for backup media. However, with the introduction of large hard drives and the typical disk space on a Windows-based computer (2GB or higher), it's no longer practical to use diskettes. For example, to fully back up a 2GB hard drive, you would need more than 1,400 diskettes! Furthermore, the amount of time involved in writing to and swapping that many diskettes in and out of the disk drive makes it impractical. However, for small amounts of personal data and specific (small) system files, such as the Registry, diskette storage is a viable option. Other backup media options include the following:

- Tape drives (different formats)
- ZIP and JAZ drives
- WORM drives (Write Once, Read Many)

Tape Drives

The most commonly used backup devices are tape drives. Magnetic tapes are available in different sizes (ranging from the 9-track reel-to-reel tapes to 1/4-inch tape cartridges, QICs, to 4mm and 8mm DAT tapes) and different capacities (ranging from about 100MB for QIC to over 10GB for 8mm DAT). There are two reasons why tapes are popular backup media:

- They are cost effective. You can get an 8mm DAT tape (14GB capacity) for less than $20.
- They are *relatively* fast. Depending on the type of tape drive and software used, a peak throughput of 100MB/minute is not uncommon.

Other Media

The other backup media, such as WORM drives (in essence, CD-ROMs), ZIP drives, and JAZ drives (from Iomega, http://www.iomega.com), are not as popular on large systems because of their limited capacity—the typical capacity is about 650MB—and, in some cases, slow speed. Although these media are not as cost effective or able to store as much data as tapes, they do offer convenience and improved performance over using tapes.

Some companies use WORM/CD-ROMs to back up their financial data so that the recorded information cannot be modified, which makes it serve as reliable audit data.

In terms of access, it is faster and more convenient to use CD-ROMs, JAZ, and so on than it is to use tapes. This is because tapes need to be accessed sequentially, but CD-ROMs and the like can be accessed randomly. What's more, tapes have a relatively short "shelf-life" compared to the other storage media (except for floppy diskettes)—years for tapes versus decades for CD-ROMs. So if you have data that needs to be archived for an extended period (typically more than three years), you should consider moving it to CD-ROMs or JAZ cartridges.

Using Microsoft Backup

Windows 98 comes with a much improved Backup utility (from Seagate Software) that includes several wizards to help you with backup and restore chores. The new Backup also supports the backup and restoration of Registry files and has built-in support for SCSI tape drives and many other backup device types.

To start the Backup program, choose Start | Programs | Accessories | System Tools | Backup. A startup dialog box similar to the one shown in Figure 9.1 is displayed; this screen is shown every time you start Backup.

FIGURE 9.1

Microsoft Backup's startup dialog box.

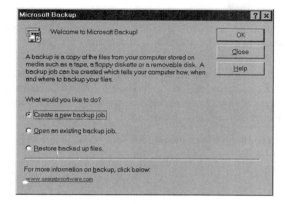

At startup, Backup checks your system to see whether you have any backup device (such as a tape drive) installed. If it didn't find any, Backup displays a dialog box asking whether you want to run the Add New Hardware wizard to install a device. If you do have a backup device installed and Backup didn't see it, you should click Yes. Otherwise, click No to continue.

The following sections cover using the Backup and Restore wizards, which are accessed by selecting the Create a New Backup Job and Restore Backed Up Files options, respectively, in Backup's startup dialog box.

Using the Backup Wizard

You can start the Backup wizard in one of two ways:

- In the Backup startup dialog box, select Create a New Backup Job and then click OK.
- In the Microsoft Backup window, choose Tools | Backup Wizard.

The first wizard dialog box, the What to Back Up dialog, offers you two choices:

- **Back Up My Computer**   This option performs a backup (full or partial) of your *local* files.
- **Back Up Selected Files, Folders and Drives**   This option performs a backup (full or partial) of selected files, folders, and drives, which can be either local *or* remote.

Using the Back Up Selected Files, Folders and Drives option, you can easily
back up your local files as well as those on the servers (including peer
servers) from across the network.

Keep in mind that backing up across a network is slower than performing
the backup on the server locally. However, in most cases, the convenience of
being able to perform backup operations from a single location far out-
weighs the extra time needed.

If you chose to back up only selected files, the next wizard dialog box allows you to
choose those files. This dialog box, shown in Figure 9.2, is very similar to the Explorer
window, but with an optional check box beside every file, folder, and drive. Click the
appropriate check box to select a file, folder, or drive to be backed up. After finishing
your selections, click Next to continue.

FIGURE 9.2

*This dialog box allows
you to select local and
remote files, folders,*

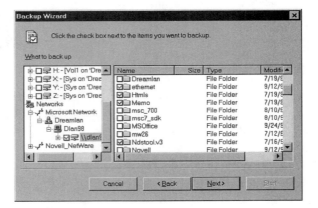

If you look closely at the dialog box, you'll notice that the check mark is
blue when a whole folder (drive) is selected for backup, but gray when only
certain files within that folder (drive) are selected for backup.

The wizard then asks whether you want to back up all selected files (full backup) or new
and changed files (partial backup). Select the option that suits your needs and click Next.

The next dialog box asks you where you want the files to be backed up. Depending on
your system configuration, you'll see one or both of the following options:

- **File**   This option allows you to back up the selected files into a single QIC backup file. You can specify the name and location of this backup file.
- **Backup Devices**   This option allows you to back up the selected files to your backup device. The available names vary, depending on the backup devices you have installed on your machine.

Choose the destination and click Next.

There are two options on the second-to-last wizard dialog box:

- **Compare Original and Backup Files to Verify Data Was Successfully Backed Up**   If this option is checked, Backup compares each backed-up file against its original to ensure that the copy was made without errors. Do keep in mind that this option doubles the amount of backup time.
- **Compress the Backup Data to Save Space**   If this option is checked, Backup compresses the backed-up files to save space on the backup media. The typical compression efficient is about 50 percent.

Choose your options and click Next.

The last dialog box of the Backup wizard shows you the options you have chosen, and enables you to enter a name for the backup job (so you can use it again later without having to re-enter all the information). Click Start to begin the backup process.

A Backup Progress window (see Figure 9.3) keeps you abreast of the operation's progress, and a dialog box is displayed when the job is finished.

FIGURE 9.3

This dialog box shows you the progress of the backup operation.

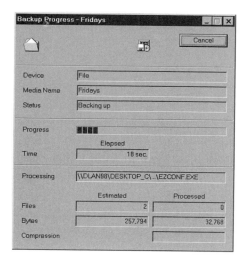

Using the Restore Wizard

If you ever need to restore a copy of your data from the backup, you can either use the Restore Wizard or perform the restore manually with the Restore tab in the Microsoft Backup dialog screen.

Bring up the Restore Wizard in one of two ways:

- In the Backup startup dialog box, select Restore Backed Up Files and then click OK.
- In the Microsoft Backup window, choose Tools | Restore Wizard.

In the first of the Restore Wizard dialog boxes, you need to select the source of your backed-up data. For example, if you previously backed up the data to C:\MYBACKUP.QIC, select this name from the Restore From list and then click Next.

The wizard then displays a list of backups, known as *backup sets*, found on the medium. If the backup medium is a file, you see only one set listed; if the medium is a tape, you can expect to see multiple backup sets if you didn't use the overwrite option when backing up. Select the backup set(s) you want to restore and then click OK.

The next dialog box is much like the file selection dialog box described in Figure 9.2. Use this dialog box to select the file or files you want to restore and then click Next.

You can select whether the files are restored to their original location or an alternative one in the next dialog box. If you select Alternate Location from the drop-down list, a new text box appears so that you can specify the new location. Click Next to continue.

> Unless you're restoring a file that was mistakenly deleted, it's best to first restore a file to an alternative location, so that you can check its contents before replacing an existing file on the system.

The wizard then asks you what should happen if the file you're restoring already exists. You have three options:

- **Do Not Replace the File on My Computer**   With this option selected, Backup does not replace any files on the destination path with backed-up files if there is a name conflict.
- **Replace the File on My Computer Only If the File Is Older**   Select this option if you want Backup to replace files on the destination path with backed-up files of the same name that have a later date.

- **Always Replace the File on My Computer**   This option allows Backup to replace any files on the destination path with backed-up files that have the same name.

Select the option you want, and then click Start. Backup prompts you to insert the media needed for the restore (even if the source is a file). Insert the media, if necessary, and then click OK.

A progress status window similar to that shown during the backup operation appears during the file restore. A dialog box is displayed when the job is finished.

9

> You *can* restore files to a remote server by using Backup.

Scheduling Backups

You should set up an automated backup schedule so the process will initiate itself periodically without manual intervention. This is important because if you need to manually start the backup procedure daily, one day you'll forget, you won't have time, or something will happen to prevent you from doing it. As dictated by Murphy's Law, that will be the one day you need a backup!

> You might want to get a backup device that holds about twice as much tape (or whatever media) as you need for a backup job so you have the option of not changing the tapes for one day.

Although Windows 98 includes a Task Scheduler that can schedule any Windows application, macros, DOS program, or even batch file, you can't, unfortunately, really use it to automatically run Backup to back up your files.

Well, the Task Scheduler *can* be used to launch Backup according to a predetermined schedule. However, Backup itself doesn't offer an easy way—say, through the use of command-line parameters—to load and run an existing job. You could, if you had the patience and know-how, create some Windows macros that launch Backup, select the job, run it, and then exit Backup. You could then use the Task Scheduler to run the macros.

You could use the Task Scheduler as a reminder for your backup operations. For example, you can schedule a task to launch Backup at 4:45 p.m. daily. With the application opened on your desktop, it serves as a reminder that you need to run a backup. Granted, it is not foolproof, but it's a workaround.

The bright side of this dilemma is that if you buy a tape drive for your backup needs, it generally comes with backup software, and most commercially available backup software has built-in schedulers. Or, if you're on a NetWare network, for example, you can set up your Windows 98 machine with the Target Service Agent service that comes with the Novell NetWare client, and have the NetWare server back up your machine for you instead.

Other Backup Tools

There are also plenty of freeware, shareware, and commercial-ware products that can help you address this backup and scheduling problem. During Hour 21, "Surfing Tools," you find out where you can locate such tools and how to get them over the Internet. However, in this section, you should be aware of at least two alternatives to Backup:

- **Seagate Software's Backup Exec Desktop 98**   When you look at the Seagate Backup Exec Desktop 98, you'll notice it has exactly the same look and feel as Backup. That's because Microsoft Backup is a scaled-down version of Backup Exec Desktop 98!

  Backup Exec has a built-in scheduler, and its integrated Emergency Recovery feature can rebuild your entire system without reinstalling the operating system or the backup software. In addition, Backup Exec supports most tape devices, CD-R and CD-RW, DVD-RAM, ZIP and JAZ drives, magneto optical, PD/CD, SuperDisk, even floppy disks, hard disks, and network drives mapped as a device using the File Specification feature. It also protects data on a network, including NetWare 3.x bindery and trustee information.

- **Novell's Target Service Agent for Windows 95/98**   Included free-of-charge with the Novell NetWare Client, the TSA service allows the Windows 98 workstation to be remotely backed up by a NetWare server across the network. All you need running on the server is a Storage Management Service (SMS)–compliant backup software engine. You can either use the SBACKUP (W32SMDR in NetWare 5) software shipped with NetWare or get an alternative.

Another popular commercial backup solution is ARCserve, from Cheyenne Software.

Summary

In this Hour, you've learned about the different backup types and gotten some information about what type of backup device best suits your particular needs. You also found out how to perform a backup and restore using Microsoft Backup's wizards. Finally, you discovered why Backup might not be the best solution for unattended backup operations and found some alternative solutions.

This Hour also concludes the coverage on Windows 98 networking. Starting with the next hour, you're going to take a trek into the Windows NT territory.

Workshop

Q&A

Q I didn't install the Windows 98 backup tools while I was installing Windows 98. Can I add them now?

A If you didn't install Backup along with Windows 98, you can add it by choosing Start | Settings | Control Panel and selecting Add/Remove Programs and then the Windows Setup tab. From the dialog box, choose System Tools, click Details, select the Backup check box, and then click OK twice. Windows 98 then asks you to put the Windows 98 CD-ROM (or diskette) in your drive; after you do, Backup will be installed.

Q What is the best time for me to perform backups on my Windows 98 peer-to-peer network?

A Regardless of whether your machine is networked or what type of network you have, you should always schedule your backup during a time period when there is little or no user activity. One reason for this is that backup procedures take up system resources—such as CPU cycles—and put a high demand on hard disk access. This could degrade the system performance. Second, in a networked environment when there are users on the system, there are always opened files on the server, which generally don't get backed up. To back up as much changed data as possible, you should shut down any applications that keep files opened constantly and also restrict user access to files while you perform your backup.

Quiz

1. What are the different backup types?

2. What is the difference between incremental backup and differential backup, if any?

3. True or False: Windows 98's Backup can back up and restore Registry files.

4. True or False: Windows 98's Backup can back up from a remote drive but can't restore to one.

PART III
NT Networks

Hour

10 NT Server Basics

11 Sharing NT Resources

12 NT Remote Access Service (RAS)

13 Accessing NetWare Resouces from Windows NT

14 Installing a Windows NT Server

15 Managing NT Servers

16 Backing Up and Restoring Data on Windows NT

17 Advanced NT Server Management

HOUR 10

NT Server Basics

This Hour, you take a look at some NT terminology and cover the following topics:

- Learning about workgroups and domains
- Looking at domain models
- Understanding the concept of users and groups
- Reviewing some ideas about security
- Looking at the options for formatting your disk partitions: FAT (File Allocation Table) and NTFS (NT File System)

Workgroups

A *workgroup* is a logical grouping of NT machines, suitable for small installations or when centralized management is not required. In the workgroup model, each machine maintains its own unique database of users and security information. The obvious advantage of the workgroup concept is its simplicity, but the disadvantage is the lack of centralized management.

For example, if you want George to access resources on two of the other machines in his workgroup, then you need to go to those two machines, create "user George," and assign the appropriate rights. Remember, each machine has its own database, and they are isolated; they do not synchronize their account information with the other machines in the workgroup. It is this lack of centralized control that makes the workgroup model useful only in very small environments.

> Windows for Workgroups and Windows 9x machines can also belong to workgroups; it's not just an NT thing!

Domains

Like a workgroup, a *domain* is also a logical grouping of NT machines for the purposes of administration and resource sharing. However, as a member of a domain, the computer has access to a central database containing user accounts and security information. This means that, unlike the workgroup model, you need to create user George only one time, not several. It is this centralized management that makes the domain model useful in larger networks.

As shown in Figure 10.1, the master copy of the database resides on a *primary domain controller*, or *PDC*. Copies of the database are kept on *backup domain controllers*, or *BDCs*. As in the movie *Highlander*, when it comes to having a PDC, there can be only one; however, you can have many backup domain controllers. Changes to the domain database are made at the PDC and then get copied to the BDC.

> So what happens if you lose your primary domain controller? Losing the PDC, although it won't make your day, isn't going to set you back too far, as long as you have a backup domain controller. Because changes to the database can be made only at the PDC, then you can't make changes, which means you can't create new users, you can't change passwords, and administration pretty much comes to a halt.

FIGURE 10.1

In the domain model, you have a master copy of the database on the primary domain controller. The backup domain controllers get a copy from the PDC.

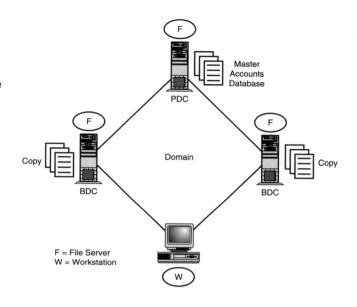

10

Either a PDC or a BDC can authenticate you to the domain at login time, so that's a relief; you can at least authenticate to the network if a PDC goes down. If the PDC is going to be down for only a few hours, no need to worry—just wait. If the PDC has decided to go south forever, then you need to promote one of the BDCs to become the PDC, and your problem is solved. (Promoting a BDC to a PDC is covered in Hour 15, "Managing NT Servers.")

 A domain controller, either PDC or BDC, doesn't necessarily have to be a dedicated machine. The domain controller could also be an Exchange server, or some other application server. But keep in mind when implementing your network design that, because either the PDC or BDC needs to authenticate you at login time, this is an extra load on the machine.

To keep things manageable, domains can establish trust relationships with each other, which is covered in Hour 17, "Advanced NT Server Management." After trust relationships are established, you can give rights to your resources to users from another domain, and vice versa. Trust relationships keep you from having to create user George in each domain.

Remember, a domain is a logical grouping. On one physical network, there might be two or more domains. You can think of trust relationships as a partitioning strategy. You either have one huge domain with lots of members, or several smaller domains, and then establish the trusts. Using trusts keeps the centralized management concept intact because you keep the concept of one user and one logon.

Single Domain Model

Refer back to Figure 10.1 for an example of a single domain model. There is only one domain, one PDC, and one or more BDCs. (Note that having a BDC isn't a requirement; technically, the network functions just fine without a BDC. But realistically, you certainly want a backup!) The single domain model is useful in small environments because you get centralized management without worrying about trust relationships.

Single Master Domain Model

In the single master domain model, one master domain contains all users and global groups. Each domain, by definition, has its own domain controller, but all the user account information is handled centrally at the master domain. The resource domains trust the master, so users and groups from the master domain can access the printers and disks in the resource domains. Figure 10.2 shows a single master domain.

FIGURE 10.2

With the single master domain model, you have one master domain where all the accounts reside. Then one or more domains contain the resources. Each arrow shows a one-way trust.

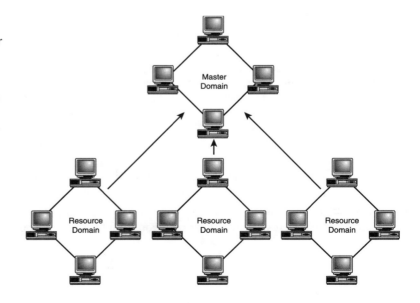

The advantage of this model is that creating and administering users and groups are centralized, but the administration of the resource domain is managed independently in each resource domain. This one is a bit strange, but think of it like this: The central office can create all the users and groups it wants, but as the administrator of the remote resource domain, you still have control over which of those users get access.

Multiple Master Domain Model

The multiple master domain model, shown in Figure 10.3, functions very much like the single master domain model, except that you have two or more master domains, instead of having all the users and groups in one domain. You can see that the number of trust relationships will have to grow. Not only do the master domains need a trust relationship, but each of the resource domains needs to trust not just one master, but all of them. This is a more complex model than the others, but it scales better for larger networks.

FIGURE 10.3

The multiple master domain model is like the single master, except the user accounts are spread across more than one domain. Each arrow indicates a one-way trust.

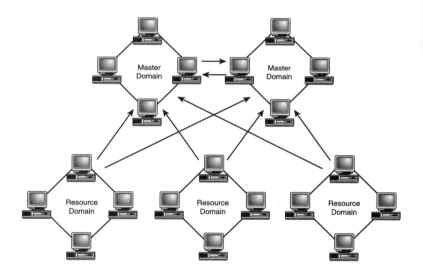

Complete Trust

The complete trust model does away with the centralized management concept to some degree. As shown in Figure 10.4, in the complete trust model, every domain has a two-way trust with the other domains, and each domain is independently administered. The complete trust model *distributes* management and control instead of centralizing it. Obviously, the number of your trust relationships is going to grow even more, increasing complexity.

In the complete trust domain model, everyone trusts everyone. Each pair of arrows indicates a two-way trust.

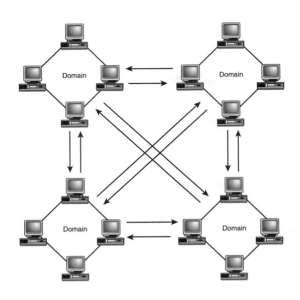

Users and Groups

A network with no users is probably the dream of all network administrators, but in the real world, it's probably not going to happen! Each user needs an account to be able to log on, and groups, or collections of these accounts, make administration quicker and easier.

User Accounts

A *user account* is your ticket to get on board the network. No account, no access. There are two types of accounts:

- Those you create yourself, such as for user George
- Built-in accounts, such as Guest or Administrator

User Manager, which is covered in more detail in Hour 15, is the NT utility used to create users and groups (see Figure 10.5).

FIGURE 10.5

User Manager is the utility for creating users and groups.

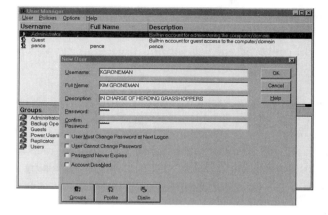

When dealing with accounts you create yourself, one of the first things you want to do is establish a naming convention. This might seem silly in a small office, where everyone knows each other, but in a larger environment, it's very important. Along with a naming convention, you should think about password restrictions. How many characters will you require for a password? Using longer passwords naturally provides greater security, but keep in mind that the administrator and the user most likely have mutually exclusive views on this subject. The users want short and simple passwords, but the administrator wants long tortuous ones to be used. The password can be up to 14 characters in NT, and the password is *case sensitive* (that means John is not the same thing as john).

User accounts are either

- **Domain accounts**   A domain account is created via User Manager for Domains, and this account is good for your single user, single login concept.

- **Local accounts**   Local accounts are created on standalone machines, or member servers, and exist only on that machine.

When a domain account is created, changes to the domain database are made only at the PDC; the BDC(s) receive a copy. You might run into a situation where you create a domain account, call the user and tell her to try it, and her login attempt fails. That's because she has contacted a BDC to authenticate, and the BDC has not yet gotten an update reflecting the new account. It's possible to force a synchronization of the PDCs and BDCs through two methods:

- With Server Manager, choose Start | Programs | Administrative Tools | Server Manager. On the Computer menu, you will see choices regarding synchronization. If you have a BDC highlighted, you have a choice to Synchronize with Primary Domain Controller. If you have the PDC highlighted, then the choice reads

Synchronize Entire Domain. The former option syncs up only the one BDC, and the latter option synchronizes all the BDCs.

- Use the command line with the `net accounts /sync` command.

Groups

Groups are collections of users. If you are a member of a group, then you have the same rights that the group has. Groups make your life vastly easier because they make your network easier to manage. For example, a typical user needs rights to applications, such as Word, Excel, and Terminal Emulation. If you create a group for these typical users (call this group `everyone`), you can give your new group the rights it needs to these applications. That way, you don't have to assign the appropriate rights to each user in the group; you can simply assign the rights to the group.

There are two types of groups:

- **Global groups**   Global groups are used to collect users.
- **Local groups**   Local groups are given rights to the resources.

The accepted method is to give the local group the right to the resource, and then add the global group to the local group (see Figure 10.6).

FIGURE 10.6

Rights to the resource are assigned to the local group, and then the global group (collection of users) is added to the local group.

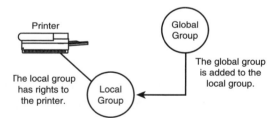

As with user accounts, there are also built-in groups, both local and global. Some of the built-in local groups are users, administrators, and guests. They have their equivalent at the domain level, with built-in global groups of domain users, domain administrators, and domain guests.

File Systems

When installing NT, you have a choice of using one of two file systems to format the disk:

- FAT (File Allocation Table), which is the venerable file system you probably associate with DOS, if your computing roots reach back that far!

- NTFS (NT File System) is new and unique to NT. Only NT can see volumes formatted with NTFS.

The main difference between FAT and NTFS is that FAT has no file-level security, which means you can't drill down to the file level and implement restrictions. NTFS, on the other hand, gives you greater control over security because it allows you to have both folder- and file-level security.

NTFS requires using NT, so any partition formatted with NTFS isn't seen if you are booting another operating system. To dual-boot between NT and another operating system (OS) such as Windows 95, you must use FAT. Dual-booting allows you to choose which OS you want to run. For example, you might have both Windows 95 and NT on the same machine. Being able to boot into multiple operating systems is a nice feature for home machines, laptops, and test machines. Because NT doesn't let you access the hardware directly, many games won't work with it; many people dual-boot for this reason. Another reason might be to keep hardware diagnostic programs on a DOS partition, which you could then boot to in the event of problems.

10

Keep in mind that neither NT nor DOS can understand FAT32, and DOS cannot understand NTFS.

All your disk partitions do not have to be formatted in the same way. You might have one partition using FAT, and the rest can be NTFS.

Oddly enough, NT calls the partition the machine boots from the *system partition*, and the partition NT loads from the *boot partition*. It's fairly common for these two partitions to be the same, meaning you would boot from the C: drive and NT would also load from the C: drive.

One suggestion is to have a 2GB or smaller FAT partition on the C: drive, acting as both the system and boot partitions. Again, that would mean you both boot and load NT from the C: drive. Why use FAT for this? Because if you have trouble, you can simply boot from a DOS disk, change to the C: drive, and edit, copy, rename, and delete files. If you used NTFS for this, you could still boot from your DOS floppy, but you couldn't change to the C: drive and fix problems. Some third-party utilities allow this, but keeping the system and boot partitions FAT makes life easier.

What if you have originally formatted with FAT and later want to take advantage of NTFS? It's possible to easily convert from FAT to NTFS by using the convert command (see Figure 10.7). This is a one-way street. It's simple to go from FAT to NTFS, but there's no option for the reverse. Moving from NTFS to FAT requires backing up the data, formatting the partition, and then restoring.

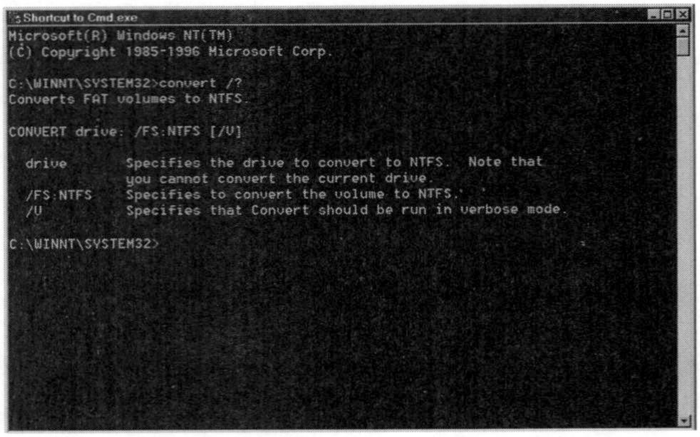

FIGURE 10.7

The convert command lets you convert from FAT to NTFS.

NTFS permissions are covered in Hour 11, "Sharing NT Resources." For now, just know that NTFS is an option, and that it can be seen only by NT.

Security

First things first: Control physical access to the file server. Without physical security, there is no security—especially today, when hot-swappable drives are common. These types of drives go in and come out very easily, so giving a thief even a few minutes alone with your server could end with your entire disk walking out the door. These hot-swappable drives can come out even when the machine is powered up, hence the term "hot swappable."

Second, maintain a password policy that requires a password (with a minimum password length), and make sure the passwords expire on a routine basis. Users have a habit of writing down passwords on those nice yellow Post-it notes and then putting them some-place clever, like underneath the keyboard (or in plain sight).

> As you learn in Hour 15, you can use User Manager to limit the times when users can log in, and even limit them to certain workstations.

10

With FAT volumes, you can't set permissions on individual files and folders. You can set permissions only on shared folders; these permissions come into play only when these shares are accessed over the network. With NTFS, you can have restrictions on individual files and folders, and the folders don't have to be shared. In fact, the NTFS permissions apply even if the machine is accessed locally. NTFS permissions are sometimes referred to as *local permissions*.

Summary

During this Hour, you looked at some basic concepts, such as workgroups and domains. Workgroups are suitable for small installations, where centralized administration is not necessary. In larger environments, domains are used. There are four types of domain models: the single domain model, the single master, the multiple master, and the complete trust model. The complete trust model distributes network management as opposed to centralizing it, and also generates a large number of trusts.

User and group accounts can be either local or global. You create users and groups with User Manager. The user account is the ticket that allows you to authenticate, or log in to the network. Group accounts—collections of users—are used to simplify administration.

There are two types of file systems you need to know about: FAT and NTFS. FAT is very common and easily accessible. NTFS requires NT. With NTFS, you have more control in terms of permissions than you have when using FAT. Also, not all the partitions need to be formatted the same way. You can have a mixture of both FAT and NTFS on the same machine. It's possible to easily convert from FAT to NTFS, but the reverse isn't possible. To go from NTFS to FAT requires that you delete and re-create the volume.

Workshop

Q&A

Q One of my partitions was formatted as FAT. I would like to change it to NTFS. Is this possible?

A Yes, you can use the `convert` command, **convert c: /fs:ntfs**, to get from FAT to NTFS. This command works in only one direction (that is, you cannot use `convert` to get from NTFS to FAT).

Q What is the maximum length of the password on a user account?

A The maximum is 14 characters, and the password is case sensitive.

Q Why would FAT be a good choice to use on my system and boot partitions?

A FAT is easily accessible. NTFS requires NT. Because these partitions are FAT, you can boot from a DOS disk and still have access to the files.

Q Our company is small. Do we have to have a domain?

A In a small environment, the workgroup model works just fine.

Q Why should you use groups when assigning rights?

A Groups make administration simpler. You can create a group and give it rights; then all you need do is add members to the group.

Quiz

1. You have just created a new user account, but the user can't log in. Everything you did looks fine. What would be a good first step in troubleshooting?

2. On your home machine, you have installed NT using NTFS. It turns out that a lot of your son's games no longer work. Is there a solution?

3. True or False: The primary domain controller was taken from your computer room by a horde of deranged programmers and thrown from the roof of the building. There is nothing you can do but start re-creating all your user accounts.

4. Of the four domain models, the _____ model requires the smallest number of trust relationships to be established.

5. Why is the primary domain controller like the movie *Highlander*?

HOUR 11

Sharing NT Resources

During this Hour, you learn about sharing NT resources and assigning permissions. Sharing a resource makes it available over the network, and you use permissions to control what users can do with the resource. The following topics are covered:

- Creating shared files and folders
- Creating shared network printers
- Assigning permissions
- Briefly explaining the little-known command prompt

Sharing Files and Folders

Why share? You might not have as a kid, but if you want users to be able to get to folders on the server, you have to start! For example, you might want to let your users share an application on your server instead of having 100 separate copies of the application on 100 separate machines, or you might want to supply a shared folder that everyone in the department can access to share data.

Just because a folder exists on the server does not mean that users can connect to it! That's where *shares* come in. You can think of a share as a "mount point." For example, if you have a folder called c:\common on the server and you want your users to be able to access this directory, then you need to *share* it. After you create the share, the folder becomes accessible from the network.

A shared folder or drive is shown in Explorer with a hand under it. When you see the hand, you know that the folder or drive is shared.

Creating Shares

You don't really *create* a share; instead, you simply start sharing. To share a folder, do the following:

1. Right-click the folder you want to share.
2. Choose Properties.
3. Select the Sharing tab.
4. Select the Shared As radio button (see Figure 11.1).
5. Enter a share name.
6. Click OK.

FIGURE 11.1

You don't really create a share; you just start sharing!

Notice that you can use this screen to limit the number of users you allow to connect to the share.

Keep in mind that not all clients can see long names or names with special characters. For example, in the screen shown in Figure 11.2, a directory named This is Three is being shared. The system reminds you that not all clients will be able to connect to this share; keep this in mind if you have any MS-DOS workstations that need to connect. If you have any DOS workstations, it's best to stick to the DOS 8.3 naming convention.

FIGURE 11.2

Not all share names can be seen by all clients.

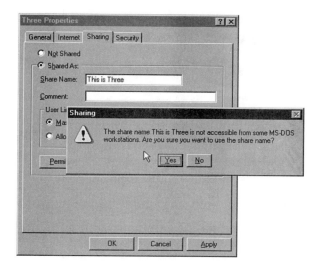

Administrative Shares

NT automatically shares the root of each volume and names the shared volume drive letter$, as shown in Figure 11.3; you can reach this dialog box by right-clicking the icon representing the drive and choosing Properties, and then selecting the Sharing tab. These are called *administrative shares*, and you as the administrator can connect to them. When you connect to the administrative share at the root of the volume, you have access to the entire volume. As shown in Figure 11.4, you cannot set the permissions on the default administrative shares (you'll learn about setting permissions for shares next).

The $ sign causes the share to be hidden, meaning that it doesn't show up when users are browsing the network. You can specify that a share be hidden simply by putting a $ sign at the end of the share name.

FIGURE 11.3

The $ sign denotes a hidden share.

FIGURE 11.4

You cannot set permissions on administrative shares.

Notice the New Share button. You can click it to share the same folder multiple times with different names.

Assigning Permissions to Shared Folders

After you've set up a folder to be shared, the next thing you want to do is assign rights (also called *permissions*) to users. For example, if you want them to be able to see what files are in the folder but not add or delete files, you might give them permission only to read.

Shared folder permissions apply only when the folder is accessed over the network! If you can log on locally, then you are accessing the folder directly, and the share permissions do not apply.

To set permissions, do the following:

1. In the Share Properties dialog box (refer back to Figure 11.1), click the Permissions button.

2. The Access Through Share Permissions screen opens (see Figure 11.5). As you can see, the group Everyone has been given Full Control permission to your newly created share. Click the Add button to open the Add Users and Groups dialog box shown in Figure 11.6; from here, you can add and remove users and groups and control their access.

The Everyone group gets Full Control permission by default in NT. In the Novell world, users start with no permissions; as the administrator, you must add them. In NT, it is just the opposite; users start with full rights, and you must take them away!

FIGURE 11.5

Here you set permissions for the share.

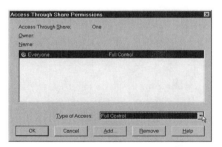

What permissions can you assign, and what does each permission mean? If you look closely at the drop-down list in Figure 11.6, you can see that you have four options:

- **No Access**   This option is the most restrictive. Users cannot open the folder or see its contents.

- **Read**   This option allows for the display folder and file names and enables users to run executables (programs), see data and attributes of files, and navigate to sub-folders.

- **Change** This option enables users to do everything permitted by the Read option, as well as the following:
    - Delete folders and files.
    - Create folders and files.
    - Change file attributes.
    - Change file data.
- **Full Control** As mentioned, this setting is the default for the Everyone group. It allows users to do everything permitted by the Change option, plus the following:
    - Change file permissions.
    - Take ownership of files (on NTFS).

FIGURE 11.6

Here you add users and groups and assign permissions.

Shared folders are the only way you can secure folders on a FAT volume. Later on, you will see that on an NTFS volume, other permissions can be applied.

As a rule of thumb, always grant only the bare minimum of permissions needed to allow users to get their jobs done. If a user just needs to read the files in a folder, then don't give him the right to delete files!

User Permissions and Group Permissions

Permissions can be assigned to either users or groups. The $64,000 question is this: What if the user George has been given read access to a share, but the Graphics group, of which George is a member, has been given change access to the same share?

This leads to the concept of *effective permissions*, which are the end result of combining these multiple permission assignments. In George's case, his effective permissions are a combination of change (given to the group) and read (given to the user George); George's effective permissions, therefore, are change permissions.

The no access permission always overrides any other permissions!

Assigning Permissions to NTFS Volumes

If you have an NTFS volume, then you can apply even more permissions. And unlike shared folder permissions, which apply only when the shared folder is accessed through the network, NTFS permissions apply even when you access the resource locally (for this reason, NTFS permissions are sometimes referred to as *local permissions*). Also, unlike shared folder permissions, which can be applied only to folders, NTFS permissions can be placed on files.

To set NTFS permissions on a file or folder, do the following:

1. Right-click the folder and choose Properties.
2. Select the Security tab (see Figure 11.7).

11

FIGURE 11.7

Use this tab to assign NTFS permissions.

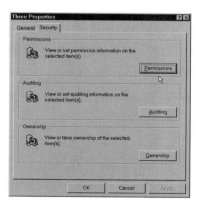

3. Click the Permissions button to open the Directory Permissions dialog box, shown in Figure 11.8.

FIGURE **11.8**

There are more NTFS permissions than there are shared folder permissions.

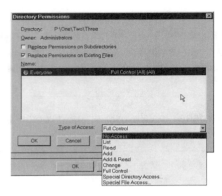

By default, the permissions you assign apply only to the directory you are working with. If you check the Replace Permissions on Subdirectories check box in the Directory Permissions dialog box, the changes flow down and apply to the subdirectories of the folder, too.

If the Replace Permissions on Existing Files check box in the Directory Permissions dialog box is cleared, then the permissions are applied to the folder only—not to the files in it.

If you take a close look at the drop-down list shown in Figure 11.8, you'll note that there are more NTFS permissions than there are shared folder permissions.

What are the NTFS permissions, and what do they mean?

- **Read (R)**   Users can read folder names, filenames, and attributes.
- **Write (W)**   Users can create files and folders, change attributes of files and folders, and change the data in a file.
- **Execute (X)**   Users can run executables.
- **Delete**   Users can delete files and folders.
- **Change Permission (P)**   Users can change the permissions of a file or folder.
- **Take Ownership (O)**   Users can take ownership of files and folders.

Having said that, does this list of NTFS permissions look anything like the drop-down list shown in Figure 11.8? No, it doesn't. This is because the drop-down list in Figure 11.8 is showing *standard permissions*, which are groupings of the individual NTFS permissions. Table 11.1 shows what each standard permission is composed of.

TABLE 11.1 STANDARD FOLDER PERMISSIONS.

Permission	Composed of These NTFS Permissions
No Access	N/A
List	RX
Read	RX
Add	WX
Add & Read	RWX
Change	RWXD
Full Control	All

The Special Directory Access and Special File Access options are covered later in this section.

In addition to standard folder permissions, there are also standard file permissions (see Figure 11.9). Table 11.2 shows the individual NTFS permissions that make up each of the standard file permissions.

FIGURE 11.9

There are also standard file permissions.

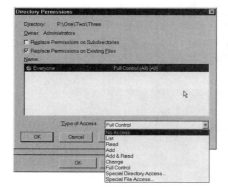

TABLE 11.2 STANDARD FILE PERMISSIONS.

Permission	Composed of These NTFS Permissions
No Access	N/A
Read	RX
Change	RWXD
Full Control	All

> Notice in both tables that for the no access standard permission, N/A (not applicable) appears in the right-hand column. This is because no access means no access!

Suppose none of the standard NTFS permissions fill your needs. In that case, you can assign special access permissions. If you refer to the drop-down list shown back in Figure 11.8, you will notice two choices not covered yet:

- **Special Directory Access**   With this type of access (see Figure 11.10), you can whip up your own batch of permissions to suit your fancy (these are the individual NTFS permissions mentioned before in the discussion on standard permissions). Just check what you want, salt lightly, and then network.
- **Special File Access**   See Figure 11.11.

FIGURE 11.10

The Special Directory Access dialog box.

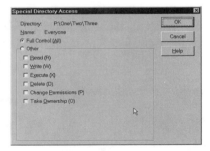

FIGURE 11.11

The Special File Access dialog box.

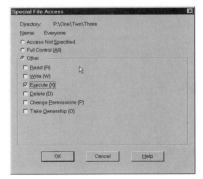

User Permissions and Group Permissions

As with shared folder permissions, you can assign NTFS permissions to both groups and users. This means that, as with shared folder permissions, the same user might receive permissions both as an individual user and as a member of a group (as was the case with user George, who was also a member of the Graphics group). There are a few simple rules when it comes to overlapping rights:

- As with shared folder permissions, no access permission always overrides any other permission.
- File permissions override folder permissions. For example, if a user has read permission to the folder, but has full control access to one of the files in that folder, then the user can write to the file because file permissions override folder permissions.
- Effective permissions are a combination of the user and group permissions.

> Each user automatically becomes the owner of the files and folders he or she creates. Owners can always change permissions of their files.

Combining Shared Folder Permissions and NTFS Permissions

Because a folder must be shared for it to be accessed from the network, share folder permissions must be assigned. But how do you handle sharing the folder and using NTFS permissions on that same folder? The answer is simple. Evaluate the user's effective permissions on the shared folder side. Then, evaluate the user's effective permissions on the NTFS side. Finally, just remember this: *The most restrictive permission is the effective permission.*

For example, suppose George has full control shared folder permissions to folder Pokey, to which he has also been assigned read NTFS permissions. The effective shared folder permissions are full control, but the effective NTFS permissions are read. The most restrictive permission is the one that applies, so George has only read access to folder Pokey.

Accessing Shared Folders

There are many ways of connecting to a shared folder; you might already be familiar with clicking the Map Network Drive toolbar button (the one that looks like a disk) to reach the screen shown in Figure 11.12. The following list describes the elements on this screen:

- **Drive**   Use this drop-down list to specify the drive letter for the share.
- **Path**   Use this drop-down list to specify the path to the share. (Or you can type the path in the form *servername**sharename*.)

11

- **Connect As**   By default, you are connected as the user name you used when you logged in. If you are connecting with a different account, then the account name you are using goes here. If the account is in a separate domain, the syntax is *domain name\account name*.

- **Reconnect at Logon**   Check this box to make the drive persistent. That way, the next time you log on, the drive will be reconnected automatically.

- **Expand by Default**   Check this box to make the list in the Shared Directories pane expand to show the computers in your domain. You should always clear this check box if you are connecting over a slow link, such as RAS.

FIGURE 11.12

Click the Map Network Drive toolbar button to open this screen.

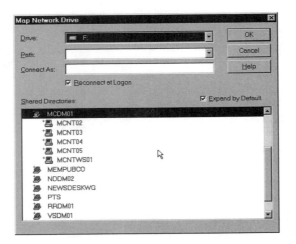

Another way to connect to a shared folder is to choose Start|Run, and enter the name of the server where the shared folder resides, as shown in Figure 11.13. Using this method is pretty slick; it opens a window showing you all the shares on the server, which you can then browse through. Also, using this method means you don't have to supply a drive letter.

FIGURE 11.13

You can also connect to a share by using the Run dialog box.

The Venerable net use Command

Old-timers often find it easier to drop to the command prompt to accomplish a task than to open several windows to get their work done. Enter the net command. There are far too many options for using the net command to cover here (they would take an entire chapter), but suppose you are at a command prompt and want to get a directory listing of a share you are not connected to. Do you have to minimize or exit the command prompt window and connect through the GUI interface, or can you connect from right where you are? Not surprisingly, you can connect from the command prompt.

Notice in Figure 11.14 that the command net use has been issued, and that the result is There are no entries in the list. (We are doing this only to show that we currently have no drives connected.) Next, we used the command net use f: \\mcnt04\c$; as you can see, the command was completed successfully. This is all you need to do to connect to a share from the command prompt. To prove that we are connected, we again issued the net use command to reveal the status of the F: drive.

FIGURE 11.14

Connecting to an Administrative share with the net use *command from a command prompt.*

11

Network Printing

As with a shared folder, a printer must be shared before it can be used by other network users. In this section, you look at creating and administering a network printer, so buckle up and get ready to print!

> **NT TERMINOLOGY**
>
> In NT-ese, the physical device that puts the ink on the paper isn't a printer; it's a *print device*. The machine attached to the print device acts as a *print server*, and the *printer* is the software interface that takes jobs from the print server and sends them to the print device. Hey, we don't cook it—we just serve it up!

Setting Up a Network Printer

To set up a printer for sharing, do the following:

1. Choose Start|Settings|Printers.

2. In the Printers screen, click Add Printer. This starts the Add Printer wizard; the first screen is shown in Figure 11.15.

FIGURE 11.15

The Add Printer wizard is used to set up your printers.

3. To create a new network printer, select the My Computer radio button, and follow the wizard's screens. When you are done, you will have a local printer.

> If you select the Network Printer Server radio button, that means you are merely connecting to a printer that already resides on another machine. The wizard asks you which network printer you want to connect to; either browse for or type in the name, and you are finished.

4. After the printer is set up, right-click the printer in the Printers screen and choose Properties.

5. Select the Sharing tab to view the screen shown in Figure 11.16.

FIGURE 11.16

Just like a folder, you share the printer and give it a name.

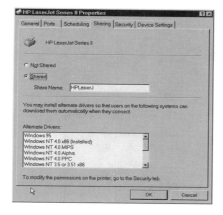

6. Enable the Shared radio button.

7. Give the shared printer a name in the Share Name text box.

The same cautions for shares about long names or names with illegal characters apply for printers.

8. Click OK.

Printer Permissions

Now that you have created, shared, and given the printer a name, you must apply permissions. To do so, follow these steps:

1. Right-click the printer in the Printers screen and choose Properties.

2. Select the Security tab to view the screen shown in Figure 11.17.

3. Click the Permissions button.

4. From the screen shown in Figure 11.18, you can add and remove users and groups and control the permissions. Set permissions as you see fit, and click OK. There are four printer permissions:

   • **No Access**   Users cannot use the printer.

   • **Print**   Users can connect to the printer, print documents, and control their own jobs (that is, they can pause, resume, and cancel print jobs). This is the default for the Everyone group.

   • **Manage Documents**   Users have print rights and can also control all the documents, not just their own.

FIGURE **11.17**

The Security tab of the Printer Properties dialog box.

- **Full Control**   Users have manage documents rights, as well as rights to share the printer, change the printer properties, delete printers, change permissions, and other administrative tasks.

FIGURE **11.18**

Assigning printer permissions.

Managing Network Printers

To manage documents, choose Start|Settings|Printers, and double-click the printer in question. This takes you to the Printers dialog box. If a user has only print rights, she can use the Document menu in this dialog box to cancel jobs, pause jobs, or check the properties of a job in the queue (see Figure 11.19). If a user has manage documents rights, she can use this dialog box to control all the jobs in the queue, not just her own.

FIGURE 11.19

The Document menu, which is used to control print jobs.

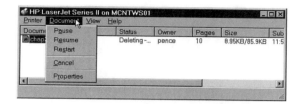

A *queue*, also called a *spooler*, is where print jobs actually go when you choose to print. If NT did not spool print jobs, only one person could print to a printer at a time. Instead, your job waits in the queue until its turn to be printed.

The Printer menu, shown in Figure 11.20, can be used to control the printer, instead of just the documents in the queue. (Remember, *printer* refers to software, not to the actual printer, which is hardware!) If you have been given the full control printer permission, then here you can pause the printer, which you might want to do if there's a problem with the print device. Or, you can purge all the documents in the queue.

FIGURE 11.20

The Printer menu, which is used to control the printer.

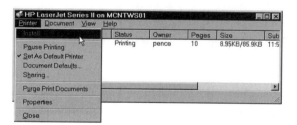

Print Server Properties

Remember, the machine with the printer attached is acting as a print server to the clients on the network. To control the server properties, choose Start|Settings|Printers, and then choose File|Server Properties. Select the Advanced tab to view the screen shown in Figure 11.21.

FIGURE 11.21

*Controlling the print
server properties.*

In this dialog box, you can set the following:

- **Spool Folder**   In this text box, you can specify the spool folder. This is the folder where print jobs reside until it is their turn to be printed.
- **Logging Options**   Use the first three check boxes to specify whether errors, warnings, or information events are logged.
- **Notification Options**   The last two check boxes enable you to specify whether the system beeps on errors of remote documents, and whether the system notifies you when remote documents are printed.

Printer Pooling

Imagine if you had three HP LaserJet print devices—one connected to LPT1, one connected to LPT2, and the third connected to COM1. Wouldn't it be great if you could configure your system to pool those resources? That way, the printer would have three output devices to send jobs to, not just one! Of course, print jobs would get out of the queue more quickly. Even if one of the printers in this example is busy, there are still two others to service the queue.

To enable printer pooling, choose Start|Settings|Printers. Right-click on the printer, choose Properties, select the Ports tab to view the screen shown in Figure 11.22, and check the Enable Printer Pooling check box.

Here are a couple of caveats about printer pooling:

- All printers in a pool must be of the same type.
- Unless you are a practical joker, place all pooled print devices together. (Of course, you could put one on every floor of your building, and enjoy watching users search for their output!)

FIGURE 11.22

On the Ports tab, you enable printer pooling.

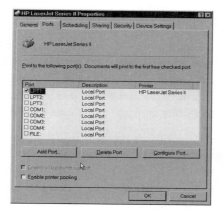

Scheduling

You can use the Scheduling tab of the Printer Properties dialog box (see Figure 11.23) to set options, including availability of the printer (for example, you might set a printer to be available only at night and have all the large jobs sent to that printer). Additionally, you can specify whether print jobs are sent directly to the printer or whether they are spooled. If you choose to spool documents, they can begin printing immediately as they enter the spool or only after the entire document is spooled.

FIGURE 11.23

The Scheduling tab of the Printer Properties dialog box.

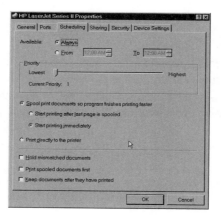

You would select the Print Directly to the Printer radio button only for a non-shared printer.

Summary

For you to be able to access a resource—such as files, folders, or printers—across the network, that resource must be shared. There are four shared folder permissions: no access, read, change, and full control. Shared folder permissions have an effect only when the folder is accessed through the network. A user's effective permissions are a combination of the ones specifically assigned to the user and the ones assigned to groups to which the user belongs.

Unlike shared folder permissions, NTFS permissions work even when the resource is accessed locally. For this reason, NTFS permissions are sometimes referred to as *local permissions*. Most often, NTFS permissions are assigned by using standard permissions. Standard permissions are collections, or groups, of individual NTFS permissions. There are seven standard folder permissions: no access, list, read, add, add and read, change, and full control. There are four standard file permissions: no access, read, change, and full control. When the standard NTFS permissions are not adequate, you can assign special NTFS permissions, which allow you to choose exactly which NTFS permissions you want to assign. Like shared folder permissions, a user's effective NTFS permissions are a combination of the rights assigned to the user and the rights assigned to the groups of which the user is a member.

When combining shared folder permissions and NTFS permissions, you must first determine the effective rights on both sides of the equation; the most restrictive permissions are the ones that apply.

Printers can also be shared, and there are permissions that apply here, too. There are four printer permissions: no access, print, manage documents, and full control. The *print device* is the actual hardware that puts ink on the paper, what one would normally call the printer. The machine with the print device attached is called the *print server*; the *printer* is really just software that sends jobs from the queue, or spooler, to the print device. *Printer pooling* is when there is more than one print device servicing a printer. This is useful in high-volume printing environments because it allows jobs to get out of the queue more quickly.

Workshop

Q&A

Q Why are NTFS permissions sometimes referred to as *local permissions*?

A Unlike shared folder permissions, which kick in only when accessed through the network, NTFS permissions still apply if the file or folder is accessed locally.

Q What is an administrative share?

A NT automatically shares the root of all volumes. These shares are hidden; they don't show up when you're browsing. This lets you, as the administrator, access the entire volume across the network, as opposed to being able to access only what has been shared.

Q What is printer pooling?

A Printer pooling is when you have a printer serviced by more than one print device. This allows print jobs to leave the spool, or queue, quicker than a single print device would.

Q What do you mean by *effective permissions*?

A Effective permissions are the bottom line, the real rights the user has. For example, if you have been assigned full control to a share as an individual, but you are also a member of a group that has been assigned no access to the same share, your effective permissions are no access.

Q What are standard NTFS permissions?

A Instead of assigning individual NTFS permissions to a file or folder, NT has prepackaged groups that generally do the job for you. The groupings of permissions are called *standard permissions*.

11

Quiz

1. Sandra is a member of the Sysop group, which has been given the shared folder permission full control over the Groneman folder. As the administrator, you assign the shared folder permission of read to the Groneman folder. What are Sandra's effective rights to the Groneman folder?

2. What permission always overrides all others?

3. True or False: When using both shared folder permissions and NTFS permissions, you first evaluate the user's effective shared folder permissions. You then evaluate the user's effective NTFS permissions. The least restrictive permissions are the ones that apply.

4. You have one department that does a very high volume of printing. Users are complaining that they often have to wait for their print output. What can you do to solve this problem?

5. True or False: NTFS folder permissions override the NTFS file permissions.

6. True or False: The command net use f: \\Dave\Parkes will connect to the Parkes share on server Dave and assign it the drive letter F.

HOUR 12

NT Remote Access Service (RAS)

Remote Access Service (RAS) provides connectivity for remote users. When RAS is installed, remote clients can establish a Dial-Up Networking connection and access resources on the network just as though they were in the same building as the server.

Even if you don't need remote access for your users, you should install RAS so that as the administrator, you can establish the connection for trouble shooting and administration purposes.

The RAS service uses the domain database, so your users are already set up to use it. You simply have to give the user permission to use RAS. You will see later this Hour how you can use the RAS administration program to give this permission (it can also be done with User Manager, covered in Hour 15, "Managing NT Servers").

This connection is naturally going to be slower than the Ethernet connection users are used to when in the building.

On NT Workstation, RAS supports only one connection, but on NT Server, RAS supports up to 256 simultaneous connections.

The Protocols

RAS supports TCP/IP, IPX, and NetBEUI, your old friends from Hour 3, "Protocols." The connection between the remote workstation and the RAS server occurs by modem using either of the following:

- **SLIP (Serial Line Internet Protocol)**   Supports TCP/IP over serial or dial-up lines. SLIP supports only IP, so if the remote clients are using IPX or NetBEUI, SLIP doesn't work.
- **PPP (Point-to-Point Protocol)**   This is an enhancement to SLIP that has more functionality. PPP supports many protocols, including the three that RAS uses: IPX, TCP/IP, and NetBEUI.

Installation

Now get RAS installed so you can work with your own machine as you take a look at the configuration screens and the RAS administration program:

1. Choose Start | Control Panel.
2. Double-click the Network icon to open the Network properties screen.
3. Select the Services tab.
4. Click Add.
5. You should see the screen shown in Figure 12.1. Highlight Remote Access Service and click OK.
6. The Setup program is going to want some files, so load up your installation CD-ROM.

FIGURE 12.1

Use the Select Network Service dialog box to add a service.

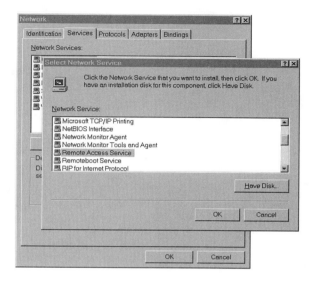

Whenever you add something, Windows is going to want the files from the Setup CD-ROM. This is very annoying because of course now you have to go and dig it up. The solution is to copy the i386 directory to the hard disk. Then, whenever Setup wants files, simply point it to c:\i386.

RAS is basically going to take your modem and make it work like a network interface card. If you haven't installed a modem yet, Setup informs you that there are no RAS-capable devices, as shown in Figure 12.2. At this time, you have the option of invoking the Modem Installer, by clicking Yes, to install the modem.

12

FIGURE 12.2

If there's no modem installed, you have the choice of invoking the Modem Installer.

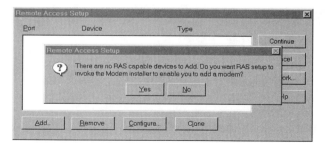

If all goes well, you should wind up with a RAS-capable device installed, as shown in Figure 12.3. Click OK to continue.

FIGURE 12.3

After the Modem Installer has run, you now have a RAS-capable device added to the system and can continue with the installation.

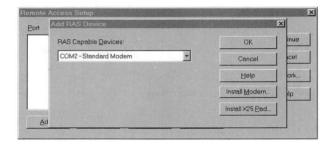

Next, you see screens for configuring protocols. RAS tries to bind all the protocols you already have running, so if you are using both IP and IPX, then you get a configuration screen for each of them. If you are running only one protocol, you get only one configuration screen. For now, just say OK to the defaults on these screens. If all goes well, you then see the screen shown in Figure 12.4; as always, Windows wants you to reboot!

FIGURE 12.4

Congratulations! RAS is now successfully installed.

Notice how Figure 12.4 tells you that you can use the Remote Access Admin? You can find this new tool by choosing Start | Programs | Administrative Tools. You'll learn more about this tool later this Hour.

Don't forget to reinstall Service Pack 3 after RAS has been set up successfully. The rule is that if you get asked for files from the CD-ROM (or in your case, the c:\i386 directory), always reinstall the service pack! This applies to any service you add, not just RAS.

Configuration

Now that you have RAS successfully installed, you need to make sure you have a handle on what protocols are being used and how they are configured. You can find this information in the the protocol configuration screens you saw during the installation. Luckily, you can access these screens at any time, not just during installation.

If you return to the Network properties screen, highlight Remote Access Service, and choose Properties, you find yourself back in RAS Setup (see Figure 12.5).

FIGURE 12.5

From the Setup screen, you can configure the port with the Configure button or the protocols with the Network button.

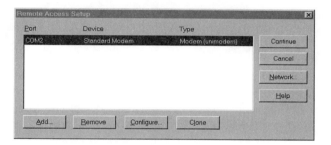

Click the Configure button to set up your RAS server to dial out only, receive calls only, or handle both dial out and receiving, as shown in Figure 12.6.

FIGURE 12.6

The port can be set to dial out only, receive only, or both.

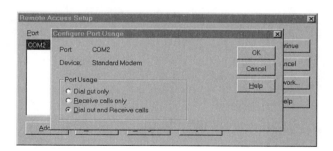

12

To configure how RAS handles protocols, click the Network button (refer to Figure 12.5). This opens the RAS Network Configuration screen, shown in Figure 12.7. What you see here depends on what protocols you have installed.

FIGURE 12.7

The Network Configuration screen shows you which protocols are enabled for dial out and also allows you to configure the protocols you have enabled.

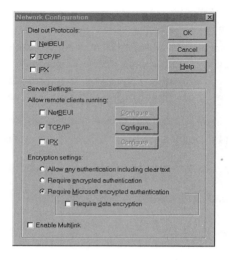

 Notice the Enable Multilink check box on the Network Configuration screen. *Multilink* is used to "bond" together more than one modem or RAS-capable device to act as one. (Think of it as taking two physical modems and turning them into one logical modem.) This increases your bandwidth and, therefore, speeds up your connection. Both the client and server must have the Multilink feature enabled for it to work.

Note that if you, as a client using Multilink, call the RAS server and your setup is such that the server must call you back, then the Multilink will fail. That's because there's room for only one entry when entering the number the server uses to call back; as a result, the server calls only one of your Multilink devices. Using Multilink with dial back can be done on the client side with ISDN (Integrated Services Digital Network), however.

Notice that TCP/IP is the only protocol checked in the Server Settings section. Click the Configure button next to the TCP/IP entry to view the screen shown in Figure 12.8.

Many of the options on this screen are self-explanatory, such as whether you allow access to the entire network or only the RAS server. If you allow access to the entire network, then your RAS server acts like a router. Your traffic comes into the server over the modem, and then the server routes the packet to its own network interface card. With this option enabled, you can access any device on the network just as you normally would. If you select the This Computer Only radio button instead of the Entire Network radio button, then all you can get to is the RAS server itself—whatever you need had better be on that box!

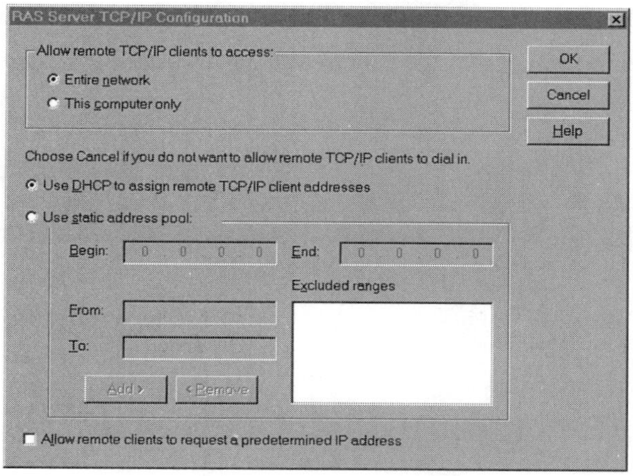

FIGURE 12.8

From the TCP/IP Configuration screen, you specify how RAS deals with users connecting through TCP/IP.

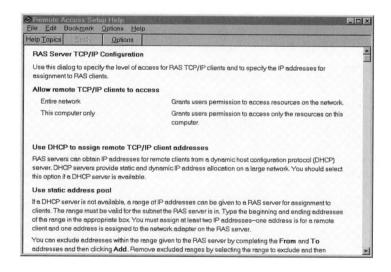

Instead of covering every possible option in detail, I suggest you click the Help button in this dialog box to learn about the other options (see Figure 12.9).

FIGURE 12.9

Take a look at the Help screen if you have a question about configuration.

12

Administration

One of the advantages of NT from an administrator's point of view is the capability of the management utilities to select the server you want to control or look at. This means it isn't necessary to actually go to the server running RAS to administer it. You can administer all your RAS servers with the Remote Access Admin:

1. Choose Start | Programs | Administrative Tools | Remote Access Admin.
2. Select the computer you want to administer from the Server menu (see Figure 12.10).

FIGURE 12.10

The main RAS admin-istration screen.

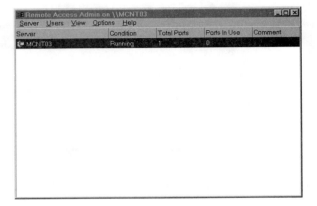

From here, you can stop, start, or pause the RAS service, or take a look at the status of your communication port. You can also see active users or assign user permissions (see Figure 12.11). (Users must be granted permission to connect via RAS, and this permission can be given either here or through User Manager.)

FIGURE 12.11

You need to not only grant permission to use RAS, but also specify how the system responds, such as set-ting call back options.

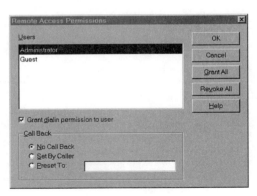

Notice that in addition to granting permission to use RAS, you can also set call back options on the Remote Access Permissions screen shown in Figure 12.11. Here, you can specify whether the server calls back, and if so, at what number. This is a useful security option to keep in mind. If you don't use call back, anyone can attempt to access your network from any phone number. With call back enabled, unless the cracker is sitting at the phone number you have entered, he's out of luck!

To check on the status of the port and see if things are working correctly, you need to choose Communication Ports from the Server menu. You then see the port or ports you defined during your installation. Choose Port Status to view information about the status of your port (see Figure 12.12). There's information about the line condition, connection statistics, device errors, and which user is currently on the port. From here, you also have the option of choosing Reset to reset the communications port.

FIGURE 12.12

The Port Status screen gives you information about your modem, line condition, and other statistics.

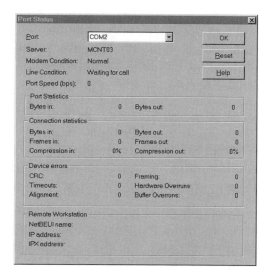

Troubleshooting

First things first: Has the service started? Always check the Event Viewer (see Figure 12.13), which is covered in more detail in Hour 15. The services and drivers enter events into the system log, which you can use to determine whether the service has started.

If you're dying to take a look at the system log now and can't wait until Hour 15, choose Start | Programs | Administrative Tools | Event Viewer. From the Log menu, select the system log. You can also double-click Services in Control Panel and check to see the current status of the services, as well as stop and restart them.

FIGURE 12.13

This is a detailed view of one of the events in the system log. Notice that the RAS service has failed to start.

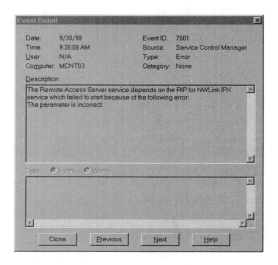

If there are authentication problems, remember that both ends have to match—not only the protocols, but also the authentication information. Take a look back at Figure 12.7 and notice the encryption settings. Start by using the simplest requirements, and then move up gradually. And don't forget it could be something as simple as the user entering the wrong password. Most people have far more passwords than they can keep up with and often forget which password goes with which system. Remember, the passwords are CASE SENSITIVE!

The Dial-Up Networking Monitor in the Control Panel gives you another window into RAS. The Status tab of the Dial-Up Networking Monitor is what you saw when running the RAS administration program. The Summary tab shows you which remote networks and users are connected and which devices are part of each connection. The Preferences tab, shown in Figure 12.14, lets you set alerts and show status lights.

FIGURE 12.14

Dial-Up Networking is another method of checking on your RAS status.

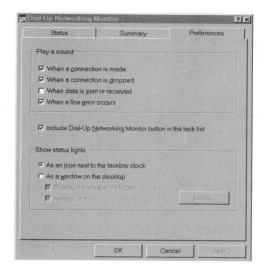

The Other End: Dial-Up Networking

Everything discussed so far has been server based. RAS runs on the server, but how do you connect to it? With Dial-Up Networking. I could devote another chapter of this size to the other end of the connection, Dial-Up Networking.

Dial-Up Networking is automatically installed when you set up RAS, provided that RAS was set for either dial out only or dial out and receive. Having set up RAS, you should have no trouble handling things on the client side. Simply open My Computer and click Dial-Up Networking. You're prompted to install your modem if necessary, and once past that, you just need to configure some entries to dial.

12

Summary

Remote Access Service (RAS) provides network access to remote users through telephone lines and modems. The phone lines become the network cabling system, and the modems act like network interface cards. The connection between the two modems uses either SLIP or PPP, most likely the latter. RAS runs on the server, and the clients make the connection with Dial-Up Networking, using the same protocols they normally run.

The installation and configuration are fairly straightforward, and the setup also installs the RAS Admin program. Using the Admin program, you can administer any RAS server on your network; you don't have to physically walk to the machine and run the Admin program there.

Multilink lets you bond two physical modems together to act as one logical modem. This gives you greater bandwidth, thus increasing the speed of your response time. NT Workstation supports one RAS connection, and NT Server supports up to 256 simultaneous connections.

Users need to be given permission to use RAS, and you also need to set up how the server responds. You will be using the existing domain database, so you don't have to create a new batch of users because you have added a new service.

RAS runs on the server and gets things ready at that end. The other side of the equation is the calling workstation. You use Dial-Up Networking to connect to the RAS server.

Workshop

Q&A

Q The head of one of my departments wants to work at home occasionally. Will RAS let him do that?

A Remote Access Service, or RAS, lets you establish a true network connection over telephone lines. The RAS server can be set to act as a router and allow access to the entire network, or it can be set to provide access to only the machine the service is running on.

Q When I try to install RAS, I get a message telling me there are no RAS-capable devices. Why is that?

A RAS is going to make your modem act like a network interface card. You see this message when you start installation and have not yet installed a modem.

Q What is Multilink?

A Multilink takes two physical modems and makes them act as one logical unit. This is done to increase bandwidth and to speed up your connection.

Q Do I need to install any special protocols at the client end to use RAS?

A No. To the clients, they authenticate to the network just as they usually do. The network connection is set up between the two modems, and then your normal protocols flow over this "network."

Quiz

1. You are certain that Dial-Up Networking is configured correctly at both the client and server. In fact, you can connect to the server from all your workstations but this one. What could be the problem?

2. True or False: When using RAS, you can access only the server that has the modem attached and RAS running.

3. RAS running on NT Workstation supports _____ connections, and RAS running on NT Server supports _____ simultaneous connections.

    A. 10, 64

    B. Who needs more than one connection, anyway?

    C. 5, 10

    D. 1, 256

4. Name two troubleshooting tools you might use to check on the RAS status.

12

HOUR 13

Accessing NetWare Resources from Windows NT

As mentioned in Hour 8, "Accessing NetWare Resources from Windows 98," Novell's NetWare is the world's most popular client/server-based network operating system. During the past few years, however, Windows NT has become the desktop operating system of choice for many corporations and even for home use by some power users. Therefore, chances are good you'll need to know how to access resources on a NetWare server from a Windows NT workstation.

During this Hour, the following topics are covered:

- Installing and configuring Microsoft's Client Service for NetWare
- Installing and configuring Novell's NetWare Client for Windows NT
- Using the clients to access NetWare resources

Microsoft's Client Service for NetWare

The steps for installing the Microsoft Client Service for NetWare are very similar to those for installing any other network service in Windows NT. The following is a step-by-step procedure that assumes you already have your network adapter installed (have your Windows NT CD-ROM handy):

1. Log in to Windows NT as Administrator or with an account that is a member of the Administrators group.

2. After you have logged in, right-click on the Network Neighborhood icon on your desktop and choose Properties from the context menu that appears. Or, you can open the Network properties sheet through the Control Panel.

3. Select the Services tab and then click Add to bring up the Select Network Service dialog box (see Figure 13.1).

4. Highlight the item Client Service for NetWare and then click OK.

5. You are asked to specify the location of the Windows NT install files. Enter the path (such as D:\i386\, assuming D: is your CD-ROM drive) and then click Continue.

6. The Setup program copies the appropriate files to your machine and then brings you back to the main window. You should see Client Service for NetWare listed as a component in the Network Services window.

7. Click Close. Click Yes to reboot your computer so the new settings take effect.

FIGURE 13.1

Select the Client Service for NetWare from this dialog box to install this service.

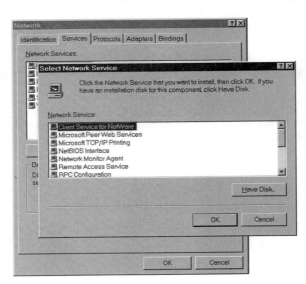

Accessing Novell Directory Services

Unlike the Microsoft Client for NetWare Networks shipped with Windows 98, you don't need to install any additional service or update to the Client Service for NetWare to gain access to the Novell Directory Services (NDS).

The Microsoft Client Service for NetWare that ships with NT 4.0 lets you log an NT workstation onto an NDS tree. However, because of the DLL libraries needed, the Microsoft client can't run the 16-bit NetWare Administrator (NWAdmin) that ships with NetWare 4; you need to use the Novell client.

Configuring the Client

When configuring the NT client, you'll notice two things that are different from the Windows 98 client:

- When you highlight the Client Service for NetWare component in the Services tab of the Network properties sheet, the Properties button is grayed out!
- You have a new icon in the Control Panel labeled "CSNW."

In Windows NT, you configure the Microsoft Client Service for NetWare through this new CSNW icon. The following steps outline the procedure for configuring the Microsoft client:

1. When your computer has finished rebooting, log on as Administrator or equivalent again.

2. During Windows NT logon (after you've entered your user name and password and clicked OK), a Select NetWare Logon dialog box appears.

3. If you access a bindery server (such as NetWare 3.12 or a NetWare 4 or NetWare 5 server via Bindery Services), click Preferred Server and enter the name of your preferred server in the Select Preferred Server text box; select None if you don't want one set, and you log on to the nearest available server instead of a specific server.

   If you're accessing NDS, click Default Tree and Context and enter the name of your NDS tree and the logon context.

4. Enable the Run Login Script check box under the Login Script Options.

5. Click OK to continue the logon process.

If you clicked Cancel in the Select NetWare Logon dialog box or want to make changes to settings you made, use the CSNW icon in the Control Panel. You can set the following properties in the CSNW dialog box (see Figure 13.2):

13

- Preferred server (if bindery mode)
- Default tree and context (if NDS mode)
- Print options, such as add form feed at end of a print job
- Enable or disable the execution of NetWare login script during logon

FIGURE 13.2

Use this dialog box to change the properties of the Client Service for NetWare.

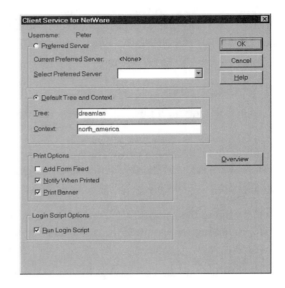

Novell Client for Windows NT

Novell's latest client is a vast improvement from previous versions. The new NetWare Client for NT offers improved NDS-based administration and desktop management tools that network administrators will find very useful.

If you have the Microsoft Client Service for NetWare installed on your Windows NT machine, Novell's installation program removes it before installing the Novell Client for Windows NT.

If you don't have NetWare 5, you can download the latest Novell Client for Windows NT from the Internet, free of charge, at http://www.novell.com/download. Be aware that it's a *very* large download. If you have a slow link to the Internet, it would be best to order the CD-ROM from Novell (http://www.novell.com/products/clientscd) for about $35.

Installing the Novell Client

Because of the number and size of the associated files (as it includes files for Z.E.N. Works), the current version of the Novell NetWare Client for Windows NT can be installed only from a CD-ROM, server, or local hard drive.

> The latest Novell Client for Windows NT (v4.5) *requires* Windows NT 4.0, and NT Service Pack 3 is recommended but isn't required.
>
> If you have Windows 3.51, you need an older version of the Novell Client for Windows NT, such as v4.11a.

The following steps assume you have the NetWare 5 client CD-ROM (you probably won't need it, but know where your Windows NT CD-ROM is just in case):

> If you're familiar with the steps for installing the Novell Client for Windows 95/98, the steps for the Novell Client for Windows NT are similar, but either a few steps are missing or their order is changed.

1. A language selection screen is displayed when you insert the CD-ROM into the drive. Click on the language you want. (At the time of this writing, the client is available only in English.)

2. Select Windows NT Client from the Clients and Z.E.N. Works Starter Pack screen, and then click Install Novell Client.

3. You have a choice of doing a typical install or a custom install. The typical install sets up the workstation for logging on to the server using either IPX or IP under NDS mode and installs the Novell Distributed Print Services (NDPS), Novell Workstation Manager, and Z.E.N. Works Application Launcher NT Service components. If you select the Typical Installation option, click Install to continue, and skip to step 7.

   The custom install first lets you choose the optional client components to install (see Figure 13.3) and then asks you to select your protocol preference.

13

FIGURE 13.3

Optional components for the Novell NT Client.

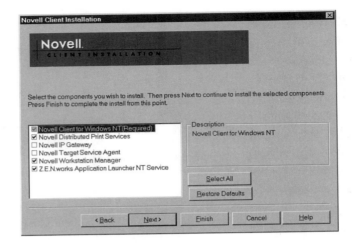

These are the available optional NT client components:

- **Novell Distributed Print Services**   This component (NDPS) enables two-way communication in real time between your workstation and your network printer.

- **Novell IP Gateway**   This component allows the workstation to access the Internet or an intranet from IPX or private IP networks through Novell IP/IPX Gateway servers.

- **Novell Target Service Agent**   This component allows a server-based backup software to back up files from the Windows NT workstation.

- **Novell Workstation Manager**   This component allows you to configure and manage NT Workstation's user accounts and desktop information (such as policy) from within NDS.

- **Z.E.N. Works Application Launcher NT Service**   This component allows Novell Application Launcher (NAL) to install applications on secure NT workstations.

4. Check the components you want and then click Continue.

It's worth mentioning here that, without going into painstaking details, you can have a single logon to both Windows NT and NDS using Workstation Manager. Workstation Manager also allows your Windows NT users to roam freely to use any Windows NT workstations without having to set up users in each Windows NT workstation's local SAM or create an NT domain.

5. The next dialog box asks you to select your protocol preference (see Figure 13.4). If you're connecting to a NetWare 4 or lower server, you can use the Custom option and select IPX as the protocol preference. If you're connecting to a NetWare 5 server, depending on whether it's configured for IP, IPX, or IP with IPX compatibility, select the protocol accordingly, and then click Next to continue.

FIGURE 13.4

The Protocol Preference Selection dialog box.

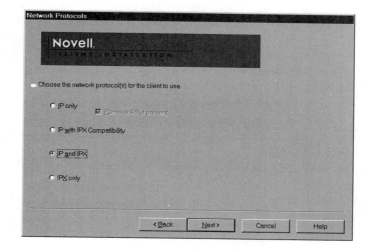

 Click the Help button in this dialog box for a detailed explanation of the protocol choices.

6. You now need to specify whether you're logging into an NDS or a bindery server (see Figure 13.5). Select the appropriate option and then click Next.

7. If you have elected to install Workstation Manager, you're prompted to specify the name of the NDS tree (see Figure 13.6). Enter the tree name and then click Next.

8. Click Finish to bring up the Software License Agreement screen and then click Yes to continue.

9. If you have the Microsoft Client Service for NetWare installed, you're prompted to confirm that it will be removed.

10. (You won't see this step if you have CSNW installed.) At the end of the install process, a dialog box appears with a recommendation that you set some properties for the client. You can click Yes to perform this operation now (see next section on how to customize the client) or click No to continue.

11. Click Reboot on the resulting dialog box to make the new settings take effect.

13

FIGURE 13.5

Use this dialog box to specify if you're going to use NDS or bindery mode to log on the NetWare server.

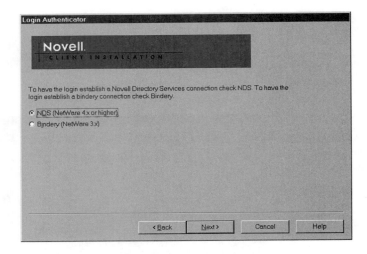

FIGURE 13.6

Use this dialog box to specify the NDS tree to be used by Workstation Manager.

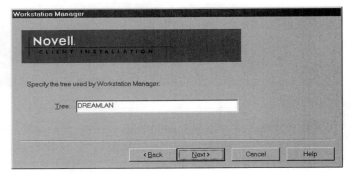

The following changes are made by the install program to your system:

- The login screen is changed as Novell's setup program replaced Microsoft's GINA (Graphical Identification and Authentication) by Novell's own NWGINA.

- Addition of a new submenu to Start|Programs called NetWare (Common). It contains four commands: NetWare Login, NetWare Scheduler, NetWare Send Message, and ReadMe.

- A system tray icon (called NetWare Services) that links to a number of NetWare commands is added to the task bar (see Figure 13.7). The icon is a red letter *N*. Additional icons might be added if you have optional components, such as Z.E.N. Works, installed.

FIGURE 13.7

Right-click the red N system tray icon to bring up the NetWare Services context menu for Windows NT.

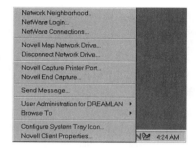

Configuring the Novell Client

Unlike the Microsoft Client Service for NetWare, the Novell NetWare Client has many configuration tabs (see Figure 13.8). You can access these tabs as follows:

- When the Novell NetWare Client installation program asks whether you want to customize the client (as described in step 10 in the previous section), click Yes.

- In the Network properties sheet, highlight the Novell Client for Windows NT component under the Services tab and then click Properties.

- From the system tray, click the red N icon and then choose Novell Client Properties from the context menu.

FIGURE 13.8

The Client configuration tab of the Novell NetWare Client for Windows NT.

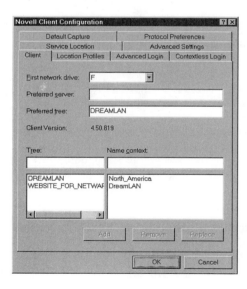

13

These configuration tabs are discussed in the following sections. You'll find most of the options and settings available here to be identical or similar to those found in the Novell Client for Windows 95/98 discussed back in Hour 8. Therefore, instead of repeating the same information, only the tabs with settings unique to Windows NT are discussed here.

Advanced Login Properties

In addition to the check boxes for the Windows NT policy location and settings that are displayed on the NetWare logon dialog box, you can also specify the name of the BMP file to be used in the welcome screen and the caption to be displayed on the upper-right area of the NetWare logon dialog box (see Figure 13.9).

FIGURE 13.9

The BMP filename specified under the Welcome screen section must be located in the \winnt4 *directory on the computer. Leave the name blank if you don't want to use any bitmap.*

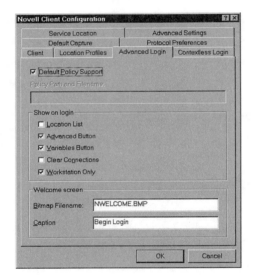

Client Properties

In the Client Properties tab (refer to Figure 13.8), other than specifying the first network drive letter, preferred server, and preferred tree, you can specify tree and name context "pairs" for each NDS tree the workstation is accessing. When you select a tree name in the logon dialog box, the name context text box is automatically filled in (and, yes, you can change that during login). This tab also displays the version of the client software.

Protocol Preferences Properties

The options offered in this tab are the same as those found in the Protocol Preferences tab available in Novell Client for Windows 95/98. However, the "look" is different (see Figure 13.10); the NT version is a lot less cluttered.

FIGURE 13.10

A different look than the same tab found in the Windows 95/98 Client.

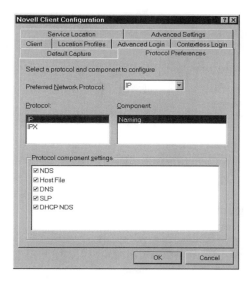

Accessing NetWare Resources

Both the Microsoft Client Service for NetWare and the Novell NetWare Client for Windows NT are tightly integrated with Windows NT's My Computer, Windows Explorer, and Network Neighborhood operations. However, the Novell NetWare Client adds some nice extensions that aren't available in Microsoft's version. Therefore, the discussions in the following sections are specific to Novell NetWare Client (unless otherwise noted). The overall concepts, however, apply to both clients.

Furthermore, most operations in My Computer, Explorer, and Network Neighborhood are similar between Windows 98 and Windows NT. Because you read about them in Hour 8, only the NT-specific features are highlighted here.

Connecting to a NetWare Server

If you're using Microsoft's NetWare client, the standard Windows NT logon screen (see Figure 13.11) is used to log on to both Windows NT and NetWare. If the user name is not found on the specified server (in bindery mode) or in the specified name context (in NDS mode), a NetWare Authentication Failure dialog box is displayed.

13

FIGURE 13.11

*The logon screen when
Microsoft Client
Service for NetWare is
used.*

If you're using the Novell NetWare Client for Windows NT instead of the standard
Windows NT logon screen, a login screen that looks similar to the one shown in Figure
13.12 is displayed. The change is caused by replacing the Microsoft GINA with a Novell
GINA. If you haven't configured your NDS tree and name context preferences or want to
change them, click Advanced in the login screen to make the selections.

FIGURE 13.12

*The login screen for
the Novell NetWare
Client for Windows NT.*

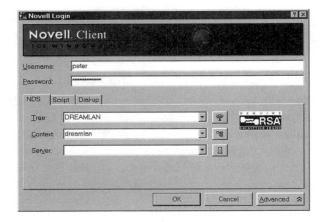

You might notice that some options are not available. You need to enable
them through the Advanced Login properties settings of the Novell
NetWare Client for Windows NT.

If you try to access a NetWare server or NDS tree without being authenticated to it first,
you're given a logon prompt (similar to the one shown back in Figure 13.12) when you
try to access its resources.

Working with NetWare Volumes

Using Windows NT, you can easily browse for NetWare resources, such as volumes, by using My Computer, Explorer, or Network Neighborhood. Novell added four integrated features to these tools for use when you're working with NetWare volumes (see Figure 13.13):

- Novell Map Network Drive
- Salvage Files
- Purge Files
- NetWare Copy

FIGURE 13.13

The Novell NetWare Client for Windows NT added four options to the context menu.

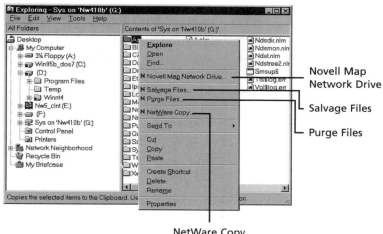

You learned about the Novell Map Network Drive feature in Hour 8, so it isn't discussed again here. The other three features are worth mentioning, though.

With the Salvage Files option, you can undelete erased files from a NetWare volume (see Figure 13.14). This is *much* easier than having to start up NWAdmin, locate the appropriate Volume object in the NDS tree, and then perform the salvage operation, or pop into a DOS prompt, fire up `filer.exe`, locate the volume, and then perform the salvage operation. The same is true for the Purge Files option (see Figure 13.15).

13

FIGURE 13.14

The Novell NetWare Client for Windows NT's Salvage Network Files dialog box.

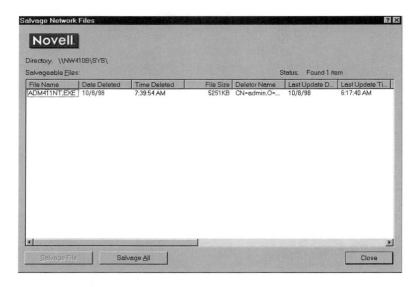

FIGURE 13.15

The Novell NetWare Client for Windows NT's Purge Network Files dialog box.

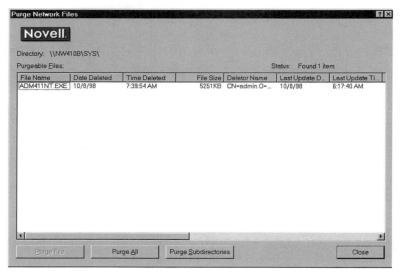

The NetWare Copy option is what you would call "the best thing since sliced bread"! Not only does it allows you to copy files from one NetWare volume to another and keep their NetWare-specific attributes, but it also lets you *assign* NetWare file attributes (such as Read Only and Immediate Compress; see Figure 13.16) to the new copy of the files. Without this feature, you need to use several steps, and it takes much longer to do the same task.

FIGURE 13.16

The Novell NetWare Client for Windows NT's File Copy Utility dialog box.

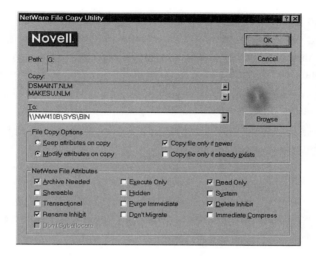

Using Windows Point and Print

The Windows Point and Print feature (discussed in Hour 8 when using Windows 98) can be configured for Windows NT 4.0, but *not* for Windows NT 3.51. The procedure for configuring Point and Print for Windows NT is the same as that for Windows 98. However, remember that for NT 4.0, you must still be a member of Power User or Administrators to install a printer driver to the local machine; otherwise, you get an error.

Summary

During this past Hour, you have learned the basics of installing and configuring the Microsoft and Novell NT Clients for NetWare networks.

In the next Hour, you find out how to install and configure a Windows NT server.

Workshop

Q&A

Q How do I install the Novell NT client from a command prompt?

A Assuming you have the NetWare 5 Client CD-ROM, run the `setupnw.exe` program from the `\products\winnt\i386` directory.

13

Q Can the Novell NT client be installed unattended?

A Yes, you can install the Novell NT client unattended by using SETUPNW /ACU or SETUPNW /U and an unattend.txt file. And you can use an unattend.txt file to install the Novell client at the same time you're installing Windows NT.

Q I can't get one of my bitmaps to display as the NT Welcome screen. How come?

A Check to see if your bitmap is 24-bit. If so, open it in PaintBrush or a similar program and resave it as either a 16-color or a 256-color bitmap, and it should work for you. It seems NT can't display 24-bit bitmaps in the Welcome screen.

Quiz

1. True or False: Microsoft Client Service for NetWare supports NDS.

2. To use Windows Point and Print to set up printers, a user must be a member of which group(s)?

3. True or False: CSNW can coexist with Novell NetWare Client for Windows NT.

4. How do you salvage a deleted file from the sys:bin directory using Network Neighborhood?

HOUR 14

Installing a Windows NT Server

This chapter might seem a bit long-winded because I don't have a lot of nice screen shots to keep you entertained. (It's awfully hard to run a screen capture program when the NT installation process has control of the system!) But hang in there—the information is important!

Also, if you can, take the time to play with the installation. Get it going, delete it all, and then do it again. Take notes. At the time, it seems like you couldn't possibly need to write down this or that because it's so obvious. But two years from now, at 3 o'clock in the morning, some notes might not seem like such a bad idea!

The following topics are covered in this Hour:

- Hardware requirements
- File system and partitioning
- Installing NT Server
- Other installation methods
- Removing NT

Hardware Requirements

Before you buy the hardware for a server, it's important that you clarify what the server will be used for. For example, if you're going to have a server acting as a RAS server with only one modem attached for occasional dial-up access, then maybe one of your existing servers is more than adequate. You could perhaps upgrade another server that's just barely able to handle the load, and then use the trickle-down theory and turn that machine into your RAS server.

On the other hand, if the machine is going to be handling file, print, and applications for 500 users, then maybe something more top-of-the-line is called for.

Administrators have strong opinions on server hardware. Many swear by clone machines and are quick to point out the money they have saved. Others buy only top-of-the-line systems from one of the major vendors, such as Compaq or HP, for reasons of support, quality, and reputation.

> Don't be penny-wise and pound-foolish. The server is a resource that every-one on the network accesses, so uptime is critical. Also, the cost of the server is spread out across the number of users. So a setup with 100 users accessing an $8,000 server runs only $80 a head, and that $8,000 server is still going to be in use two years or more from now, which reduces the cost even more. Purchasing a $2,000 clone certainly costs less at the time, but is cost the most important variable in the equation?

The minimum hardware requirements for NT are as follows (keep in mind that the minimum is not necessarily the ideal):

- CPU: 486/33 or higher
- Memory: 16MB for NT Server, 12MB for NT Workstation
- Disk space: 125MB for NT Server, 110MB for NT Workstation
- Display: VGA or higher
- CD-ROM
- High-density floppy disk drive

Did I mention that "minimum hardware requirements" might not be realistic? Just making sure!

The HCL

Make sure the hardware you buy is on Microsoft's Hardware Compatibility List (HCL). Microsoft supports only hardware on the HCL, so keep that in mind if you ever need to give Bill a call!

The HCL is a list of computers and computer hardware that have been tested with Windows NT for compatibility. Microsoft Product Support Services uses the HCL to determine if a computer is supported for use with Windows NT.

You can find the latest Microsoft Windows NT HCL by pointing your browser to `http://www.microsoft.com/hwtest/hcl/default.htm`; the start page for this site is shown in Figure 14.1.

FIGURE 14.1

You can search the HCL at Microsoft's Web site to see if your hardware is compatible.

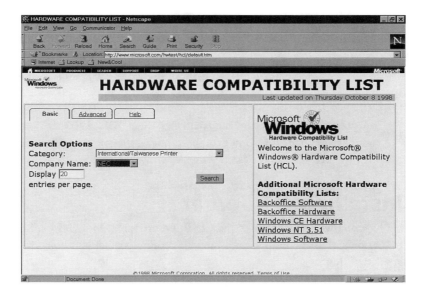

If the URL is no longer active, simply search the Microsoft site for "hardware compatibility list."

File System and Partitioning

14

Early on in the installation process, you have to make a decision about which partition to install NT on. The setup process also gives you the option of creating and deleting partitions, so starting with a blank disk is fine.

> Remember that NT calls the partition it boots from the *system partition* and that the partition loads the operating system files from the *boot partition*. This isn't exactly obvious; you would think it's the other way around.

You need to create at least one partition, and it can be both the system and boot partition. After it's created, it must be formatted, and here's another choice you have to make:

- Formatted as FAT, the partition can easily be accessed simply by booting from DOS.
- Formatted as NTFS, the partition requires NT to be accessed.

> Keep in mind that if file-level security is required, a partition must be NTFS. Also, it's possible to go from FAT to NTFS, but not the other way around. You can go from NTFS to FAT, but doing so requires that you restore your files from tape because reformatting wipes the partition clean!

A good recommendation is a small (less than 2GB) FAT partition for both the NT boot and system partition. Don't forget to mirror this partition, as covered in Hour 17, "Advanced NT Server Management."

Installing NT Server

Along with your copy of the CD-ROM are three floppy disks. Simply boot from the first one and then continue on. Make the required decisions about creating and formatting a partition.

When you're past the hardware portion of the installation, it's time for more decisions. Setup asks for the following:

- A licensing mode (per server or per seat)
- A computer name (maximum of 15 characters)
- Server type (PDC, BDC, or standalone)
- An administrator password

You are also asked if you want to create an emergency repair disk and which optional components you want to install.

Licensing Modes

You have two choices about licensing modes:

- **Per server**   Per server licensing assigns the designated number of CALs (client access licenses) to this server.
- **Per seat**   With per seat licensing, a client access license applies to a specific computer, or seat, not to a server connection. After the CAL is assigned to the computer, it can then access any Windows NT server on the network. When you use per seat mode, an unlimited number of computers with client access licenses can connect to each server.

If you have installed in per server mode and specified 50 concurrent connections, then only 50 users can connect. The 51st user who tries to connect will get an error message; another user who's already connected will have to disconnect before this user can get in.

> Each resource you access on the server doesn't take up a separate license count. In other words, if you are accessing \\server\mydata and are also printing to \\server\the_printer, then this counts as only one connection to the server.

If you have any doubt during the installation as to which mode to choose from, choose per server. The Licensing folder in Control Panel gives you a one-time opportunity to convert from per server to per seat, but you can't go from per seat to per server.

Sample Setup

As an example, take a look at MagicNet Network Consulting, which has one NT server. MagicNet has set up this server using the per server licensing mode for 25 connections. That is, it has 25 CALs assigned to this server, which means 25 users can connect. Because MagicNet only has 25 workstations, this is fine.

Because of the overwhelming success of the main product it sells, the NDS Toolkit, MagicNet is going to add another server. At this point, it can do one of the following:

- Install the new server using per server, and then buy another 25 CALs and asssign them to the new server. Ouch! Why should MagicNet have to buy another 25 client access licenses, when it has only 25 workstations? That's a total of 50 CALs for only 25 machines!
- Convert the first server from per server to per seat. Install the second server using per seat licensing mode. Now the CALs are not assigned to the servers, but to the seats, or workstations, or clients. And these client access licenses allow them to access either server!

14

Looks like the second choice might be the way to go.

Server Types

As mentioned, three server type options are available during the installation:

- **PDC (Primary Domain Controller)** If this is the first server in the domain, choose PDC. The PDC holds the master copy of the accounts database for the domain. Every domain requires a PDC, and as they say in my favorite movie, *Highlander*, "There can be only one."

- **BDC (Backup Domain Controller)** A BDC receives a copy of the accounts database from the PDC. You want at least one backup domain controller, and more than one is not unusual at all. A BDC can authenticate users to the network, so if the primary domain controller fails, you still have access. A BDC can also be promoted to PDC if the need arises, as you will see in Hour 15, "Managing NT Servers."

- **Standalone (Member Server)** A standalone, or member server, is a fully functioning server and a member of the domain, but it does not authenticate users to the network. Member servers are often used as dedicated application servers. You can't take a member server and change its role to either PDC or BDC without reinstalling NT.

> If you're installing into an existing domain, then the PDC already exists. You choose either BDC or member server.

Installing Networking

When you're past the question and answer period, the Setup Wizard launches the networking portion of the setup. You are asked the following:

- **Do you want to install networking?** If you choose to install networking, you are asked whether this computer is on a LAN, whether it dials into a network, or both.

- **Do you want to install the Web server?** Choosing Yes installs Microsoft Internet Information Server, also known as IIS.

- **What NIC is in the server?** Let Setup find your NIC automatically. If the NIC doesn't get detected correctly, specify it manually, and be ready with the newest drivers from the manufacturer's Web site.

- **What protocols do you want to use?** The choices are TCP/IP, IPX/SPX compatible, and NetBEUI.

- **Are you joining a domain? And if so, which one?** If you are joining a domain, there's an option to create a computer account in the domain during this portion of Setup.

Alternative Installation Methods

Whenever you add a service, such as RAS, to your server, you're prompted for the installation CD-ROM. This can be a pain, causing you to scramble to find it among the jumble and confusion of your office. A helpful workaround is to copy the \i386 directory from the CD-ROM to the server's hard disk. Then, when prompted, you can simply point to c:\i386. Or, if there are already servers on the network, you can copy the files to the server and run the installation from there or share the installation CD-ROM at an existing server.

After the files are copied to the hard disk, you can run winnt.exe to create the three floppy disks that come with the CD-ROM. You are then asked to insert the first disk into the machine and reboot.

If you're running the installation from a server (this is called a *server-based installation*), then winnt.exe creates the floppy disks, copies the files down to a temporary directory, and then has you put in the first disk and reboot.

Many switches can be used with winnt.exe, including the following:

- **/OX** Don't do anything but create the three boot disks needed for the installation. You can use this option if you have lost your original three floppy disks and want to re-create them. You can then use them to proceed with a CD-ROM–based installation.

- **/X** Don't create the three boot disks. Use this option if you already have the three boot disks and want to speed things up.

- **/B** Floppies! We don't need no stinking floppies! This switch is for installing with no floppy disks, so winnt.exe runs without creating them. Instead, it creates some magical temporary files in lieu of having to put in the floppy disks.

For even more switches and options, type **WINNT** **/?** at the command prompt.

14

Removing NT

Why does the installation hour have a section on removing NT? Well, you might want to completely remove NT so you can use the machine for another purpose, or to get a completely fresh installation, or maybe just for the fun of it!

To remove NT from a FAT partition:

1. Boot from a DOS disk that you have copied sys.com onto.

2. At the A: command prompt, enter the command **sys c:**.

3. Take out the floppy and reboot. The machine restarts with the version of DOS that you had on the floppy disk. The only thing to do now is clean up the files from the NT installation.

To remove NT from an NTFS partition, the simplest method is to run the Setup program from the three floppy disks mentioned earlier. When it's time to select or create a partition, highlight the NTFS partition and press D to delete it. Press the F3 key to exit the Setup program.

NT is now gone, but the files are still there. To get the space back, the following are fair game for deletion:

- The boot.ini file in C:\
- C:\winnt and all subdirectories
- Any paging files, such as c:\pagefile.sys
- NT*.* in C:\
- The bootsec.dos file in C:\, if it exists
- Any Windows NT folders under the Program Files folder

Some of these files might be flagged as system, hidden, and read only, so take that into account. Either change the settings in Explorer to show them, or type the ATTRIB command at the command prompt.

Summary

Before buying server hardware, it's important to analyze what services the server is expected to provide and how many users will be accessing the new machine. Regardless of whether you fall into the clone camp or the name-brand camp, make sure the hardware is on Microsoft's Hardware Compatibility List. The minimum hardware requirements as published are just that: minimums. Buy the best and fastest equipment you can afford for your servers.

The partition that NT boots from is called the system partition, and the partition that the operating system files are loaded from is called the boot partition. During the installation, you have to create at least one partition and make the decision as to what file system to use when formatting it. FAT partitions are easily accessible in the event of problems, and an NTFS partition requires NT to be seen. Only NTFS volumes provide file-level security.

There are three types of NT servers: PDC, BDC, and standalone. Every domain must have at least one PDC. One or more BDCs is also recommended. There are two licensing modes: per server and per seat. You can go from per server to per seat once and only once, but you cannot go from per seat to per server. Client access licenses are assigned to the servers in per server mode, and you can think of them being assigned to the workstations in per seat mode.

You can start your installation from a shared directory on the server, known as a server-based installation, by connecting to the share and using the `winnt.exe` program. This also works directly from the C: prompt.

How you remove NT depends on which file system is used at the time of the installation. If the file system is FAT, merely type **sys C:**, and then reboot. The only thing left to do then is clean up the NT files to get the disk space back. If the file system was NTFS, then the simplest method is to run the Setup program from the three floppy disks; when it's time to deal with the partitions, use the Setup program to delete the NTFS partition.

Workshop

Q&A

Q Are the minimum hardware requirements as published realistic?

A Absolutely not! They are extreme minimums. You can't expect to get performance from a 486/33 with 16MB of memory.

Q Are there any advantages to using FAT for my system and boot partition as opposed to NTFS?

A The FAT partition is easily accessible in the event of problems. You can boot DOS and change to the C: drive to move, copy, or delete files. NTFS requires NT.

Q Is there more than one primary domain controller in a domain?

A No. The PDC is like the theme of the movie *Highlander*; there can be only one!

14

Q Why would I install NT Server as a member server?

A A member server does not participate in authenticating users to the network. This allows it to devote resources to more dedicated tasks, such as being an application server.

Q What are the two licensing modes?

A Per server and per seat.

Q I have a machine that does not have a CD-ROM. How do I install NT?

A You need to perform a server-based installation. Copy the \i386 directory to the server and share it. Then connect to the share and run winnt.exe.

Quiz

1. You have lost the three floppy disks that came with your NT CD-ROM. You can

   A. Quit your job as a network administrator and take up bartending.

   B. Open a call with Microsoft.

   C. Run WINNT /OX.

   D. Call Novell.

2. True or False: To remove an NT installation on an NTFS partition, you can boot to DOS and type sys C:.

3. True or False: To have file-level security, the files in question must be on a FAT partition.

4. Because the primary domain controller has the master copy of the accounts database, you can make sure this information is protected by installing a _____.

5. A server has been set up for per seat licensing, but management has made a decision to change it to per server licensing. True or False: You can easily do this.

6. What is the HCL?

7. True or False: It's not possible to install NT without using the three floppy disks.

8. True or False: After a partition has been formatted using FAT, it can be changed to NTFS.

Hour **15**

Managing NT Servers

If you have just had the administrator position dumped on you, which isn't an uncommon situation, then this Hour is for you. It covers the following:

- Installing Service Pack 3, the latest service pack you need to keep your server current
- User Manager, for creating and managing user and group accounts
- Server Manager, which is much like User Manager except that it's used to manage computer accounts
- Event Viewer, for viewing the system logs

Then you take a quick tour through the Network dialog box and the Services control panel and wrap it all up by learning how to promote a backup domain controller to a primary domain controller.

Service Packs

When you consider the millions of lines of code in NT Server and the myriad types of hardware it must be able to support, it's no wonder the software needs to be patched after its release. A *service pack* is a collection of bug fixes and other fixes made to the system. (Of course, these new fixes then induce a fresh crop of bugs, and the cycle continues.) The current NT service pack is Service Pack 3.

> Service packs are cumulative, so putting on SP3 (Service Pack 3) is all you need to do; you do not have to install SP1, then SP2, and so on.

Installing SP3

The readme file that comes with SP3 is 26 pages long, 10 pages of which list the bugs that have been fixed. Before you do anything, print out the readme file that comes with the service pack and READ it! Then do the following:

1. Insert the service pack CD-ROM.
2. From either the Web interface or a command prompt, run `spsetup` from the `\i386` directory. You should see the screen shown in Figure 15.1. Click Next to continue.

FIGURE 15.1

Beginning the installa-tion of SP3.

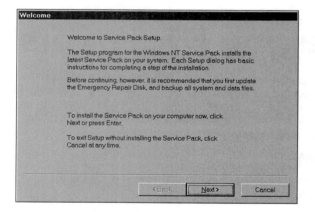

3. From the next screen, shown in Figure 15.2, you can either install the service pack or uninstall a previously installed service pack. Select the Install the Service Pack radio button.
4. The Setup program gives you the option of creating an uninstall directory, as shown in Figure 15.3. It's important that you create an uninstall directory so you can use the uninstall feature shown in Figure 15.2. Click Next to continue.

This directory, $NTServicePackUninstall$, will be created under the \winnt directory and require about 60MB of free space.

15

FIGURE 15.2

At this screen, you have the option to uninstall a previously installed service pack.

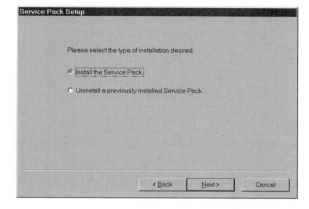

FIGURE 15.3

Creating an uninstall directory is very important!

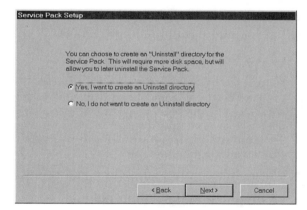

5. The dialog box shown in Figure 15.4 shows the progress of creating the uninstall directory.

FIGURE 15.4

Before the service pack files are copied, your original files are copied to \winnt\$NTService PackUninstall$.

6. After the uninstall directory is created, you see the screen shown in Figure 15.5. Here, you decide whether to replace the 128-bit security file from your original installation of NT with the 40-bit security file found in Service Pack 3. A discussion of these security issues is beyond the scope of this book, so look over the readme files that come with SP3 if you need help deciding which file to use.

FIGURE 15.5

*The install prompts
you about the*
`schannel.dll` *file.*

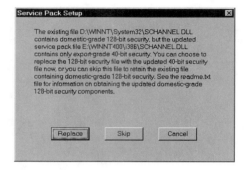

7. After the service pack is installed, it's time to reboot (see Figure 15.6). Notice the cautionary message above the OK button: If you change or add any components to your system, you need to reapply the service pack!

Suppose you have the server up and running with SP3 and decide to add the DHCP server service. During its installation, you're prompted for the original NT CD-ROM to copy the appropriate DHCP files, but the files being copied are the original, unpatched ones. This is why you must reapply the service pack after adding any new service that prompts you for the original NT files—to update the added files.

FIGURE 15.6

*The system has been
patched, and it's time
to reboot.*

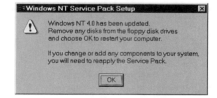

Uninstalling SP3

If you chose to create an uninstall directory (refer back to Figure 15.3), which I hope you did, then getting back to where you were before SP3 was installed is fairly simple:

1. Insert the service pack CD-ROM.

2. From either the Web interface or a command prompt, run `spsetup` from the `\i386` directory.

3. Click Next.

4. From the screen shown back in Figure 15.2, select the Uninstall a Previously Installed Service Pack radio button.

After the system restarts, the files from the uninstall directory are placed on your system, and the Registry settings are returned to where they were before SP3 was applied.

User Manager

You can use User Manager to do the following:

- Define the account policy
- Create user and group accounts
- Manage user and group accounts
- Establish trust relationships (see Hour 17, "Advanced NT Server Management")

Defining the Account Policy

Your account policy should take several security-related issues into consideration. For example, you should do the following:

- Require a minimum password length. The longer the password, the harder it is to break.

- Do not allow blank passwords. That is, you should require users to enter characters as passwords instead of leaving the password field blank.

- Set an expiration for passwords so that they must be changed on a regular basis.

- When it's time for a user to change her password, you should not allow her to just reuse her existing one. Also, you should keep a history so that users can't simply alternate between two passwords. A history tracks the recent passwords used and does not allow them to be reused.

- Lock out accounts after failed login attempts, and allow only the administrator to unlock any locked accounts.

- Forcibly disconnect users if they exceed their allowed access times.

You can control these by the settings in the Account Policy dialog box, shown in Figure 15.7. Start User Manager, and after clicking the Policies button, select Account.

FIGURE 15.7

The Account Policy dialog box.

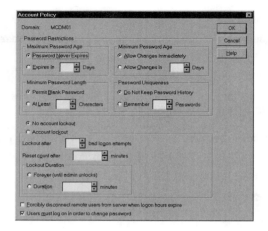

The Account Policy dialog box has two main sections:

- Password Restrictions
- Account Lockout

The Password Restriction section offers the following settings:

- **Maximum Password Age**   Set the password to never expire, or have it expire every x days.
- **Minimum Password Length**   Either permit blank passwords, or specify how long the password must be.
- **Minimum Password Age**   Set how long a password must be used before it can be changed. This setting must be less than the Maximum Password age. Do not allow immediate changes if you're going to implement a password history or password uniqueness.
- **Password Uniqueness**   If you keep a password history, then users can't reuse an old password until the number you enter here has been reached.

The Account Lockout section offers the following settings:

- **No Account Lockout**   If this is checked, the account will not be locked no matter how many failed login attempts have been made.
- **Account Locked**   If this is set, the following parameters apply:
  - **Lockout After**   Set the number of bad logon attempts here. After that number is exceeded, the account will be locked.

15

- **Reset Count After**   This counts the number of bad logon attempts within a set time interval. If no bad logon attempts occur within the specified time interval, then the bad logon attempt count is returned to zero.
- **Lockout Duration**   Either set this to forever, which means that you as the administrator must unlock the account, or enter a number of minutes. For example, if you set this to 30 minutes, then you do not have to unlock the account; after 30 minutes, the system will unlock the account itself.

In addition to the Password Restrictions and Account Lockout sections, the following check boxes appear in the Account Policy dialog box:

- **Forcibly Disconnect Remote Users from Server When Logon Hours Expire** If this check box is selected, users are disconnected when the allowable logon hours expire. If this check box is left blank, then users aren't disconnected, but can't establish any new connections.
- **Users Must Log On in Order to Change Password**   If this check box is selected, then users cannot change their own expired passwords; you as the administrator must change them (if a user's password has expired, there's no way she can change it because she has to log on to do so). If this check box is left blank, then users can change their own expired passwords.

Creating Accounts

To create a new user account, use the dialog box shown in Figure 15.8. Start User Manager, and choose User|New User. Simply fill in the blanks and then click Add.

FIGURE 15.8

*Creating a new user
with User Manager.*

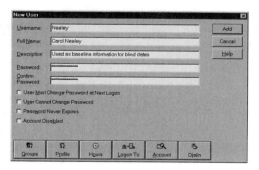

Fill in the following text fields in the New User dialog box:

- **Username (required)**   Enter a unique name for the account.
- **Full Name (optional)**   This field is used for documentation purposes. For example, suppose you create a user account called BSG7. When you create it, you proba-

bly know who BSG7 is, but a year later, you might not remember. If the Full Name field is filled in, your problems are solved!

- **Description (optional)** This field is also used for documentation. The description can be any text describing the user account or the user.

- **Password** This field can be up to 14 characters long and is the password for the account.

- **Confirm Password** If you enter a password, use this field to confirm that it was entered correctly.

In addition to the text fields mentioned, the New User screen has the following check boxes:

- **User Must Change Password at Next Logon** This check box is checked by default. This option is a good security check that can be used to make sure only the user knows her password. After all, if you, as the administrator, set the password, then you know what the password is. If this box is left checked, then the user must change her password the first time the account is used; only she will know what she changed the password to.

- **User Cannot Change Password** If more than one person uses the account, then you don't want one of them to be able to change the password.

- **Password Never Expires** There could be some accounts whose passwords should never expire—an account used by a service such as Exchange is an example.

- **Account Disabled** Checking this box disables the account until this check box is cleared. This can be useful if you create a new account for an employee who won't arrive at your company for several weeks. You might also disable an account when someone leaves the company and his or her replacement will be using the same account. After the replacement is hired, you could then enable the account.

Notice the series of buttons at the bottom of the New User screen shown in Figure 15.8:

- **Groups** Click this button to view the group memberships of the user and to add and remove group memberships (see Figure 15.9). The groups to which the user belongs are shown in the Members Of list. To add a group, highlight it in the Not Member Of list, and then click Add. To remove the user from a group, highlight it in Members Of and click Remove.

FIGURE 15.9

At this screen, you manage the group membership of the user.

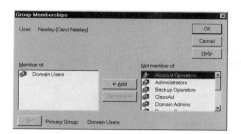

15

- **Profile**   Click this button to add a user profile path, a login script name, or a home directory (all of these are optional). A *profile* is a collection of settings that define things such as network connections or the appearance of the desktop. Profiles can also be used to restrict what users can access. For example, you might not mind them changing the appearance of the desktop, but you might not want them arbitrarily changing the type of monitor they have, thus causing you problems. The User Environment Profile dialog box, shown in Figure 15.10, offers the following settings:

  - **User Profile Path**   Enter the network path to the user's profile. The path follows the form *server name\profile folder name\user name*.

  - **Login Script Name**   If a login script is assigned, it runs each time the user logs in. This could be a batch, or .CMD file, or an executable.

  - **Home Directory**   If assigned, this setting becomes the default directory for File Open and Save As dialog boxes, for the command prompt, and for any applications that can't specify default working directories.

  - **Connect To**   You can specify a shared network directory as the user's home directory. Then when the user logs in, he's connected to this share using the drive letter you specify.

FIGURE 15.10

Controlling the user environment profile.

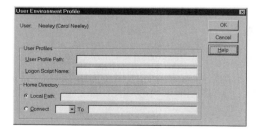

- **Hours**   Click the Hours button to set the times when the user is allowed to log on to the network. In the screen shown in 15.11, use the mouse to highlight times, and then choose Allow or Disallow.

Unless the Forcibly Disconnect Remote Users from Server When Logon Hours Expire option in the Account Policy dialog box is checked, the user isn't disconnected if she is on when her time is up, but she can't make any new connections.

FIGURE 15.11

The times when Carol Neeley is allowed to log on.

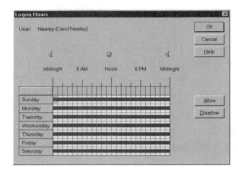

- **Logon To**   You might want to allow the user to log on only to specific workstations; you can specify this by clicking the Logon To button. In the screen shown in Figure 15.12, you specify whether the user can log on to all workstations, or you can enter up to eight computers the user can use.

FIGURE 15.12

You can control which machines users can log on to.

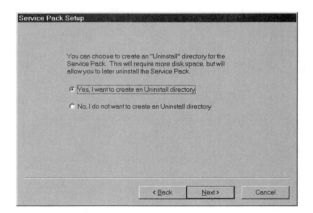

- **Account**   Click this button to set if and when an account expires (see Figure 15.13). If you specify that the account should expire and enter a date, the system automatically disables the account on that date. You can also set the account type in the Account Information dialog box. A global account is for regular users in your domain. When you create a local account, however, the account is created *only* in the accounts database of that single computer. With a local account, a user can log on to and access resources only on that computer.

FIGURE 15.13

The Account Information dialog box.

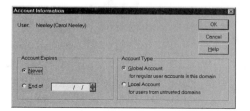

- **Dialin** Click this button to grant dial-in permissions to the user (see Figure 15.14). If the Grant Dialin Permission to User check box is selected, then the following three options apply:
    - **No Call Back** When the user connects, the RAS server will not hang up and call the user back. This call would be on the user's dime.
    - **Set By Caller** After connecting, the user can specify a phone number for the RAS server to call. The RAS server will then dial the user; this time, the charge will be on the RAS server's dime.
    - **Preset To** This forces the user to access the RAS server from a specific phone number. The RAS server will call back only to that number, so the user has to be there. This prevents individuals from accessing the RAS server from any old number.

FIGURE 15.14

The Dialin button is used to grant dial-in permission.

Managing Accounts

The User Rights Policy dialog box, shown in Figure 15.15, is used to manage the rights of user and group accounts. To use this dialog box, select the right in question from the drop-down list, click the Add button, and then select the user you want to grant rights to.

FIGURE 15.15

The User Rights Policy dialog box.

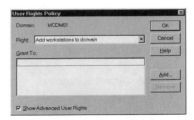

Unlike a *permission*, which applies to a user's ability to perform actions on a specific object, a *right* authorizes a user to perform certain actions to the system as a whole. If the user does not have appropriate rights to perform an action, then the system blocks any attempts to perform that action. For example, the Back Up Files and Directories right would allow a user to back up files and directories of the computer and would supersede any file and directory permissions.

It might be simpler to assign the user's accounts to one of the built-in groups that already have the needed rights than to administer the user rights policy.

Server Manager

Just as User Manager for Domains is used to manage user and group accounts, Server Manager, shown in Figure 15.16, is used to manage computer accounts in the domain. Before a computer running NT can participate in domain security, it must have a computer account added to the domain.

FIGURE 15.16

Server Manager is used to manage computer accounts in the domain.

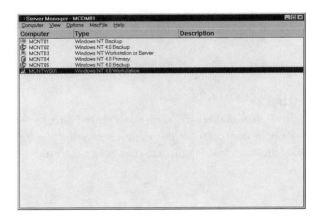

If you double-click one of the servers in the list, you can access the Properties tab for
that server (see Figure 15.17).

FIGURE 15.17

*The Properties tab for
a selected server.*

From here, you have many of the same buttons you saw in User Manager:

- **Users**   Click this button to see the number of connected users and the computer
  name of the machine they are using (see Figure 15.18). In this dialog box, you can
  also disconnect selected users or disconnect everyone.

- **Shares**   Click this button to view which users are connected to a particular share
  and the path to that share (see Figure 15.19). You can disconnect individual users
  using the share or disconnect everyone using the share.

FIGURE 15.18

*Viewing the user ses-
sions on a selected
server.*

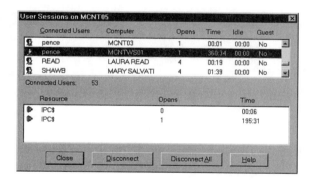

FIGURE 15.19

*Viewing the shared
resources of a selected
server.*

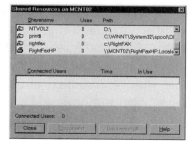

Clicking the Shares button gives you some data and control, but you might also consider choosing Computer | Shared Directories from the menu bar. The screen you see after clicking the Shares button is network oriented, but the screen you see after choosing Computer | Shared Directories is more administrative and informational. From it, you can see the properties of a share, stop sharing, and even create a new share.

- **In Use**   Click this button to view the open resources on a selected server (see Figure 15.20). You can see what's open and who opened the resource. From here, you can also close individual resources or close them all.

FIGURE 15.20

Viewing the open resources on a server.

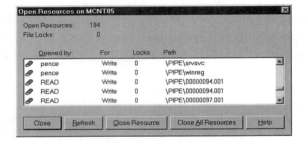

Event Viewer

Your system uses *log files* to track all types of events. There are three types of log files:

- **System**   The system log file tracks events triggered by the operation system itself, such as warnings or errors. What's written here is dictated by the operating system.
- **Application**   The application log file tracks events generated by applications, such as MSExchange. As with system logs, the events written to the application log file are a function of the program itself. Many applications have a default level of event logging, with the option to turn on more advanced logging for troubleshooting purposes.
- **Security**   The success or failure of the events you have chosen to audit is recorded in the security log.

You should make checking log files part of your normal routine and always check them when troubleshooting. To view the log files, you use Event Viewer. Do the following:

1. Choose Start | Programs | Administrative Tools | Event Viewer to see the screen shown in Figure 15.21.
2. To drill down for more detail, double-click the entry for which you want more information. You see a screen like the one shown in Figure 15.22.

FIGURE 15.21

The Event Viewer is used to see the log files. This is the summary view.

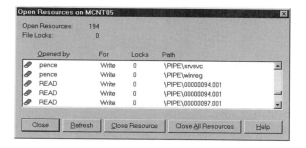

FIGURE 15.22

To view the event detail, double-click the entry in the summary view.

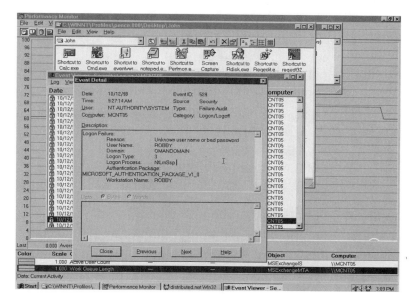

You will be coming back to Event Viewer auditing in Hour 17 because you use Event Viewer to look at the security log, where the results of your auditing are written. Hour 17 covers clearing, archiving, and overwriting the log files, in addition to controlling the size you allow these files to reach. In this section, however, you take a look at two features of Event Viewer not covered in Hour 17:

- The Find function
- The Filter control

The Find Function

Because log files can grow quite large and have many, many entries, the ability to search is very important. If you choose Find from Event Viewer's View menu, you see the options to search the log file and jump to the events you're interested in (see Figure 15.23). For example, if you're interested only in events where the source is Print, you can set up your search to find only those events and to quickly jump from entry to entry without having to scroll through the entire log.

FIGURE 15.23

The Find function lets you jump quickly to the events you're interested in.

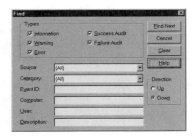

These are the available options to fine-tune your search:

- **Information**   Events are logged by successful operations of major server services, such as a program loading successfully.
- **Warning**   Select this option to view warnings or events that have been logged that might cause future problems.
- **Error**   These are significant problems, such as a service failing to load.
- **Success Audit**   Select this option to view successful security access attempts.
- **Failure Audit**   Select this option to view security access attempts that failed.
- **Source**   The software that logged the event, which can be either an application or a part of the system (such as a device driver).
- **Category**   A classification of the event; classifications are defined by the source. For example, one of the categories for the source Security Account Manager is Logon/Logoff.
- **Event ID**   Each event has a number to identify it.
- **Computer**   The name of the computer where the logged event occurred. This field is not case sensitive.
- **User**   Here you specify text that matches what's in the User Name field. It's not case sensitive.
- **Description**   Each event has an event detail associated with it. This field lets you search for text in the event detail.

The Filter View

The Find function is helpful, but just lets you jump from entry to entry without having to scroll. A Filter view, on the other hand, applies a filter so that you see only those events that match your criteria. For example, in Figure 15.24, you're about to filter the display to show only events where the source is NTBackup. The other options are the same as those in the Find function—the only exceptions are the View From and View Through options, where you can set the time frame you're interested in seeing. After you click OK, the filter is applied, as shown in Figure 15.25.

FIGURE 15.24

You can filter the display to show only what you're after.

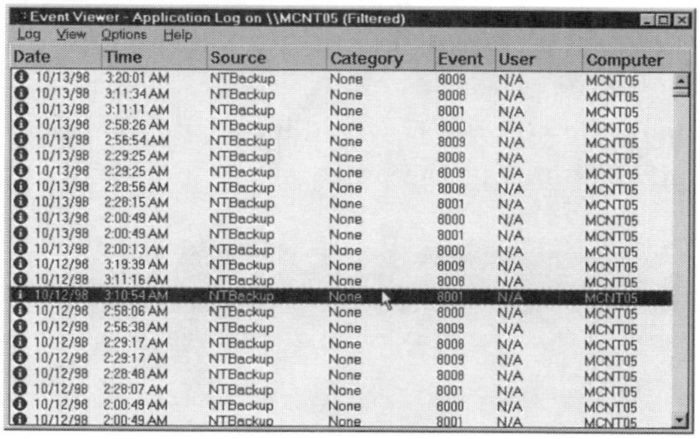

FIGURE 15.25

After the filter is applied, you see in the summary view only those events that meet your criteria.

The Network Dialog Box

There are two ways to open the Network dialog box:

- Double-click the Network icon in the Control Panel.
- Right-click the Network Neighborhood icon on your desktop and choose Properties.

When you open the Network dialog box, you see several tabs:

- **Identification**   In this tab, you set the computer name and specify whether the machine is a member of a domain or workgroup (see Figure 15.26). The computer name shown is the NetBIOS name of the workstation. This is normally the same as the host name you can set under TCP/IP properties, but it doesn't have to be. The Change button is used to change the name of the workstation and to join or leave a domain.

FIGURE 15.26

The Identification tab.

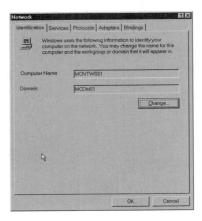

- **Services**   In this tab, shown in Figure 15.27, you can add and remove services. You can also see the properties of the services, if they can be configured. If you have more than one networking client installed, you also see the Network Access Order button; click it to set the order in which resources are accessed.

FIGURE 15.27

The Services tab.

- **Protocols**   Use this tab to add and remove protocols. You can also look at the properties of the protocols here (see Figure 15.28).

FIGURE 15.28

The Protocols tab.

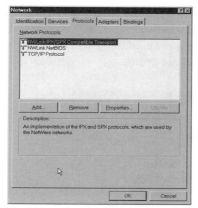

- **Adapters**   In this tab, shown in Figure 15.29, you add or remove network interface cards (NICs). You can also see the properties of the NIC, such as the resources
  it's using, like the interrupt or I/O port. Click the Update button to update the driver for the adapter.

FIGURE 15.29

The Adapters tab.

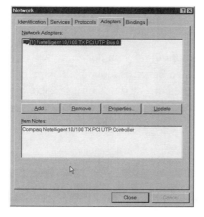

When troubleshooting network-related issues, check the vendor's Web site
for updated drivers. Applying them should be one of the first things you try.

- **Bindings**   A *binding* is a connection, or association, between the NIC, the driver
  for the card, and the services installed. In the Bindings tab, you can enable or disable bindings or change the order in which the machine accesses resources. For

example, notice in Figure 15.30 that the workstation service talks to the WINS client using TCP/IP and that this grouping is then bound to the actual NIC. The Enable and Disable buttons are used, obviously, to enable or disable the binding; the Move Up and Move Down buttons are used to change the access order.

FIGURE 15.30

The Bindings tab.

Services

In the Network dialog box, you saw a Services tab, which is used to add and remove services. To manage the services running on your server, however, you need to go to Control Panel and double-click the Services icon. This opens the screen shown in Figure 15.31. From here, you can see the current status of a service, along with how it's configured to start up. You can also start and stop services. For example, when troubleshooting, you might want to stop a service such as RAS to see whether a fresh start alleviates the problem.

FIGURE 15.31

The Services dialog box.

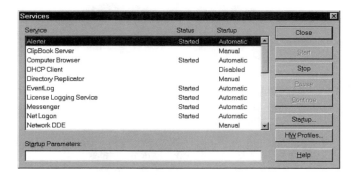

Sometimes, you might want to manually start a service as opposed to running it all the time. If you highlight a service in the Services dialog box and then click the Startup button, you see the Service dialog box shown in Figure 15.32. From here, you can disable the service or set it to start automatically. If you select Automatic, then every time the server comes online, the service starts. If you select Manual, then you have to go to the Services dialog box shown in Figure 15.31, highlight the service, and choose Start. You can also control how the service interacts with the system. For example, you might want a particular service to use a particular account; you would force this by selecting This Account and then filling in the information.

FIGURE 15.32

You can control the startup parameters of a service.

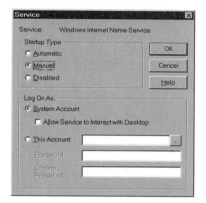

Promoting a BDC to PDC

As you know, there's only one primary domain controller (PDC) in a domain. The PDC holds the master copy of the domain's database, which is automatically replicated to the backup domain controllers (BDCs) every five minutes. Because a BDC can authenticate users to the network, users can log in even if the PDC is offline. But because changes to the database can be made only at the PDC, you can't perform any account administration if the PDC is offline—you can't create or delete accounts or even change a password.

If the PDC is going to be down for only a short period, you don't need to do anything. But if the PDC is going to be offline for a long time, you should promote one of the BDCs to assume the role of the PDC. There are two scenarios to consider:

- Planned changes to PDC status
- Unplanned changes to PDC status

Planned Changes to PDC Status

You might want to promote a more powerful machine to act as the PDC, or you might be planning to remove the machine that's currently the PDC. In either case, because both machines are online, the process is simple:

1. Run Server Manager.

2. Highlight the BDC you want to promote to PDC.

3. From the Computer menu, shown in Figure 15.33, choose Promote to Primary Domain Controller.

FIGURE 15.33

Server Manager is used to promote a BDC to a PDC.

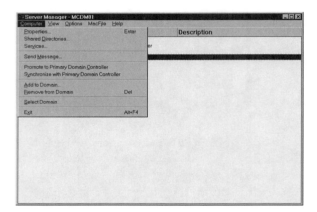

4. You get a message indicating that this process might take a few minutes and that all connections to both the BDC and PDC will be closed. You are asked to confirm this action. Click Yes.

5. The BDC is automatically promoted to PDC, and the former PDC is demoted to BDC status.

Unplanned Changes to PDC Status

A worst-case scenario is if the PDC goes offline unexpectedly, perhaps caused by a hardware failure or an abend. In this case, you can still promote one of the BDCs to become the PDC, but the process isn't as automatic. Because both machines are not online, you have to do a bit more.

You start by promoting one of the BDCs to become a PDC, just as in the previous section. However, when the original PDC is brought back online, it's going to realize that there's a new PDC. This makes the original PDC unhappy—specifically, the NetLogon service will not start on the original PDC. At this point, you need to demote the original PDC to become a BDC:

1. Highlight the original PDC in Server Manager.

2. The Promote to Primary Domain Controller choice on the Computer menu changes to Demote to Backup Domain Controller. Select this option.

3. The original PDC is demoted to BDC status.

> After the system has stabilized, you can make the machines resume their former roles by following the steps outlined in the preceding section.

Summary

A *service pack* is a collection of updated files used to fix bugs in the operating system. The latest service pack for NT is, at the time of this publication, Service Pack 3, more commonly referred to as SP3. It's important to reapply SP3 whenever you make changes to your system that ask for the files from the original CD-ROM. Also, make sure you create the uninstall directory, which you can use to back out in the event of problems.

User Manager is used to create, delete, and manage user and group accounts. The account policy, which determines how passwords and lockout options are handled, is also set here. You learned how to create a user account and explored the buttons used to manage the account.

Server Manager is similar to User Manager, except Server Manager is used to create, delete, and manage computer accounts in the domain. As in User Manager, you can get to the properties of a server; once again, you have buttons you can click to drill down for more information. Server Manager is also used to promote a BDC to act as the PDC.

The Event Viewer is used to view the log files; there are three types: application, security, and system. Make viewing the log files part of your normal routine and always look at them when troubleshooting. You took a look at the Find function, which lets you search for specific entries, and at the Filter control, which filters the display for you.

The Network dialog box is used to manage the networking side of your system. Here you add and remove adapters and add, remove, and configure protocols and bindings. The Services tab in the Network dialog box is used to add and remove services, which is not the same as the Services icon in Control Panel.

The Services icon in Control Panel is used to view the current status of a service and to stop and start services. You can also control the startup options for a service, as well as the account used by the service.

Workshop

Q&A

Q **What is the difference between the Services dialog box that I get to by clicking the Services icon in Control Panel and the Services tab in the Network dialog box?**

A The Services tab in the Network dialog box is used to add and remove services. The Services dialog box that you get to through the Services icon in Control Panel is used to manage the services—to see their current status and to stop and start them.

Q **Why do I need to reinstall SP3 when I add a service?**

A When you add a service, the install wizard asks for the location of the original NT files, generally from the CD-ROM or the \i386 directory if you have copied the CD-ROM to the server's hard disk. These files are older than the ones in the service pack, so you need to reapply it.

Q **How can I keep users from using the same password over and over?**

A You need to set Password Uniqueness for some number. This keeps a history of the user's last x number of passwords; users can't reuse a password until it has fallen off the history list.

Q **Is it possible to have Event Viewer show only certain types of events? Right now, I have to scroll through a lot of entries I have no interest in.**

A You can set a filter, which shows you only entries that meet the criteria you set.

Quiz

1. If you promote a BDC to PDC while both machines are online, the process is automatic. If you promote a BDC to PDC while the PDC is offline, then what happens?

2. You have logon hours set for a user to end at 4:00 p.m exactly. The user is logged on, and 4:00 p.m. comes and goes without disconnecting the user, which is not what you wanted. How do you fix this?

3. A password can be up to _____ characters in length.

4. True or False: Server Manager can be used to create a share on a server.

5. You currently have WINS installed on a server, but you don't want it running. It currently starts up whenever the server starts. How do you fix this?

HOUR 16

Backing Up and Restoring Data on Windows NT

After reading Hour 9, "Backing Up and Restoring Data on Windows 98," you already know the basics about backing up and restoring files on Windows 98. The same concepts apply to Windows NT. However, you should be aware of a few extra points, covered in this Hour, when backing up and restoring Windows NT files and systems.

During this Hour, you learn about the following:

- Fault-tolerance features in Windows NT Server
- Using Microsoft Windows NT Backup
- Backing up and restoring Windows NT's Registry
- Automating Windows NT backups
- Do's and don'ts about Windows NT backup
- Third-party backup tools

Windows NT Server Fault Tolerance

Because you're going to read more about the fault-tolerance features available in Windows NT Server in the next Hour, here's just a quick capsule view of how these features can help you in terms of server backup and recovery.

The idea of using the hard drive as a backup medium has the advantage of speed. However, to fully back up your system, you basically need to more than double your disk capacity (so that you have a "multi-generation" backup), which can be quite expensive. Fortunately, many operating systems, including Windows NT Server, support disk mirroring and/or disk duplexing.

Disk Mirroring and Duplexing

With *disk mirroring*, you have one or more hard drives duplicating the data of the primary drive, and all these drives are connected to the same controller. When the operating system does a write-to-disk, data is written to both the primary and secondary drives. When a read operation takes place, the data is supplied from either the primary or the secondary drive because they contain exactly the same information. If the primary drive fails, the mirror (secondary) drive takes over transparently without any loss of data or downtime—you can limp along until the end of the day before taking the system down to effect repairs. However, in this configuration, the single point-of-failure is the hard drive controller.

Alternatively, you can put the secondary mirror drive(s) on a separate controller so that even if the controller of the primary drive fails, it does not affect the secondary drive(s). This is known as *duplexing*. Another advantage of duplexing is that because you now have two disk channels to the same data, disk I/O performance is increased, especially in terms of file reads.

RAID 5

A third way of using hard drives involves *redundancy* rather than backup, but the end result is the same: data loss is prevented. Instead of standard hard drive controllers, you can use RAID (*redundant array of inexpensive disks*) controllers. There are different levels of RAID, and RAID 1 is equivalent to disk mirroring. It is common for high-performance servers holding important data to use RAID 5, where three or more disks are used to form an array (a single logical disk). In the event of a single disk failure, RAID 5 can rebuild the data from the remaining disks (while running at a degraded performance).

Many operating systems, including Windows NT Server, support RAID through software. However, it's recommended that you use a hardware-based solution because it's typically faster.

Using Microsoft Windows NT Backup

16

Similar to Windows 98's Backup utility, Windows NT's Backup is a scaled-down licensed version of Backup Exec for NT from Seagate Software. Do keep in mind that NT Backup will not back up the following:

- Files that you do not have permission to read
- The Registry on remote computers
- Open files locked by user applications
- Files that are temporary in nature, such as PAGEFILE.SYS, WIN386.SWP, 386SPART.PAR, BACKUP.LOG, and RESTORE.LOG, which are neither backed up nor restored by Windows NT Backup

The list of skipped files is hard-coded into Windows NT Backup and can't be changed.

To start NT Backup, choose Start|Programs|Administrative Tools (Common)|Backup. At startup, NT Backup checks your system to see whether you have tape drives installed. If it didn't find any, NT Backup displays an error dialog box, shown in Figure 16.1. Although Windows 98 enables you to create a backup "archive file" when you don't have a tape drive installed, NT Backup doesn't offer you that option—you *must* have a tape drive to have NT Backup back up your Windows NT machine.

Because Windows NT is geared toward power users, NT Backup doesn't have any Backup or Restore wizards. Fortunately, however, the interface is quite easy to understand and use, so wizards aren't really necessary. The following two sections summarize the steps for performing backup and restore operations with NT Backup.

FIGURE 16.1

Microsoft NT Backup requires that you have a tape drive installed.

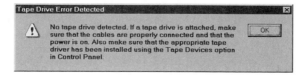

> Windows NT security doesn't permit you to back up files (including hidden files) and directories that you don't own or have no access to.

Backing Up Files

You can easily back up either all files on a drive or selected files to tape (each backup session creates a *set* on the tape). Use the following steps to back up the whole drive:

1. In the Drives window, check the box beside the drive you want to back up.
2. On the Operations pull-down menu, select Backup. (Or, if you have configured the toolbar to be displayed, click the Backup button.)

If, however, you want to back up only selected files, use the following procedure:

1. In the Drives window, double-click the drive where the files are located.
2. Check the box beside the filename you want to back up (see Figure 16.2).

FIGURE 16.2

Select the files you want to back up using this dialog box.

3. Repeat step 2 for each file you want to back up. You can combine steps 2 and 3 by first selecting all the files you want to back up and then choosing Select|Check from the menu.
4. On the Operations pull-down menu, select Backup. (Or, if you have configured the toolbar to be displayed, click the Backup button.)

After the Backup option is selected, the Backup Information dialog box is displayed (see Figure 16.3). In this dialog box, you can select or set the following options:

- Type of backup operation.
- If there is already a backup set on the tape, specify whether the new backup is appended to or replaces the current backup set.

- Whether the local Registry is to be backed up.
- Whether a verification should be done after the backup is finished.
- Whether hardware compression is to be used.
- Whether the backed-up data should be restricted to the file owner or administrator.
- Whether a log file should be created and, if so, how much information should be logged.
- A tape name.
- A description for the backup session.

16

FIGURE 16.3

Use the Backup Information dialog box to set the backup options.

After you have made your selections, click OK to start the backup. A Backup Status dialog box (see Figure 16.4) is displayed, showing you the names of the drive, directory, and files that are being backed up, as well as a status message.

When the backup is done, click OK to close the Backup Status dialog box.

FIGURE 16.4

The Backup Status dialog box.

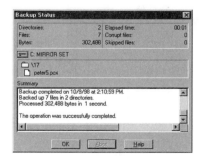

Restoring Files

To restore data from a tape, you need to first load the catalog of backup sets from the tape. Then you can restore either the entire tape set or selected files within that tape set. To restore a whole tape or one of the backup sets on the tape, use the following procedure:

1. Choose Operations|Catalog from the menu to load the tape catalog of backup sets from the tape.

2. In the left panel of the Tapes window, check the tape, backup set, or files you want to restore.

3. In the right-hand panel of the Tapes window, check the backup set you want.

4. Choose Operations|Restore from the menu (or you can click the Restore button on the toolbar).

To restore selected files from a tape set, use the same steps outlined here, but select the files from the catalog of the tape set instead of selecting the catalog for the tape itself.

After the Restore option is selected, the Restore Information dialog box is displayed (see Figure 16.5). In this dialog box, you can select or set the Restore options, such as whether the Registry and file permissions should be restored. Make your selections, and then click OK to continue.

FIGURE 16.5

The Restore Information dialog box

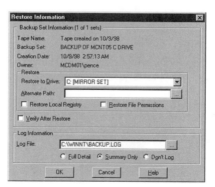

A Restore Status dialog box (see Figure 16.6) opens, showing you the names of the drive, directory, and files being restored, as well as a status message.

FIGURE 16.6

The Restore Status dialog box.

16

Automating Windows NT Backup

The Windows NT Backup utility doesn't include a built-in scheduler, but Windows NT 4.0 itself offers a system, called AT, that you can use to schedule backups. Follow these steps:

1. Start the Schedule service in the Services application of the Windows NT Control Panel.

2. Change the Schedule Startup settings to Automatic by double-clicking the entry and selecting Automatic in the Startup Type window. This loads the Schedule service each time Windows NT boots.

3. Using a text editor (say, WordPad), create a CMD file that contains the command options for the backup operation. For example, a FULLBAK.CMD file that contains

   ```
   ntbackup backup c: /t normal /d "November 12, 1998 Full Backup"
   ➥/b /l "c:\backup.log"
   ```

   would launch NT Backup to perform a backup of the C: drive, including the local Registry, overwriting any existing data on the tape. It then labels the backup November 12, 1998 Full Backup and creates a log file called c:\backup.log.

4. Launch the command prompt from the Start button's Programs menu item and add the CMD file to the automated schedule with this command line:

   ```
   at 23:00 /every:m,w,f fullbak.cmd
   ```

   This sample AT string executes the FULLBAK.CMD file every Monday, Wednesday, and Friday at 11:00 p.m.

For a list of AT task-addition command details, type AT /? at a DOS command prompt.

If you like an easier-to-use GUI-based scheduler (because AT isn't very user-friendly), there's the WINAT Command Scheduler included in the NT Resource Kit. You'll read more about WINAT in Hour 23, "Support Resources."

Backing Up and Restoring Windows NT Registry

The Windows NT Registry is a large data file that contains most of NT 4.0's system configuration information in a less-than-user-friendly format. Most people are afraid to look at the Registry, much less edit it. However, if you accidentally corrupt it, your system could become a *very* expensive paperweight. For your own sanity, be sure to back up your Registry regularly, especially before you install a new application, apply a systems update (such as a Service Pack), or make changes to the Registry. If the installation kills your system, you might be able to recover by using the older version of the Registry.

> Windows 98 also stores its system configuration information in its Registry. Therefore, the concepts discussed here for Windows NT apply equally to Windows 98 systems.

There are at least three ways in which you can back up the Registry; they are explained in the following sections.

> Microsoft supposedly built the rollback.exe utility to permit a clean return to a previous Registry version. **Don't use this utility under any circumstances!** It's been known to effectively destroy your Registry and force you to perform a clean install; rollback is meant for OEM resellers to preload NT on their machines when a "clean" Registry is wanted.

Using Windows NT Backup

The Registry of the machine running Windows NT Backup can be backed up in one of two ways:

- When you're setting up the backup session, select the Backup Local Registry check box in the Backup Information dialog box.
- If you're using the AT scheduler, include the /b parameter as one of the command-line parameters.

Keep in mind, however, that Windows NT Backup can't back up another machine's Registry over the network. A backup must be run from the machine to which the tape drive is physically attached; because tape drives can't be shared on a network, NT Backup can back up only a local Registry.

To restore the Registry previously backed up by Windows NT Backup, select the Restore Local Registry check box in the Restore Information dialog box after you've decided which backup set to restore the data from.

16

Using Registry Editor

Probably the best way to back up the Registry is by using the Registry editor. Unlike many of the other tools and utilities of Windows NT, the Registry editor does not appear in any window or menu listing; you have to launch it from the Start button's Run command or from a DOS command prompt.

Windows NT 4.0 includes two Registry editors: Regedit (located in the `\WINNT4` directory) and Regedt32 (found in the `\WINNT4\SYSTEM32` directory). Both utilities let you view and edit the Registry, but there are some subtle differences, as shown in Table 16.1.

TABLE 16.1 DIFFERENCES BETWEEN REGEDIT AND REGEDT32.

Regedit	Regedt32
Displays the Registry as a single, multilevel tree (see Figure 16.7)	Displays each key in a separate window (see Figure 16.8)[sr]
Can perform a search on the entire Registry	Can search only within a single key
Able to act only on the Registry	Able to save and restore single keys and sub-elements of the Registry
Does not support security	Supports security on Registry data
Can't customize display	Can change appearance of data display
Supports key values of the type `string`, `binary`, and `DWORD`	Supports key values of the type `string`, `binary`, `DWORD`, and `multistring`

FIGURE **16.7**

Regedit displays the Registry as a single large tree.

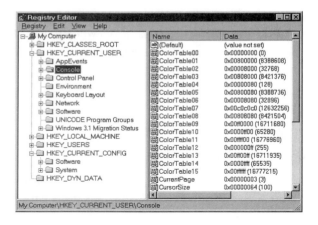

FIGURE **16.8**

Regedt32 displays each Registry key in its own window, much like Sysedit in Windows 3.x.

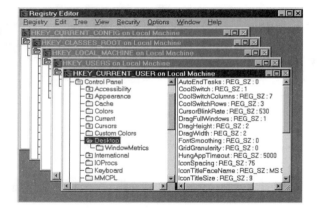

The following steps illustrate how to use Regedt32 to back up your Registry:

1. Highlight the name of one of the five main subtrees or any sub-element item (key) or tree (key branch).

2. Choose Registry|Save Key from the pull-down menu bar.

3. Type the name of the key or key branch you are storing, and then click Save.

4. Copy the stored files onto floppy disks or other storage media.

5. Repeat steps 1–4 for the other subtrees you want to back up.

To back up your Registry using Regedit, choose Registry|Export Registry File from its pull-down menu bar. Similarly, to restore a previously saved Registry, choose Registry|Import Registry File from the menu bar.

If you have a recent Registry backup, then restoring your system shouldn't be too difficult. If you can still boot and launch the Registry editor, you can restore parts of the Registry as follows:

1. Unload (remove) the key to be restored.
2. Restore the key from the saved files.
3. Reload the key.

However, Registry keys that are integral to current system operation can't be restored in this manner. If you've gotten yourself into a situation where the computer won't boot, you can try the Last Known Good Configuration option discussed in the next section.

Using Last Known Good Configuration

If you edit the Registry or perform some other operation that causes your NT 4.0 system to stop functioning properly, you might be able to restore the system by using the Last Known Good Configuration (LKGC). The LKGC is saved each time a successful user login occurs. To return to the LKGC, reboot your NT 4.0 system and watch the boot process: When the message `Press spacebar NOW to invoke Hardware Profile/Last Known Good menu` appears, press the spacebar, and then press the L key to use the LKGC configuration. Your system should return to its state at the last successful user login.

General Windows NT Backup Notes

In the following sections are some general tips and notes you should consider when doing backups of your Windows NT Server and Workstations.

Make Sure Registry Is Backed Up

Because the Windows NT Registry is such an important part of the operating system, make sure it's included in *all* your backup sessions. You should also use RDISK to create a set of Emergency Repair Disks (ERD) containing up-to-date system information, including a copy of the Registry, on a regular basis. This allows you to repair a failed disk boot sector and damaged Registry, should the need arise. Having good backup on tapes doesn't do you much good if your system can't boot.

Permissions and Rights Required

It is advisable to create a special account, such as SYSBACKUP, and make it a member of the Backup Operators group. This automatically gives SYSBACKUP the correct rights to back up and restore all files and directories. For greater protection of your system, a separate account for backups without restore rights could be useful because the backup process is not as drastic as restore, which can overwrite files and should be used with great care.

If the Scheduler service is running under the system account, it has only guest privileges on remote shares. If the service runs under the special SYSBACKUP account instead, you can assign full access to all remote shares to that account only. Otherwise, giving read access to the Backup Operators group would mean that any backup operator can access the remote shares, where sensitive files might be stored, through Explorer.

 Beware that members of the Backup Operators group automatically have user rights to log on locally, shut down the system, back up files and directories, and restore files and directories.

Backing Up Remote Windows NT Registry and Shares

NT Backup doesn't understand UNC naming, so it can't back up a remote drive named `\\Peter_Desktop\directory`. To back up network drives using NT Backup, the `net use` command is needed to connect to a remote share. After the network drive is established, the backup can then be performed on the drive letter used. When you're done, `net use /D` disconnects the drive.

Although NT Backup can back up the local Registry, it can't back up another machine's Registry over the network. Fortunately, there's a workaround: On each remote machine whose Registry you want to back up, use the AT or WINAT scheduler to export a copy of the Registry out to a file by using the `Regback.exe` utility available from the Windows NT Resource Kit. Include this file in the backup. To be restored, the file copy would have to be restored from the backup and then re-imported into the Registry.

Disconnecting Users

It is strongly advised that you close down as many files as you can during the backup time because most backup software can't back up open files. You can do this manually or use a batch file and the Scheduler to disconnect any attached users from shares, stop all Windows NT services that have databases open, such as WINS, DHCP, Exchange, SQL, and so on, just before the backup starts, and then resume the stopped services after the backup is done.

LFN Support

LFN stands for Long File Name. Windows 95/98 and Windows NT allow you to create a file whose name is longer than the traditional "8.3" DOS limit. It is imperative that the backup solution you use for your Windows 9x and Windows NT backup support LFN. If not, when you restore any files, you'll lose all the long filenames. This can get your computer in serious trouble because it can't find the names it needs, which could require you to uninstall every program you have and reinstall them. What's worse, you could corrupt the Registry with no way to restore it.

NTFS Support

For backup software to back up a drive, it must be able to "see" it first, and that depends on the file system used to format the disk and the file system supported by the backup software. Windows 98 can use 16-bit FAT (FAT16) or 32-bit FAT (FAT32); Windows NT supports FAT16 and NTFS. Therefore, a DOS-based backup software can't see an NTFS drive, so it can't back up any data on it. Consequently, you must make sure the backup software you use supports the type of file systems used on your Windows NT machine.

FAT is the generic term for the data structure used by operating systems to keep track of disk sectors.

Third-Party Backup Tools for Windows NT

Unless you're just backing up a single Windows NT machine (Server or Workstation), NT Backup isn't an ideal backup solution. There are many third-party commercial and shareware products available for Windows NT. The following are just a few:

- **Backup Exec for Windows NT from Seagate Software**   Its integrated wizards step you through routine operations and a GUI that simplifies management tasks. The product offers virus detection and cleaning and Agent Accelerator technology to maximize performance and provide data security. Visit http://www.nsmg. seagatesoftware.com/bewinnt/ for more information.

- **ARCserve*IT* from Computer Associates**   ARCserve*IT* is a multiplatform backup solution that supports both the Windows NT and UNIX platforms. With the help of Backup Agents, ARCserve*IT* can back up databases (such as Oracle) while the database or messaging server is active and in use. In addition, each database or messaging server is backed up separately. In multiple database and messaging servers, one database can be restored without interruption of the others on the same server. Visit http://www.cai.com/arcserveit/ for more information.

- **HP OpenView OmniBack II for Windows NT**   It offers seamless integration and allows protection of MS BackOffice data and use of existing MS BackOffice-based management processes. OmniBack II's online backup for MS SQL Server,

MS SMS (System Management Server), and SAP R/3 business data guarantees high application availability. Visit `http://www.hp.com/openview/products/obntpb.html` for more information.

- **NovaNet 7 for Windows NT**   This product has powerful features like flexible administration, true background operation, concurrent devices within jobs, and more. NovaNet can run multiple jobs with multiple devices on both NT and NetWare platforms, making NovaNet the only backup software that adapts to your network configuration. NovaNet even reads ARCserve 4.x and 6.x tapes. NovaNet's optional modules, such as NovaNet Open File Manager, can make copies of open files (such as Microsoft Mail and Oracle databases) for purposes other than backup, such as copying a live database to another machine for training or testing purposes. Visit `http://novanet.novastor.com/datasheets/nnet7_ds.html` for more information.

Summary

During this past Hour, you've learned about some of the fault-tolerance features available in Windows NT Server and how to use Windows NT Backup and AT to automate your backups. You also learned about Windows NT Registry and Registry editors, as well as how to back up and restore the Registry. Last, you discovered some of the issues you need to consider when backing up Windows NT systems.

In the next Hour, you get to learn about some advanced Windows NT concepts, such as domain trusts.

Workshop

Q&A

Q I hear that it's possible to "make" NT Backup back up open files by changing a key in the Registry. Which key is that?

A It's true that you can make a change in the Registry that allows open files to be backed up, but the restored version might be corrupted. Therefore, it's strongly recommended that you get a third-party backup software that can back up and restore open files without messing around with the Registry.

Q **My backups keep skipping these two directories on the D: drive. I even select-ed the whole drive for backup, but that didn't help. What's wrong?**

A Remember, Windows NT does not let you back up files that you don't own or have no rights to. Check that you have the proper access permission to those two direc-tories.

Q **Where can I find the list of command-line options for Windows NT Backup?**

A The complete command-line instructions are listed in the Windows NT Backup help documentation under the topic "Using Batch Files to Do Backups."

16

Quiz

1. What two Windows NT utilities can you use to automate backups?

2. How do you automate backing up the Windows NT Registry with NT Backup?

3. What does FAT stand for?

4. Which Registry editor displays each key in a separate window?

5. What does LKGC stand for and what can it do for you?

HOUR 17

Advanced NT Server Management

This Hour you take a look at the following:

- **Trust relationships** They let you connect your isolated domains so that you can share resources and have a single login.
- **Auditing** Auditing lets you track events such as failed or successful logins so that you can keep a closer eye on the network.
- **WINS** WINS, or Windows Internet Name Service, is used to resolve NetBIOS names to IP addresses. When using a name to connect to a resource, it always comes down to name resolution in the end.
- **Disk management** This topic should be near to the hearts of all administrators because the disks are where the data is!

Trust Relationships

A trust relationship is set up between domains to allow access. Without a trust relationship, a domain is an isolated island; the users in a domain can access only what's on the "island" with them. But when you have a trust relationship, you build a bridge between the islands. Now you can cross the bridge and get to the coconuts and palm trees on another island, and you can let the inhabitants of the other island use the coconuts from your island.

Trusts can be either one-way or two-way. An example of one-way trust is if I trust you enough to let you use my VCR, but you don't trust me enough to loan me a wrench. With two-way trust, you know you can use my VCR and have no qualms about letting me use your wrench.

> Use the smallest number of trust relationships you can get away with to keep administration simple.

> Trusts can be established only between domains, so if you have only a single domain to deal with, there will be no trusts.

Trust relationships are nontransitive. If, like me, you've already forgotten your high school algebra, *transitive* says that if A=B and B=C, then A=C. Trusts don't work this way. If A trusts B and B trusts C, that does not mean A trusts C. For that to happen, you have to set up another trust between A and C.

Groups and Trust Relationships

Now take a few minutes to go over groups. If people have similar job requirements, it makes sense to place them all in a group. For example, if everyone in the company requires email, then you can create an email group and give that group the appropriate rights to the email directories. Then, when you have a new employee, all you have to do is make him or her a member of this group and the rights are all taken care of.

There are two types of group accounts:

- Global
- Local

By global, I don't mean you can add anyone to the group from anywhere. Instead, it means the group can be used across trust relationships. That means a global group can be assigned rights in more than one domain. Global groups can contain user accounts from only a single domain (the domain in which the global group was created).

Global groups can contain only user accounts. They can't contain other groups.

By local, I mean that the group can be assigned rights and permissions to resources only in the domain in which the local group exists. Local groups can contain the following:

- User accounts from the domain
- Global groups from the domain
- Both user accounts and global groups from another domain, assuming the trust relationship exists

A local group can't contain other local groups.

No matter what type of domain model is used, you always want to create a local group and give it the rights to the resources in question, such as a printer. Then you create a global group and make the global group a member of the local group. This might seem strange, but it does ease management. The only thing you have to do is add and remove user accounts from the global group; you don't have to worry about the local groups or permissions. The global group is just a collection of user accounts. In and of itself, the global group has no rights. The rights come from the local group, which the global group is made a member of.

Establishing One-Way Trust

Trusts are set up through User Manager for Domains (choose Policies | Trust Relationships) with the following two steps:

1. The administrator of the trusted domain adds the trusting domain.
2. The administrator of the trusting domain adds the trusted domain.

Suppose you have two domains: Jamaica and Haiti. You want Haiti to trust Jamaica. That makes Haiti the trusting domain and Jamaica the trusted domain. So in the screen shown in Figure 17.1, the administrator of Jamaica (the trusted domain) enters the domain name Haiti (the trusting domain) and enters the password in both the Initial Password and Confirm Password fields. This password, a security feature, is made up by the initiating administrator of this process, who must give it to the administrator at the other end. Unless you know the password, the trust relationship cannot be established.

The name can be typed in either uppercase or lowercase, but it's always displayed in uppercase.

After the trust is established, the system automatically changes this password (more on this in a second).

You can't remove only one side of the trust relationship and then try to re-establish it using this password. To re-establish the trust, you need to completely remove both sides of the relationship and then re-create it from scratch.

FIGURE 17.1

Here, you add a domain to your domain's list of trusting domains.

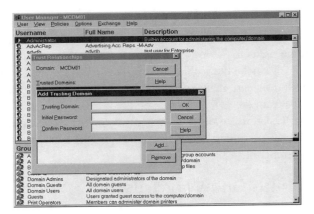

Second, the administrator of the trusting domain (Haiti) adds the trusted domain (Jamaica), as shown in Figure 17.2. That means Haiti is saying that it trusts Jamaica and that the accounts in the Jamaica domain are trusted to use the resources in the Haiti domain, but not vice versa.

The password is case sensitive and needs to be the same as the password that was entered in the Add Trusting Domain dialog box. Again, the system automatically changes this password.

FIGURE 17.2

A domain is added to the domain's list of trusted domains.

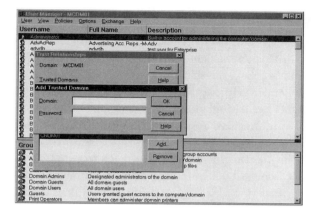

If the system is going to automatically change the password, then what's the point? This is another form of security, in which the administrator of the trusted domain can control creating trust relationships. As long as a PDC or BDC is running on each side, the trust remains. If all the domain controllers are down, then when one comes up, the trust is re-established. In the event of a problem, the trust has to be broken and re-established, at which time the administrators make up another password to use.

Establishing Two-Way Trust

A two-way trust is really just two one-way trusts. If you've managed to establish one-way trust, establishing two-way trust is easy. Just perform the exact same steps, but reverse the roles! This time, Jamaica is the trusting domain, and Haiti is the trusted domain. When the two-way trust is established, you can see the same domain name showing up under both trusted and trusting domains.

The PDC in a trusting domain establishes a secure channel with a domain controller in a trusted domain. Pass-through authentication then occurs over this secure channel.

When trusts are set up correctly, you just need to log in and supply a password one time to access the resources you have rights to.

Trust Management

There aren't many tools out there that enable you to monitor trust relationships, but there is the Domain Monitor that's included with the NT Resource Kit (see Figure 17.3). The Domain Monitor checks the status of servers in a specified domain and its secure channel status to the domain controller and to domain controllers in trusted domains. If any status shows errors, Domain Monitor displays status icons, plus the domain controller name and list of trusted domains. You can find the cause of errors by checking the error numbers reported in the Windows NT Messages database. When errors occur in connection with a problem domain, you can disconnect and reconnect to try to correct the error by clicking the Disconnect button in the Domain Controller Status dialog box.

> For more help on Domain Monitor, browse the online help (you must have the Resource Kit installed and Domain Monitor must be running).

FIGURE 17.3

The Domain Monitor, included with the Resource Kit, shows the status of the trust relationships.

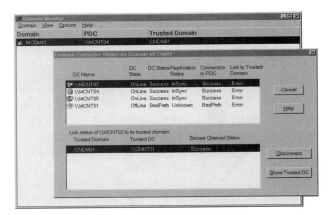

BROKEN TRUST

A broken trust could be caused by physical problems, such as the actual cabling. Renaming one of the domains can also break the trust. Also, the NetLogon service has to be running for trusts to be recognized, but if it was stopped, you would probably see other problems before worrying about your trusts!

If all else fails, delete the trust relationship and re-create it.

Also included in the Resource Kit is the NLTEST utility, which gives you information about an existing trust and even resets a trust's secure channel, as shown in Figure 17.4.

FIGURE 17.4

The NLTEST utility, included in the Resource Kit, gives you information about your trust.

```
Shortcut to Cmd.exe
Usage: nltest [/OPTIONS]

    /SERVER:<ServerName> - Specify <ServerName>

    /QUERY - Query <ServerName> netlogon service
    /REPL - Force replication on <ServerName> BDC
    /SYNC - Force SYNC on <ServerName> BDC
    /PDC_REPL - Force UAS change message from <ServerName> PDC

    /SC_QUERY:<DomainName> - Query secure channel for <Domain> on <ServerNam
    /SC_RESET:<DomainName> - Reset secure channel for <Domain> on <ServerNam
    /DCLIST:<DomainName> - Get list of DC's for <Domain>
    /DCNAME:<DomainName> - Get the PDC name for <DomainName>
    /DCTRUST:<DomainName> - Get name of DC is used for  trust of <DomainName
    /WHOWILL:<Domain>* <User> [<Iteration>] - See if <Domain> will log on <U

    /FINDUSER:<User> - See which trusted <Domain> will log on <User>
    /TRANSPORT_NOTIFY - Notify of netlogon of new transport

    /RID:<HexRid> - RID to encrypt Password with
    /USER:<UserName> - Query User info on <ServerName>

    /TIME:<Hex LSL> <Hex MSL> - Convert NT GMT time to ascii
    /LOGON_QUERY - Query number of cumulative logon attempts
    /TRUSTED_DOMAINS - Query names of domains trusted by workstation

    /BDC_QUERY:<DomainName> - Query replication status of BDCs for <DomainNa
    /SIM_SYNC:<DomainName> <MachineName> - Simulate full sync replication

    /LIST_DELTAS:<FileName> - display the content of given change log file
    /LIST_REDO:<FileName> - display the content of given redo log file
```

17

For example, suppose the wizard domain trusts the dragon domain. NLTEST can be used to show this trust relationship:

```
C:\>nltest /trusted_domains
Trusted domain list:
    dragon
The command completed successfully
To determine the Domain Controllers in the wizard domain:
C:\>nltest /dclist:wizard
List of DCs in Domain wizard
    \\WizardPDC (PDC)
    \\Wizard01
The command completed successfully
```

To determine the domain controllers in the dragon domain, try this:

```
C:\>nltest /dclist:dragon
List of DCs in Domain dragon
    \\DragonPDC (PDC)
The command completed successfully
```

For more information about the NLTEST utility, refer to the nltest.txt file in the c:\ntreskit directory (you must have the Resource Kit installed).

Another Resource Kit utility is Netdom, a command-line utility for managing domains that lets you perform tasks such as establishing trust relationships, resetting secure channels on BDCs, managing computer accounts, and more. For more information on Netdom, execute the netdom.hlp file in c:\ntreskit (you must have the Resource Kit installed).

Auditing

The first step in auditing is to formulate your audit policy, which means you need to determine in advance exactly what you want to keep track of. This decision isn't cast in stone, so you can go back later and make changes. For example, if you initially decide that you don't need to audit successful logons, and then later decide that you do want to audit these events, you can make the necessary change to your audit policy.

The events you choose to monitor are written to the security log; you use Event Viewer to look at the logs.

You want to set a policy that will deliver meaningful data. Acquiring too much information is as bad as not acquiring enough, so think in terms of keeping the information manageable. As the administrator, add viewing the logs to your list of routine maintenance tasks.

Keep in mind that auditing is extra overhead on the system, so don't track things just because you can. For example, instead of monitoring successful logins, it might be more useful for you to monitor failed ones. Also, because all the events are written to the security log, the log can fill up quickly. Imagine the entries in the log if you were tracking the successful use of a printer that everyone in a large department used!

Setting the Audit Policy

Only administrators can audit files, printers, and directories on a domain controller. On a standalone, or member, server, you need to be an administrator on that computer to audit it. The audit policy is set by choosing User Manager | Policies | Audit Policy, as shown in Figure 17.5.

FIGURE 17.5

The audit policy is set in User Manager.

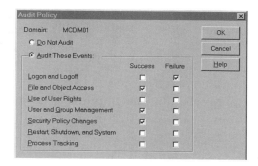

You must first decide whether you want to audit success, failure, or both on the following seven types of events:

- **Logon and Logoff**   This event tracks when users log on and off.
- **File and Object Access**   This event tracks when files and objects are accessed.

> For you to be able to audit files and directories, they must reside on an NTFS partition.

- **Use of User Rights**   This event tracks when a user has exercised a right.
- **User and Group Management**   This event tracks whether a user account was deleted, renamed, or disabled or had a password changed, or whether a group account was created, changed, or deleted.
- **Security Policy Changes**   This event tracks whether the audit policy was changed and whether changes were made to the trust relationships or to user rights.
- **Restart, Shutdown, and System**   This event tracks whether a computer was shut down or restarted, or whether an event has occurred that affects the system security.
- **Process Tracking**   This event tracks program activation and handles duplication, indirect object access, and process exit.

Auditing Files and Directories

Before you can audit files and directories, they must be on an NTFS partition. Setting file and object access in your audit policy is step one in auditing files and directories. After this tracking is enabled, you then have to go to the Properties dialog box of the file or directory and, in the Security tab, specify what to audit. You must set what to track on each file and directory because these settings are not global.

Again, keep system overhead in mind and remember that you as the administrator have to wade through the entries created. For example, if you decide to track the success of the Execute event, and you have this set on a program that everyone in the company runs daily, you're going to generate some events! You can always go back to the File Auditing screen and make changes later. On the other hand, be sure to audit such things as read access to sensitive data. You definitely want to see who is reading the payroll file, for example.

When you're at the File Auditing screen, shown in Figure 17.6, you can track the success, failure, or both of the following six events:

- **Read**   For a directory, the display of properties, such as permissions, owner, and filenames; on a file, the data or properties.

- **Write**   For a directory, the creation of files or directories or changes made to the properties; on a file, changes to the data itself or the properties.

- **Execute**   On files and directories, display of the properties; on files, the actual running of the program.

- **Delete**   On both files and directories, deletion.

- **Change Permissions**   On both files and directories, changes made to the permissions.

- **Take Ownership**   On both files and directories, changes to the owner of the file or directory.

FIGURE 17.6

You can track the success or failure of actions to the file.

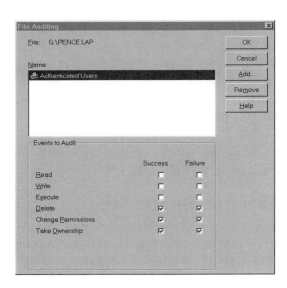

If, instead of looking at the file auditing properties, you had chosen to audit a directory instead, then the screen shown in Figure 17.6 would look slightly different. The same six events are available, but there are two additional check boxes:

- **Replace Auditing on Subdirectories**   Select this check box if you want the changes to apply to the files in the subdirectories, too.

- **Replace Auditing on Existing Files**   If you clear this check box, then the changes apply only to the directory itself.

When you're at the File or Directory Auditing screen, the first thing you need to do is to select the users and groups whose access you are going to track. Click the Add button, and the Add Users and Groups dialog box appears. From here, select which users and groups to track. Don't hesitate to click the Help button to get a description of each event. (In the real world, it's not necessary to memorize this type of thing; that's why the online help is there!)

Auditing Printers

Like files and directories, the first step in auditing printers is to enable tracking file and object access in your audit policy. You then have to set this on each printer you want to audit. Right-click the printer, choose Properties, select the Security tab, and then click the Audit button.

You can track the success or failure of the following five events, as shown in Figure 17.7:

- **Print**   The printer was used.

- **Full Control**   Events that affect the control of the printer, such as pausing, restarting, moving print jobs, or changes to sharing.

- **Delete**   Print jobs have been deleted.

- **Change Permissions**   Changes have been made to the printer permissions.

- **Take Ownership**   Changes have been made to the ownership of the printer.

> Again, keep in mind what information you really need. Failure to print generally brings a phone call from the user long before anyone takes a look at the logs in Event Viewer!

As with file auditing, the first thing you need to do with printer auditing is select the users or groups you're going to track. After they are added in the Add Users and Groups dialog box, then you set the tracking for success, failure, or both of the printer events.

FIGURE 17.7

You can track the success, failure, or both of five events for printers.

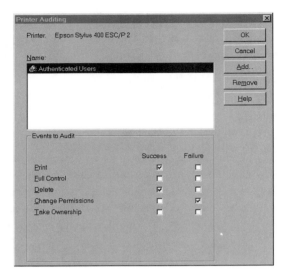

Viewing the Log Files

To view the log files, you use Event Viewer. Choose Start | Programs | Administrative Tools | Event Viewer. There are three types of log files:

- **System** The system log file tracks events triggered by the operation system itself, such as warnings or errors. What's written here is dictated by the operating system; you don't make these choices.

- **Application** The application log file tracks events generated by applications, such as MSExchange. As with system files, the events written are a function of the program itself.

> If you're running MSExchange, then you are already familiar with the types of entries written in application logs. Many applications have a default level of event logging, with the option to turn on more advanced logging for troubleshooting purposes.

- **Security** The security log file is what you're interested in when checking audited events. The success or failure of the events you have chosen to audit is recorded here.

To select which log file to view, choose it from the Log menu. As with many of the NT utilities, you don't have to go to each machine to view the event log. From the Log menu, choose Select Computer and select the machine you want to view. Notice in Figure 17.8 how many entries have been written—and how quickly. This is from only a few minutes, while the changes to auditing were made for this chapter. If you were tracking a heavily used resource, such as a departmental printer, there would be a veritable flood of entries!

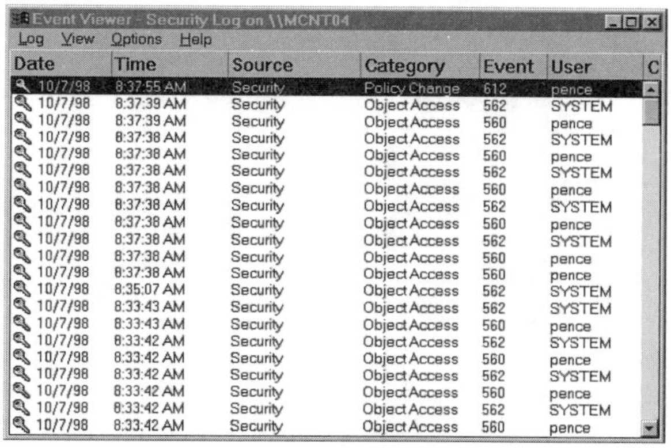

FIGURE 17.8

The results of your audit policy are recorded in the security log, which you look at by using Event Viewer.

In Figure 17.8, you see that a policy change has been made. To drill down and get more details, simply double-click the entry, as shown in Figure 17.9. Of particular importance is that not only do you see the new policy, but you also know who did it.

FIGURE 17.9

The details of the event you have chosen from the security log.

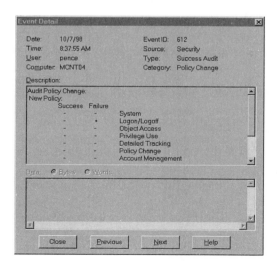

Managing the Log Files

You have control over the log files and how they are handled by the system. When you're in Event Viewer, choose Event Log Settings. The log file selections you choose in the Event Log Settings dialog box, shown in Figure 17.10, are a function of your environment. In an extremely high-security environment, you might want to archive all the logs and then begin creating new ones. In a low-security environment, simply overwriting events might be fine.

FIGURE 17.10

The Event Log Settings dialog box lets you control how the system handles the log files.

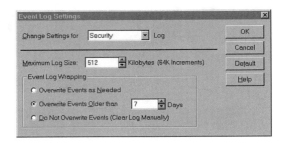

A drop-down list lets you select which log file you want to manage. You can set the maximum log file size here, too. The log file can be from a minimum of 64KB to a maximum of 4,194,240KB. You have three choices on how to handle the log files:

- **Overwrite Events as Needed**   This does exactly what it says. When the log is full, events begin to get overwritten.

- **Overwrite Events Older Than *X* Days**   Enter the number of days here, and those events are overwritten.

- **Do Not Overwrite Events (Clear Log Manually)**   If this is selected, you have to manually clear or archive the log files.

To clear a log file, choose Clear All Events from the Log menu. You get several warnings about this, but after you okay them, the log file is cleared. To archive a log file, choose Save As from the Log menu, and then enter a path and filename. To view an archived file, choose Open and then enter the path and filename.

Notice in Figure 17.11 that the security log has been cleared. As a result, an entry is generated. This is good for you in terms of security. If another administrator can clear the audit log, then a rogue administrator could clear the log to hide unethical activity, such as accessing a file that he shouldn't. Clearing the log covers his tracks, but can't hide the fact that he covered his tracks! You can drill down to get details on this event and see who is responsible, as shown in Figure 17.12.

FIGURE 17.11

The security log has been cleared, and an entry is made as a result.

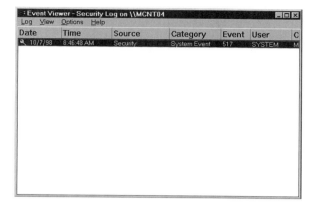

FIGURE 17.12

You can drill down and get details on exactly who cleared the audit log.

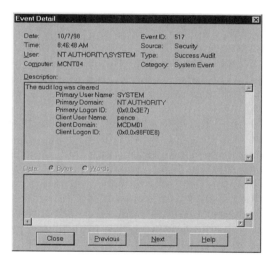

Windows Internet Name Service (WINS)

Hardware addresses and IP addresses are fine for computers, but human life forms prefer something a bit friendlier: names. WINS, short for Windows Internet Name Service, helps you out with this preference. The computer's NetBIOS name is what you see if you right-click Network Neighborhood and then select the Identification tab (see Figure 17.13).

When you use the NetBIOS name of a resource, it needs to be resolved in some fashion; this resolution is the purpose of WINS. The computers that have WINS enabled register themselves with the WINS server. Later on, to resolve a name, they ask the WINS server something along the lines of "Who is Peter?" (Peter being the NetBIOS name). The server answers "Peter is 206.101.138.49," and then you can proceed from there.

Earlier I mentioned broadcast packets. The problem with broadcast packets is that not only do they generate extra traffic on the wire, but they also slow things down. Each workstation has to pass the broadcast packet up the protocol stack far enough for a decision to be made, and then either ignore the broadcast or deal with it.

Without using WINS for name resolution, you have to rely on broadcasts. When you need to resolve the question of "Who is Peter?" you must broadcast to everyone instead of sending a directed packet to the WINS server. In addition, the workstation also broadcasts when it first comes up to make sure it's okay to use the name. And again, at shutdown time, you have another broadcast to free up the name. All this broadcast traffic can be eliminated by using WINS.

Although you can use a static file called lmhosts instead of WINS to map computer names to IP addresses, static is static. You have to maintain this file on each computer, and if an address changes, you have to change all the lmhosts files on the network. WINS, on the other hand, is dynamic. The machines register themselves with the server when they come up, and then later release themselves when shutting down. So from the client side, the workstations register themselves, direct queries to the server to resolve names, and then later release their registration when shutting down. At the client, you simply need to add an entry for the WINS server, as shown in Figure 17.14. As you will see in Hour 19, "Troubleshooting," when you look at name resolution order, NT examines the hosts file if configured to do so. This file is used to resolve the names of TCP/IP resources that do not connect through the NetBIOS interface. By default, the NetBIOS name is the same as the host name.

FIGURE 17.14

At the client, you merely need to add an entry for the address of the WINS server.

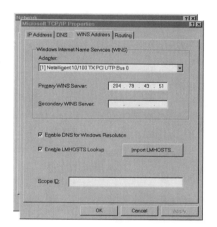

The address of the WINS server is one of the TCP/IP properties you can define. If you're using DHCP (Dynamic Host Configuration Protocol) on your network, the DHCP server can be configured to hand out this address, which simplifies management even more. This way, if the address of your WINS server changes, instead of having to go to each machine where the address is hard-wired, you have to make the change in only one location.

Notice in Figure 17.14 that you have the option of putting in an address for a secondary WINS server. Later, you will see that you can replicate the WINS database to another server for fault tolerance. If your primary server goes offline, abends, or is taken down, your name resolution will still work. The workstations then query their secondary server.

Installing WINS

The installation of WINS, like all services, occurs through the Services tab of the Network properties dialog box. Simply select Windows Internet Name Service, and then click Add (see Figure 17.15). As always, you need to reboot, and you need to reinstall Service Pack 3. After WINS is installed, you see an addition to the Start | Programs | Administrative Tools menu: WINS Manager.

FIGURE 17.15

WINS is simple to install and works right out of the box.

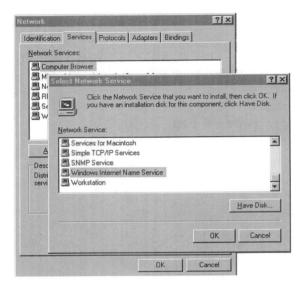

You can also create your own shortcut to WINSadmn.exe to run the program.

WINS Manager

Like many of the Microsoft utilities, you don't have to physically go to the server running WINS to manage it. You can add the server to the copy of the manager you have running, perhaps on an NT workstation, and manage the service remotely. The WINS Manager, shown in Figure 17.16, is used to administer and configure WINS.

To provide redundancy, you can place a copy of your database on another WINS server; this process is known as *replication*. A replication partner can be one of two types:

- **A push partner**   A push partner pushes the updates of its database to its replication partner.
- **A pull partner**   A pull partner asks its replication partner for updates.

You can also configure the server to do both—push and pull.

FIGURE 17.16

The WINS Manager program, WINSadmn.exe.

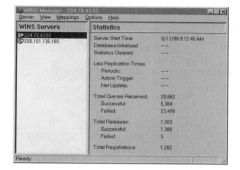

Figure 17.17 shows some of the replication options. For example, you can add and delete replication partners and specify what to show in the list. You can replicate now or send a trigger.

FIGURE 17.17

The available WINS replication options. Choose Server | Replication Partners from the Manager menu.

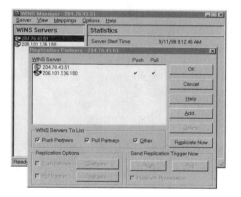

If you drill down by clicking the Configure button, you have the opportunity to set the update count, as shown in Figure 17.18. The update count acts as a throttle. Instead of sending every single change every time a change occurs, you can specify how many changes must occur before the replication partners are notified. As always, don't hesitate to click the Help button for detailed explanations of the options.

FIGURE **17.18**

The update count allows you to specify how many changes must be made to the database before replication partners are informed.

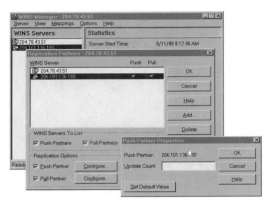

To actually see the contents of the database (as shown in Figure 17.19), choose Mappings | Show Database from the WINS Manager menu. From here, you can show all mappings or only the mappings from a selected owner, along with the sort options. Clicking Delete Owner removes all references to the selected server, along with removing all database entries owned by that server.

FIGURE **17.19**

To actually view the database entries, choose Mappings | Show Database.

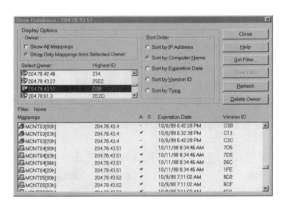

Notice the A column and the S column. A check mark in the A column tells you that the entry is active (that is, the workstation has registered with the server); a mark in the S column tells you that the entry is static (that is, it's one you have manually entered). The version ID, assigned by the server during name registration, is also used by the replication partners to find new records.

Before closing the screen shown in Figure 17.19, take a closer look—you will see more than one entry for each computer name. The clients actually register with the WINS server three or more times, and the numbers in the brackets are the different services. For the computer named MCNT04, you have four entries showing in the database:

- **MCNT04[00h]**   This name is registered for the WINS client workstation name.
- **MCNT04[03h]**   This name is registered for the Messenger Service on the WINS.
- **MCNT04[06h]**   This name is registered for the RAS service.
- **MCNT04[20h]**   This name is registered for the Server Service on the WINS client.

There are many more options in the WINS Manager than what have been covered in this chapter, so don't hesitate to poke around and use the Help. Also note that you can stop and start the WINS service just like any other service: with the Services icon in Control Panel.

Backing Up the WINS Database

To back up the WINS database, do the following:

1. Choose Mappings | Backup Database.
2. Enter the location of the folder for the backup files.
3. Click OK.

After the backup folder is specified, the server automatically backs up the database every 24 hours.

> If you look at the WINS Manager Help, you can see that it says the backup will occur every three hours. If Easter eggs can make it into production software, I suppose you shouldn't begrudge the occasional mistake in online documentation!

> The actual name of the WINS database is WINS.mdb, and it's found in \winnt\system32\WINS. You can view the properties of this file to determine its size.

Disk Administration

Before you can really delve into disk management, you need to understand partitioning. In this section, you're going to learn exactly what a disk partition is. After you have a handle on that, then you can take a look at some of the features in NT, including the following:

- Stripe sets
- Volume sets
- Mirroring
- Stripe sets with parity

Partitions

The normal office in corporate America today is a large space broken up into cubicles, supplying much fodder for Dilbert cartoons. Translating this to computers, if the large room is your hard disk, then the cubicles are the partitions. Even though each cubicle is part of the large room, each "partition" can be dealt with independently. One cubicle dweller might be neat, but the cubicle next to him or her might be in continual chaos.

Disk partitions are like cubicles. You can take a large disk and break it up into partitions, each of which can be dealt with separately. Partitions are created from free space on the disk. Most people are probably familiar with having only one partition, which takes up their entire C: drive.

There are two types of partitions (see Figure 17.20):

- **Primary**   A primary partition is one you can format with a particular file system and actually load an operating system from. There can be a maximum of four primary partitions on a disk. Multiple primary partitions allow you to boot up into differing operating systems. You could have a FAT partition for your Windows 95, another for your NT system, and an NTFS partition where you have installed NT (remember, in NT, they call the partition you boot from the *system partition* and the partition NT loads from the *boot partition*). Each of the primary partitions is assigned a drive letter.

- **Extended**   An extended partition is like the Highlander: There can be only one. An extended partition is not formatted like a primary partition; instead, it's broken up into logical drives, each of which is formatted. Because there can be only one, if you have free space and intend to create an extended partition, use all your free space to do it with. It can then be broken up into logical drives.

FIGURE 17.20

You can have a maximum of four primary partitions or three primary and one extended.

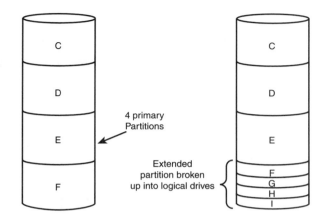

4 primary Partitions

Extended partition broken up into logical drives

Managing Partitions

All disk management is done with windisk.exe, which is in \winnt\system32. You can also choose Start | Programs | Administrative Tools | Disk Administrator. The first time Disk Administrator is run, you see the following message:

```
Disk administrator has determined that this is the first time Disk
Administrator has been run, or that one or more disks have been added
to your computer.
```

Or you might see this message:

```
No signature found on Disk X. Writing a signature is a safe operation that
will not affect your ability to access this disk from other operating
systems.
```

Click Yes or OK regardless of which dialog box appears. You are then looking at the Disk Administrator screen shown in Figure 17.21. You use Disk Administrator to create partitions, delete partitions, format partitions, assign drive letters, and implement fault tolerance.

In Hour 10, "NT Server Basics," I discussed having a small FAT partition for both your NT boot and system partitions. The reasoning was that if you needed to access the disk, you could do so from a DOS boot disk, change from A: to C:, and move, copy, delete, and edit files. Take another look at Figure 17.21, and figure out what you're looking at.

17

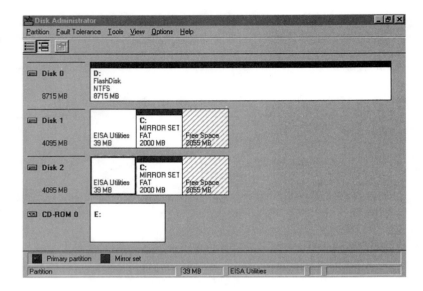

FIGURE **17.21**

Disk administration is done with windisk.exe, *the Disk Administrator program.*

There are three drives in this server. Disk 0 is an 8,715MB drive. It is actually an external RAID array, but as far as NT is concerned, it's one disk that has been formatted with NTFS. Disk 0 has only one partition. Disk 1 and Disk 2 look suspiciously alike, and there's a good reason for this: They are mirrored drives. Disk 1 and Disk 2 have two partitions:

- **The EISA utilities partition**   This partition lets you boot up into the EISA configuration, which you need to do when configuring the machine (such as adding or removing adapters).

- **A 2GB partition formatted with the FAT file system**   On this partition, you have your NT system and boot partitions.

Notice that both Disk 1 and Disk 2 have 2,055MB of free space on them. You could use this space for a variety of things, such as a stripe set, a volume set, or simply another partition. For example, if you highlight the free space on Disk 1, you can create another partition (see Figure 17.22). You can do the same thing on Disk 2. Each of these partitions would get a drive letter.

FIGURE 17.22

Now the free space has been broken up into a stripe set and a volume set.

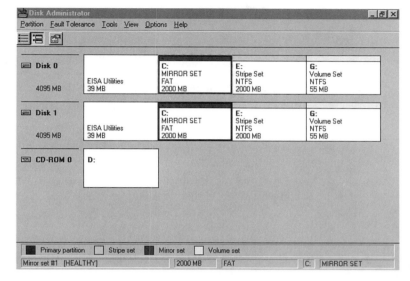

Stripe Sets

A stripe set allows you to take free space on more than one disk and combine these blocks of free space into one volume. For example, suppose you have three disks in your server, and each has 100MB of free space. You could create three 100MB volumes, or you might find it more beneficial to create one 300MB stripe set. Stripe sets are one way to collect and use the bits of free space you have on the server's disks.

A stripe set requires free space on at least two (although up to 32 are allowed) physically separate drives. The data is *striped*, or written, across the set. The free space used on each disk needs to be approximately the same size, else the space used on each disk will be the lowest common denominator, or the smallest bit of free space you choose. In other words, if you take 100MB of free space on Drive A and only 10MB of free space on Drive B, and go to create a stripe set, then the 10MB of free space is the lowest and you will use that on each disk.

Because the stripe set is being implemented by the OS, or NT, then the NT system and boot partitions cannot be on a stripe set. You need the OS to see the stripe set, so you certainly can't expect to be able to boot from it! Finally, if the stripe set is on disks that allow simultaneous access, a stripe set can improve I/O (input and output) because a command can be processed by the disks at the same time, instead of sequentially.

A stripe set provides no fault tolerance. In fact, the loss of a single drive in the set will be the death knell of your stripe set. Be prepared to replace the failed disk, re-create the set, and restore from tape.

Volume Sets

If you refer back to Figure 17.22, you'll notice that a volume set has been created. Like the stripe set, a volume set can use from 2 to 32 areas of free space. But there are some major differences. You can create a volume set on the same drive, if you like, but the stripe set requires at least two physical drives. Unlike the stripe set, the volume set completely fills one member of the set before moving on to the next. There's no simultaneous I/O or performance benefit.

A good thing about volume sets is that the pieces of free space that become members do not have to be the same size. You could have 50MB of free space on one disk, 200MB on another, and 75MB on a third. You could create three small volumes, but a better strategy might be to combine all these fragments into one larger and more useful volume of 325MB.

> A volume set gives you no fault tolerance. A loss of any one disk takes out the entire volume, so use a volume set only for scratch data, or be prepared to re-create and restore from tape. In fact, a volume set is highly susceptible to failure because losing only one disk breaks the entire set.

As with a stripe set, you can't load your OS from a volume set. The only thing that recognizes a volume set is the NT operating system, so if you need the OS to recognize the volume, the OS has to come up first! Table 17.1 compares volume sets and stripe sets.

TABLE 17.1   VOLUME SET AND STRIPE SET COMPARISON.

Attribute	Volume Set	Stripe Set
Hold the system or boot partition	No	No
Improve I/O	No	Yes
Free segments used about the same size	No	Yes
One member filled, then the next	Yes	No
Combine disks, such as SCSI and IDE	Yes	Yes
Maximum number of members	32	32

Mirroring

Neither the stripe set nor the volume set gives you any redundancy. The only thing mentioned in that respect is *mirroring*, also referred to as *RAID 1*. Mirroring is just that: You take a partition on disk A and mirror it to disk B. Every time the OS writes to A, it writes the same data to B (Figure 17.23 shows the difference between mirroring and disk duplexing). You can add further protection by having disk A on its own SCSI controller and disk B on its own controller. This protects you against not only disk failure, but also controller failure.

FIGURE 17.23

Disk mirroring uses only one disk controller. Disk duplexing is also mirroring, except adding a second disk controller improves performance and adds protection.

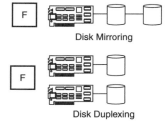

Disk Mirroring

Disk Duplexing

F = File Server
☐ = Disk

RAID

RAID, short for *redundant array of inexpensive disks*, has five levels ranging from RAID 1 (disk mirroring) to RAID 5 (striping with parity, discussed in the next section). Basically, a RAID array takes a collection of physical disks and presents them to the OS as one logical disk.

Cost-wise, mirroring is expensive because you get to use only 50 percent of the storage you've purchased. For example, to mirror a 4GB drive, you need to purchase another 4GB drive. You've bought a total of 8GB, but can store only 4GB of data. Then again, if you're talking about critical data, money might not be the most important variable in the equation.

Mirroring doesn't improve write performance because you have to write to both disks at the same time. Each drive can perform a read operation independently, so mirroring improves your read access.

Stripe Set with Parity

RAID 5, striping with parity, is like the stripe set discussed earlier, except there's also *parity* information being written. Because the parity information is striped across the drives along with the data, you can lose one of the drives and still continue to function—the parity information gives the system enough information to supply the missing data.

NT calls this software implementation of RAID 5 a *stripe set plus parity*. Keep in mind the words *software implementation*. Because the OS is implementing the array, it does add overhead and, therefore, has an effect on performance. So consider implementing RAID in the hardware; to the OS, it appears as just one disk. Server vendors, such as Compaq and other big players, have the capability of implementing RAID in the hardware, or you might consider an external RAID array. In any case, the objective is to take the load off the operating system.

From a financial standpoint, the more disks you have in your array, the less the parity information costs you. In other words, with three drives in the array, you effectively have one-third of your available space going to parity information. With five drives, you have four available for your data and only one-fifth going to parity.

No matter how many disks you have in your stripe set with parity, you can recover data only if no more than one disk is lost. If two or more disks are lost, it's time to restore from tape. So if you lose one disk, then you're still okay, but it's time to move quickly at this point and repair the damage. You can read and write to a set with a lost partition as though it were healthy, but the stripe set no longer has any fault tolerance. If you lose any of the remaining partitions, then it's once again time for a tape restore.

The status bar in Disk Administrator indicates stripe set condition. When a partition in the set is selected, Disk Administrator displays information about the set in the lower-left corner of the window, as in:

```
Stripe set with parity #0 [HEALTHY]
```

[HEALTHY] is what you want to see. Here's other status information you might see:

- **[NEW]**   You have created the stripe set, but the system has not been shut down and restarted to begin the actual creation.

- **[INITIALIZING]**   After the system comes back up and the stripe set is being generated, you're in the initialization stage.

- **[RECOVERABLE]**   You have lost one of the partitions in the set, but the rest are okay, or one partition isn't in sync with the others.

The Fault Tolerance Menu

To implement either mirroring or a stripe set with parity, click on the free space you're going to use in the Disk Administrator. Then, holding down the Ctrl key, click on the other areas of free space. Finally, open the Fault Tolerance menu, where you see the following choices:

- Establish Mirror
- Break Mirror
- Create Stripe Set with Parity
- Regenerate

The Create Stripe Set with Parity and the Establish Mirror options should be self-explanatory after the reading ordeal you have just subjected yourself to. But what about the Break Mirror and Regenerate options?

In your stripe set with parity, you can lose a disk and still continue to function. However, because the system uses the parity information to re-create the missing data, your performance is slower. Also, at this point, your stripe set is at risk because you can afford to lose only one drive from the set. To fix things, replace the failed disk, click on the free space you are going to use, and then choose Regenerate from the Fault Tolerance menu.

To recover from a mirror failure, you must first break the mirror (choose Break Mirror). Then delete the failed partition, replace the disk, and use the free space to re-establish the mirror set.

Boot.ini and ARC Paths

There's a hidden text file in the root of the system partition called boot.ini (see Figure 17.24). This file, created during the installation of NT, points to the operating system files.

FIGURE 17.24

The boot.ini *file points to your operating system. It might need to be modified with an emergency boot disk to get the system up after a disk failure.*

That strange information in Figure 17.24 is an ARC path (*ARC* is short for *advanced RISC computing*). Imagine that you have your normal boot and system partition and, being the excellent administrator that you are, you have this critical partition mirrored to another disk. Now suppose you lose the primary partition of this mirrored pair because of disk failure. Your system won't boot. If you could somehow create an NT boot disk (which you will do shortly) and edit the boot.ini file to point to the remaining good half of the mirror, then you would be back in business. But what in the boot.ini file should you edit? You need to interpret that rather cryptic-looking file:

- **multi/SCSI**   This is an either/or entry. If you're using a SCSI controller that does-n't have the BIOS enabled, it reads SCSI. Otherwise, it reads multi.

- **(x)**   The number of the controller. If there's more than one controller, the first one to load up gets the number 0, the second the number 1, and so on.

- **disk(x)**   This setting is always 0 for multi. For a SCSI controller, *x* equals the SCSI bus number.

- **rdisk(x)**   This is the disk number. This parameter is ignored by SCSI.

- **partition(x)**   This is the number of the partition. Partition numbering starts with the number 1.

> When I'm talking about SCSI in the boot.ini file, I mean only that you're using a SCSI controller that doesn't have the BIOS enabled. A system can have only SCSI drives in it, and the boot.ini file can still show multi. Also, the boot.ini file is flagged as a system and read-only file, so to edit it, you have to remove these attributes.

Now that the secret decoder ring is in your hands, what's your boot.ini file saying to you? The first line reads as follows:

```
multi(0)disk(0)partition(2)\WINNT="Windows NT Server Version 4.00".
➥Multi(0)
```

This means you have a SCSI controller and the BIOS is enabled. The (0) tells you it is the first controller. You can ignore the disk(0) portion of the line because, for multicon-trollers, disk is always set to 0. rdisk(0) indicates that the disk number is 0, and parti-tion(2) means that partition 2 is the partition with your NT files on it. Clear as mud?

And why partition 2? If you look back at your setup, shown in Figure 17.21, you see that partition 1 contains your EISA configuration utilities and that partition 2 is a mirror set.

This mirror set contains your operating system files. Now your boot.ini file is pointing you to partition number 2 on disk 0. If you lose disk 0, your system isn't going to come up. You know how to edit the boot.ini file to make things point to the good partition—now if you only had an NT boot disk!

Partition Numbering

NT assigns partition numbers to all the primary partitions first, and then the logical drives of the extended partitions. This is of particular importance because you could create a partition but wind up unable to boot! Imagine you have only one disk in the system, and you have created on that disk a primary partition and an extended partition. The primary would be partition 1 and the extended would be partition 2. You have your boot partition, where NT loads from, on your extended partition.

Now suppose you add another disk to the system and create a primary partition on it. Because primary partitions are assigned numbers before extended partitions, you now have partition 1 on disk 1, partition 2 on disk 2, and what was your original partition 2, the extended partition, still on disk 1 (see Figure 17.25). However, notice that the partition number of the extended partition has changed. Where would the boot.ini file be pointing? The wrong place! The boot.ini file in this case needs to be modified for reasons that have nothing to do with disk failure.

FIGURE 17.25

Primary partitions are numbered before extended partitions. Here, creating another partition has caused the partition number of the boot partition to change.

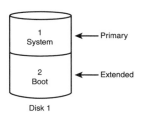

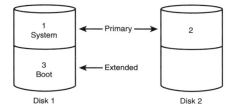

NT Boot Disk

An NT boot disk enables you to get the system back up by booting off a floppy disk and having the boot.ini file on the disk point to the backup partition. To create a boot disk, start by formatting a floppy disk on a machine running either NT Workstation or NT Server. Then copy the following files, some of which are hidden (you can set Explorer to show all files and then make the copy):

- ntldr
- ntdetect.com
- boot.ini
- ntbootdd.sys (this file needs to be copied only if you are using a SCSI system with the BIOS disabled)

Boot up with the floppy disk and test it. Even if you have only one drive in the system, you might still have problems with the boot sectors on that drive; being able to boot from a floppy disk can get you up and going. If you have more than one drive and are mirroring, then practice editing the boot.ini file and coming up from your mirrored partition.

Summary

Trust relationships are created between domains to allow access. Without a trust relationship, the only resources you can access are those in your own domain. Trusts are either one-way or two-way. One-way trusts allow access only in one direction; two-way trusts are actually two one-way trusts. When assigning rights involving trust relationships, always create a local group with rights to the resource and then add a global group to the local group. Trusts are created with User Manager for Domains.

The first step in auditing is to formulate the audit policy, which should be defined with the goal of delivering meaningful yet manageable information. Too much data can be just as troublesome as not having enough. Checking the logs from Event Viewer should be part of your normal maintenance routine.

To audit files and directories, you must first enable file and object access in your policy, and the files must be on an NTFS partition. Auditing must then be set on the individual files and directories you want to audit. The same holds true for printers. You must choose the printer and select the events you want to track.

Log files are viewed by using Event Viewer and can be set to circular login mode, in which events are overwritten automatically, or you can set the system to force the administrator to deal with them manually. You can also control the size you want the log files to grow to. If the audit log is cleared, an event indicates that. This security feature keeps an administrator from clearing his or her tracks in the event of unethical behavior.

WINS, or Windows Internet Name Service, is a dynamic method of resolving NetBIOS, or computer names, to IP addresses. A workstation using WINS registers itself with the WINS server when it comes online, and then later releases this registration at shutdown. When a name needs to be resolved, the workstation directs a query to the WINS server instead of using broadcasts. WINS is managed with the WINS Manager program. For redundancy, you can have your WINS server replicate the database to another server. This replication allows your name resolution to continue to function if your primary server is down. Workstations register themselves with the server more than once, depending on the services running.

Disk administration is done with the Disk Administrator program. From here, you create, label, format, and perform all disk-related activities. There can be a maximum of four primary partitions or three primaries and one extended partition per disk. Primary partitions are numbered first, and then any logical drives in extended partitions.

NT has two levels of fault tolerance: mirroring (RAID 1) and stripe set with parity (RAID 5). Mirroring is the simpler of the two and more costly. You can add more redundancy by giving each disk in the mirrored set its own disk controller, which is known as *duplexing*. A stripe set with parity stripes the data across the array. You can lose a disk from the array and still access it as though it were healthy, but at that point, the redundancy is gone. The loss of another disk would be a show-stopper. It would be better to implement RAID at the hardware level, where it appears to NT simply as one disk, than to implement it at the software level, which causes overhead on the system and thus a performance hit.

You can use free space to create volume sets and stripe sets. They offer no fault tolerance but are a convenient way to collect pieces of unused space into useful storage space. Make an NT boot disk and test it!

Workshop

Q&A

Q I have wound up with free space on each of my three disks. Is there any way to collect it all into one large volume?

A That's the perfect scenario for a volume set, especially if the sizes of the free space segments do not match closely.

Q What is WINS and why do I need it?

A Windows Internet Name Service is a dynamic method of resolving computer, or NetBIOS, names to IP addresses. You always need some form of name resolution, and WINS prevents the need for broadcast packets.

Q **What's the difference between a one-way and a two-way trust relationship?**

A A one-way trust is when I trust you, but you don't trust me. That means you can use my resources, but I can't use yours. A two-way trust is just two one-way trusts.

Q **I can't seem to get file auditing to work. It's simply not an option.**

A First, the files must be on an NTFS partition. Second, file and object access must be enabled in your audit policy.

Q **I think I'm auditing, but where do I go to view the log files?**

A The log files are viewed by using Event Viewer. Choose the security log.

Q **Why would I want to mirror my disks? Buying two and just being able to use one seems like a waste.**

A Mirroring gives you fault tolerance. With only one drive in the system, if it goes, you're down. With mirrored disks, the system continues to function until you can replace the failed disk and re-create the mirror set.

Q **Trust relationships are diagrammed with arrows. In what direction should the arrow point?**

A The arrow always points to people whom you trust, so it points away from the trusting domain and toward the trusted domain.

Q **What is the `boot.ini` file?**

A The `boot.ini` file points NT to the boot partition. NT looks here to continue loading.

Quiz

1. There are printers at the corporate office that you would like to send jobs to, and corporate would like to send jobs to your printer. However, they are two separate domains. What's the solution?

2. What are the types of log files?

3. What's the maximum size of a log file?

4. True or False: A volume set can be created on one physical drive.

5. A stripe set can have a maximum of _____ members.

6. NT offers two forms of fault tolerance: RAID 1 and RAID 5. They are also known as _____ and _____.

7. True or False: A stripe set protects you from the loss of one of your disks.

8. When your WINS server goes down, things go all to pieces. Users can't attach to the resources they need. What's the solution?

PART IV

Beyond the Basics

Hour

18 DHCP

19 Troubleshooting

20 Connecting Your Windows 98 Desktop
    to the Internet

21 Surfing Tools

22 Connecting Your Network to the Internet

23 Support Resources

24 Online Resources

Hour **18**

DHCP

When using the IP protocol, each machine must be assigned a unique IP address. These addresses can be assigned in one of the following ways:

- **Statically** If you statically assign IP addresses, you must visit each machine and enter the address information by hand—this method is often referred to as *hard-wiring* the address. It's then up to you as the administrator to document this information in a spreadsheet or database and to track all the moves, adds, and changes. (Of course, documentation has a tendency to fall by the wayside; before you know it, your spreadsheet will be out of date and inaccurate.) Also, if a machine is moved to another subnet, it won't work until you enter new information that's correct for the new subnet.

- **Dynamically** By using DHCP, IP addresses can be *dynamically* assigned. That means the IP address is not hard-wired into each workstation. Instead, when a workstation comes online, it asks for an address; your NT server (acting as a DHCP server) then assigns it an address to use for a period of time (called a *lease*). This greatly simplifies administration.

In addition to using DHCP to assign addresses, you can use it to hand out other pertinent bits of information, such as the default gateway and the address of the WINS service.

Hour 3, "Protocols," touched on DHCP from a theoretical point of view. This Hour covers the following topics:

- Installing and configuring DHCP
- Creating a scope
- Creating client reservations
- Managing the DHCP server

Installation and Configuration

Client-side configuration of DHCP is simple; just follow these steps:

1. Choose Start|Settings|Control Panel.
2. Double-click the Network icon.
3. Select the Protocols tab.
4. Highlight TCP/IP and then click Properties.
5. Check the Obtain an IP Address from a DHCP Server check box in the IP Address tab (see Figure 18.1).

FIGURE 18.1

Setting the workstation to use DHCP.

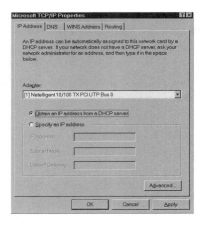

To install DHCP on the server, follow these steps:

1. Choose Start|Settings|Control Panel.

2. Double-click the Network icon.

3. Select the Services tab.

4. Click Add, and then select DHCP from the list.

5. The DHCP server cannot be a DHCP client, which means that the server requires the IP protocol and a static IP address. Fill in the appropriate information in the dialog box.

6. DHCP is installed, and you're prompted to reboot. Don't forget to reapply Service Pack 3; its installation is covered in Hour 15, "Managing NT Servers."

After DHCP is installed, you see a new addition to NT's administrative tools: DHCP Manager (see Figure 18.2).

FIGURE 18.2

DHCP Manager is installed when the DHCP service is added.

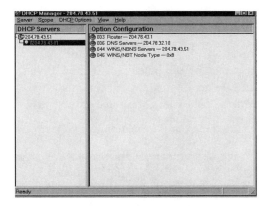

18

Creating the Scope

Now that you have DHCP installed, you need to create and configure a scope. A *scope* is a range, or pool, of IP addresses that the server can hand out to the clients as addresses are requested. To create the scope, do the following:

1. Choose Start|Programs|Administrative Tools|DHCP Manager.

2. Double-click Local Machine.

3. From the Scope menu, choose Create.

4. You then see the Scope Properties dialog box shown in Figure 18.3 (except that the screen you see is blank). Available fields in this dialog box are as follows:

- **IP Address Pool Start Address and End Address**   Here you define the range of IP addresses that the server hands out to clients. The scope includes the addresses entered for the start and end of the scope.

- **Subnet Mask**   Here you enter the correct subnet mask for your addresses. If you remember from Hour 3, the default subnet masks are 255.0.0.0 for Class A, 255.255.0.0 for Class B, and 255.255.255.0 for Class C. Refer to Table 3.1 in Hour 3 for a refresher on address classes and subnet masks.

- **Exclusion Range Start Address and End Address**   Here you define addresses that the DHCP server does *not* hand out. To exclude a range, enter the start and end of the range and then click Add. To exclude an individual IP address, enter the address in the Start Address field, leave the End Address field blank, and click Add.

> You can exclude more than one range or IP address.

- **Lease Duration**   If you do not want a time limit on how long the lease is good for, enable the Unlimited radio button. If you want to set a time limit on the lease, select Limited To and enter the number of days, hours, and minutes. The default lease length is three days.

5. When you have filled in your information, click OK to create the scope.

FIGURE 18.3

The scope is the range of IP addresses that the server can hand out to clients.

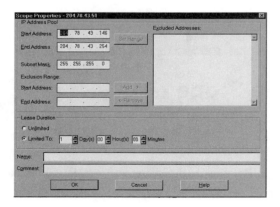

Notice in Figure 18.3 that instead of entering an IP Address Pool Start Address of
204.78.43.1 (which, with an End Address of 204.78.43.254, would have designated the
entire range of available addresses for the pool), 204.78.43.146 was entered. This is
because certain machines, such as servers, should not be DHCP clients; therefore, the IP
addresses of those machines shouldn't appear in the pool of available addresses. By starting the pool at .146, you have addresses available for the DHCP clients and addresses
available that you can hard-wire for those machines not using DHCP. This keeps you
from having to manually exclude addresses in the scope properties.

Scope Options

Now that your scope has been created, the server has a pool of IP addresses to hand out
to DHCP clients. Remember, though, that you can take advantage of DHCP by handing
out other important information, such as the default gateway or router, the address of the
WINS server, and more. These pieces of information are called *scope options*.

There are three types of scope options:

- **Global options**   These options pertain to all clients. When all workstations need
  the same piece of information, you add that piece of information as a global
  option.

- **Scope options**   These options apply only to clients of that particular scope. If you
  have more than one scope defined, you might use scope options to hand out information unique to that subnet, such as the default router. Scope options override
  global options.

- **Client options**   If you have reserved IP addresses for specific clients (discussed
  later this hour), then you can have options that apply only to those specific clients.
  Client options override both scope and global options.

To add and configure the options, do the following:

1. Open DHCP Manager by choosing Start|Programs|Administrative Tools|DHCP
   Manager.

2. From the DHCP Options menu, choose Global, Scope, or Client to open the dialog
   box shown in Figure 18.4.

18

FIGURE 18.4

Unused options are listed on the left, and active options are listed on the right. You can tell that the server is handing out the addresses of the router, DNS server, and WINS server and the WINS/NBT node type because they appear in the Active Options list.

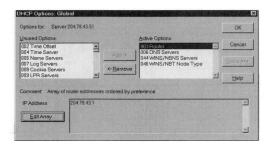

3. To add an option, highlight it in the Unused Options list and click Add.

4. To remove an active option, highlight it in the Active Options list and click Remove.

5. Click the Value button to view the value of the active option. For example, notice in Figure 18.4 that active option 003 is highlighted. Clicking the Value button displays the router's IP address in the field at the bottom of the dialog box (the address is 204.78.43.1).

6. To change the router's address or add more than one router, click the Edit Array button to open the IP Address Array Editor, shown in Figure 18.5.

7. Enter the new address, click Add, and then click OK.

FIGURE 18.5

You can edit the values of the options that are handed out.

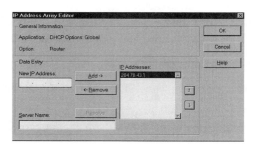

Now for some more about the 046 WINS/NBT Node Type option in the Active Options list shown in Figure 18.4. If you highlight this item, you can see that some cryptic options become available (see Figure 18.6):

- **0×1 = B-node**   B-node, or *broadcast node*, uses broadcast packets for both name registration and name resolution. This is not a good option because you can wind up with too many broadcasts flooding the network; besides, as you have seen, most routers don't forward broadcast packets.

> Microsoft B-node is slightly modified. First, the workstations check the `lmhosts` cache, then they try broadcasting, and then they parse the `lmhosts` file.

- **0×2 = P-node**   P-node, or *peer node*, does not use broadcast at all. Instead, workstations register themselves with a NetBIOS name server (WINS). They also use the WINS server for name resolution. The problem with P-node is that if the WINS server is unavailable, names cannot be resolved.

- **0×4 = M-node**   M-node, or *mixed node*, uses a combination of B-node and P-node. First, B-node is used and then P-node. M-node is better than P-node because if the WINS server is unavailable, names can still be resolved.

- **0×8 = H-node**   H-node, or *hybrid node*, also uses B-node and P-node, except it uses broadcasts only as a last resort. H-node always uses P-node (contacting the WINS server) and then broadcasts only if using P-node fails. The system can also be configured to use the `lmhosts` file before using broadcasts if P-node fails.

18

> When a workstation is configured to use WINS for name resolution, it uses H-node for name registration by default.

FIGURE 18.6

Using the WINS/NBT Node Type option, you can specify the type of NetBIOS name resolution to be used.

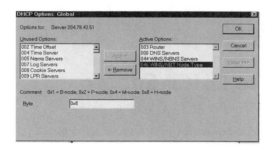

> See Hour 19, "Troubleshooting," for more information on name resolution order.

Client Reservations

You might have some client machines that you want static addresses for. Instead of manually hard-wiring addresses into these machines, you can use a *client reservation*. When a machine with a client reservation requests a lease from the DHCP server, the server recognizes the MAC address of the client requesting the lease and knows that this particular MAC address is supposed to receive a certain IP address.

To create a client reservation, do the following:

1. Open DHCP Manager by choosing Start|Programs|Administrative Tools|DHCP Manager.
2. Choose Scope|Add Reservations to open the dialog box shown in Figure 18.7.
3. Type the IP address you want reserved in the IP Address text field.
4. In the Unique Identifier field, type the MAC address of the client's NIC.

 If you enter the MAC address incorrectly, the server doesn't recognize the reservation, so it gives the client any one of its available addresses.

5. If you want, type the name of the user of the client machine and a description of the user or machine.
6. When you're finished, click Add.

FIGURE 18.7

Creating a client reservation.

Managing the DHCP Server

Managing your DHCP server might entail the following:

- Tracking whether certain leases in a scope are active
- Gleaning extra information about active leases
- Reconciling the DHCP database with the Registry
- Altering the DHCP database's automatic backup interval

All these tasks can be accomplished from the DHCP Manager.

Tracking which leases in a scope are active is easy. Simply do the following:

1. Open DHCP Manager by choosing Start|Programs|Administrative Tools|DHCP Manager.

2. Double-click the scope (next to the lightbulb) in the lefthand pane of the main DHCP Manager screen to open the Active Leases dialog box for that scope, as shown in Figure 18.8. Here you can see how many addresses are active, who each address is leased to, and how many addresses in the pool remain available. You can easily change the sort order of the display or set it to show reservations only.

FIGURE 18.8

Viewing the active leases.

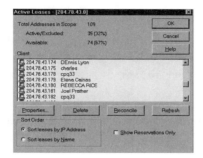

To glean more information about one of the active leases, just highlight the active lease from the Client list in the screen shown in Figure 18.8 and click Properties. This opens the Client Properties dialog box, shown in Figure 18.9 Notice that this address has been given to user Eric Tolbert. You can see when the lease expires and, as an added bonus, the Unique Identifier field supplies the MAC address of the NIC on Eric Tolbert's machine.

FIGURE 18.9

The client properties of lease 204.78.43.185.

To reconcile the DHCP database with the Registry, click the Reconcile button in the Active Leases dialog box (refer to Figure 18.8). Clicking this button runs a consistency check and lists inconsistent addresses. With an *inconsistent address*, the Registry shows the address as being leased, but the DHCP database does not.

The consistency check is performed at the scope level, so if you have more than one scope, the check needs to be run separately for each scope.

What and where are the files that make up the DHCP database? The actual database file is dhcp.mdb, and it's located in the \winnt\system32\dhcp directory.

The database is automatically backed up every 60 minutes. If you want to change this interval, you must manually edit the Registry; of course, the usual cautions apply. The BackupInterval value is located under the following key:

```
HKEY_LOCAL_MACHINE\SYSTEM\CurrentControlSet\Services\DHCPServer\Parameters
➥\BackupInterval
```

You can see in Figure 18.10 that the default setting for BackupInterval is 0x3c, which is hexadecimal for 60 minutes. If you're weak in counting in hexadecimal, then fire up calc.exe, the calculator, and change the view from standard to scientific. This lets you enter a number in decimal and then check the Hex box, and voilá—a number in hex!

FIGURE 18.10

The backup interval must be manually set by editing the Registry. The default is 60 minutes.

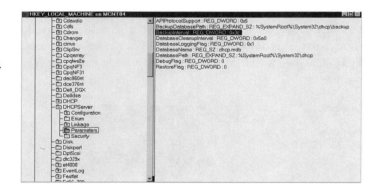

Summary

When using the IP protocol, each machine must have a unique IP address assigned to it. DHCP, short for Dynamic Host Configuration Protocol, can dynamically hand out addresses from a scope, or pool, of available addresses. After the scope is created, you can leverage the power of DHCP by handing out information other than just addresses, such as the default gateway or router, the address of the WINS server, or the address of a domain name server. These extra bits of information are called *scope options*.

You can create client reservations, where the MAC address of the requesting client is used to associate the request with a particular IP address you have reserved.

You can use DHCP Manager to manage your DHCP server. Managing your server might entail such chores as tracking whether certain leases in a scope are active, gleaning extra information about active leases, reconciling the DHCP database with the Registry, and altering the DHCP database's automatic backup interval.

Workshop

Q&A

Q Why use DHCP?

A DHCP simplifies administration by handing out IP addresses, which means you don't have to hard-wire those addresses at each machine. In addition, you can use DHCP to hand out other bits of information, such as the correct default gateway for the client to use.

Q We have an entire Class C address space, but we don't want some of our machines to be DHCP clients. How do we handle that?

A You have several options. The machines could be DHCP clients and still receive the same address by using client reservations, or you could exclude those addresses when configuring the scope. Finally, you could simply start the range of the scope at a number that leaves some addresses available for the DHCP server to use and the rest free for you to hard-wire.

Q What is a scope?

A A scope is a pool, or collection, of IP addresses that the server can hand out to DHCP clients.

Q What is a scope option?

A A scope option is "extra" information that the server can deliver above and beyond just handing out addresses.

18

Quiz

1. The three types of scope options are _____, _____, and _____.

2. True or False: Scope options override global options.

3. You have two separate networks. The workstations are set up to use DHCP to get their addresses and other information, such as the default gateway. Each network has its own DHCP server, and you move a machine from one network to another. True or False: You need to reconfigure the workstation after you have moved it for it to function correctly.

4. A _____ node type does not use broadcasts.

5. The DHCP database is automatically backed up every _____ minutes by default.

Hour 19

Troubleshooting

Network problems? The first thing to do is stay calm. In this Hour, you're going to take a look at the following:

- Browsing and Network Neighborhood
- Troubleshooting utilities
- Name resolution

Browsing and Network Neighborhood

Network Neighborhood enables you to browse a list—called the *browse list*—of all available resources. This Hour, you take a quick look at how browsing works. Although this Hour's coverage is by no means comprehensive, you should begin to understand why some machines show up in your Network Neighborhood even though you can't connect to them (and why you might be able to connect to services that don't appear in your Network Neighborhood).

> Even though a computer might show up when you're browsing Network Neighborhood, this doesn't necessarily mean you can connect to that computer. For example, a machine that has been off for some time might show up in the browse list, but a machine that's active might not show up at all.

The Browse List

There are four types of machines involved with generating a browse list (or lack thereof):

- **Non-browser**   A computer that has been told not to maintain a browse list or net work resource list.

- **Potential browser**   A computer that *can* maintain a browse list.

- **Backup browser**   A computer that definitely has a browse list. The backup browser contacts the master browser every 15 minutes to get the latest copy of the browse list. Later, when contacted by a browser client, the backup browser hands its copy of the list over to the browser client.

- **Master browser**   A computer that keeps *the* browse list. The master browser is responsible for collecting the list; it then hands it to the backup browsers.

If a machine—such as an NT server, a Windows 98 machine with file sharing enabled, or an NT workstation—has shared resources available, it informs the master browser of that every 12 minutes. If the machine with the resources fails to check in after 12 minutes, the master browser lets that slide—likewise if the machine fails to check in after 24 minutes. But if the machine with the resources fails to check in after 36 minutes, the master browser chops the machine with the resources from the browse list (the list of available resources). This means the resource is removed from Network Neighborhood.

Browsing Network Neighborhood

When you browse Network Neighborhood, here's what happens:

1. Your machine contacts the master browser.
2. The master browser gives you the name of three backup browsers.
3. Your machine contacts one of the backup browsers and asks for a list of machines offering resources.
4. The backup browser obliges, giving you the browse list.
5. You contact one of the servers on the browse list to get information about what resources it offers.

Here's the problem: Remember your forgiving friend, the master browser? It gives servers that advertise resources three chances, or 36 minutes, to check in. If a server has been disconnected from the network, it still appears in the browse list for up to 36 minutes. Consider, too, that the backup browser gets a copy of the browse list only every 15 minutes. That means it's possible for a nonexistent resource to appear in Network Neighborhood for up to 51 minutes (the 36 minutes that the master browser lets slide, plus the 15 minutes for the backup browser to get an updated copy)!

The moral of this story: Just because a resource shows up in your Network Neighborhood doesn't mean the resource is available. And conversely, you might be able to connect with no problems to a resource that doesn't show up in the list!

Utilities That Can Help

The first thing to figure out when faced with a computer problem is whether the problem is with just this one workstation or the problem is affecting everyone. If only one user is having the problem, then look to the configuration of that particular machine. If more than one user is having the problem, don't waste your time looking at the individual workstations; look for network problems instead. The next important thing to find out is when the problem started. Often, users have problems for days or weeks without reporting them. Finally, determine whether any changes have recently been made to the system, such as adding new applications.

After you know who's being affected, how long the problem has been going on, and what—if any—changes have been made, and you're armed with your knowledge of the following utilities, it's time to become Sherlock Holmes and follow the clues! This section covers the following tools:

- The `winipcfg` tool
- The `ipconfig /all` command
- The `ping` command
- NT Diagnostics
- Server Manager
- The `nbtstat` command
- The `tracert` command
- The `route` command
- The `arp` command
- Performance Monitor

19

- Task Manager
- Event Viewer/event logs

The `winipcfg` Tool

A user calls complaining about being unable to access the Internet or machines on a remote network. Your first thought is that perhaps the user's default gateway or subnet mask is set incorrectly. (If you remember from Hour 3, "Protocols," the subnet mask is used to determine whether the destination IP address is on the same network as the sending machine. If the sender specifies that the packet is destined for a remote network, then the packet is sent to the workstation's default gateway to be forwarded to the remote network.) How can you quickly get the information you need about this user's configuration?

One way is to look at the properties of the TCP/IP protocol, but a simpler method is to simply run the `winipcfg` utility (see Figure 19.1) by choosing Start|Run|Winipcfg. With a quick glance at the information supplied by `winipcfg`, you can determine whether the problem is with the workstation's configuration or the problem lies elsewhere. Information you can get from `winipcfg` includes the following:

- The host, or workstation name
- The address of the DNS server
- The node type
- The adapter's hardware address
- The workstation's IP address
- The subnet mask
- The default gateway
- The DHCP server's address and lease information
- The address of the WINS server(s)

 The `winipcfg` tool is available only for Windows 95 and 98. If you run NT, you need to use the `ipconfig` tool, covered in the next section.

 The `winipcfg` tool also lets you release and renew a lease if you're using DHCP on the network.

FIGURE 19.1

The winipcfg *tool gives you an instant look at the workstation's configuration.*

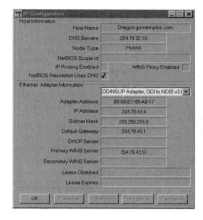

The `ipconfig /all` Command

On the NT platform, you don't get the nice GUI troubleshooting tool you get with Windows 9x, but all the information you can glean from `winipcfg` is still there. To get this information, simply drop to a command line and run the `ipconfig /all` command. The syntax of this command is as follows:

```
ipconfig [/? | /all | /release [adapter] | /renew [adapter]]
```

Table 19.1 explains what each parameter means.

TABLE 19.1 THE `ipconfig /all` PARAMETERS

Parameter	Description
/?	Displays the `ipconfig` help.
/all	Displays full configuration information.
/release	Releases the IP address for the specified adapter.
/renew	Renews the IP address for the specified adapter.

19

Note that the last two switches, `/release` and `/renew`, apply only when using DHCP. The default is to display only the IP address, subnet mask, and default gateway for each adapter bound to TCP/IP.

Listing 19.1 shows the result of running `ipconfig /all`. The listing contains the same information you got from `winipcfg`; it just doesn't look as pretty.

LISTING 19.1 RESULTS OF RUNNING ipconfig /all

```
Host Name . . . . . . . . . : mcnt03.gomemphis.com
DNS Servers . . . . . . . . : 204.78.32.10
Node Type . . . . . . . . . : Hybrid
NetBIOS Scope ID. . . . . . :
IP Routing Enabled. . . . . : Yes
WINS Proxy Enabled. . . . . : No
NetBIOS Resolution Uses DNS : No
Ethernet adapter AMDPCN1:
Description . . . . . . . . : AMD PCNET Family Ethernet Adapter
Physical Address. . . . . . : 00-00-E1-09-A9-17
DHCP Enabled. . . . . . . . : No
IP Address. . . . . . . . . : 204.78.43.4
Subnet Mask . . . . . . . . : 255.255.255.0
Default Gateway . . . . . . : 204.78.43.1
Primary WINS Server . . . . : 204.78.43.51
```

The `ipconfig` tool gives you the option of releasing and renewing IP address leases if you're using DHCP.

The `ping` Command

The `ping` command is, to paraphrase the immortal Red Green, the "handyman's secret weapon." It should always be your first line of attack when troubleshooting IP problems.

Pretend you're standing on the edge of the Grand Canyon, and you give a shout. Barring some freakish act of physics, you will hear an echo. Likewise, when you Ping another host, you essentially give it a shout; the remote host send you back the echo, or reply.

The `ping` command can be extremely useful for troubleshooting because it works at a low level compared to the application. For example, suppose you receive a phone call from a user who tells you her application, which uses TCP/IP, isn't working. You try to Ping her machine, but fail. This tells you that the problem doesn't lie in the application; instead, it lies in one of the lower-level functions of the computer. If you remember from Hour 3, when the OSI model was covered, the application layer is way up at the top. The `ping` command, on the other hand, uses ICMP, or Internet Control Message Protocol, which rides on IP at layer 3.

As shown in Figure 19.2, you can Ping by using an IP address or a host name. When troubleshooting a problem like the one in the preceding paragraph, you should first try to Ping your destination with the IP address. If this works, try to Ping it by using the name. If using the IP address works but the name doesn't, then you know it's a name resolution problem, which is covered later this hour. PING is a command-line utility; if you're Pinging by name, this is the syntax:

```
C:\Windows>ping Elvis
```

This works if the computer you are Pinging is on your own subnet. For networks with more than one subnet, or to Ping non-Windows hosts, you must use a fully qualified domain name, such as `elvis.graceland.com`, and have a DNS server available to resolve the name.

If you're Pinging by IP address, this is the syntax:

```
C:\Windows>ping 205.174.133.15
```

When Pinging by name, the name needs to be resolved in some fashion. When using the IP address to Ping, there's no need for any form of name resolution. If you can Ping by number and not by name, then you might look at the status of your DNS server.

FIGURE 19.2

Using the ping *command, the handyman's secret weapon!*

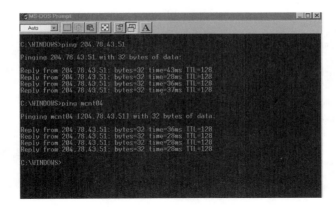

19

If you can't Ping a remote host, try to Ping your own address. If you can't get an answer from Pinging your own IP address, then try the local loopback address (127.0.0.1). You should get a response similar to the following:

```
Pinging 127.0.0.1 with 32 bytes of data:
Reply from 127.0.0.1: bytes=32 time=<10ms TTL=128
Reply from 127.0.0.1: bytes=32 time=<10ms TTL=128
Reply from 127.0.0.1: bytes=32 time=<10ms TTL=128
Reply from 127.0.0.1: bytes=32 time=<10ms TTL=128
```

If you cannot Ping the local loopback address, then TCP/IP is not properly installed, and the problem lies in the workstation's configuration.

There are several switches available for the ping command. The -t switch is especially useful because it Pings the remote host continuously until interrupted—for example, ping 204.78.59.42 -t. To view the switches available with the ping command, drop to a command prompt and enter the command ping all by its lonely self.

> This is a strange thing. You can generally get help for the command-line utilities by using the /? switch, such as ipconfig /?, that was discussed earlier. However, if you enter the command ping /?, then PING will happily take off and try to reach /?! So to get help with PING, enter the command with no parameters at all.

NT Diagnostics

A wealth of information is available from the NT Diagnostics program, shown in Figure 19.3. To reach this screen, do the following:

1. Choose Start|Programs|Administrative Tools|NT Diagnostics.

2. Select the Network tab.

3. Click the Statistics button.

As you can see from the scrollbar in Figure 19.3, what's showing on the screen is only a fraction of the available network statistics.

FIGURE 19.3

The Network tab of the NT Diagnostics program.

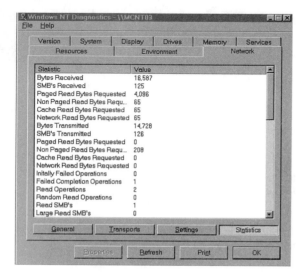

Figure 19.4 shows the NT Diagnostics program's Memory tab, where you can get information about your server's memory. Of importance here is the pagefile information. You can instantly see the location of the pagefile, its size, and the peak usage. Also notice the Print button; don't make the mistake of clicking it for every tab you look at. Clicking the Print button once, from any tab, prints out *all* the information.

The pagefile is used as virtual memory. It's actually a file on the hard drive that NT treats as memory. When NT needs more "real" memory, it writes to the pagefile to free up physical memory.

FIGURE 19.4

The Memory tab of the NT Diagnostics program.

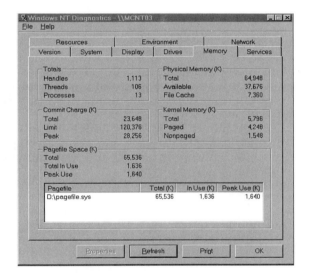

Server Manager

Because Server Manager is covered in Hour 15, "Managing NT Servers," it's just touched on here. Like the other administration tools, you get to Server Manager by choosing Start | Programs | Administrative Tools. After Server Manager is running, you're immediately assured that the server is up and talking. In Figure 19.5, you doubled-clicked server MCNT05 in the main Server Manager window and can now look at users, shares, resources in use, replication, and alerts. This can be useful information if you're troubleshooting.

19

FIGURE **19.5**

*Server Manager lets
you monitor aspects
of your NT server.*

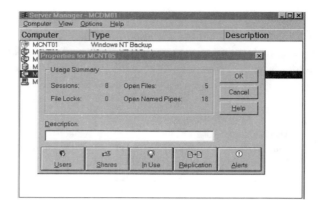

Figure 19.6 shows the result of drilling down by clicking the In Use button. Here, you can see files on the server that are open.

FIGURE **19.6**

*The open resources
displayed by clicking
the In Use button.*

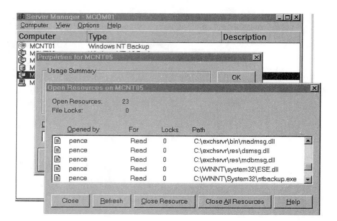

The nbtstat Command

You can also use nbtstat, a command-line utility that can be used to display protocol statistics as well as current TCP/IP connections that are using NBT or NetBIOS over TCP/IP. As shown in Figure 19.7, there are several switches for the command.

FIGURE 19.7

The switches available for the nbstat *command.*

One use for this command is to purge and reload the remote name cache, or to display the contents of the remote name cache, as shown in Figure 19.8. If you make a change to your lmhosts file, which contains a list of machines and their IP addresses, you can purge and reload the NetBIOS remote name cache table by using the command nbtstat -R instead of rebooting and reloading.

FIGURE 19.8

Running nbtstat -c *shows you the NetBIOS remote name cache table, which is useful for name resolution purposes.*

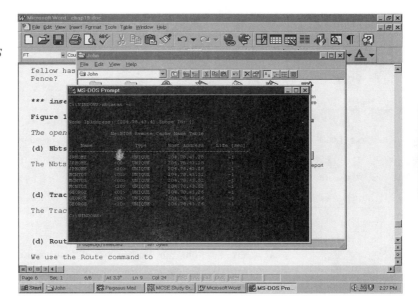

19

The tracert Command

The tracert command can be used to determine where a packet stopped on the network or to view the route the packet has taken. This command is useful for troubleshooting large networks where a packet might take one of several paths to arrive at a certain destination or where many intermediate routers are involved. It can also be used to identify the slow points in the system the packet is traversing. For example, in Figure 19.9, tracert has been used to see whether there's a valid path to jpence.com.

FIGURE 19.9

The tracert *command "traces the route."*

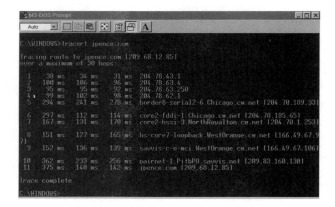

The syntax of the tracert command is as follows:

tracert [-d] [-h maximum_hops] [-j host-list] [-w timeout] target_name

Table 19.2 explains what each parameter means.

TABLE 19.2 THE TRACERT PARAMETERS

Parameter	Description
-d	Specifies not resolving addresses to host names.
-h maximum_hops	Specifies the maximum number of hops to search for target.
-j host-list	Specifies loose source route along the host list.
-w timeout	Waits the number of milliseconds specified by timeout for each reply.
target_name	Name or IP address of the target host.

Several command-line switches can be used with tracert, but they are usually not needed for standard troubleshooting.

The route Command

The route command is used to display and manipulate the route table. Any computer using TCP/IP as a network protocol has a route table; the route a network packet takes from one computer to another using TCP/IP is determined by the route table of the sending computer. The computer's route table is automatically rebuilt every time it's restarted.

As the network administrator, you can add persistent (static) entries to the computer's route table. Persistent entries "stick" and are automatically reinserted in the route table each time it's rebuilt.

The `route` command can be used with switches, including the following:

- **route print**   Displays the route table (see Figure 19.10).
- **route add**   Adds a route.
- **route delete**   Deletes a route.
- **route change**   Modifies an existing route.

FIGURE 19.10

The route print *command shows the current routing table.*

19

You might have a bit of a problem getting the route command to display options. If you type route /?, you naturally get a list of all the command-line switches for the route command, but they scroll off the screen before you can get a look at them! Typing route /? ¦ more doesn't work either, nor does route /? > thisfile. One workaround is to right-click on the title bar of your command prompt, choose Properties, and then Layout. You can set the height of the screen buffer size to, say, 500. This creates a vertical scrollbar in your command prompt window that lets you scroll up and down, so you can see the switches that have rolled off the screen.

The arp Command

Suppose you want to send a packet to the IP address 204.78.43.4, but your NIC, which operates way down on the physical layer of the OSI model, needs the destination machine's MAC address—the actual physical address burned into the destination machine's NIC—not the IP address. Fortunately, it uses the Address Resolution Protocol, or ARP, to get the hardware address that corresponds to the IP address.

The *ARP cache* is a table of IP addresses that have recently been resolved to MAC addresses. Recently resolved names are stored in cache to prevent machines from having to rediscover the MAC address for every packet. If an entry in the ARP cache is incorrect, the packet is sent to the wrong destination.

You can use the command arp -a to view the ARP cache, as shown in Figure 19.11; use arp -d to delete any incorrect entries. For more information on the available switches, run the command arp /?.

FIGURE 19.11

Use the command arp -a *to view the ARP cache.*

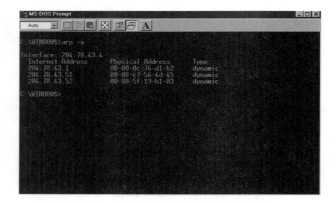

Performance Monitor

Performance Monitor is a wonderful tool for getting extremely specific information about server performance. Think of the millions of statistics available from a server: those related to disk space and usage, those related to memory, those related to network traffic and utilization…the list is endless. Instead of having some sort of enormous drop-down list, Performance Monitor groups statistics together; these groupings are called *objects*.

> Which object you monitor depends on your objectives. For example, if you're trying to track memory-related issues to see whether more memory needs to be added to the server, don't look at the network traffic statistics!

After you've opened Performance Monitor (choose Start | Programs | Administrative Tools | Performance Monitor) and selected the server you want to monitor, you choose the object you want to track. For example, in Figure 19.12, the processor object has been chosen, so you just see information related to processors.

FIGURE 19.12

Performance Monitor gives you an incredible amount of information about your server's performance.

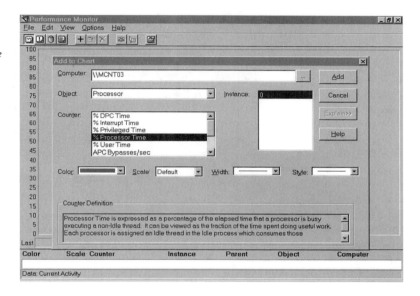

After you've chosen an object, you must select the counter you want to monitor. (Click the Explain button for an explanation of the counter you have selected from the Counter list. As you can see in Figure 19.12, a definition of the counter appears at the bottom of the Add to Chart dialog box.)

When you have selected what you want to monitor, click the Add button and then sit back and watch the show (see Figure 19.13). Each counter has its own scale and shows up in a different color.

19

FIGURE **19.13**

Monitoring two counters related to the processor object and one counter related to the server.

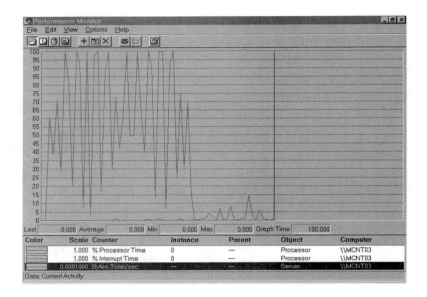

Keep in mind that this is overhead on the system, so don't monitor indiscriminately. You want only useful information. Or, to put it more elegantly, don't have a server monitor itself—always monitor remotely!

Some applications, such as MSExchange, add counters and objects, allowing you to monitor application-specific statistics.

To control the chart view and sampling rate, choose Chart from the Options menu (see Figure 19.14). For example, suppose you're monitoring the size of a message queue. A periodic update of once per second might be gross overkill; a more realistic time slice might be once every 15 or 30 seconds.

The Chart Options dialog box also lets you select appearance-related details, such as whether the grid lines appear.

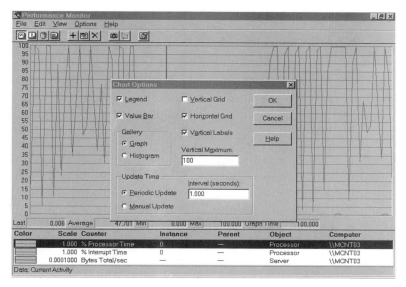

Task Manager

The Task Manager, shown in Figure 19.15, gives you a quick look at CPU usage and
memory utilization. To start Task Manager, press Ctrl+Alt+Del and then click the Task
Manager button. If you select the Processes tab (see Figure 19.16), you can view the
active processes and even terminate tasks.

FIGURE **19.15**

*Task Manager showing
memory and CPU
usage.*

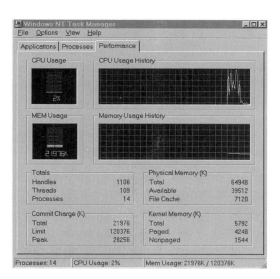

19

FIGURE **19.16**

Task Manager showing active processes.

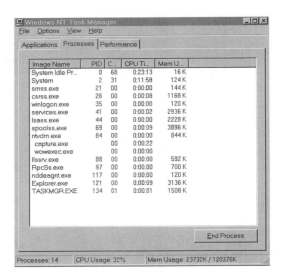

Event Viewer and the Event Logs

The Event Viewer (more specifically, the security log) is covered fairly thoroughly in Hour 17, "Advanced NT Server Management," when auditing is discussed. For troubleshooting purposes, however, you should always take a look at the system log. Many times, such as when a service fails to start, you find an entry in the log. Usually, the real problem is that one of the things the service depends on to start hasn't started. Make it a point to keep an eye on the event logs frequently—and *always* when you are troubleshooting.

Name Resolution

Earlier, when discussing the nbtstat command used to view the remote name cache table, I mentioned name resolution. *Name resolution* refers to the process of converting the computer's NetBIOS name to its IP address (and, ultimately, as discussed in the section about the arp command, to the MAC address).

For example, if you go to map a drive by typing \\mcnt05\c$ to connect to the hidden administrative share on the machine named mcnt05, NT tries to resolve this name in the following order:

1. It checks the NetBIOS name cache to see whether the name is already resolved. (You looked at this cache earlier this Hour in the section about using the nbtstat command.) If the name is in cache, then presto—it's resolved. No network activity is involved.

2. If the name isn't in cache, then three attempts are made to contact the NetBIOS name server (if one is configured). The WINS server discussed in Hour 17 is the NetBIOS name server in this case.

3. If the server still hasn't had success, then three broadcasts are sent, asking every machine on the network "Who is mcnt05?" Most routers are configured to not forward broadcasts, so the broadcasts are sent only to machines on the local network.

4. If no machines respond to the broadcast, the lmhosts file is parsed (read). If the name is here, it's then resolved (more about the lmhosts file in the next section).

5. If you still haven't had success resolving the name, NT gives host name resolution methods a try, so this step involves parsing the hosts file (more about the hosts file later this Hour).

6. If there's no entry in the hosts file, then the domain name server (DNS) is tried (provided that the Enable DNS for Windows Resolution check box, shown in Figure 19.17, on the Microsoft TCP/IP Properties dialog box is checked). A domain name server works very much like a WINS server (refer to Hour 17), except that a DNS server registers names like www.jpence.com or pc1959.jpence.com as opposed to local NetBIOS names, such as JohnsPC.

FIGURE 19.17

You can enable DNS for Windows resolution.

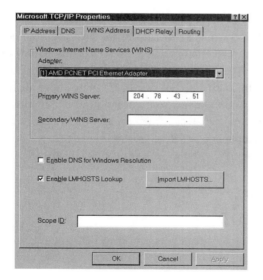

19

If none of these methods is successful, NT returns an error, which makes you swear mightily and jump up and down, wondering how you ever got into this line of work!

The `lmhosts` File

The `lmhosts` file is an ASCII text file that the system parses to see if the name you're trying to resolve has been entered there. Basically, the `lmhosts` file is simply a list of names and addresses. In `\winnt\system32\drivers\etc`, NT contains an `lmhosts.sam` file, which is self-documenting. The actual `lmhosts` file needs to be named `lmhosts`, not `lmhosts.sam`, but you can simply copy the `lmhosts.sam` file to `lmhosts` and then edit the file as needed.

If you take a look at the `lmhosts.sam` file, you'll probably notice that it looks a bit complicated. This looks a bit simpler:

```
204.78.43.52  mcnt05 #PRE  #DOM:mcdm01
```

That's it—the entire `lmhosts` file. In this instance, there's only one entry, and it's preloaded. As a point of interest, the *LM* stands for LAN Manager, which was the forerunner of Windows NT. `Lmhosts` is necessary because NetBEUI and NetBIOS are not routable protocols. This system of `lmhosts` files has been around for a long, long time and will work with all Windows and DOS workstations running a Microsoft TCP/IP stack.

The `hosts` File

By default, the NetBIOS name is the same as the host name (of course, that doesn't mean that host names and NetBIOS names are always the same). Host name resolution resolves the names of TCP/IP resources that don't connect through the NetBIOS interface. An example of this is a Web browser or IP applications such as PING, FTP, and Telnet. When troubleshooting name resolution issues, it's important to know whether the application is resolving a NetBIOS name or a host name. Like the `lmhosts.sam` file, NT also comes with a sample `hosts` file in `\winnt\system32\drivers\etc`. Check it out on your system. You'll see it's nothing but a simple ASCII text file listing addresses and names.

Network Monitor

If you really want to know what's going on with your system, you have to look at the wire. When you can capture and display packets and start to understand what you're seeing, then there's no network problem you can't solve. Network Monitor is a protocol analyzer; using it is like putting a phone tap on your network. A protocol analyzer captures and displays every packet on the network. Network Monitor needs to be installed like all the other services. Go to the Services tab of the Network Properties screen and then add Network Monitor Tools and Agent. After it's installed, you will have a new addition in the Administrative Tools menu: Network Monitor. Start Network Monitor, and then click the Start Capture button on the toolbar.

> There's no better way to learn networking than to use a protocol analyzer and study the captures.

In Figure 19.18, Network Monitor has been started and has a capture running. A command was issued from server \\mcnt03 to map a drive to server \\mcnt05. The capture was then stopped and displayed, as shown in Figure 19.18. Here, you're looking at the summary view of each frame after the capture is stopped.

FIGURE 19.18

Network Monitor with a capture running.

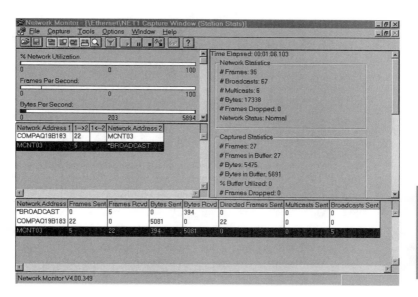

Notice that the first frame in Figure 19.19 is an ARP request, with the source computer being MCNT03 and the destination being a broadcast. Why ARP? Hint: Remember the one-line lmhosts file in the previous lmhosts section? And remember from the name resolution section that the remote name cache is tried before anything else? If the name is preloaded, then it's in the cache. You can start to see now how it all ties together! Because MCNT03 already knows the IP address of MCNT05, now you need the hardware (MAC) address of MCNT05—and isn't that what ARP does for you?

FIGURE **19.19**

The summary view of each frame captured.

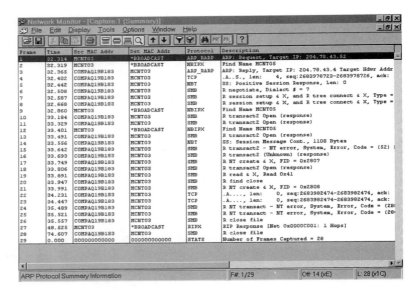

Why a broadcast destination? You know only the IP address you are trying to reach. To send a packet, however, your NIC needs the destination MAC address, so you have no choice but to broadcast. All the machines will see the broadcast packet, but only one will answer the call.

Figure 19.20 goes a step further, showing the detail view of the ARP frame. You can see that the sender's hardware and protocol addresses have been supplied so that when 204.78.43.52 answers, it can send the response directly to you. Also notice that even though you know the destination protocol address of 204.78.43.52, the destination, or target, hardware address is all zeros. This is what MCNT05 fills in for you in the ARP reply. Additionally, you can see that frame #3 is the ARP reply. This time, it's a directed packet from the Compaq Fast Ethernet NIC in MCNT05 to MCNT03.

Summary

What shows up when browsing Network Neighborhood can't be trusted. As a browser client, you get a list of backup browsers from the master browser, and then you get a browse list. Finally, you contact the actual server on the list to see what resources that server is offering. Because of the timing of servers advertising their availability, and the timing of backup browsers getting a copy of the browse list from the master browser, resources that aren't available might show up for as long as 51 minutes.

FIGURE 19.20

Drilling down to look at the detail view of the ARP packet.

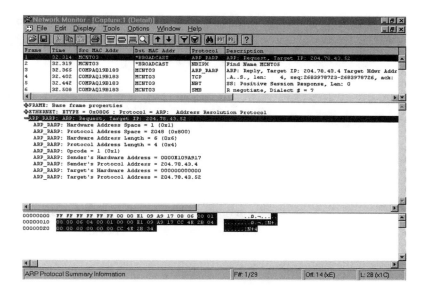

You then had a quick introduction to some utilities, both command-line tools and GUI programs. These utilities can help you troubleshoot your system by gathering information you need to solve the problem, whether it's related to name resolution or to other issues.

Network Monitor lets you put a "phone tap" on your network wiring and actually capture and display conversations between machines. When you have the ability to capture packets and understand the trace, there's no network problem you can't solve.

19

Workshop

Q&A

Q Do I need to be able to see resources when browsing Network Neighborhood to connect to them?

A Absolutely not. It's possible for resources to show up in the browse list when they are not available, and vice versa.

Q What is `ping`?

A The `ping` command is like sonar for your network. You "Ping" your destination, and you should get an answer, or "echo," back to verify connectivity.

Q **Is it possible to identify the route a packet is taking from source to destination?**

A This can be done with the tracert utility.

Q **What is ARP?**

A ARP is the Address Resolution Protocol. After you have the IP address the destination for your data, you need the hardware, or MAC address, to send it. ARP is used to get this information.

Q **What is the lmhosts file?**

A The lmhosts file is an ASCII text file containing mappings of NetBIOS names to IP addresses.

Q **Is it possible to actually see what's happening on the wire?**

A The Network Monitor program, a protocol analyzer, can be used to capture and display what's happening on the wire. These frames can then be analyzed to understand the conversation.

Quiz

1. It's possible for a resource to show up when you're browsing Network Neighborhood for up to _____ minutes after the resource has become unavailable.

2. True or False: As a browser client, you get the available resources, the browse list, from the master browser.

3. True or False: On an NT workstation, to get the current IP configuration, you run the winipcfg program.

4. To document your NT server, you might use what utility?

5. The nbtstat -c command gives you what information?

6. True or False: ARP is the protocol used to find an IP address when you know the destination hardware address.

7. To get real-time statistical information about your server, you could run _____.

HOUR **20**

Connecting Your Windows 98 Desktop to the Internet

Overview

If you've read Parts II and III before getting here, you already know everything you need to connect your Windows 98 and Windows NT desktops into a LAN. This Hour shows you how to connect your desktop to the "big network" known as the Internet.

Because most of you are using Windows 98 at home to connect to the Internet, this Hour covers the necessary information using Windows 98 as the vehicle; however, the same concepts apply to Windows NT. The following topics are covered:

- Selecting and installing a modem
- Selecting an ISP (Internet Service Provider)

- Installing and configuring Dial-Up Networking (DUN)
- Troubleshooting your Internet connection

Selecting and Installing a Modem

To make an informed decision on choosing a modem, you should know what a modem is and what the standards are. A *modem* (an acronym for *modulator-demodulator*) is a device that enables a computer to transmit data over telephone lines. Computer information is stored digitally, but information transmitted over telephone lines is transmitted in the form of analog waves. A modem converts between these two forms.

Modems come in two types: external and internal. An external modem can be attached to any computer that has a serial port, which almost all personal computers have. There are also modems that come as an expansion board you can insert into a vacant slot. They are generally referred to as *internal modems*. When deciding between an external modem and an internal modem, here are some questions you should think about:

- Do you have an empty slot in your computer for an internal modem?
- Do you sometimes need to move the modem from one computer to another?
- Do you have room in your work area for an external modem?
- Do you have a serial port that can be tied up by the external modem?

 If your computer has a USB port, consider buying a USB modem because it provides much higher throughput than a standard modem can. There are also parallel port modems, but they're not as common as the serial port–based modem.

If you're not mechanically inclined or have a pet (such as a cat) that roams near your computer, an internal modem is generally a better choice.

 When buying an external high-speed modem, you should check to see if your computer has a 16550 or better UART. If not, you can't run the modem at its highest speed. Fortunately, just about every new computer you buy today has the new UART. For more information about what a UART is, refer back to Hour 4, "Direct Cable Connection Network."

Modem Basics

To be comfortable when you're selecting and working with modems, you should be familiar with the following terms:

- **Bps**   How fast the modem can transmit and receive data. At slow rates, modems are measured in terms of baud rates. The slowest rate is 300 baud (about 25 cps, or characters per second). At higher speeds, modems are measured in terms of bits per second (bps). At the time of this writing, the fastest modems run at 57,600bps (56Kbps), although they can achieve even higher data transfer rates by compressing the data. Obviously, the faster the transmission rate, the faster you can send and receive data.

> You can't receive data any faster than it's being sent. If, for example, the device sending data to your computer is sending it at 2,400bps, you must receive it at 2,400bps. It doesn't always pay, therefore, to be on the "bleeding edge" and have a very fast modem if the other modem you're communicating with is a slower model. In addition, some telephone lines can't transmit data reliably at very high rates.

- **Data compression**   Some modems perform data compression, which enables them to send data at faster rates. However, the modem at the receiving end must be able to decompress the data using the same compression technique.
- **Full/half duplex**   *Full duplex* refers to the transmission of data in two directions simultaneously. For example, a telephone is a full-duplex device because both parties can talk at once. In contrast, a walkie-talkie is a *half-duplex* device because only one party can transmit at a time.
- **Flash memory**   Some modems come with flash memory rather than conventional ROM (Read-Only Memory), which means that the communications protocols can be easily updated if necessary.
- **FAX capability**   Most modern modems are FAX modems (as well as voice/data), which means they can send and receive faxes.

Modem Standards

Although the modem interfaces are standardized, there are different protocols for formatting data to be transmitted over telephone lines. Some, like CCITT V.34, are official standards, but others have been developed by private companies. Most modems have built-in support for the more common protocols—at least at slow data transmission

20

speeds, most modems can communicate with each other. At high transmission speeds, however, the protocols are less standardized. The popular data communication standards used by modems are shown in Table 20.1.

CCITT is the abbreviation of Comité Consultatif International Téléphonique et Télégraphique, an organization that sets international communications standards. CCITT, now known as ITU (International Telecommunication Union, the parent organization) has defined many important standards for data communications, including FAX standards.

TABLE 20.1   DATA COMMUNICATIONS PROTOCOLS.

Protocol	Maximum Transmission Rate	Duplex Mode
Bell 103	300bps	Full
CCITT V.21	300bps	Full
Bell 212A	1,200bps	Full
ITU V.22	1,200bps	Half
ITU V.22bis	2,400bps	Full
ITU V.29	9,600bps	Half
ITU V.32	9,600bps	Full
ITU V.32bis	14.4Kbps	Full
ITU V.34	36.6Kbps	Full
ITU V.90	56.6Kbps	Full

Here's a brief description of each of the protocols:

- **V.21**   The standard for full-duplex communication at 300 baud in Japan and Europe. In the United States, Bell 103 is used in place of V.21.
- **V.22**   The standard for half-duplex communication at 1,200bps in Japan and Europe. In the United States, the protocol defined by Bell 212A is more common.
- **V.22bis**   The worldwide standard for full-duplex modems sending and receiving data across telephone lines at 1,200 or 2,400bps.
- **V.29**   The standard for half-duplex modems sending and receiving data across telephone lines at 1,200, 2,400, 4,800, or 9,600bps. This is the protocol used by FAX modems.
- **V.32**   The standard for full-duplex modems sending and receiving data across phone lines at 4,800 or 9,600bps. V.32 modems automatically adjust their transmission speeds based on the quality of the lines.

- **V.32bis**   The V.32 protocol extended to speeds of 7,200, 12,000, and 14,400bps.
- **V.34**   The standard for full-duplex modems sending and receiving data across phone lines at up to 28.8Kbps. V.34 modems automatically adjust their transmission speeds based on the quality of the lines.
- **V.90**   The standard for full-duplex modems sending and receiving data across phone lines at up to 57,600bps.

There are also two data compression standards you might encounter:

- **V.42**   An error-detection standard for high-speed modems. V.42 can be used with digital telephone networks.
- **V.42bis**   A data compression protocol that can enable modems to achieve a data transfer rate of 34,000bps.

The next time you see a modem being advertised as "conforming to V.90 and supporting V.42," you know what that means!

Installing a Modem

Before you can use any communication software, such as HyperTerminal, you need to tell Windows 98 what kind of modem you have. The exact steps for installing a modem differ slightly depending on whether you've already installed a modem in Windows 98. If the modem was connected to the computer when Windows 98 was being installed, chances are good that the modem was detected and the modem driver installed.

The following steps take you through installing your first modem in Windows 98—it's assumed your modem has been physically installed on the computer:

1. Double-click the Modems icon in Control Panel to bring up the Install New Modem Wizard.

2. If your computer is a laptop, the first dialog box asks for the type of modem to install: PCMCIA modem card or Other. Select the appropriate type and then click Next.

3. If you selected PCMCIA modem card, you're prompted to insert the card. After you've done so, skip to step 8.

4. If the modem isn't yet attached to the computer, enable the Don't Detect My Modem; I Will Select It from a List check box. Otherwise, leave it unchecked. Click Next to continue.

5. If you've asked Windows 98 to detect the modem, it queries all your serial ports to see whether a modem is attached. When it's done, it displays the name of the modem it found. If the displayed information is incorrect, click Change. Otherwise, click Next and skip to step 7.

20

6. If you're manually selecting the modem, you see the dialog box shown in Figure 20.1. As you did when installing network adapters, use the Manufacturers and Models lists to highlight your modem, and then click Next. If your modem isn't in the list, you have two choices. First, you can select (Standard Modem Types) from the Manufacturers list and choose one of the standard modems from the Models list that corresponds to the speed of your modem. Second, if you have a driver disk for your modem from the manufacturer, click Have Disk and follow the onscreen prompts.

FIGURE 20.1

Select your modem in this dialog box.

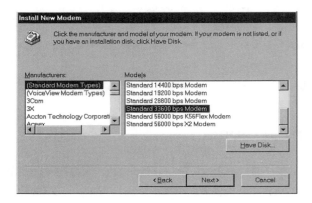

7. The next dialog box (see Figure 20.2) asks you to select a serial port. Highlight the appropriate port and click Next. If dialing properties (such as your area code and long distance access methods) weren't previously defined, you're asked to enter them.

FIGURE 20.2

Select a serial port in this dialog box.

8. After Windows 98 installs your modem, click Finish.

After you've installed your first modem, the Modems Properties dialog box (see Figure 20.3) is displayed. Also, the next time you open the Modems icon, Windows 98 displays the Modems Properties dialog box.

FIGURE 20.3

The Modems Properties dialog box lists your currently installed modem. PCMCIA modems have a card icon to their left; regular modems are identified by a telephone icon.

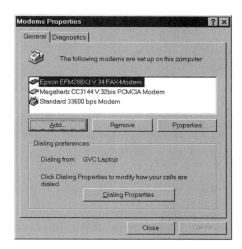

To add a modem from the Modems Properties dialog box, click the Add button and follow the steps outlined previously. If you need to change the settings of a particular modem, highlight it from the display list and click Properties. To remove an installed modem, highlight the modem and click Remove.

If you have call waiting on your telephone line, you should disable it before initiating a data call with your modem. To do this, click the Dialing Properties button in the Modems Properties dialog box, and enable the To Disable Call Waiting, Dial: check box. From its drop-down list, select the appropriate sequence. If you're unsure, check with your local phone company. If the sequence you need is not one of the listed ones (*70, 70#, or 1170), simply enter yours in the text box. Click Apply or OK to save the change.

Choosing an Internet Service Provider

One of the most challenging aspects of using the Internet is not the learning curve on how to use a dozen new programs or even finding out about all the interesting places to explore. The biggest challenge for most is finding Internet access.

20

Before you can surf the Net, you need to have access to a computer that's part of the network. This is much like buying a telephone—it doesn't work right out of the box. Before you can make that first call, you need to have arranged for service from your local telephone company. Similarly, you can't just connect into the Internet until you gain access to a computer that's part of the Net.

The Internet's equivalent of the phone company is an ISP, short for Internet Service Provider.

What Is an ISP?

An ISP is a company that gives you access to the Internet. For a monthly fee, it gives you a software package, a user name, a password, and an access phone number to its network (known as *Point of Presence*, or POP), which is in turn connected to the Internet.

In addition to serving individuals, ISPs also serve companies to supply a direct connection from the company's networks to the Internet. You find out more on how to connect your network to an ISP in Hour 22, "Connecting Your Network to the Internet."

ISP Features

Depending on whether you're looking for an ISP as a home user or a business, your ISP should offer certain features. As a home or small-business (where only a few people need to access the Internet simultaneously) user, your ISP should offer the following options:

- **PPP or SLIP dial-up access**   Point-to-Point Protocol (PPP) and Serial Line Internet Protocol (SLIP) are two types of dial-up IP links that connect your computer directly to the Internet while you're online—PPP dial-up access is the most common. You can run applications such as FTP, Telnet, Internet Explorer, and other Internet tools locally from your own computer. In essence, your computer becomes part of the Internet.

- **Multiple dial-up access numbers**   To make it easier for users, ISPs set up a "hunt group" on their bank of dial-up phone numbers so you need to know and dial only one number to gain access. However, depending on the service class you subscribe to, there might be additional access phone numbers you can use if the "public" one is busy.

- **Good dial-up modem port-to-user ratio**   Ideally, you'd like a ratio of 1-port-to-1-user. However, that's impractical, so ISPs generally maintain a ratio of 1-port-to-5-users or 1-port-to-10-users.

- **Local access**   The ISP's monthly charge might not be your only cost. If your ISP doesn't have a telephone number that's a local call from your location, you have to pay long-distance or toll telephone charges; all services that offer toll-free access using 800 and 888 numbers result in an extra charge on your regular connection charge.

- **Amount of disk storage** This option affects how much email you can receive. If you're using the ISP connect for business use, make sure you have lots of disk space (say, 5 or 10MB). Remember that because you get your email only when you connect to your ISP, it's stored on the ISP's server when it first arrives. Some ISPs count the space taken up by your email as part of your disk quota.

- **Web site storage** Almost all ISPs offer Web hosting service of one type or another. Even for individual users, ISPs often offer a 2 to 5MB Web site storage space so you can put up your own personal Web site. You should check to see if this disk space allotment is separate from or in addition to the regular disk storage space mentioned previously.

- **Speed** Your 56K modem won't justify its cost if your ISP doesn't support 56K connections. Find out what speeds are supported and if it has plans to support 56K (if it's not currently supported).

If your company needs to connect a large group of people who require simultaneous, extremely fast connections to the Net, dial-up access is not the best choice. If you need to connect 15 users who require simultaneous and permanent Internet connections, you should give serious consideration to dedicated lines. You find out how to do this later in Hour 22. Most of the preceding points still apply if you use a dedicated line, and here are some additional considerations:

- **Types of high-speed dedicated connections** There are different speeds for dedicated leased lines, such as T1 (1.544Mbps), fractional-T1 (56Kbps), 64Kbps ISDN (Integrated Services Digital Network), and 128Kbps ISDN. Some ISPs also offer dedicated dial-ups over POTS (plain old telephone service) so you can leave your modem connected 24 hours per day, seven days a week, instead of the additional expense associated with leased lines. Your ISP should have a reasonably priced option that fits your needs.

- **Global dial-in access** If your users need to travel to different parts of the country or the world, your chosen ISP should provide local dial-up or toll-free dial-up access from all over the globe so your users can easily call into your network and check for email and so on.

- **Reliability** Nothing in the world is more frustrating than trying to send an urgent proposal to a client by email only to find you can't get through to your ISP. Although there are scheduled downtimes (usually during the wee hours of the night), you should be able to hit the Net during normal business hours without any problems. If you often have trouble getting through during normal business hours, it's time to look for a different ISP.

20

Alternatives to Dial-Up Connections

Instead of the more expensive dedicated leased-line technology such as T1, ISDNs are often a favorite alternative. Depending on your location, you can get ISDN service for home use for as low as $20/month. However, to get it (often through telephone companies), your local telephone company must support digital switches and run special lines to your location. ISDN service might be offered as a metered service, in which you get so much traffic for a base rate and then additional costs when you go over, or you can get it for a flat fee regardless of the amount of traffic. Because digital service is required, you might not be able to get ISDN service into older apartment buildings or remote locations.

Recently, two new dedicated leased line–type technologies have been implemented by ISPs that can be considered alternatives to ISDN. One is cable modem and the other is ADSL (pronounced as separate letters; short for Asymmetric Digital Subscriber Line). A cable modem, generally supplied by the ISP, connects to your TV cable outlet, and you plug a cross-over 10BaseT Ethernet cable between your computer's Ethernet card and the cable modem. (At the time of this writing, only Ethernet is supported for cable modem use.) Cable modem service is generally available only in the newer areas of larger cities because the TV cable network needs to be running over fiber-optics.

ADSL is a new technology that allows more data to be sent over existing copper telephone lines (POTS). It supports data rates from 1.5 to 9Mbps when receiving data (known as the downstream rate) and from 16 to 640Kbps when sending data (known as the upstream rate).

Like cable modem connections, ADSL requires a special ADSL modem. It isn't currently available to the general public except in some major cities, but many believe it will be one of the more popular choices for Internet access over the next few years.

Among the three options mentioned here, cable modems seem to be the most popular choice today because it's much easier to get cable service than, for example, ISDN service.

On the other hand, given the low cost of 56K modems (much less than $200), you might be tempted to opt for a dedicated 56K dial-up connection for your office's Internet connection. This would generally be enough for Web browsing and email, but do remember that 56K refers to *download* speeds only. Because these modems upload data at a relatively modest 28.8Kbps or 33.6Kbps, they're not ideal for two-way, data-intensive applications. If you plan to video-conference or serve a Web site from your office, consider going with 64Kbps ISDN instead.

Comparing ISPs

Offering access to the Internet represents a rapidly growing class of business, and ISPs come in all forms, sizes and shapes. As a result, prices vary widely, but so do levels of service, reliability, and the odds that your ISP will be around at the end of the month. Here are five of the most common questions you should ask when choosing an ISP:

- How do I separate the sheep from the goats?
- How much should I pay?
- What if I have to move?
- Is it local or national?
- Should I wait?

Here are some answers (including caveats) to these questions.

How do I separate the sheep from the goats? Consider these issues:

- Find somebody with experience who's been using an ISP for at least three months and approves strongly of it (and isn't a shareholder in that ISP).

- Find out the port-to-user ratio of the ISP. This number is often publicized by the ISP, so you can easily find out. Pick one that has a ratio of about 15 or fewer users per modem.

- Find out what kind of a "pipe" the ISP has out to the Internet (56K, T1, 10Mbps, and so on) and, combined with the first two issues listed here, pick the ISP with the largest pipe. Some ISPs "piggyback" off other ISPs' connections, so if an ISP has a direct high-speed (T3 or better) connection to the Internet backbone, it's a winner.

- Find out how many employees the ISP has and what range of services is offered. In general, the wider the base, the more likely it is that your service level and reliability will remain high.

- If all else fails, pick the one with the name you like best or the one that's been in business the longest.

20

How much should I pay? Not too little and not too much. As the saying goes: "You get what you pay for…eventually." In some large cities, you can pay as little as $20.00 per month for unlimited hours. In this case, the ISP trusts that the "average" user is on for little more than an hour a day, which is generally *not* the case.

To provide high-quality service and make a decent living, an ISP might charge anywhere from $1.00 to $2.00 per hour in most cities. Everything changes rapidly in this business, however, and if the ISP doesn't make a profit, three things happen: The users-per-modem ratio creeps up, the level of service declines, and the equipment in use becomes unreliable and obsolete.

One standard piece of advice is to never sign up for the yearly rate, however attractive. Try a month first, and then perhaps three months. You don't want to be stuck with a "lemon."

What if I have to move? It's not the end of the world. The Internet was designed for mobility. You take with you your experience, your data, and your software tools.

What you leave behind is your email address of *username@domain*; if you have your own domain, however, you can have it transferred to the new ISP. The more important that is, the more care you should take in your initial selection. A good ISP makes your move easier if you do decide to jump ship and will set up an alias for a short time so that your email gets forwarded automatically.

Is it local or national? In the next 12 months, there will be many new entrants into the ISP business. A lot of national and international firms are telling their investors that they're going to get rich by becoming the GM of Internet provisioning. Well, do the U.S.-based readers remember Prodigy? (And do the Canadian readers remember Unitel?) If you need to access the Net from different cities or countries, it would serve you better to pick an ISP that has global POPs.

Big is not necessarily better, but if "Big" is losing a lot of money trying to buy market share, then maybe you ought to take advantage. If you do have to make this choice, remember the other advice here about selecting and divorcing from an ISP. Bear in mind that the port-to-user ratio will likely be poor and that there will probably be congested traffic on the ISP's link to the Internet.

Should I wait? No. This is the simplest question to answer. Only if you live in a town where there's only one ISP and it's charging more than $3.00 an hour should you wait. If there's only one ISP, then there's probably a reason for that in the short term. In the longer term, some competition will arrive. If you live in an urban area where there are several ISPs, then prices are probably already reasonable. Besides, like computer hardware, there's always something newer tomorrow, and you can end up waiting forever!

Is your head pounding yet from all this information? Grab yourself a cup of coffee, call up some friends who are already on the Net, and find out who their ISPs are and what they think of them.

If you have an ISP now, how does it rate when you apply the five selection criteria to your own ISP and your friends' ISPs?

Dial-Up Networking

The component in Windows 98 and Windows NT that enables you to connect your computer to a network (such as the Internet) through a modem is called *Dial-Up Networking*, more commonly referred to as DUN. In this section, you find out how to set up DUN for your Internet access.

Setting Up DUN

Setting up and configuring DUN on your Windows 98 machine for Internet access involves four steps, each explained in more detail in the following sections:

1. Install the Dial-Up Adapter, if needed.

2. Configure the Dial-Up Adapter.

3. Create a new DUN *connectoid*, which is a profile that contains information for a given server you're connecting to.

4. Configure the connectoid. Then you can copy a connectoid shortcut to your desktop so that all you need to do to make a connection is double-click the connectoid icon.

> If you didn't install the DUN component when installing Windows 98, refer to the "Q&A" section to see how to install it from your Windows source disk.

Installing the Dial-Up Adapter

Windows 98 automatically installs the Dial-Up Adapter when DUN is installed. If for some reason it isn't listed in the Network properties sheet, you can manually install it as follows:

1. Open the Network icon from the Control Panel.

2. In the Network properties sheet, click Add.

3. In the Select Network Component Type dialog box, highlight Adapter and click Add.

4. In the Select Network Adapters dialog box, highlight Microsoft in the Manufacturers list and then highlight Dial-Up Adapter in the Network Adapters list.

5. Click OK to return to the Network properties sheet.

20

You should now see Dial-Up Adapter listed as one of the installed network components.

Configuring the Dial-Up Adapter

After the Dial-Up Adapter is installed, you need to perform the following tasks to configure it:

- If the TCP/IP protocol isn't installed, you need to install it and bind it to the Dial-Up Adapter. Refer to Hour 5, "Installing a Two-Node Peer-to-Peer Windows 98 Network," for details. (However, you don't need to configure the TCP/IP properties associated with the Dial-Up Adapter. That's taken care of by the connectoids discussed in the following section.)

> If you're using DUN to connect a RAS server (such as a Windows NT computer), you need to make sure that a common protocol is used between the remote computer and the RAS server and that this common protocol is bound to the Dial-Up Adapter.

- The next task is setting Dial-Up Adapter properties. There are four that you can configure. You'll find them listed in the Advanced tab of the Dial-Up Adapter properties sheet (see Figure 20.4):

  Enable Point To Point IP   Use this setting to enable or disable PPP over the Dial-Up Adapter. If you set it to No, SLIP is used instead.

  IP Packet Size   Use this property to select the relative size (known as an MTU, Maximum Transfer Unit) of the IP packets used by the Dial-Up Adapter. Generally, the larger the packet size, the better the performance. However, depending on the configuration of the remote system, a large MTU could actually cause connection problems if the other side can't handle your MTU. This parameter should generally be left at its default setting unless you have good reason to change it.

  Record a Log File   If you select Yes, DUN creates a text file named `ppplog.txt` in your main Windows 98 folder and uses this file to maintain a record of each session.

> Because of the extra overhead posted by maintaining the log file, you shouldn't enable it except for troubleshooting purposes.

Use IPX Header Compression   This setting is useful only if you're calling into a server that supports IPX and supports IPX header compression. It has no effect on your Internet connections.

FIGURE 20.4

The Advanced tab of the Dial-Up Adapter Properties dialog box.

Creating a New DUN Connectoid

With the Dial-Up Adapter installed and configured, you're now ready to create your connectoid. Each connectoid corresponds to a profile for a server you'll be calling and contains settings such as the phone number, server type (such as PPP or SLIP), and the modem to use.

You can access DUN in one of two ways:

- Open the DUN folder in My Computer.
- Choose Start | Programs | Accessories | Communications | Dial-Up Networking.

The first time you start DUN, the Make New Connection Wizard automatically starts up and give you a little introduction. Click Next.

Otherwise, the DUN folder opens up and shows your existing connectoids (see Figure 20.5). To create a new connectoid, start the wizard with one of the following two methods:

- Double-click the Make New Connection icon.
- Choose Connections | Make New Connection.

20

FIGURE 20.5

The DUN folder show-ing your existing connectoids.

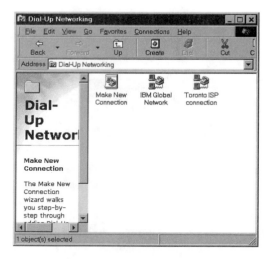

 If you haven't installed a modem at this point, the Install New Modem Wizard is launched by the Make New Connection Wizard.

The first of the Make New Connection dialog boxes asks you to enter a name to identify the connection and select the modem you want to use for this connection (see Figure 20.6). Click the Configure button if you need to adjust any modem settings. When you're done, click Next.

FIGURE 20.6

Use this dialog box to enter a name for your connection and select a modem.

The wizard then displays the dialog box shown in Figure 20.7. Enter the area code, telephone number, and country code for the server you're connecting to, and then click Next. In the final dialog box, click Finish.

FIGURE 20.7

Enter the telephone number for your server in this dialog box.

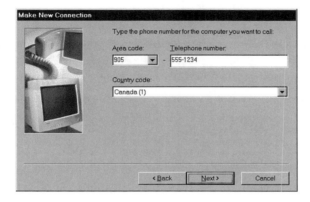

Configuring the Connectoid

You now need to customize the connectoid you just created. For example, you need to specify how the IP address is to be assigned and what the IP addresses for the DNS servers are. To change the connectoid's properties, highlight its icon in the DUN folder, and then either choose File|Properties or right-click the icon and select Properties from the context menu. You then see the dialog box shown in Figure 20.8.

FIGURE 20.8

The properties sheet of a DUN connectoid. The Server Types tab is shown here.

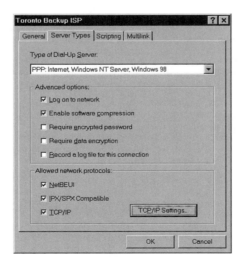

20

Most of the settings you see are straightforward. You generally need to change properties only in the Server Types tab. The relevant ones are as follows:

- **Type of Dial-Up Server**   Use the drop-down list to specify the dial-up protocol (such as PPP) to use with this dial-up server.

- **Log On to Network**   If this is checked, DUN attempts to log on to the dial-up server with the user name and password you used to log on to Windows 98. Unless your Windows 98 and your Internet logons share the same user name and password, it's best to leave this unchecked.

- **Enable Software Compression**   When this is checked, data is compressed before it's transmitted between your computer and the server. Compression occurs only if both computers are using compatible compression protocols.

- **Record a Log File for This Connection**   When this is checked, DUN maintains a log of all connection activity.

- **Allowed Network Protocols**   You can specify which of the three protocols (NetBEUI, IPX, and TCP/IP) is used with this connectoid. For Internet connections, you need only TCP/IP.

You also need to define the connection-specific TCP/IP properties by clicking the TCP/IP Settings button (see Figure 20.9). Unless you have a dedicated dial-up connection with your ISP, your IP address and name server (DNS) addresses are generally assigned by the dial-up server. You should make sure the following three selections are made, unless otherwise instructed by your ISP:

- Server Assigned IP Address.
- Server Assigned Name Server Addresses.
- Use Default Gateway on Remote Network. This setting causes your computer to route IP traffic to the WAN connection by default.

When connecting to the Internet through PPP, you should also check the Use IP Header Compression check box because it allows DUN to optimize data transfer between computers by compressing the IP header information.

FIGURE 20.9

Specify your connection-specific TCP/IP properties in this dialog box.

TCP/IP Settings

- ⦿ Server assigned IP address
- ○ Specify an IP address
  - IP address: 0 . 0 . 0 . 0

- ⦿ Server assigned name server addresses
- ○ Specify name server addresses
  - Primary DNS: 0 . 0 . 0 . 0
  - Secondary DNS: 0 . 0 . 0 . 0
  - Primary WINS: 0 . 0 . 0 . 0
  - Secondary WINS: 0 . 0 . 0 . 0

- ☑ Use IP header compression
- ☑ Use default gateway on remote network

OK   Cancel

If your ISP supports the PPP Multilink Protocol (and not many ISPs do at the time of this writing) dial-up access, you can use the Multilink tab to specify additional devices to use with the connectoid (see Figure 20.10). PPP Multilink Protocol, or *multilink channel aggregation*, is a standard technology that enables you to combine the bandwidth of two or more PPP connections and use the extended bandwidth as one. For example, if you have two 56K modems attached to two separate telephone lines, multilink PPP establishes a connection on both lines and then manages simultaneous data transfer on the two lines; you have an effective bandwidth of 112Kbps.

FIGURE 20.10

Use this dialog box to specify additional devices for your multilink PPP connection.

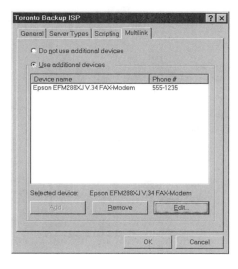

Toronto Backup ISP

General | Server Types | Scripting | Multilink

- ○ Do not use additional devices
- ⦿ Use additional devices

Device name	Phone #
Epson EFM288XJ V.34 FAX-Modem	555-1235

Selected device: Epson EFM288XJ V.34 FAX-Modem

Add...   Remove   Edit...

OK   Cancel

20

The multilink PPP technology has been in use by the ISDN community for several years to combine two 64Kbps B channels to provide a maximum transmission speed of 128Kbps.

To set up a multilink PPP connection, follow these steps:

1. Display the Multilink tab of the connectoid.
2. Select the option for Use Additional Devices.
3. Click Add to bring up the Edit Extra Device dialog box.
4. Use the drop-down Device Name list to select another modem or device (such as an ISDN modem), enter the telephone number the device should dial, and then click OK.
5. Repeat steps 3 and 4 to add more devices.

Because you need to specify a user name and password when logging on to your ISP, in the Scripting tab you can specify a script that runs after the connection to your ISP is established to automate the logon (see Figure 20.11). You can easily customize the sample scripts included with Windows 98 for your use, or you can contact your ISP's technical support for a DUN script that has already been customized for its environment. (If you're using CompuServe as your ISP, you can use the `cis.scp` script as is without any changes.)

FIGURE 20.11

Use the Scripting tab to specify a script to automate the logon process to your ISP.

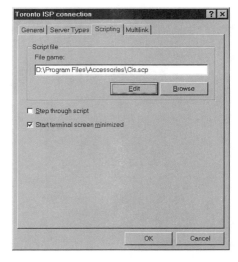

Turning Off File and Print Sharing

There's one more thing to check on before testing your ISP connection. Recall from Hour 6, "Sharing Windows 98 Resources," that when you have the File and Print Sharing service enabled, other users on your network can access any folders, drives, and printers you have shared. If you bound the File and Print Sharing service to your Dial-Up Adapter's TCP/IP protocol, you'll be making your shared resources available to the Internet as a whole, so *anyone* on the Internet can access your shares!

For someone on the Internet to gain access to your shares over your DUN connection, the following conditions must be satisfied:

- The remote user's computer must be running Microsoft Networking.
- The remote user needs to know your IP address and the NetBIOS name of your computer.
- The remote user needs to have an entry in his or her own lmhosts file that includes your IP address and NetBIOS name.

> The lmhosts file, similar to the hosts file, was discussed in Hour 19, "Troubleshooting."

When these conditions are met (which isn't difficult for someone who knows what he or she is doing), the remote user can access your shares by using the NET commands from a DOS prompt.

It's because of this potential security risk that Windows 98 does a check before making a DUN connection that uses IP. It checks to make sure your TCP/IP protocol bound to the Dial-Up Adapter isn't also bound to the File and Print Sharing service.

To protect yourself, make sure the File and Print Sharing service is not bound to the TCP/IP protocol of your Dial-Up Adapter. If your connection to the Internet is through a LAN connection, ensure that the File and Print Sharing service is not bound to the TCP/IP protocol of your network adapter. You can, however, still share resources by using another protocol, such as NetBEUI.

20

> If your network uses TCP/IP only, then it might be impractical to disable the File and Print Sharing service. Your alternative is to set up a reasonable level of security (such as using share-level or user-level security) to protect the resources you share.

Connecting to the Internet

With the security issue taken care of, you're now ready to connect to your ISP by using DUN. You can use any one of the following methods to make the connection

- Double-click the connectoid icon in the DUN folder.
- Highlight the connectoid icon and choose Connections|Connect.
- Right-click the connectoid icon and select Connect from the context menu.

Depending on the DUN setting, the Connect To dialog box (see Figure 20.12) is displayed. Enter your user name and password. This information is passed to the script as part of the logon process. When you're ready to make the connection, click Connect.

FIGURE 20.12

You can make some last-minute changes in the Connect To dialog box before making the connection.

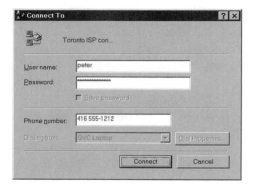

The Connect To dialog box can be bypassed if you uncheck the Prompt for Information Before Dialing check box in the DUN settings. To open the DUN settings dialog box, choose Communications|Settings.

All being well, you should hear your modem burst into life when DUN establishes the connection with your ISP!

If your logon script is working correctly, you then see the brief message "Verifying user name and password" as DUN establishes your connection, and then the Connection Established dialog box is displayed (see Figure 20.13).

FIGURE 20.13

The dialog box show-ing you've successfully made a DUN connec-tion.

Congratulations! Your computer is now a full-fledged peer of the Internet. You can surf the Net using Internet Explorer and other Internet toys. You'll find a discussion of the most common Internet surfing tools in Hour 21, "Surfing Tools."

If you want to check the time duration of your session or disconnect from the network, double-click the DUN icon in the system tray to bring up the dialog box shown in Figure 20.14.

FIGURE 20.14

The DUN connection status dialog box.

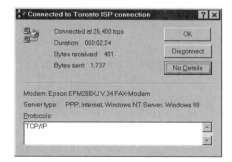

You owe yourself a pat on the back and a nice cup of java for the effort of getting your Windows 98 machine connected to the Internet.

Why don't you fire up Internet Explorer by double-clicking its icon on your desktop to get a quick preview of what's in store for you in Hour 21? With everything working correctly, you should see the home page of `http://home.microsoft.com` displayed.

20

Using the Internet Connection Wizard

Wouldn't it be nice if you had a wizard to guide you through the steps described earlier? If you're using Windows 98, you're in luck! The Internet Connection Wizard gives you an easy way to get your Windows 98 machine connected to the Internet. (If you're using Windows NT, sorry, but you have to slog through the steps for setting up DUN the old-fashioned way.)

In addition to walking you through the setup step-by-step, the wizard also helps you set up service accounts, such as ISP, Internet email, news, and directory service accounts. Otherwise, you have to manually configure those accounts separately. You can launch the Internet Connection Wizard by using one of the following methods:

> The wizard uses the term *account* to refer to the user name you have for your ISP as well as the configuration information necessary for Internet services, such as email and news.

- Open the Connect to the Internet icon on your Windows 98 desktop. (The icon is removed after you've gone through the wizard once.)
- Open the Internet Explorer icon on your Windows 98 desktop. (This method works only once. After you've gone through the wizard, opening the icon launches Internet Explorer.)
- Choose Start|Programs|Internet Explorer|Connection Wizard.

The opening dialog box offers you three choices:

- **I Want to Sign Up and Configure My Computer for a New Internet Account** Select this option if you don't have an existing ISP account.
- **I Have an Existing Internet Account Through My Phone Line or Local Area Network (LAN)** Select this option if you have an existing ISP account and just need to configure Windows 98.
- **My Computer Is Already Set Up for the Internet** Select this option if you already have an Internet connection set up. This choice exits the wizard right away.

Make your selection and click Next. The rest of this section assumes you selected the second option: I Have an Existing Internet Account Through My Phone Line or Local Area Network (LAN).

At this point or later in the process, depending on your machine's configuration, you might have to deal with the following:

- If you haven't already installed the Dial-Up Adapter or a modem, Windows 98 walks you through the necessary steps to install them.

- If you have more than one modem installed, the wizard displays the Choose Modem dialog box asking you to select the modem you want to use for your Internet connection.

- If you have TCP/IP installed and bound to the Dial-Up Adapter and the File and Print Sharing service bound to the TCP/IP of the Dial-Up Adapter, the wizard pops up a warning about a security issue (see the previous "Turning Off File and Print Sharing" section). Click OK to disable the file and print sharing, and click OK again to restart your computer.

With the basics taken care of, the wizard displays a dialog box (see Figure 20.15) asking if you're accessing the Internet through an ISP/LAN or using an online service such as The Microsoft Network. If you choose the online service option, the next dialog box indicates you should configure your online service by double-clicking its icon on the desktop or in the Online Services folder. Windows 98 is shipped with the setup kits for these services:

- America Online
- AT&T WorldNet Service
- CompuServe
- Prodigy Internet

If your service isn't listed, you need to install the software supplied by your online service provider.

20

FIGURE 20.15

Use this dialog box to select your connection type.

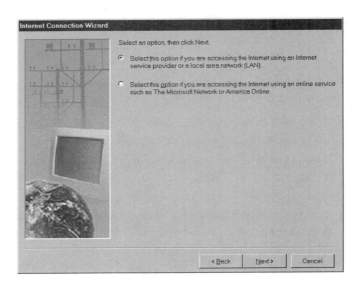

If you've picked the ISP or a LAN option, the next dialog box asks you to indicate whether you're using your telephone line or your LAN. Make your selection and then click Next.

Setting Up Your DUN Connectoid

If you're using a modem connection and have more than one modem defined, the wizard asks you to pick a modem. If you don't have any modems defined, the Install New Modem Wizard is launched. Follow the steps outlined in the previous "Installing a Modem" section.

If you've already created one or more DUN connectoids, the wizard asks whether you want to use one of them or create a new one (see Figure 20.16). The following assumes you're creating a new connectoid, so select Create a New Dial-Up Connection and then click Next.

The next dialog box asks for telephone and area code information for your ISP. Enter the information and then click Next. In the next dialog box (see Figure 20.17), enter the user name and password assigned by your ISP and then click Next.

FIGURE 20.16

Use this dialog box to select whether you're creating a new DUN connectoid or using an existing one for connecting to the Internet.

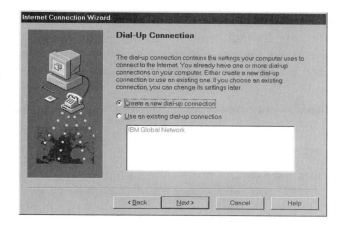

FIGURE 20.17

Enter the user name and password assigned by your ISP.

You're then asked if you need to adjust any advanced settings (such as connection type and IP address) for the connection. Select Yes and click Next. The next few dialog screens deal with the following:

- **Connection Type**   Whether your connection is a PPP or SLIP connection.
- **Logon Procedure**   Whether you need to enter information into a logon screen. You can assign a script to help automate the logon process.

20

- **IP Address**   Whether your ISP assigns you a new IP address automatically every time you connect or assigns a fixed IP number.
- **DNS Server Address**   Whether your ISP assigns you the IP address of its DNS server automatically every time you connect or you need to configure it before-hand.
- **Dial-Up Connection Name**   Enter a name to identify your new DUN connectoid.

After entering the name for your new connectoid, click Next to continue.

You are then asked three more questions if you selected the Connect Using My Local Area Network (LAN) option earlier. The three extra dialog boxes are for the following:

- **Proxy Server**   If your network has a proxy server, select Yes.
- **Proxy Server Name**   Enter the name of your proxy server and the port, if you selected Yes in the Proxy Server dialog box.
- **Proxy Server Exceptions**   List the IP addresses for which you don't want to use a proxy server.

> A proxy server can provide network security and enhance network performance. You'll read more about proxy servers in Hour 22.

Setting Up Your Internet Mail Service

The wizard next asks whether you want to configure your Internet email. Just about every ISP in the world offers email as part of the basic package, so you should select Yes and then click Next.

If you have previously installed and configured an email client, the wizard detects that and asks whether you'd like to create a new account or use an existing one. The following assumes you're creating a new account, so select Create a New Internet Mail Account and then click Next.

The next few dialog boxes ask you for the following information:

- **Your Name**   This is the name that appears in the From: field of your outgoing email messages.
- **Internet E-mail Address**   This is your email address as assigned by your ISP or email administrator.

- **E-mail Server Names** This is where you specify the type of your ISP's mail server (POP3 or IMAP) and the names of your incoming and outgoing mail servers (see Figure 20.18).

- **Internet Mail Logon** This is where you enter the user name and password required to access your email.

- **Friendly Name** Enter a name to identify this email account.

FIGURE 20.18

Enter the names of your incoming and outgoing mail servers in this dialog box.

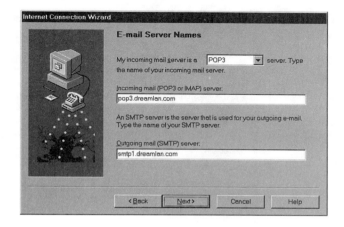

Setting Up Your Internet News Service

The wizard next asks whether you want to configure your Internet news service. If you want to access Usenet newsgroups, select Yes and then click Next. (For more information on Usenet newsgroups, see Hour 21.)

The next few dialog boxes ask you for the following information:

- **Your Name** This is the name that appears in the From: field of your outgoing email or newsgroup articles. It should be the same as the one you used for the email account earlier.

- **Internet News E-mail Address** This is your email address as assigned by your ISP or email administrator. It should be the same as the one you used for the email account earlier.

> One thing you'll find out rather quickly when using newsgroups is your potential for being *spammed*—getting flooded by junk mail. A common practice to avoid being spammed is to enter a modified email address in this field, such as *realname*@no-spam@*domain_name*.

20

- **Internet News Server Name**   This is where you specify the name of your news server (see Figure 20.19).
- **Internet News Server Logon**   If your news server requires you to log on, enter your user name and password in this dialog box.
- **Friendly Name**   Enter a name to identify this news account.

FIGURE 20.19

Enter the name of your news server in this dialog box.

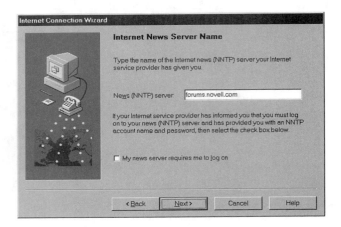

Setting Up Your Directory Service

The last set of wizard dialog boxes pertains to configuring your Internet directory service. If you want to access an LDAP (Lightweight Directory Access Protocol) database on the Internet, select Yes and then click Next. (For more information about LDAP, see the "Q&A" section.)

You can either create a new directory service provider or choose an existing one. A number of predefined LDAP providers are included with the wizard (see Figure 20.20).

FIGURE 20.20

Choose to use an existing LDAP provider or create a new one in this dialog box.

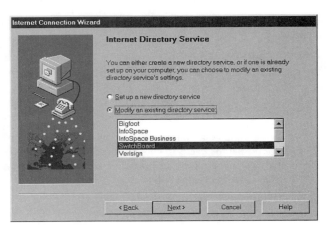

The next few dialog boxes ask you for the following information:

- **Internet Directory Server Name**   This is where you specify the name of your directory service (LDAP) server (see Figure 20.21).
- **Internet Directory Server Logon**   If your LDAP server requires you to log on, enter your user name and password in this dialog box.
- **Check E-mail Addresses**   Select whether you want your email program to check the email addresses of your message recipients using the specified LDAP server.
- **Friendly Name**   Enter a name to identify this news account.

FIGURE 20.21

Enter the name of your LDAP server in this dialog box.

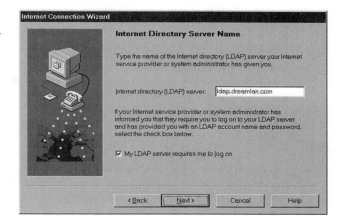

Finally, you're done! Click Finish to complete the configuration. You should find a new connection in your DUN folder.

Troubleshooting DUN

If anything goes wrong during the logon process, don't panic! It's probably caused by something simple, such as an incorrect password. If you still have a problem connecting, first check the configuration options (such as compression) and then check out your COM port; if the modem dials, you can be fairly sure the serial port configuration is okay. Another common cause of logon problems is the script. Try disabling the script (refer to the dialog box shown in Figure 20.11 earlier) and log on manually. That helps narrow down the possibilities.

When you try to connect to your ISP, you might see a dialog box saying this:

"Dial-Up Networking could not negotiate a compatible set of network protocols you specified in the Server Types settings. Check your network configuration in the Control Panel, and then try the connection again."

20

If you see that, check your network protocols to make sure you have TCP/IP bound to the Dial-Up Adapter.

You might run into a conflict between using DUN and accessing NetWare servers. Two possible symptoms of this problem are as follows:

- While using Novell's client when trying to establish a connection through a Dial-Up Adapter to the Internet through a modem, the error "You are currently using NetWare servers, which will be inaccessible if you establish this connection" was returned.
- After DUN establishes a connection to an ISP (or other service, such as an NT RAS server) using IP, the workstation is prompted to log on to the local NetWare network even though the workstation is already logged on to the NetWare network.

The reason for the conflict is that the Novell client doesn't route any protocol between two network cards or between a network card and a modem port. As a result, the Novell client does not allow the same protocol to be active on two different ports at the same time. You can have two different protocols active on two different ports at the same time, such as IPX on your network card and TCP/IP on a modem port, but not IPX on both.

The solution is rather straightforward. First of all, go to the properties of the connectoid used for this connection and select the Server Types tab. In the Allowed Network Protocols section, remove IPX from the protocol list, and in the Advanced Options section, uncheck the Log On to Network check box. Next, open the Network icon from the Control Panel, highlight the Dial-Up Adapter, and do the following:

1. Click the Properties button.
2. Select the Bindings tab.
3. Uncheck all bindings except for the binding to IP.
4. Click OK, and restart the computer as needed.

Troubleshooting the ISP Connection

If you can't connect to your ISP or you can connect to the ISP but not to the Net, you should determine whether your DUN configuration is correct (are you able to call into a RAS server or connect to a different ISP?). The problem could well be on your ISP side.

First, you can check the obvious, such as the following:

- **User Name and Password** Some ISPs' logon procedures are case sensitive.
- **Encryption** Not all ISPs support the encryption schemes used by DUN. Try turning the password and data encryption off (in the Server Types tab of your DUN connectoid's properties sheet).
- **Modem Compatibility** If you have a 56K modem, make sure it's compatible with your ISP's. For example, a 56K X2 modem can't talk to a 56KFlex modem.

If you still can't find the problem, you can use the tools mentioned in the following sections. (Hour 19 had a more detailed discussion of PING and Tracert.)

Using a Different Dialer

Some ISPs (such as IBM Global Network; see Figure 20.22) offer their own dialer to help you connect to their POPs. DUN should work with any ISP, but if you're having trouble establishing the connection, try the dialer supplied by the ISP. In some cases, the ISP's dialer has been optimized, so you might get a better throughput than you do when using DUN.

FIGURE 20.22

IBM Global Network's dialer software.

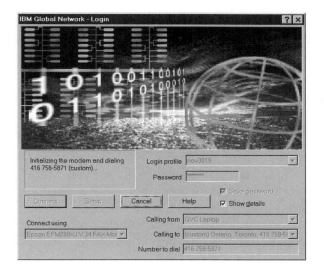

Online services, such as CompuServe, generally offer their own software for Internet connectivity as well. So, again, try the software supplied by the online service provider should you have trouble using DUN. There are also third-party dialers, which have different automation features built in. Perhaps the best known of them is Trumpet. You can get more information about the Trumpet suite of software from this site:

```
http://www.trumpet.com/
```

Using PING

As described in previous Hours (especially Hour 19), if you can't reach a particular host on the network (Internet), you can try using the PING utility to see whether the host is available. This is the basic syntax for PING:

```
ping hostname
```

20

In this line, *hostname* is the name or IP address of the host you're trying to reach.

If you can't Ping a remote host, see if you can Ping one of the servers (such as the DNS server) at your ISP's location. This helps determine whether the problem is between you and your ISP or further down in the network. If you don't know the IP address or the name of any of your ISP's servers, you can use the winipcfg utility (discussed in the section "Using winipcfg") to look up the IP addresses of your ISP's DNS servers.

Using Tracert

If you can't Ping a remote host, it could be that the reply packets to your Ping are getting held up somewhere in the network. The Tracert (trace route) utility can be used to find out how far away (in terms of *hops*; each hop is a router connection) a remote host is from you and the round-trip times between your computer and each hop. This is the basic syntax for Tracert:

```
tracert hostname
```

In this line, *hostname* is the name or IP address of the host you're trying to reach.

Using Tracert can help you to identify where along the path between your computer and the remote host the communication runs into a bottleneck (because that's the last entry in the Tracert output). For example, say you can't browse http://www.dreamlan.com. You issued a trace route command for www.dreamlan.com and received the following output:

```
Tracing route to dreamlan.com [209.68.53.219]
over a maximum of 30 hops:

  1    135 ms    130 ms    129 ms   toro1br1-tr51.on.ca.ibm.net
       [129.37.152.57]
  2    158 ms    152 ms    152 ms   beth1br2-0-1.md.us.ibm.net [165.87.29.2]
  3    157 ms    160 ms    160 ms   165.87.230.86
  4    157 ms    159 ms    163 ms   165.87.28.117
  5    164 ms    164 ms    171 ms   nyc-uunet.ny.us.ibm.net [165.87.220.13]
  6     *         *         *       Request timed out.
  7     *         *         *       Request timed out.
  8     *         *         *       Request timed out.
  9     *         *         *       Request timed out.
 10     *         *         *       Request timed out.
       .
       .
       .
 30     *         *         *       Request timed out.

Trace complete.
```

The "Request timed out" messages mean there's a network problem between nyc-uunet.ny.us.ibm.net and its next hop, which explains why you can't browse that Web site.

Using `winipcfg`

As previously discussed in Hour 19, included with Windows 98 is a utility called `winipcfg` (Windows IP configuration) that displays the current TCP/IP configuration of your computer. To bring up the IP Configuration dialog box (see Figure 20.23), use one of these two methods:

- Choose Start|Run, enter **winipcfg**, and click OK.
- Run `winipcfg` from a DOS command prompt.

FIGURE 20.23

The `winipcfg` *utility can display a lot of your Windows 98 TCP/IP configuration.*

The `winipcfg` utility tells you the IP configuration, such as IP address and DNS server addresses, for each installed network adapter in your Windows 98 computer. By clicking the button beside the DNS Servers entry, you can cycle through the IP addresses of the different DNS servers your connection uses.

The `winipcfg` utility summarizes all your current IP-related information into a single screen so that when you talk to your ISP's or LAN's technical support, you have all the information readily available.

For Windows NT users, use `ipconfig` instead; you need to run it from a command prompt.

20

Summary

In this Hour, you've learned how to select and install a modem in Windows 98 and gotten some tips about selecting an ISP for your Internet access. You also discovered how to install and configure DUN—both the hard way and the easy way (using the Internet Connection Wizard). And finally, you learned some tips and tricks on troubleshooting your Internet connection with some TCP/IP utilities, such as PING and Tracert.

In the next Hour, you learn about some useful Internet surfing tools and some cool sites to visit on the Net.

Workshop

Q&A

Q What's PCMCIA?

A PCMCIA, short for Personal Computer Memory Card International Association (pronounced as separate letters), is an organization that developed a standard for small, credit card–sized devices, called PC Cards. Originally designed for adding memory to portable computers, the PCMCIA standard has been expanded several times and is now suitable for many types of devices, such as modems and network cards. Although *PC Cards* is the proper term for the devices, they are commonly referred to as "PCMCIA cards."

Q My ISP offers both PPP and SLIP dial-up access. Does it matter which one I use?

A If you have the choice of PPP or SLIP, choose PPP because it's better implemented and a little faster than SLIP.

Q I didn't install the Dial-Up Networking component when installing Windows 98. How do I add it now?

A Just follow these steps. Bring up the Control Panel dialog box by choosing Start|Settings|Control Panel. Double-click Add/Remove Programs and then select Communications from the Windows Setup tab. Check the Dial-Up Networking check box and then click OK.

Q **Is there somewhere I can find out what scripting commands are available for the DUN scripting tool?**

A For a complete listing of DUN scripting commands, see the `script.doc` file in your main Windows 98 folder.

Q **What's LDAP?**

A LDAP is a set of protocols for accessing information directories. It's based on the standards in the X.500 standard, but it's much simpler and supports TCP/IP. Because it's a simpler version of X.500, LDAP is sometimes called "X.500-lite."

Although not yet widely implemented, LDAP should eventually make it possible for almost any application running on practically any computer platform to get directory information, such as email addresses and public keys. Because LDAP is an open protocol, applications don't need to worry about the type of server hosting the directory.

Quiz

1. How can you determine what protocols are active after you've connected to a dial-up server?

2. What's the name of the wizard that can help you set up your Internet connections?

3. How can you determine the dynamic IP address assigned by your ISP?

4. What tool can you use to determine how many hops there are between your computer and www.microsoft.com?

5. How many hops are you from www.dreamlan.com and from www.jpence.com?

20

HOUR 21

Surfing Tools

You read about the Internet, Web browsers, FTP, and so on in the first part of this book. After reading the previous Hour, you have your Windows 98 desktop connected to the Internet, and you're probably itching to get some action! This is the time to learn about the essential Internet tools, your "survival gear" for the World Wide Web.

Some service providers, such as America Online (AOL), supply their customers with collections of Internet programs. This is an easy way to get started because most of the programs are already configured with the appropriate options for your ISP. On the other hand, you can use the wide array of Internet applications included with Windows 98 and Windows NT.

Although the Web surfing utilities discussed here are based on Windows 98, they are also available for Windows NT and even Windows 3.x. Therefore, regardless of your desktop platform, this Hour's for you! During this Hour, the following topics are covered:

- Web browsers
- Accessing Internet resources
- Sending and receiving email

- Newsgroups
- Shopping in cyberspace

Browsers

To access the World Wide Web, you need a Web browser, which is the client half of the Web's client/server environment (the Web server being the other half of the equation). A Web browser is a powerful tool that performs many functions; for that reason, many power users consider a Web browser the "Swiss Army knife" of Internet tools. Here are some of the functions a Web browser performs:

- **Navigation aids**   These features give you the ability to move forward and backward within the links, open new documents (links), search for words within the current document, add the location of the current document to the bookmarks, and so on.
- **User presentation options**   These features enable toggling options, such as selecting font sets and colors as well as imaging loading.
- **Services**   Although most people use the browser simply to view documents, it also offers other services, such as printing current documents, saving current documents to local storage, reading and composing email, searching and retrieving information from Gopher servers, Telnetting to remote computers, and so on.
- **Plug-ins**   By including plug-in add-ons, you can, among other things, listen to audio files and play back movies.

Because you move around (navigate) the Web by using a browser, a Web browser is also known as a Web *navigator*. A variety of Web browsers are available to run on Windows platforms. The two most common Windows-based browsers, Microsoft Internet Explorer and Netscape Communicator, are discussed in the following sections.

Internet Explorer

Microsoft's Internet Explorer, frequently shortened to *IE* (or *IE4* in reference to the version), is an integral part of the Windows 98 operating system. You can launch IE with one of the following methods (see Figure 21.1):

- Click on the Launch Internet Explorer Browser icon in the Quick Launch toolbar.
- Double-click the Internet Explorer icon in the desktop.
- Choose Start | Programs | Internet Explorer | Internet Explorer.

FIGURE 21.1

Three ways to launch Internet Explorer on a Windows 98 machine.

Shortcut item

Quick Launch icon

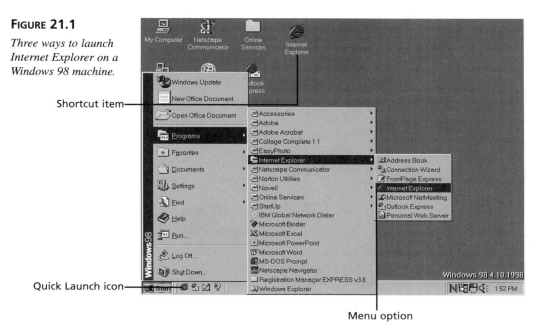

Menu option

When you start up Internet Explorer, the opening screen is similar to the one shown in Figure 21.2. The page is from `http://home.microsoft.com`. The very first page displayed by a Web site is known as the *home page*, and it generally contains introductory information about the site. A Web site's home page is much like the table of contents for a book.

Internet Explorer has many buttons and pull-down menus. The following is a summary of the main features of the IE display screen:

- **Title bar**   This top line of the screen shows the title of the currently displayed Web page. (If you're familiar with Web page design, this is the text enclosed by the `<TITLE></TITLE>` tags.)

- **Pull-down menus**   They contain many options, such as customization settings and navigation aids.

- **Function buttons**   Shortcut point-and-click access to many of the frequently used pull-down menu options.

- **Address bar**   This text bar shows you the URL (Uniform Resource Locator) of the currently displayed Web page. You can also enter URLs into the Address bar to move to another Web page or site.

- **Links bar**   A set of toolbar buttons that represent five predefined Web sites.

21

- **Content area**   This area is where the body of the Web page is displayed.
- **Hypertext links**   Links to other Web documents or to other locations within the same Web page. The mouse pointer turns into a hand when it's placed over a hypertext link. (Hypertext links are also called *hyperlinks*.)
- **Status bar**   Shows you the current status of IE, such as whether it's contacting a server or downloading a file.
- **Current zone**   Shows you the *security zone* of the current Web page.

FIGURE 21.2

Internet Explorer showing http://home. microsoft.com*'s home page.*

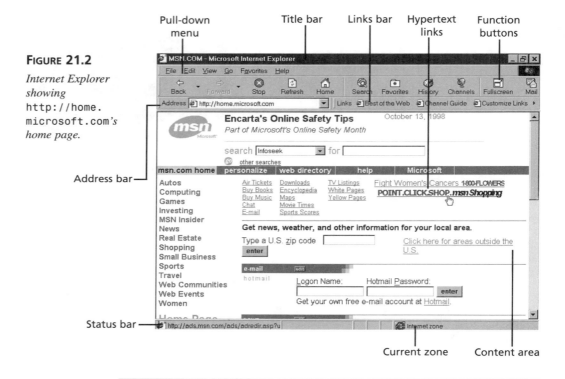

IE allows you to divide the Internet world into zones, and you can assign a Web site to a zone with a suitable security level. For example, you'd assign a Low security level to all your intranet Web sites where most programs and files can be downloaded with little or no notification. On the other hand, you might assign a Medium security rating to your intranet Web sites (where warnings are generated before running potentially damaging content) because you're doing Web site development work. For more information about IE's security features, see its online help.

The following are some ways you can use IE to navigate around the World Wide Web:

- **Entering a URL**   If you know the URL of the Web site you want to visit, click inside the Address bar, delete the current URL, enter the one you want, and press Enter. Or you can use File | Open (or press Ctrl+O) to bring up the Open dialog box (see Figure 21.3) and enter the URL there.

FIGURE 21.3

Enter the URL you want in the Open dialog box. You can also use the drop-down list to see a list of previously entered URLs.

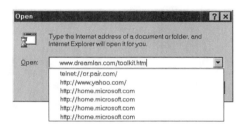

- **Following a hyperlink**   Frequently, you see some text displayed in an underlined font that's a different color from the rest of the Web document. Also, when you move the mouse pointer over the underlined text and it turns into a hand, it's a hyperlink that takes you to another part of the same document, a different document, or a different Web site.

- **Using the History bar**   IE remembers your recently visited URLs so you can go back to them easily. Click the History button in the toolbar to display the list (see Figure 21.4). You can also choose View | Explorer Bar | History to display the History bar.

FIGURE 21.4

Internet Explorer remembers your recently visited URLs in a history list.

History button

21

- **Using a search engine** If you don't know where you can find information on a particular topic, you can use one of the many search engines available on the Internet. Click the Search button or choose Go | Search the Web to bring up the Search bar. (If you're asked whether you want to install the Internet Search Enhancements control, click Yes.)

  The Search bar usually displays a random search engine (known as Provider-of-the-day). You can select a different search engine from the drop-down list shown in Figure 21.5.

FIGURE 21.5

Internet Explorer's Search bar gives you access to many popular search engines.

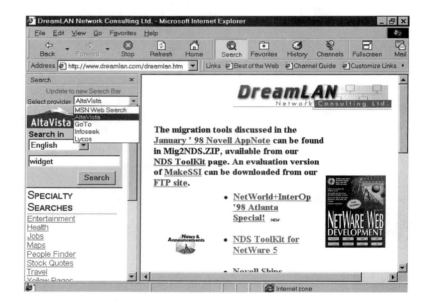

One of the original Internet search engine sites is Yahoo! (http://www.yahoo.com). Other search engine sites include AltaVista (http://www.altavista.digitial.com), Infoseek (http://www.infos-eek.com), and Deja News (http://www.dejanews.com), to name just a few.

- **Using an Internet shortcut** Like program shortcuts, you can create Internet shortcuts for your frequently visited URLs. You can create an Internet shortcut for the currently displayed Web page by simply dragging the page icon that appears in the Address bar (to the left of the URL; see Figure 21.6) and drop it on the desktop (or whatever folder you want to use to store the shortcuts).

FIGURE 21.6

Drag the page icon to the desktop to create an Internet shortcut to the currently displayed Web page.

Page icon ────

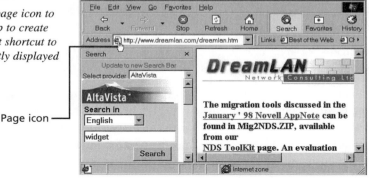

Note that the Internet shortcut feature is unique to the Windows 98 and Windows NT operating systems.

Internet Explorer has many more features, such as *subscriptions* and *active channels*, that can't be covered in detail here because of limited space. There's nothing better than hands-on experience, however, so take the time to explore and work with IE at your leisure.

Netscape Communicator

Netscape Communicator, from Netscape Communications Corporation, is an open email, groupware, and browser suite that offers a complete set of tools for easily communicating, sharing, and accessing information on your intranet or the Internet. The Netscape Communicator Standard Edition, available free of charge, includes the following components:

- **Netscape Navigator**   An easy-to-use Web browser software.
- **Netscape Messenger**   Use it to compose, send, and receive email through SMTP and POP3 protocols.
- **Netscape Collabra**   A newsreader that allows you to access discussion groups to collaborate with coworkers and leverage corporate knowledge more easily and effectively.
- **Netscape Composer**   An HTML editor for creating and publishing richly formatted Web documents with ease.
- **Netscape Netcaster**   Use it to experience dynamic, personalized information sent to you through the best channels on the Web.
- **Netscape Conference**   Communicate with coworkers using real-time voice and information collaboration.

21

- **Netscape AOL Instant Messenger** It allows you to instantly exchange messages with friends, family, and colleagues. It works much like a chat room, but is limited to one-to-one communications.

You can download Netscape Communicator from `http://www.netscape.com`. If you need only Netscape Navigator, it's available as a standalone from the same Web site.

A sample opening screen of Netscape Navigator is shown in Figure 21.7. As you can see (by comparing it with Figure 21.2), the feature set offered by Netscape Navigator is similar to what's available in Internet Explorer. For example, you can create an Internet shortcut of the currently displayed Web page by dragging and dropping the Page Proxy icon (to the left of the Location field) onto the desktop. (In IE, the Page Proxy icon was referred to simply as the "page icon.")

Page Proxy icon

FIGURE 21.7

Netscape Navigator showing Netscape's home page at `http://home.netscape.com`.

One feature available in Netscape isn't readily found in Internet Explorer. If you have several people using the same workstation, you can easily set up sharing a copy of Communicator with other users by using profiles to keep each user's email accounts, settings, preferences, bookmarks, and stored messages separate. Each user has a unique profile.

To begin, exit Navigator completely. Then from the Start menu, choose Programs | Netscape Communicator | Utilities | User Profile Manager. When the Profile Manager launches, you see a list of currently defined profiles (see Figure 21.8). To create a new profile, click New and then follow the step-by-step directions for setting up your individual profile. When more than one profile is defined, each time you launch Communicator, you can select the profile you want to use (see Figure 21.9).

FIGURE 21.8

Use the Profile Manager to manage multiple Netscape Messenger user profiles.

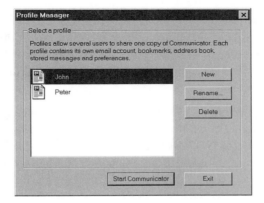

FIGURE 21.9

Select the appropriate user profile to be used with Netscape Messenger.

Others

Other than IE and Netscape, many more Web browsers are available for the Windows platform as freeware and shareware. Here are some examples:

- **NCSA Mosaic** (http://www.ncsa.uiuc.edu/SDG/Software/mosaic-w/) A free Web browser from the National Center for Supercomputing Applications (NCSA), University of Illinois at Urbana-Champaign.

21

- **1X Browser** (http://www.bendigo.net.au/~sti/)   Despite its very small size, 1X can provide frames support, caching, outgoing email, FTP downloads, bookmarks, and extended history. You can also use 1X to check your bookmarks for new site content while you browse, compare your PC's clock against an Internet time server, display different graphics file formats, and play sound files.

- **HexaBit JUNIOR** (http://www.hexabit.com/junior/)   A Web browser designed for kids, featuring a cool, easy-to-use interface. JUNIOR has parental controls, so your kids can surf safely.

- **Wildcat! Navigator** (http://204.250.9.131/public/default.htm)   This is a set of freely distributable Windows client programs. The Wildcat! Navigator Connection Manager supports modem connections, TCP/IP LAN connections, and Internet connections. This suite of programs runs under Windows 3.1x, Windows 95, and Windows NT.

- **WebSurfer for Windows 95** (http://www.netmanage.com)   A free Web browser from NetManager. The latest version offers support for plug-ins. Although it's called WebSurfer for Windows 95, it works with any 32-bit TCP/IP protocol stack, including Microsoft Windows 95 or Windows NT, Chameleon 5.0, and other vendors.

Surfing the Net

The Internet has a wealth of information that can be overwhelming, and the data is available in many forms: Web documents, files you can download, searchable online databases, and so on. In this section, you learn a few tricks and tips on where to look for information and how to retrieve it after you find it.

Browsing the World Wide Web

The application-level protocol used by the World Wide Web is called *Hypertext Transfer Protocol*, or *HTTP*. Consequently, the addresses of Web resources (such as documents) have a prefix of http://. This prefix instructs Web browsers to use HTTP as the communication protocol. However, to save you some typing, many Web browsers (such as IE and Netscape Navigator) allow you to simply enter the URL without the http:// portion—it's implied, if not specified. Instead of http://home.microsoft.com, for example, you can simply enter home.microsoft.com into IE's Address bar.

Web Site Naming Conventions

Many Web sites' URLs start with www, such as http://www.dreamlan.com or http://www.jpence.com. However, a host on the Internet can be called by *any* name (as long as it's not offensive). Including www in the name is simply a (good) convention that many Web sites use, but it's *not* a requirement that a Web site be named www.*domain_name*. Therefore, you shouldn't automatically ignore a host named `cnn.com` as a possible Web site just because it doesn't have www as part of its name.

> What makes a server a Web server is the Web server software it runs. The server's name has no bearing on the services (such as Web serving) offered by a given server.

When in Doubt, Use a Search Engine

The first thing new—and experienced, too—Internet users usually do when they need to look for a specific type of Web site or subject is to visit a search engine or indexing database. There are many such sites on the Internet; some of the more popular ones are listed here:

- **AltaVista** (`http://www.altavista.digital.com`)   This search engine is operated by Digital Equipment Corporation (now Compaq Computers).
- **Excite** (`http://www.excite.com`)   This search engine's database indexes the entire Web page instead of partially extracting information for indexing, so it gives you a more accurate representation of what's on the page.
- **Infoseek** (`http://www.infoseek.com`)   This search engine site not only indexes Web pages but also lets you search for images (such as photographs and logos) and browse through Usenet newsgroups for messages.
- **Yahoo!** (`http://www.yahoo.com`)   This is the original search engine site on the Internet.

The preceding list is made up of general search engine sites, but some search engines specialize in regional information, such as the following:

- **Alku** (`http://alku.hrsk.edu.fi`)   Provides links to Finnish Web sites, with information in Finnish.
- **Ananzi** (`http://www.ananzi.co.za`)   A search engine dedicated to the South African domain.
- **India Search Engine** (`http://www.indiasearchengine.com`)   Indexes Indian publications and Web sites.
- **Montana Pathfinder** (`http://pathfinder.mt-usa.com:8080`)   A search engine dedicated to the state of Montana.
- **Swiss Search** (`http://www.search.ch`)   A full-text search engine for Switzerland.

21

- **TechnoFIND** (`http://www2.technofind.com.sg/TF/index.html`)   A search facility for Singaporean Web sites (see Figure 21.10).

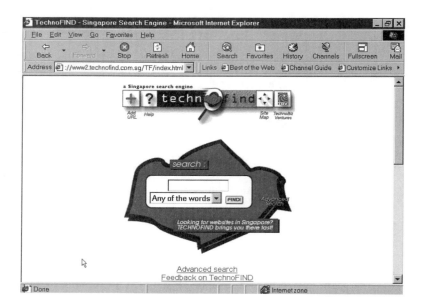

As you can see, there's a diverse range of search engines available to serve your needs. You can find a long list of them at this URL:

```
http://dir.yahoo.com/Computers_and_Internet/Internet/World_Wide_Web/
↪Searching_the_Web/Search_Engines/
```

Downloading Files with FTP

Typically you have three ways to retrieve a file from the Internet:

- Downloading the file through HTTP
- Downloading the file through FTP
- Having the file emailed to you

The first two methods are more common. However, the major disadvantage of downloading the file through HTTP is that HTTP is designed to be a "lightweight" (therefore fast) protocol, so it doesn't have any built-in error recovery. If you encounter any error during a file transfer, you end up with a corrupted file, or the download is aborted and you get no file.

The more traditional method is to use FTP to download files because it has built-in error checking and recovery. The regular FTP process requires you to use an FTP client and have a valid user name and password on the FTP server. Many FTP servers support what's known as *anonymous FTP*. If you don't have a user name and password for an FTP server (and you wouldn't for the majority of FTP servers on the Internet), try anonymous as the user name and your email address as the password. This generally gives you read-only permission on the FTP server, which is all you need to download files.

An FTP command-line utility (ftp.exe) is included with Windows 98 and Windows NT. The idea behind the FTP client is that you connect to a remote FTP server and then use commands to change directories, display files, and transfer files. It's much like working with files by using the DOS prompt.

A typical DOS-based FTP session has the following steps:

1. Start the FTP client and connect to the remote FTP server.
2. Authenticate to the server.
3. Change to the directory you want to download files from.
4. Set any necessary file transfer options.
5. Download the file or files.
6. End the FTP session.

The following sample FTP session (notice that user input is in boldface) illustrates how you use the Windows 98 FTP utility to download a file called nw5prod.htm that's in the pub/updates/nw/nw5 directory from Novell's FTP site (ftp.novell.com):

```
D:\>ftp ftp.novell.com
Connected to ftp.novell.com.
220 nemesis FTP server (Version wu-2.4.2-academ[BETA-14](4) Tue Oct 14
17:57:04
➥MDT 1997) ready.
User (ftp.novell.com:(none)): anonymous
331 Guest login ok, send your complete email address as password.
(password not
➥echoed)
230-###################################################################
230-
230-Welcome to ftp.novell.com, slip129-37-163-167.on.ca.ibm.net!
230-
230-The concurrent ftp connection limit is currently set at 450. You
230-are user 92 of 450.
230-
230-Feel free to browse around, but most of our guests will want to
```

21

```
230-proceed directly to pub/updates, where our complete set of patches/
230-file updates is located in an intuitive structure based on the
230-Novell product you are supporting. This set of files is updated
230-nightly from our internal support database.
230-
230-FTP mirror sites of ftp.novell.com are: ftp.novell.com.au,
230-ftp.novell.de with more to come. If you get a chance, check out
230-our World Wide Web sites: support.novell.com, support.novell.de,
230-support.novell.com.au where Novell Technical Information Databases
230-and support files are updated nightly.
230-
230-Enjoy!
230-webmaster_support@novell.com
230-
230 Guest login ok, access restrictions apply.
ftp> cd pub/updates/nw/nw5
250-nw5        NetWare 5
250-
250 CWD command successful.
ftp> get nw5prod.htm
200 PORT command successful.
150 Opening ASCII mode data connection for nw5prod.htm (13576 bytes).
226 Transfer complete.
ftp: 14059 bytes received in 2.80Seconds 5.02Kbytes/sec.
ftp> quit
221 Goodbye.
D:\>
```

As you can see, except for the power users who like command-line formats, most people use a graphical FTP client. There are several commercial, shareware, and freeware graphical FTP clients available that can make FTP downloading much easier (for example, you can download a file from a remote host to your computer by simply dragging and dropping between windows; see Figure 22.11). Commercial options include Novell's LAN WorkPlace for Windows and NetManager's Chameleon. One of the best sources for finding shareware and freeware graphical FTP clients is the Consummate Winsock Applications Web site:

```
http://cws.internet.com/32ftp.html
```

FIGURE 21.11

Rapid Filer is a graphical FTP client.

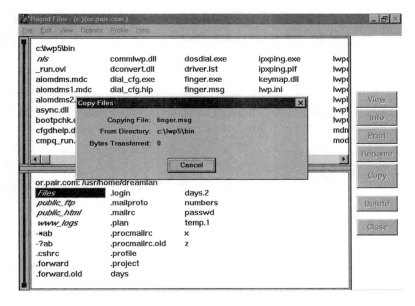

Accessing Remote Hosts with Telnet

Telnet is a terminal emulation protocol that allows you to log on to a remote host over the network and use its services as though you were sitting at a locally attached terminal. For example, you can use Telnet to log on to a library card catalog database (see Figure 21.12).

FIGURE 21.12

A library catalog system.

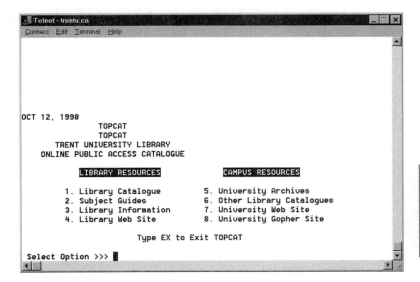

21

A Telnet client is included with both Windows 98 and Windows NT. To run the Windows 98 Telnet client, choose Start I Run, enter **Telnet**, and click OK, or from a DOS prompt, type **telnet** and then press Return. To connect to a remote host, choose Connect I Remote System to open the Connect dialog box (see Figure 21.13). You need to specify the following options:

- **Host Name**   Enter the host name or an IP address for the remote host you want to connect to.
- **Port**   Select the TCP port to be used for the connection. Most systems use TCP port 23 (the Telnet port), but you can enter a specific port number if the remote system doesn't use the standard Telnet port.
- **Term Type**   Use the drop-down list to specify the terminal type string to be sent to the host. Most UNIX hosts use this information to set the correct terminal type for your session.

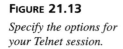

FIGURE 21.13

Specify the options for your Telnet session.

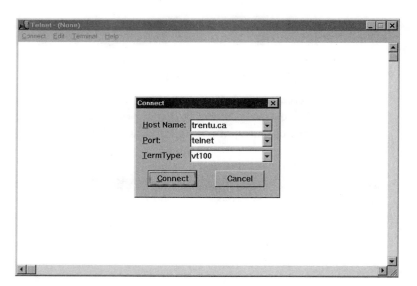

After you enter your options, click Connect to initiate the Telnet session. Depending on the services offered by the remote host, you might need to specify a user name and password to log on.

You can also establish a Telnet session with your Web browser by entering a URL in the form of `telnet://hostname`. Because a Web browser generally doesn't have a Telnet client built in, however, it calls an external Telnet program. In Windows 98, for example, the Telnet utility is used.

To end the Telnet session, choose Connect I Disconnect.

You must be anxious to jump onto the Internet and get some action. All right, then. Go fire up your workstation, and while it's booting up, grab yourself some java. Now, connect to the Internet and look around! Check out some of the following sites:

> http://www.dilbert.com
>
> http://www.microsoft.com
>
> http://home.microsoft.com
>
> http://www.yahoo.com

Music fans can start at http://www.sonymusic.com, and sports fans should check out the following:

> http://www.nascar.com
>
> http://www.nfl.com
>
> http://www.nba.com
>
> http://www.espn.com

Sending and Receiving Email

If you had to list five things people use the Internet for, electronic mail (email) would be among the top three. As a matter of fact, many people feel as though part of their life is missing if they can't access their email for an extended period. Indeed, many companies rely heavily on email as part of their day-to-day business operations.

Email Protocols

When exchanging email over the Internet (or your intranet), you often come across three terms: SMTP, POP3, and IMAP4. A brief discussion of these terms is in the following sections.

21

SMTP

SMTP is short for *Simple Mail Transfer Protocol*, a protocol for sending email messages between servers. Most email systems that send mail over the Internet use SMTP to send messages from one server to another; the messages can then be retrieved with an email client (such as Outlook Express) using either the POP or IMAP protocol. In addition, SMTP is generally used to send messages from a mail client to a mail server. This is why you need to specify both the POP or IMAP server and the SMTP server when you configure your email application.

POP

POP is short for *Post Office Protocol*, a protocol used to retrieve email from a mail server. Most email applications (sometimes called *email clients*) use the POP protocol, although some can use the newer IMAP. There are two versions of POP. The first, called POP2, became a standard in the mid-1980s and requires SMTP to send messages. The newer version, POP3, can be used with or without SMTP. Most modern email clients support POP3.

IMAP

IMAP, short for *Internet Message Access Protocol*, is a protocol originally developed at Stanford University in 1986 that's used for retrieving email messages. The latest version, IMAP4, is similar to POP3 but supports some additional features. For example, with IMAP4, you can search through your email messages for keywords while the messages are still on the mail server. You can then choose which messages to download to your machine. Like POP, IMAP uses SMTP for communication between the email client and server.

Using Outlook Express

Included with Windows 98 is Outlook Express, Microsoft's email client software. If you're running Windows NT, a copy of Outlook is included with it, too. The following discussion assumes you have set up both your Internet connection and your email account. If not, refer to Hour 20, "Connecting Your Windows 98 Desktop to the Internet," for details.

You can start up Outlook Express with any one of the following methods:

- Double-click the Outlook Express icon on your desktop.
- Click the Launch Outlook Express icon in the task bar's Quick Launch area.
- Choose Start | Programs | Internet Explorer | Outlook Express.
- In Internet Explorer, choose Go | Mail.

The first time you launch Outlook Express, it displays the Browse for Folder dialog box, asking you where you'd like your incoming messages stored. The default folder is your \Windows\Application Data\Microsoft\Outlook Express subfolder. If you want to use a different folder, use the folder tree to select the new location and then click OK.

The Outlook Express window has two major components: the Folder List on the left and the Content Area on the right (see Figure 21.14).

FIGURE 21.14

The Outlook Express window.

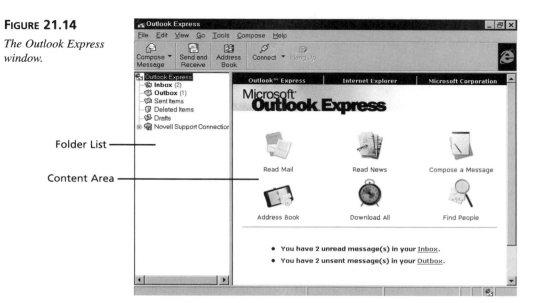

The Folder List shows the folders used by Outlook Express for storing messages:

- **Inbox** For incoming messages.
- **Outbox** For pending outgoing messages.
- **Sent Items** For messages that have been sent.
- **Deleted Items** For messages you have deleted. Like the Windows Recycle Bin, this is a temporary deletion area.
- **Drafts** For messages you've saved but haven't sent.

If you set up one or more Usenet news accounts, there's a folder for each. In the example shown in Figure 21.14, the Novell Support Connection folder is such an account.

It's fairly simple to send and receive email with Outlook Express. To send a basic email message, follow these steps:

21

1. Click the Compose Message button in the toolbar.

2. In the To, Cc, and Bcc boxes, type the email address of each recipient, separated by a comma or semicolon.

   To include addresses from the Address Book, click the To icon in the New Message window, and then select the names you want.

3. In the Subject box, type a message title.

4. Type your message, and then click Send. If you're composing a message offline for sending later, choose File I Send Later to save the message to the Outbox folder. After you've connected to the Internet, choose Tools I Send to send any messages in your Outbox.

You can configure Outlook Express to check for new messages on your mail server automatically. This is controlled by a setting in the Options dialog box; the default is every 30 minutes. To change the setting, open the Options dialog box by choosing Tools I Options.

Each new message that arrives is stored in the Inbox and appears in a bold font. To view a message, highlight it in the message list. Outlook Express then displays the message in the lower half of the Content Area. To reply to the message you're currently reading, simply click the Reply to Author (or Reply to All) button on the toolbar.

Other Email Clients

Because email is such an important part of so many businesses, there's a lot of email software available commercially, through the shareware channel, or as freeware. Perhaps the best-known of the freeware email clients is Pegasus Mail for Microsoft Windows (see Figure 21.15) by David Harris. You can find the latest version of Pegasus Mail and add-ons for it at this URL:

http://www.pegasus.usa.com.

Most Web browsers, such as Netscape, have an email client built in.

FIGURE 21.15

*The Pegasus email
client.*

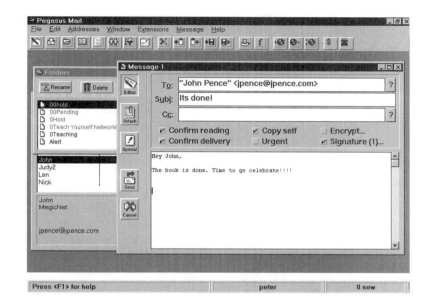

You can find a comprehensive listing of email software (and other email-related applications) at this URL:

`http://www.email-software.com`

Newsgroups

Long before the World Wide Web, Usenet was one of the major services offered by the Internet. *Usenet* is a collection of discussion groups, commonly referred to as *newsgroups*; people can use these groups to participate in a public dialogue with everyone else on the network. Usenet carries a wide variety of topics, almost any imaginable (and some nonimaginable ones!). Given that more than 25,000 newsgroups are available, you're bound to find at least *one* that piques your interest.

For those readers familiar with bulletin board systems (BBS) or online services, such as CompuServe and AOL, newsgroups are very much like the discussion sections and forums on these services.

21

Starting in the late 1990s, many companies took their technical support efforts to the Internet, using newsgroups as the vehicle. You'll learn about Microsoft-specific newsgroups in Hour 24, "Online Resources."

Usenet Basics

To get the most of your time on Usenet and cut down on the number of "flames" you might get, you should be aware of the following Usenet basics and guidelines:

- **Article**   Each individual message in a newsgroup discussion is referred to as an *article*.

- **Cross-posting**   Posting the same message to more than one newsgroup is called *cross-posting* because sometimes messages can apply to more than one newsgroup. However, some users cross-post regularly, which can be annoying to those who encounter the same message several times. As a general rule, don't cross-post unless your message really belongs in several locations.

- **Flames**   *Flame* is one of the most commonly encountered Usenet terms. A flame happens when one user gets mad at another and sends sarcastic, insulting, or downright nasty comments. A flame is usually triggered by a silly comment or a major breach of the newsgroup's rules.

- **Follow-up**   A response to an article.

- **Moderated newsgroups**   Some newsgroups don't allow postings released for distribution without the article first being examined by someone (the moderator). These groups are called *moderated newsgroups*. The moderator has the authority to refuse acceptance of an article if the subject is irrelevant to the group, doesn't contribute anything useful, or is considered in poor taste.

- **Newsgroup naming convention**   Usenet newsgroups are divided into several classifications. Each newsgroup's name leads off with an identifier that tells what type of newsgroup it is, followed by a more specific name. Here are the major groups:

alt	Groups with a more limited distribution than standard Usenet newsgroups, but usually much freer in content
biz	Business-related groups
comp	Computer- and software-related groups
misc	Newsgroups that don't readily fall under any other category
news	General news and topical subjects
rec	Groups aimed toward arts, hobbies, and recreational activities

sci	Scientific subjects, such as physics
soc	Groups dealing with social issues and socializing
talk	Debate-oriented groups that encourage lengthy discussions

The second part of the newsgroup name identifies the major subject area. For example, comp.os deals with computer operating systems. However, most subjects have further subgroups dedicated to more specific aspects of the general topic.

- **Newsreader**   The software you use to read a newsgroup's articles and to post your own articles.

- **Post**   To send an article to a newsgroup.

- **Smileys**   A *smiley* is a combination of characters that represents a facial expression. A smiley is used to emphasize that you're saying something in jest or tongue-in-cheek. A typical smiley looks like :-). Viewed from the side, it looks like two eyes, a nose, and a smiling mouth. You'll see many different variations that convey the same basic meaning.

- **Shouting**   Most articles are properly typed using a mix of uppercase and lowercase letters, just as you see in this book. However, when a user wants to emphasize something, such as an important word or phrase, it's usually written in capital letters. This is the Usenet equivalent of SHOUTING, and it's considered bad form to shout excessively.

- **Subscribe**   In a newsreader, you need to *subscribe* to a newsgroup to read its articles. If you no longer want to read the group's articles, you need to *unsubscribe* from the group.

- **Thread**   A series of articles related to the same subject line. A *thread* always begins with an original article (known as the *root* article) and then progresses through one or more follow-ups.

Newsreaders

Newsreaders are a special kind of email software. Besides communicating with news servers by using the news protocol, newsreaders can link related articles into a thread so you can more easily follow a particular discussion. What's more, newsreaders allow you to download just the messages you want (instead of all of them), read, and compose your follow-ups offline so you're not racking up your ISP connect charges.

Newsreading capabilities are built into many of the Web browsers, such as Netscape Communicator (see Figure 21.16). However, if you want a dedicated newsreader (because they tend to have more features), several are available for Windows, such as the following:

21

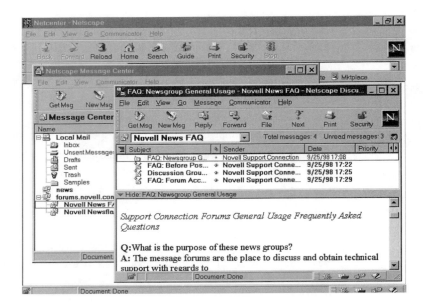

FIGURE **21.16**

Newsreader windows in Netscape Communicator.

- Virtual Access (http://www.atlantic-coast.com/cgi-bin/sellonline/va.htm)
- Gravity (http://www.anawave.com)
- Agent (http://www.forteinc.com)

Some email applications, such as Microsoft Outlook, also support reading and posting news articles. As a matter of fact, when you access a news URL using Internet Explorer on Windows 98, Outlook Express is launched as the newsreader.

Configuring Your Newsreader

Although each newsreader differs in its setup method, there are some general guidelines. The following information needs to be provided (see Figure 21.17):

- Supply the name of the news server.
- Indicate the port used by the news server (port 119 is the default).
- Specify whether authentication is needed to access the news server.

FIGURE 21.17

Configuring the access of a news server with Netscape.

After you have the news server defined in your reader, you then need to subscribe to individual newsgroups before you can read and post messages.

The following procedure outlines how to configure Outlook Express as your newsreader; it's assumed you've already set up an Outlook Express account for your news server as described in Hour 20:

1. Launch Outlook Express by either double-clicking the shortcut on your desktop or choosing Start | Programs | Internet Explorer | Outlook Express.

2. In Outlook Express's Folder List window, click on the folder that corresponds to your news server.

   The first time you do this, Outlook Express asks whether you want to view a list of the available newsgroups. Click Yes so Outlook Express can connect to your news server and download the list of newsgroups available on the server. The Newsgroup dialog box is then displayed (see Figure 21.18). (Note that the news server list appears only if you've defined multiple news servers.)

FIGURE 21.18

This dialog box lists all the newsgroups available on the selected news server.

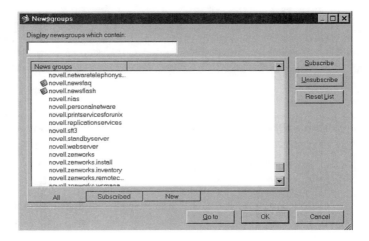

21

To bring up the list of available newsgroups later, click the Newsgroup button on the toolbar (or choose Tools | Newsgroups).

3. The newsgroups you've subscribed to are indicated by a newspaper icon appearing to the left of the newsgroup (refer back to Figure 21.18). Double-click the newsgroup to toggle between subscribe and unsubscribe status, or you can highlight the newsgroup and then click the Subscribe or Unsubscribe button.

4. Click OK to save your changes and close the Newsgroups dialog box.

Reading, Replying, and Posting Messages to a Newsgroup

There are two ways in which you can read newsgroup articles:

- **Online**   Working online means you're connected to the news server continuously. You can download message headers and body text at any time, and highlighting a message downloads it immediately. This is the general mode of operation if you have a LAN connection to your news server.

- **Offline**   Working offline means you connect to the news server only for brief periods. The normal mode of operation for working offline is to first connect and grab the available message headers (subject titles) from the newsgroups you have subscribed to. Then, while you're disconnected, examine the subjects and mark those you want to retrieve and read. You then reconnect and download the marked messages.

To connect to your news server when using a dial-up connection, click the Connect button on the toolbar, or choose File | Connect | *servername* (*servername* is the account name of the news server). There's no need to connect if you have a LAN connection because Outlook Express establishes the connection automatically, but you can prevent this by choosing File | Work Offline.

After you've connected to the server, you can download the message headers and messages in several ways. Here are some of the methods:

- To download all headers in a newsgroup automatically, click the newsgroup in the folder list.

- To download new headers in a newsgroup, right-click the newsgroup, click Mark for Retrieval, and then click New Headers. A small, blue arrow is placed to the left of the newsgroup. Choose Tools | Download *servername* to start the download.

- To download a particular message, right-click the message of interest and click

Mark Message for Download. A small, blue arrow is placed to the left of the message. Choose Tools | Download *servername* to start the download.

- To download a particular thread, right-click any message within the thread. A small, blue arrow is placed to the left of each message in the thread. Choose Tools | Download *servername* to start the download.

When you're done, disconnect from your news server by clicking the Hang Up button on the toolbar or choosing File | Hang Up.

There are two categories of Usenet articles: a new message or a follow-up (reply) message. To compose a new message, do the following:

1. Select the newsgroup you want to post the message to.
2. Choose Compose | New Message or click the Compose Message button on the toolbar.
3. In the New Message dialog box (see Figure 21.19), enter a subject to identify your message.
4. Enter your message in the text box.
5. Click the Post button to send the message right away (you need to be connected to the server to do this). Or choose File | Send Later to place the message in the Outbox folder ready to be sent when you connect to the server next time.

To send queued message, choose Tools | Send after you've connected to the Internet.

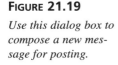

FIGURE 21.19

Use this dialog box to compose a new message for posting.

21

To post a follow-up message, use the following steps:

1. Highlight the original message in the message list.

2. Click the Reply to Group button in the toolbar (or choose Compose | Reply to Newsgroup) to bring up the message window (see Figure 21.20).

3. Cut out any unnecessary text from the original message.

4. Enter your own text in the message body.

5. Click the Post button to send the message right away (you need to be connected to the server to do this). Or choose File | Send Later to place the message in the Outbox folder ready to be sent when you connect to the server next time.

FIGURE 21.20

Use this dialog box to compose a follow-up message to the newsgroup.

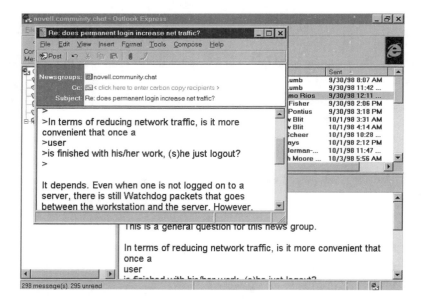

If you selected the Reply to Author option instead of Reply to Newsgroup, your article isn't posted to the newsgroup. It's sent as an email to the author of the message you're replying to.

Net Security

You're probably aware of the risk of virus-infected files downloaded or obtained from dubious sources. (You find out how to guard against viruses from the Internet in Hour 22, "Connecting Your Network to the Internet.") However, have you given much thought to the security risks you might be exposed to when surfing around the Internet? Given that you have no control over the servers you access on the Internet, some education about Internet security is in order.

When you visit a Web site, certain things go on behind the scenes that you're not usually aware of, such as the following:

- Do you know that a Web site might be collecting your personal information, such as email address, without asking you first?
- Do you know what the key icon at the bottom-left corner of your Netscape Navigator window or the lock symbol in the lower-right corner of your Internet Explorer window means when you visit certain Web sites?
- Are you exposing yourself to any risk when you visit a Web site that has some cool Java applets?

If you're not sure of the answer to any of these questions, read on.

Want a Cookie?

You probably won't notice that a Web site has given you a cookie every time you visit. A *cookie* is a message given to a Web browser by a Web server. The browser stores the message in a text file called `cookies.txt`. The message is then sent back to the server each time the browser requests a page from the server.

The main purpose of cookies is to identify users and possibly prepare customized Web pages for them. When you enter a Web site using cookies, you might be asked to fill out a form supplying information such as your name and interests. This information is packaged into a cookie and sent to your Web browser, which stores it for later use. The next time you go to the same Web site, your browser sends the cookie to the Web server. The server can use this information to offer you custom Web pages. So, for example, instead of seeing just a generic welcome page, you might see a welcome page that greets you with your name.

The name *cookie* is derived from UNIX objects called *magic cookies*. These are tokens attached to a user or program; they change depending on the areas entered by the user or program. Cookies are sometimes called *persistent cookies*, too, because they typically stay in the browser for long periods.

21

Although having a remote site store data on your hard disk seems ominous, cookies aren't a threat to security. In fact, they are often used in ways that can enhance your time on the Web. Most leading browsers, including Netscape Navigator and Microsoft Internet Explorer, can be configured to display a dialog box every time a server wants to give you a cookie.

If you take a look at the `cookies.txt` file, you'll see the information is benign. The `cookies.txt` file is stored in the same folder as Netscape Navigator or Internet Explorer. It's a text file, so you can easily view it.

If you're still not convinced about the security issue, bear in mind that each time you enter a site, your browser already tells the server a lot about you, such as which browser you're using and your IP address. If you're still worried, you can always delete the `cookies.txt` file after each session!

Cookie technology is often used by Web sites that offer online commerce, typically to store your selections as you browse the products. Each item you choose (put into your shopping "basket") is stored in your `cookies.txt` file. The store can erase that information from your file when you're finished or keep it there for retrieval next time you shop. That way you can be greeted with a message such as "Peter, welcome back! Don't miss today's special on 56K modems."

As long as the Web site plays according to the rules and uses the collected information responsibly, cookies are rather safe. The only drawback is that your `cookies.txt` file can grow to be fairly large.

What's SSL?

The ever-growing demand for Web sites to offer online shopping and "secure transactions" when credit card and other sensitive data need to be transmitted between the Web browser and the server has led to the development of a couple of new protocols. SSL, short for *Secure Sockets Layer*, is a protocol developed by Netscape for transmitting private documents through the Internet. SSL works by using a private key to encrypt data that's transferred over the SSL connection. Both Netscape Navigator and Internet Explorer support SSL, and many Web sites use the protocol to get confidential user information, such as credit card numbers. By convention, Web pages that require an SSL connection start with `https://` instead of `http://`.

When Internet Explorer displays a secure Web page (whose URL starts with `https://`), a lock icon is displayed in the lower-right corner of the browser window. Similarly, Netscape Navigator displays a key icon in the lower-left corner of the browser window.

Another protocol for transmitting data securely over the World Wide Web is *Secure HTTP* (S-HTTP). Although SSL creates a secure connection between a client and a server, over which any amount of data can be sent securely, S-HTTP is designed to transmit individual messages securely. SSL and S-HTTP, therefore, can be seen as complementary rather than competing technologies. Both the SSL and S-HTTP protocols have been submitted to the Internet Engineering Task Force (IETF) for approval as Internet standards.

For additional security, many Web sites use digital certificates. A digital certificate or "Web site certificate" states that a specific Web site is secure and genuine. It ensures that no other Web site can assume the identity of the original secure site. Web site certificates are also dated when they are issued. When you try to open an organization's Web site, Internet Explorer verifies that the Internet address stored in the certificate is correct and that the current date precedes the expiration date. If the information is not current and valid, Internet Explorer can display a warning.

Therefore, if the Web site you're doing your shopping on offers secured transactions and uses digital certificates to identify itself, you can be fairly confident that your data can't be decrypted by a third party, even if your transmission was intercepted.

Shopping on the Internet

Other than securing your data transmission over the network, you should give the following suggestions some consideration before going shopping in the cybermalls:

- Give your credit card information only to Web sites of established companies. For example, if the Web site doesn't offer you a way to contact the company's customer service department by phone or fax, you should be wary, even if SSL or S-HTTP is used.

- Don't use your regular credit card for Internet shopping. Get a separate credit card that has a low credit limit, say $250. This should be enough for doing most purchasing on the Internet, but if, for whatever reason, someone else got hold of your credit card number, you're at most $250 out-of-pocket.

- Keep good records of your Internet credit card transactions. Reputable companies send you order confirmation via email and can send you a hardcopy receipt on request.

- When your credit card statement arrives, go over it very carefully and verify its accuracy. If there are transactions you didn't know about, contact the card's issuer immediately and ask for records for clarification.

21

Is Java Safe?

Many Web sites now use Java applets or JavaScripts to enhance their appearance and add interactive functionality. However, you don't know what the applets or scripts do until your browser runs them, and if the programmer has malicious intent, it would be too late. So is Java or JavaScript safe? Before answering that question, you should know the difference between the two.

Java, developed by Sun Microsystems, is an object-oriented language similar to C++, but simplified to eliminate language features that cause common programming errors. Java was designed to be used in a networked and distributed environment.

Java source code files (files with a .java extension) are compiled into a format called *bytecode* (files with a .class extension), which can then be executed by a Java interpreter (the *Java Virtual Machine*, JVM). Small Java applications, called Java *applets*, can be downloaded from a Web server and run on your computer by a Java-compatible Web browser, such as Netscape Navigator or Microsoft Internet Explorer.

Although Sun made security one of the chief requirements for the language and has been promoting Java as a "secure" programming language, Java applets still run a risk of being messed with.

Researchers at Princeton University and the University of Washington have been able to breach several aspects of Java's built-in defenses. Although Sun has quickly plugged security leaks as they have appeared, the incidents showed that Java is fallible.

Still, you should remember that all these security flaws have been found by *researchers*—there are no reports so far of any real criminal stealing or tampering with data by exploiting a Java security hole. Of course, that doesn't mean it couldn't happen, but if it were easy, you'd have heard about some real crimes by now.

Even though it's not impregnable, most security experts still regard Java as fundamentally more secure than other kinds of executable code, most notably Microsoft's ActiveX technology.

Java applets—but not ActiveX components—use a sandbox security model. This means applets run within a confined environment, with no way to access files or memory that the applets aren't using. This is supposed to ensure that applets can't be programmed to corrupt data, delete files, or reformat your hard drive.

However, Sun acknowledges that its sandbox can limit the capabilities of Java applets. The company has recently begun to modify its security model to allow applets to venture outside the sandbox for specific functions such as writing data to a hard disk.

The sandbox is not being eliminated, but Sun is starting to rely more on *trust*, the security model ActiveX uses. Applets can now be stamped with digital certificates that verify the author's identity. If an applet ends up damaging your computer, you can track down its publisher. The browser also warns you if it encountered an applet from an unknown source. As long as you stick with applets from only "trusted" vendors or Web sites, you can greatly reduce the risk.

Still, safe network computing is an oxymoron. The Internet exposes Java applets to the general public, and, unfortunately, some portion of that public likes to make trouble. Safety belts don't make you completely safe in a car, and the sandbox doesn't make you completely safe on the Net. All things considered, however, Java has so far proved itself to be reasonably secure, so don't let concern about security keep you awake at night.

> If you're paranoid, you can configure your browser to not run Java applets at all or limit the type of resources an applet can access on your computer. In Internet Explorer, you do that by using the Java permissions in the Security Settings dialog box.

Is JavaScript Safe?

JavaScript is a scripting language developed by Netscape to enable Web authors to design interactive Web sites. Although it shares many of the features and structure of the full Java language, it was developed independently. JavaScript can interact with HTML source code, enabling Web authors to spice up their sites with dynamic content. It's endorsed by several software companies and is an open language anyone can use without buying a license. JavaScript is supported by recent browsers from Netscape and Microsoft, although Internet Explorer supports only a subset, which Microsoft calls Jscript.

JavaScripts aren't compiled and can be viewed as part of the source of the HTML document. Therefore, you can configure your browser to not run the JavaScript but simply load the Web page. Then view the JavaScript source to see if it does anything suspicious. If not, then you can enable JavaScript execution and reload the Web page. In general, however, JavaScripts are safe to run.

Summary

During this Hour, you've learned that a Web browser is a "jack of all trades" Internet tool. It's not limited to just accessing Web sites; you can also use a Web browser to download files using FTP, read and send email, and access newsgroups. You also discov-

21

ered how to use Outlook Express as both an email client and a newsreader. Finally, you found out what cookies and SSL are and gained some knowledge about security concerns when using the Internet.

In the next Hour, you're going to find out how you can connect your network to the Internet.

Workshop

Q&A

Q How do I change my Internet shortcuts if the URL is out of date?

A Because Internet shortcuts are simply text files that use the URL as a filename extension, you can change the URL by opening the URL file in Notepad or WordPad.

Q Is Internet Explorer included with operating systems other than Windows 98?

A IE is included with Windows NT, too. Starting in September 1998, IE (as well as Netscape Navigator) is bundled with Novell's NetWare 5 operating system.

Q Can I create a shortcut for my Telnet sessions?

A Yes, you can. The command syntax is `telnet` *host* [*port*].

Q How come my ISP doesn't offer the alt.autos.antique newsgroup? I thought newsgroups were circulated worldwide.

A The `alt.*` newsgroups are usually selectively circulated, depending on the news server. Because of the sometimes questionable contents in the `alt.*` newsgroups, many ISPs don't carry them. However, if you find a public news server that distributes your `alt` newsgroup, you can subscribe to it.

Q I don't always have access to an FTP client but always have a Web browser. How do I use a browser to download a file from an FTP server?

A As long as the FTP server supports anonymous FTP and you know the exact path and name of the file, you can use a URL in the form `ftp://`*hostname*/*pathname*/*filename* to download the file. For example, to download a file called `update1.zip` that's in `public/changes` on a host called `ftp.dreamlan.com`, you enter **ftp://ftp.dreamlan.com/public/changes/update1.zip** as the URL to your browser; the browser logs in using `anonymous` as the user name and sends your email address as the password.

Quiz

1. What tool(s) can you use to download the latest version of Netscape Messenger from `ftp.netscape.com`?

2. What is anonymous FTP?

3. What service is available when you Telnet to `madlab.sprl.umich.edu`?

4. What is the purpose of the Draft folder in Outlook Express?

21

Hour **22**

Connecting Your Network to the Internet

You've learned how to connect your desktop to the Internet, but what if you want to connect your company's network, too? It's not uncommon these days to link a company's network to the Internet so that everyone can access the Net through the LAN instead of having to install separate modems and additional telephone lines for those users who need Internet access. But how do you go about doing that? What do you need? You'll find out in this Hour.

The following topics are covered:

- Hardware needed to facilitate the connection
- Software configuration needed to facilitate the connection
- Network security concerns
- Usage policy

What Do You Need?

After you've made the decision of connecting your network to the Internet, you need to consider some logistics and administrative issues:

- Hardware requirements
- IP addressing
- Internet domain name
- Other required services
- Desktop TCP/IP configuration

Do You Need a Router?

The Internet is made up of different networks, each with its own IP network address. You know from Hour 2, "Networking Basics," that a router is required to connect different networks, so it's natural to ask the question:

"Do I need a router, more specifically a dedicated router, to connect my network to the Internet?"

The answer is yes and no. Yes, a router *is* needed to connect your network to the Internet, through your ISP. However, it's not immediately clear whether you'll need a router on your site (but your ISP might insist on one). Most installations do have a router on their premises that's connected to a router port at the ISP's site (see Figure 22.1). But no, you *don't* need a router on site because some ISPs offer you the option of using one of their router ports directly.

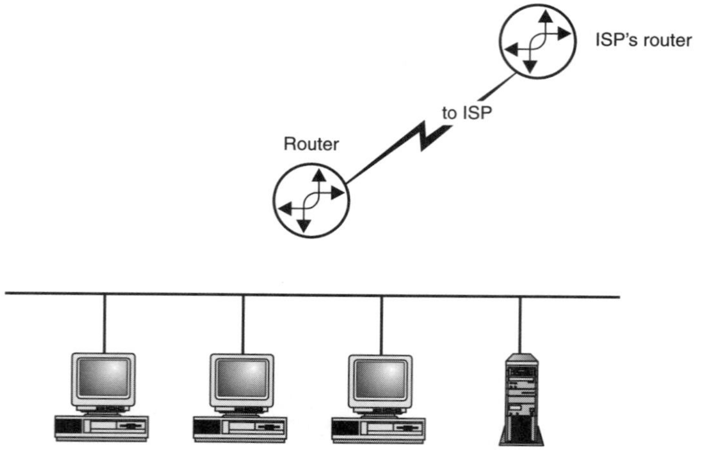

FIGURE 22.1

Connecting your LAN to the Internet through routers.

22

What's more, most servers can act as an IP router. Unless your ISP specifically requires a dedicated router, you might choose to use your server as the router, if it's not too heavily used. However, for security reasons (refer to the "Security Concerns" section later) and to have better control, most sites opt to maintain a dedicated router (which also acts as a firewall) on site.

Additional Equipment Required

Depending on what type of connection you're getting between your network and your ISP, you might need some equipment in addition to the router. For example, if you're going with a dedicated leased line, such as a T1, you need a CSU/DSU (Channel Service Unit/Data Service Unit) to connect your router to the leased line.

> The CSU is a device that connects a terminal (or a router port) to a digital line. The DSU is a device that performs protective and diagnostic functions for a telecommunications line. Typically, the two devices are packaged as a single unit (hence the name CSU/DSU). You can think of it as a very high-speed digital modem. Such a device is required for both ends of a T-1 or T-3 connection, and the units at both ends must be from the same manufacturer.

Some ISPs supply and maintain the router and the necessary requirements (such as the CSU/DSU) on both sides of the connection. Other providers insist that you buy and maintain all the equipment that's on "your" side of the connection. In the latter case, you should get the hardware recommendations from your ISP before you make any purchases to be sure that the equipment you buy is compatible with the ISP's equipment.

IP Address Considerations

Each network that's directly connected to the Internet is required to have an officially designated IP network address. Because you're connecting your network to a worldwide collection of systems, you need a unique set of IP addresses that identify your machines. Unless you've gotten a registered IP *network* address from the InterNIC (Internet Network Information Center; the folks who handle IP network address registrations), you'll probably be stuck with just one or two IP *host* addresses assigned to you by your ISP. What's worse, you might have already set up your IP infrastructure (using an arbitrary IP network address) before you decide that you need to connect to the Internet and now you need to change 150 addresses! Don't panic—there are easy fixes for these two issues.

Let's deal with the easier of the two problems first. Depending on the number of IP devices you need to manage, using a DHCP server to centrally assign and manage the IP address assignment is the best solution. The details on installing a DHCP server and configuring the clients to use it have been previously covered in Hour 18, "DHCP."

As for a lack of registered IP addresses, the easiest fix is generally to use a router that supports NAT. Short for *Network Address Translation*, *NAT* is an Internet standard that enables a LAN to use one set of IP addresses for internal traffic and a second set of addresses for external traffic. A NAT box located where the LAN meets the Internet makes all the necessary IP address translations (see Figure 22.2).

FIGURE 22.2

A NAT device can translate IP addresses between public and private networks.

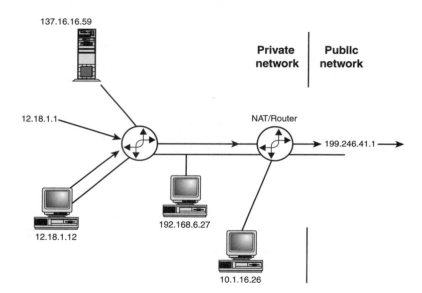

The main feature of NAT is to enable an organization to use the reserved IP network addresses (such as the 10.0.0.0 Class A network) or any IP network addresses, while still permitting clients or servers on this network to access, or be accessed by, the public Internet. It does this through a mechanism that substitutes a globally registered IP address into the source IP address part of a message leaving the private network, and restores the private IP address into the destination part of a reply message entering the private network. For example, take a look at the translatation table shown in Table 22.1.

TABLE 22.1 A SAMPLE NAT TRANSLATION TABLE.

Host Name	Private IP Address	Public IP Address
peter	12.18.1.12	199.246.41.1
john	10.1.16.26	199.246.41.2
nt1	192.168.6.27	199.246.41.3
nw1	137.16.16.59	199.246.41.4

A message originating at peter has 12.18.1.12 in the source IP address part of the message header. As it passes through the NAT to the Internet, the NAT substitutes 199.246.41.1 into that part of the header and recalculates the message checksums. The message is then sent to the addressed host on the "outside" as though it originated from the public address. When a message arrives at the NAT from the Internet addressed to 199.246.41.1, the private IP address of peter is substituted into the destination part of the message header, the checksums are recalculated, and the message is delivered to peter.

Notice that even though the four internal hosts in this example are spread across different IP networks , their public IP addresses have been consolidated into a very small section of the external IP network.

Internet Domain Name

Although not a necessity, when you connect your network to the Internet, you should get an *Internet domain name*. Having one equates to your company's presence on the Internet. For individuals, a domain name might be a novelty, but for a business that's connected to the Net, a domain name is a must. It allows someone to find your Web site or send you an email, for example.

Every domain name has a suffix that indicates which top-level domain (TLD) it belongs to. There are only a limited number of such domains; here are some examples:

- gov for U.S. government agencies
- edu for educational institutions (such as universities)
- org for organizations (nonprofit)
- mil for U.S. military installations
- com for commercial businesses
- net for network organizations (such as ISPs)

There are also TLDs for countries, such as the following:

- `ca` for Canada
- `fi` for Finland
- `jp` for Japan
- `nl` for The Netherlands
- `th` for Thailand
- `us` for United States

Because of a shortage of domain names at the top level, the Internet Ad Hoc Committee (IAHC) proposed six new top-level domains, which began being used in 1998:

- `store` for merchants
- `web` for organizations that emphasize Web activities
- `arts` for arts and cultural-oriented entities
- `rec` for recreation/entertainment sources
- `info` for information services organizations
- `nom` for individuals

The InterNIC handles all `edu`, `org`, `com`, and `net` domain name registrations. To apply for a domain name, you need to fill out an application and return it to the InterNIC by email or apply online through the Web. Here is the InterNIC Web site's URL:

`http://rs.internic.net`

Your ISP can also help you apply for a domain name. As a matter of fact, you should not apply for a domain name until you have your ISP's go-ahead. The reason is as follows: To "own" a domain name, you need to have two DNS servers—one acting as the primary DNS for your domain, and the other as a secondary DNS. You need to supply the IP addresses of these two DNS servers as part of your domain name application. In most cases, your ISP "hosts" your domain name on its DNS servers on your behalf. This is why you need your ISP's cooperation, and this is also why you can't apply for a domain name until you have signed up with an ISP (unless you have a registered IP network address).

If you want to have your own DNS servers, you can use the DNS Service on your Windows NT server. A broad outline of the necessary steps to install and configure a Windows NT server as a DNS server is given in the following sections. An in-depth discussion about DNS, however, is beyond the scope of this book.

Installing a Windows NT DNS Server

The DNS Service can be installed on a Windows NT server, but not on a Windows NT workstation. It's installed as follows:

1. Choose Start|Settings|Control Panel|Network.

2. Select the Services tab and then click Add.

3. Select Microsoft DNS Server and click OK.

4. The software is installed. Click OK when you're prompted to reboot the server.

Configuring the DNS Server

The DNS server is configured by using DNS Manager. This applet is added to the Administrative Tools group when the DNS Service is installed. Use the following steps to configure your domain:

1. Start the DNS Manager by choosing Start|Programs|Administrative Tools|DNS Manager.

2. From the DNS menu, choose New Server and enter the IP address of the DNS server, such as 199.246.41.20, and then click OK.

3. The server is then displayed with a CACHE sub part.

4. Choose New Zone from the DNS menu.

5. Select Primary (if this is the first DNS server) and click Next.

6. Enter the domain name, such as dreamlan.com, and then press Tab. DNS Manager fills in the Zone File Name. Click Next to continue.

7. Click Finish.

8. Next, a zone for reverse lookups must be created, so choose New Zone from the DNS menu.

9. Select Primary and click Next, and then enter the name of the first three octets of the domain's IP address plus in-addr.arpa. For example, if the domain's IP network address is 158.234.26, the entry would be 26.234.158.in-addr.arpa. (Note that the order of the three octets is reversed.) In this example, it would be 41.246.199.in-addr.arpa. Press Tab for the filename to be filled in automatically, click Next, and then click Finish.

10. Add a record for the DNS server by right-clicking the domain and choosing New Record.

11. Enter the name of the machine, such as dragon1, enter an IP address, such as 199.246.41.20, and click OK.

12. If you press F5 and examine the 41.246.199.in-addr.arpa domain, a record should be automatically added for dragon1 there, too.

Managing the DNS Database

The DNS Manager applet is used to manage the DNS database. Use the following procedure to add a record for a server named webserver whose IP address is 199.246.41.55 to the DNS:

1. Start the DNS Manager by choosing Start|Programs|Administrative Tools|DNS Manager.
2. Right-click on the domain, and choose New Record.
3. Enter the server name (webserver), and then enter 199.246.41.55 as the IP address.
4. Make sure the Create Associated PTR Record option is checked.
5. Click OK.

You can use the nslookup (name server lookup) utility to test the addition. Start a command prompt and enter the following:

```
nslookup webserver
```

The IP address of webserver is displayed. Also try the reverse translation by entering this:

```
nslookup 199.246.41.55
```

The name webserver is displayed.

Other Required Services

After you have your LAN link to the Internet up, one of the first things your users scream for is Internet email. Chances are you already have an email system in-house for local use. What you now need is a SMTP gateway to link your email system to the Internet. Depending on what you're using, the SMTP support might already be built in. Otherwise, you need to get the add-on. You need to add some records (known as MX records) into your DNS database to facilitate email routing. After this is all done, your users can send and receive Internet email by using *username@domain_name* as their email address.

One other often-requested service is a Web site. It could simply be for internal use, and such a Web site is sometimes referred to as the "innerWeb." Or, your marketing and sales people might hound you to get a Web site up and running for the rest of the world to see, and perhaps start doing some e-commerce. You can use the Internet Information Server (IIS), a Web server, that comes with Windows NT to set up your Web site.

Desktop Configuration

In Hour 20, "Connecting Your Windows 98 Desktop to the Internet," you learned that you can use the Internet Connection Wizard to set up a Windows 98 machine to connect to the Internet either by modem (telephone line) or LAN. When connecting with a LAN, IP configurations such as the IP address, DNS server address, gateway address, and so on must be preconfigured or issued by a DHCP server. Therefore, if you don't have a DHCP server, you need to manually configure each desktop and make sure you keep good records of what IP address is used on which computer and that there are no duplications.

When configuring the TCP/IP properties for your network card, you should make sure the following three selections are correctly set:

- If you don't have a DHCP server, select Specify an IP Address and then enter the appropriate information in the IP Address tab of the TCP/IP Properties dialog box (see Figure 22.3). Otherwise, select Obtain an IP Address Automatically.
- If you have access to a DNS server, select the Enable DNS option and then enter the associated DNS information in the DNS Configuration tab of the TCP/IP Properties dialog box (see Figure 22.4). Otherwise, select Disable DNS.
- Enter the IP address of the router port that's local to the network your computer is on in the Gateway tab of the TCP/IP Properties dialog box (see Figure 22.5). Using the example shown in Figure 22.2, the IP address for the gateway for host `12.18.1.12` is `12.18.1.1`.

FIGURE 22.3

The IP address information for the network card when using a LAN connection to access the Internet.

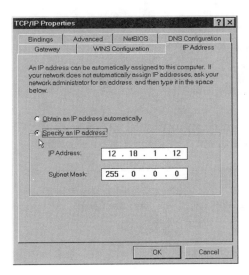

FIGURE 22.4

The DNS information for the network card when using a LAN connection to access the Internet.

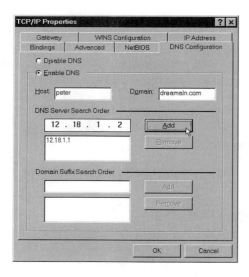

FIGURE 22.5

The gateway properties for the network card when using a LAN connection to access the Internet.

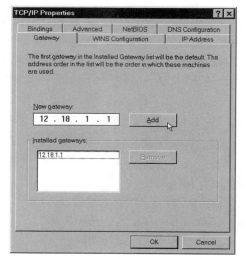

It's essential that you have correctly specified a gateway IP address for your desktops. Otherwise, the users can't access the Internet.

Security Concerns

For any network, security is always of prime concern, but whether network and server security is your *top* concern depends greatly on the type of your business you're in and how critical the information stored on your servers is.

As a network grows, there are more "points of intrusion." After your network is connected to the Internet, your possible points of intrusion are suddenly increased a million-fold—not only do you need to keep an eye out for the workstations on your network, but you also have to consider the more than 30 million people, from all over the world, who could now gain access to your network!

What makes it worse is that information can be leaked from the inside of your network to the Internet. For example, with PWS, the Web server that ships with Windows 98, any Windows 98 user can easily turn her desktop into a Web server and unknowingly allow confidential company information to be published to the World Wide Web!

As long as you're entertaining the idea of connecting your LAN to the Internet or have already connected to the Net, you should consider installing a proxy server or firewall between your network and the Internet to secure your network from outsiders and to control what Internet sites and services your users can access.

What's a Proxy Server?

A *proxy server* sits between a client application, such as a Web browser, and a real server (see Figure 22.6). One of the functions of a proxy server is to intercept all requests from the client that are going to the real server to see if it should forward or filter the request based on some administrator-entered criteria. For example, a company might use a proxy server to prevent its employees from accessing a specific set of Web sites.

FIGURE 22.6

Components of a proxy server.

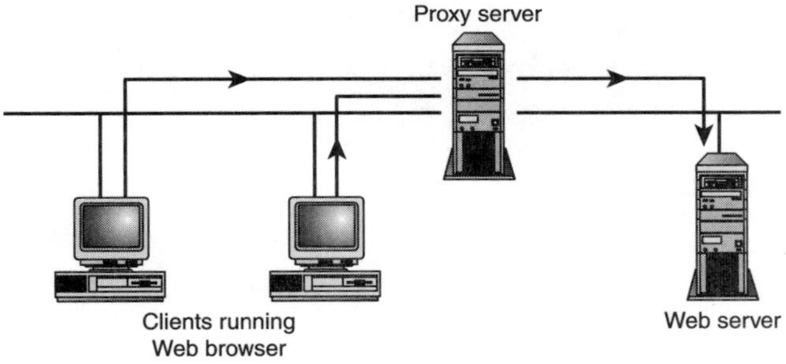

Proxy server

Clients running
Web browser

Web server

Proxy servers are also known as *application-level gateways* (see the following "What's a Firewall?" section) because they apply security mechanisms to specific applications, such as FTP and Web servers. All outgoing communications involving a proxy server show the address of the proxy server instead of the individual client's address. That means, as far as the real server is concerned, it's serving only one client instead of multiple clients. Consequently, accessing the Internet through a proxy server not only allows you to control what sites your users can access, but also prevents your company's internal network information (such as IP addresses) from being exported to the outside network.

A side benefit of a proxy server is enhanced performance in Web access. This benefit is discussed in more detail in the "Speeding Up Web Access" section later.

What's a Firewall?

A *firewall* is a system (often UNIX based) designed to prevent unauthorized access to or from a private network. Firewalls can be implemented in both hardware and software, or a combination of both. Firewalls are frequently used to prevent unauthorized Internet users from accessing private networks connected to the Internet, especially intranets. All messages entering or leaving the intranet pass through the firewall, which examines each message and blocks those that don't meet the specified security criteria.

There are several types of firewalls. Some firewalls are simply routers with packet-filtering capabilities, and the NAT discussed in the previous "IP Address Considerations" section is another type of firewall. True firewalls, however, take a multilevel approach by including packet-filtering as well as application-level gateways and circuit-level gateways.

In network-security jargon, firewalls and gateways are not the same, but the terms are often used rather casually. A firewall, in general, consists of several components, as shown in Figure 22.7. The filters (known as *security screens*) block the transmission of certain classes of traffic (such as HTTP or FTP). A gateway, on the other hand, is one or more machines that supply relay services (acting as a proxy) to compensate for the effects of the filter.

FIGURE 22.7

Components of a fire-wall.

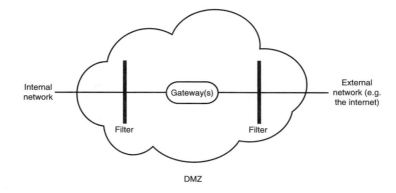

DMZ

The network region where the gateway resides is often called the *demilitarized zone* (*DMZ*). A gateway in the DMZ is sometimes assisted by an internal gateway (that is, two gateways can reside in the DMZ with one designated as the "internal" gateway and the other as the "outside" gateway). Typically, the internal gateway has more open communication through the inside screen than the outside gateway has to other internal hosts. In general, the outside screen is used to protect the gateway(s) from attack, and the inside screen, acting as a backup screen, is used to protect the internal network against the consequences of compromised gateways. Some of the more common types of security gateways are listed in Table 22.2.

TABLE 22.2 TYPES OF SECURITY GATEWAYS.

Gateway type	Description
Application-level gateway	Known as a forwarder, but more commonly referred to as a proxy server. It applies security mechanisms to specific applications, such as FTP and Telnet servers. This is very effective, but can impose a performance degradation.
Circuit-level gateway	Also known as a transparent proxy server. It relays TCP or UDP connections. A client on the internal network connects to a port on the gateway, which connects to some host on the other side of the gateway (in the outside network). During the session, the gateway copies the data between the two ports; after the connection has been made, packets can flow between the client and the host without further checking.
Packet-filtering gateway	It examines each packet entering or leaving the network and accepts or rejects the packet based on user-defined rules. Packet filtering is fairly effective and transparent to users, but it's difficult and labor-intensive to configure. In addition, it is susceptible to IP spoofing.

continues

TABLE 22.2   CONTINUED

Gateway type	Description
Screening router	It is the basic component of most firewalls. For example, it can filter TCP/IP traffic and restrict access so that only traffic between authorized hosts or network IP addresses is allowed to pass.

 IP spoofing is also known as *address spoofing*. See the "Q&A" section for more details.

A firewall is considered to be the first line of defense in protecting private network information. Many networks use a firewall that has application-level gateway (proxy) capability so that no internal network information (such as an IP address) is passed to the public network.

The following are some of the leading firewall products:

- BlackHole from Milky Networks Corporation (`http://www.milky.com`)
- BorderWare Firewall Server from Border Network Technology (`http://www.border.com`)
- Cyberguard Firewall from Harris Computer Systems (`http://www.hcsc.com`)
- Eagle from Raptor Systems (`http://www.raptor.com`)
- Firewall-1 from Checkpoint (`http://www.checkpoint.com`)

Virus Threats

Although a firewall or proxy server can deter would-be intruders from your network, they do nothing against computer viruses. A computer virus is a unique type of program that has the ability to self-replicate and store a copy of itself in another part of a computer system (usually on a hard drive, but it can also embed itself into another program). A virus program can be spread to other computers either by the transfer of an infected file or by direct access to other computers. With the vast amount of files available for easy download on the Internet, it's likely that one of your users could download an infected file unknowingly, and in turn infect your whole network. What's more, email attachments have become potential carriers of the dreaded new macro virus. The more you leverage networking and interconnections as a corporate advantage, the more you open your systems up to intrusion and viral infection. How can you prevent virus infection?

A macro virus is a set of macro commands for a particular application, such as Microsoft Word, that performs its dirty deed when you open the infected file attachment. One of the first and probably the most common macro viruses is the Microsoft Word macro virus, `Word.concept` (often referred to as the "concept macro virus"). It spreads by adding a macro to the global template `NORMAL.DOT`. The macro changes any file saved with Save As into a template file that includes the virus code.

The standard measures you can take to keep a standalone PC from getting infected also apply to the network environment. For example, you should install desktop- and server-based anti-virus products, such as:

- Dr. Solomon's Anti-Virus Toolkit from Ontrack Computer Systems Inc. (`http://www.drsolomon.com`)
- VirusScan from Network Associates (formerly McAfee Associates; `http://www.nai.com`)
- InnocuLAN from Cheyenne Software (`http://www.cheyenne.com`)
- Symantec Norton AntiVirus (`http://www.symantec.com/nav/`)
- Virus Protect from Intel (`http://www.intel.com`)

Furthermore, if you have a firewall or an email (SMTP) gateway, the following products can trap troublesome files and prevent them from reaching your workstations and servers:

- InterScan E-Mail Virus Wall from Trend Micro Devices (`http://www.antivirus.com`)
- MIMEsweeper from Integralis (`http://www.integralis.com`)
- WebShield from Network Associates, Inc. (`http://www.nai.com`)

Worthy of additional mention is WebShield's companion product, WebScanX. WebShield runs on a firewall; however, WebScanX not only detects and blocks viruses transmitted through Internet downloads, but also scans email attachments, stopping viruses before they have a chance to infect your system. What's more, WebScanX can block known hostile ActiveX and Java applets while letting useful ones continue to operate.

Usage Policy

For many years, human resources (HR) departments of companies have had what's known as an Acceptable Use Policy (AUP). It's often camouflaged as the employee manual you get when you join the organization. The AUP outlines the expected and appropriate behavior in the workplace. Very often, the AUP is supplemented with a Acceptable Computer Use Policy that outlines the expected and appropriate use of computer and related resources. Just about every AUP can be summarized as follows:

> "Work while at work, and use company property and resources for work-related uses only."

The Internet placed an interesting twist on the AUP, however. Where or how do you draw the line of acceptable use for accessing the Internet? The Internet is a major source of valuable information and is fast becoming a prime vehicle for conducting business (such as e-commerce). At the same time, the Internet can be a time waster or even a means of unethical or illegal behavior.

You need to work with your HR department on editing your current AUP to take into account the Internet. Much of it is common sense, but your usage policy should include not only Web browsing policy, but also an email usage guideline. You must spell out *very clearly* what's expected of your users and the consequences of violating the AUP.

You might consider using technological means (such as firewalls, discussed in the "Security Concerns" section earlier) to augment your AUP in preventing employees from retrieving offensive or illegal materials from the Internet.

Speeding Up Web Access

Have you ever heard of people referring to the WWW as the "World Wide Wait"? This symptom is most evident when you have a slow link (33.8Kbps or less) to the Internet. But even if you have a fast "pipe" (such as a T1), you can still run into the World Wide Wait problem. Fortunately, you can drastically improve your Web access performance by using a proxy server.

The proxy server is generally installed at your network's border (the point where your network meets other networks, such as the Internet). It establishes a cache (a very high-speed block of RAM) on the server where it stores information that users request from Internet or intranet Web servers. When users request that information again, the proxy server retrieves it quickly from this local cache. Because the proxy server doesn't have to establish an Internet connection or go to an overburdened intranet Web server to retrieve cached information, users get that information much more quickly.

The Internet services you enjoy as you browse the World Wide Web and your private intranets were originally designed without caching in mind. Of course, the designers at CERN (European Laboratory for Particle Physics) could not have anticipated the grand scale their original technologies would be taken to on the World Wide Web. But the impact of this oversight is tremendous when you consider the Internet's repetitive usage patterns and the potential benefits caching can offer in such an environment.

Consider the following characteristics of Internet/intranet access that can greatly benefit from caching:

- The access patterns of the Internet's global user community closely resemble the kind of patterns seen by videocassette rental businesses, in which 10 percent of the videos account for 90 percent of the rental business. In other words, the overwhelming majority of traffic on the Internet comes from relatively few, but extremely popular, sites. If the contents of these sites were cached in locations around the world, access times could be significantly increased for users around the globe.

- The access patterns of individual organizations and workgroups within organizations are also repetitive in nature. Workgroups tend to share similar responsibilities and interests, so they need access to similar sets of information. Corporate intranets are, therefore, another ideal environment for caching shared content.

Proxy servers generally support one or more of the following three types of caching:

- Proxy caching
- Hierarchical caching
- Web server acceleration

Proxy Caching

Proxy caching is an integral part of the proxy services you implement at your organization's Internet "border" (the connecting point between your network and the Internet). Proxy caching works as follows (see Figure 22.8):

1. A user issues a request for a file named DOC.HTM. This request is sent to the proxy cache over, for example, a 10Mbps Ethernet LAN segment. In this case, the request results in a "cache miss" because the proxy cache has never serviced a request for that document before.

2. The proxy cache initiates a request for DOC.HTM from the origin Web server on behalf of the user. This request is sent over the Internet until it arrives at the origin server.

3. The origin Web server responds to the proxy's request by sending DOC.HTM. The proxy then places DOC.HTM in its cache.

4. The proxy cache responds to the original user request with DOC.HTM.

5. When the same user (or any other user) issues a request for DOC.HTM, the request results in a "cache hit" because the proxy has kept a copy of the document in its cache.

6. In this case, the proxy replies immediately to the user request because it has DOC.HTM in cache. The proxy's response is transmitted at 10Mbps to the user, eliminating the need to fetch the document again from the origin server across the Internet.

FIGURE 22.8

A proxy cache saves repeatedly used objects to speed access and reduce Internet traffic.

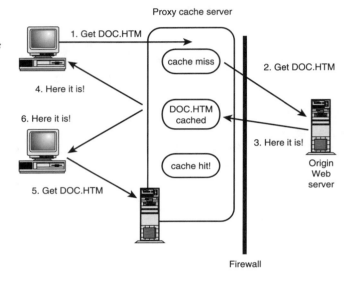

 A Web *object* refers to the components (such as a GIF image file) that make up a Web page.

The proxy cache also honors Time-To-Live (TTL) tags that dictate the length of time an object can remain in cache before it must be refreshed from the origin Web server. When the TTL expires on an object, the proxy cache Pings the origin Web server with an "if modified since" request. If the document has been modified, the proxy cache replaces the old object in its cache with a new one from the origin Web server. Dynamic requests for real-time data and other on-the-fly types of requests are not cached so that consumers always get the latest information.

When the proxy cache is operational and filled with content that's repeatedly accessed by your user community, the reduction of traffic on your Internet connection caused by browsing the same content can drastically reduce your bandwidth requirements and free your existing connections for fetching new content and servicing dynamic, non-cacheable requests.

This provides the performance you need to offset the unavoidable penalty you pay for access controls and content filtering. If your users do heavy-duty Web browsing, a proxy cache server is a must.

Proxy Cache Hierarchies

In large organizations, the advantages of a proxy cache can be multiplied by placing additional caches throughout the organization. Multiple proxy caches can be configured in a hierarchy to move shared content closer to those who use it. With a cache hierarchy in place, first-time accesses and cache misses can be fetched from other caches within your network, instead of returning all the way to the origin Web server in your intranet or on the Internet. Using a hierarchy, you have the added advantage of caching popular intranet content on the remote end of WAN links, thus improving performance for remote users and reducing the amount of traffic going across those links.

An organization with distributed workgroups across large LANs or WANs is an ideal candidate for a proxy cache hierarchy. In addition, these proxy caches communicate with each other to resolve cache misses before going to the origin Web server. You define the structure of a cache hierarchy by designating each proxy cache's peers and parents.

Both peers and parents can share their cache contents with one another, but only parents can fetch documents that don't exist in the hierarchy. When a proxy cache in the hierarchy encounters a cache miss (meaning a user requested a document that's not in its cache), the cache asks its peers and parents if they have the document. If the answer to one or more of these queries is yes, the cache fetches the document from the cache that was able to respond the fastest and has the highest priority. If none of its peers or parents has the requested document, the cache asks one of its parents to fetch the document from the origin Web server. This way, documents enter the organization through the top of the hierarchy and flow down into the hierarchy as they are requested.

Web Server Acceleration

Web servers can be a bottleneck in your intranet or Internet infrastructures. A busy Web server can quickly run out of connection capacity and often results in slow response times. In sites where performance is important, the only options usually considered are to upgrade to a more expensive Web server system or to split the content set across multiple Web servers. Neither of these options makes sense when caching offers such an elegant, cost-effective means to overcome the problem.

Some proxy servers can be configured as a "Web server accelerator." It eliminates the Web server's bottleneck by placing a dedicated cache *in front* of the Web server and handling requests for all of the Web server's cacheable content directly from its own cache.

22

Therefore, instead of the traditional proxy cache where it's located inside the firewall of the "requester's side," the reverse-proxy is located outside the firewall of the "provider's side" (see Figure 22.9).

FIGURE 22.9

The Web server accelerator offloads much of the Web server's workload and responds to requests at cached speeds.

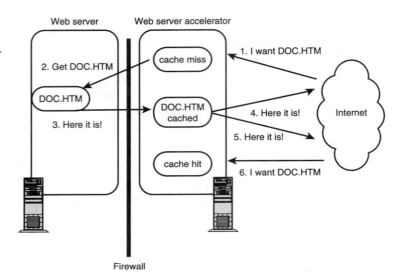

After this material is fetched from the Web server and cached in the Web server accelerator, the accelerator can handle all the requests for that content. This leaves the small percentage of dynamic requests to be "passed through" the accelerator for the origin Web server to process. Reverse-proxy caching works as follows (refer back to Figure 22.9):

1. An Internet user issues a request for a file named DOC.HTM from your Web server. This request is intercepted by the Web server accelerator. In this case, the request results in a "cache miss" because the Web server accelerator has never serviced a request for that document before.

2. The Web server accelerator initiates a request for DOC.HTM from your Web server on behalf of the remote user.

3. Your Web server responds to the Web server accelerator's request by sending it DOC.HTM. This transmission is much faster than a response to a browser. The Web server accelerator then places DOC.HTM in its cache.

4. The Web server accelerator responds to the original user request with DOC.HTM.

5. Now when the same user (or any other user) issues a request for DOC.HTM, the request results in a "cache hit" because the Web server accelerator has kept a copy of the document in its cache.

22

6. In this case, the Web server accelerator replies immediately to the browser request because it already has DOC.HTM cached. The proxy's response eliminates the need to fetch the document again from the origin Web server.

In most cases, the accelerator offloads 95–100 percent of the traffic previously handled by the Web server. This not only eliminates the need to upgrade your Web server to improve performance, but also leaves you with an underutilized Web server system and ample capacity for future growth. It might not sound like much if you have only one Web server because you're moving the load from one server (the Web server) to another server (the Web accelerator), but if you have more than one Web server being serviced by the accelerator, that starts to translate into some serious dollar-savings.

Summary

In this Hour, you've learned that in order to connect your network to the Internet, you need a router. And to protect your network from unwanted visitors from the Internet, a firewall is a must. Furthermore, you might have to reconfigure your network's IP addressing infrastructure or get a router that also supports NAT. Additionally, other administrative details, such as domain name registration, need to be taken care of. Finally, you learned that a firewall that incorporates proxy cache capabilities can dramatically speed up your WWW browsing.

In the next Hour, you find out where to find and use support resources, such as the Windows NT Resource Kit, for dealing with Windows 98 and Windows NT.

Workshop

Q&A

Q A firewall for home use is generally out of the question. What can I do to prevent my kids from accessing certain sites on the Internet?

A There are a number of workstation-based "censorware" products you can use to block your kids from accessing undesirable material online. The following are some examples:

- CyberPatrol (http://www.cyberpatrol.com)
- CyberSitter (http://www.solidoak.com/cysitter.htm)
- NetNanny (http://www.netnanny.com)
- SurfWatch (http://www.surfwatch.com)
- The Internet Filter (http://turnercom.com/if)

Q What's IP spoofing?

A IP or address spoofing makes use of TCP/IP's assumption, without verification, that the source address of any IP packet is valid. Therefore, it's possible to fake the source address of an incoming packet to fool the packet-filtering firewall into thinking the data is coming from an authorized system.

Q How can I find out if a domain name has already been registered?

A You can do a name search at `http://rs.internic.net` to find out if a domain name has been claimed or not.

Q Can I restrict my users to only browsing the WWW without being able to download any files by FTP?

A Yes, by using a firewall. Most firewalls allow you to configure what high-level application protocol to block. Therefore, you can allow HTTP to pass through, but not FTP. However, keep in mind that some Web sites allow file downloads through HTTP as well as FTP.

Quiz

1. If you're to host your own domain name, how many DNS servers do you need?

2. Define NAT and explain its main feature.

3. True or False: Anyone can apply for a domain name in the `edu` name space.

4. How can you find out the IP address for `www.microsoft.com`?

5. To speed up WWW browsing for your users, which proxy would you use? Proxy cache or reverse-proxy cache?

HOUR 23

Support Resources

Support is a topic near and dear to the hearts of all administrators. When your hardware is completely down, perhaps because of a failed power supply in the server, the problem and solution are obvious. When the hardware is just flaky—that is, operating, but operating oddly—things get a bit tougher because the symptoms become strange and varied.

But nothing compares to the complexity of software! If you've ever wished you had a guru to talk to when you were digging into solving an obscure problem, then TechNet needs to be your first line of defense. If you support Windows, then you need TechNet—and no, I'm not getting a kickback from Microsoft for this pitch!

This Hour covers the following topics:

- Finding out what TechNet offers
- Installing and using TechNet
- Fine-tuning queries for troubleshooting
- Getting the Resource Kit

TechNet

A subscription to TechNet gets you 12 issues—one each month. The first shipment you get contains everything you need to get up-to-date, including all the service packs, utilities, drivers, patches, library archives, and a binder to put it all in. Every month, you then get at least two CD-ROM updates in each issue to keep current. Table 23.1 lists what you get with TechNet.

TABLE 23.1 MICROSOFT TECHNET'S FEATURES.

Feature	Description
Microsoft Knowledge Base	The same support information used by Microsoft support. Over 60,000 issues and resolutions in a searchable database.
Resource Kits	Extra references and utilities. All the Resource Kits are included.
Technical Information	Technical notes, tips, and facts.
Drivers and Patches	Updated monthly. Drivers, patches, and utilities.
Service Packs	Essential fixes and tools and additional drivers.
Case Studies	How other companies have implemented Microsoft solutions. White Papers In-depth analysis of Microsoft technologies.
Evaluation and Reviewers Guides	How to evaluate Microsoft products and how to justify new technologies.
Training Materials	Training resources to help you and end users deploy and use the products.
Total Cost of Ownership Information	A collection of articles exploring TCO.

Unless you're in the habit of reading white papers in your free time, you are probably more interested in the concrete benefits. These are the service packs, which you don't have to download; the Resource Kits, which you don't have to buy separately; and the Knowledge Base, which can be searched.

Purchasing TechNet

You can get more information on TechNet at www.microsoft.com/TechNet. At this site, you can place an order online, or you can call Microsoft at 1-800-344-2121, extension 3118.

The cost is $299 for a single-user license and $699 for a server license. The single-user license allows you to load TechNet onto a single computer and access the information, and the server license lets you load TechNet on the server so all the users connected to it can access the information.

Installing and Using TechNet

Installing TechNet is simple: Just pop in the CD-ROM and run Setup. The only choices you have to make are the directory to install to and the type of installation, as shown in Figure 23.1.

FIGURE 23.1

The TechNet installation. Choose the type of install and the directory, and that's it!

The maximum install takes only a little more disk space, so just choose that and move on. (The minimum install runs a bit slower because some of the files are still on the CD-ROM, and the custom install lets you choose from a very few options, such as installing Help.)

After it's running, you see the main screen, shown in Figure 23.2.

23

FIGURE 23.2

The TechNet main window.

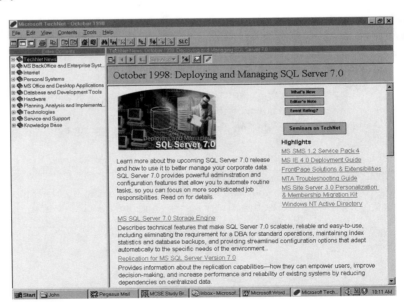

Take the time to look over the help or just start poking around. A few of the query options are covered soon. For now, however, click the icon that looks like a pair of binoculars, and you see the query dialog box, shown in Figure 23.3. After it opens, search on name resolution.

FIGURE 23.3

The TechNet Query dialog box.

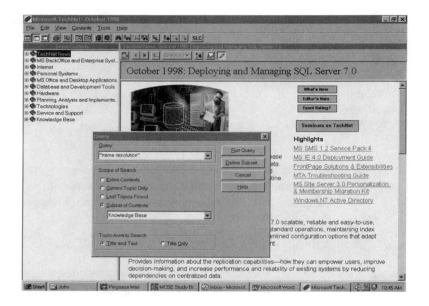

As shown in Figure 23.4, searching for name resolution yields 402 hits.

It's possible to make your query more specific, but for now, assume the information you're after is shown on the screen in Figure 23.4. You can "drill down" and display the results by either double-clicking the entry or clicking the Display button (see Figure 23.5).

If you need to refine the parameters to try to get more specific results, click the New Query button and enter new parameters.

FIGURE 23.4

The search has returned 402 hits.

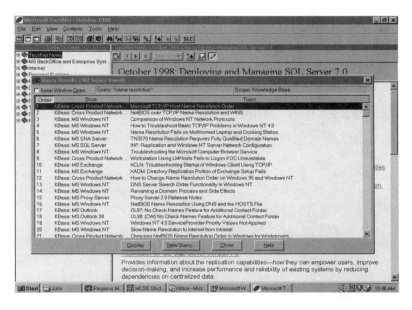

FIGURE 23.5

At last, the information you're after!

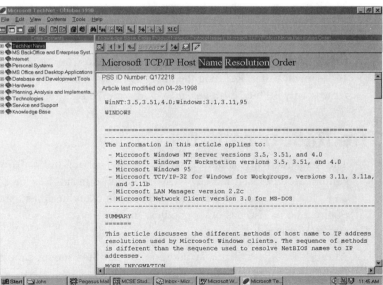

You can most likely get the same results by searching on the Microsoft Web site, but you have to deal with slow Internet access. But then again, what if you are on location and don't have Internet access? Or maybe your Internet access is the problem you're trying to fix!

Refining Queries

There are many ways to refine your query to limit the number of hits you get. Suppose, for example, you want to limit your name resolution search to information about the TCP/IP name resolution order. Table 23.2 lists your refinement options.

TABLE 23.2 QUERY OPTIONS.

Type of Query	Example	Will Return
Word	`jump`	Jump, jumped, jumps (the word and its variations)
Phrase	`"network card"`	Network card (without quotes, you would get results that contain *network* and *card*)
Wildcard	`tab*`	Tab, table, and so on
Boolean AND	`network AND`	The words *network*, *card*, and card AND *interface* in the same topic `interface`
Boolean OR	`network OR card`	The words *network*, or *card*, or OR interface *interface*
Boolean NOT	`font NOT truetype`	Information on fonts that are not TrueType
NEAR operator	`John NEAR Pence`	The words *john* and *pence* in the same topic NEAR each other.

Refining your query to `"name resolution" AND TCP/IP` reduces the number of hits to 164—much better. Refining the query to `"name resolution" AND TCP/IP AND router` returns only 39 hits, even easier to deal with. You get the idea.

The Resource Kit

The Resource Kit is another "must have" for network administrators. The installation is simple: Merely insert the CD-ROM and choose Install Resource Kit, as shown in Figure 23.6. Not only does the Resource Kit contain useful utilities, but, as you can see in Figure 23.6, it also has other goodies, such as desktop themes, crystal reports, and Web admininistration.

After it's installed, there's an addition to your Start menu; choosing Start | Programs | Resource Kit takes you to the utilities with a graphical interface. The default installation is to c:\ntreskit; if you drop to a command prompt and look around in that directory, you see many more command-line utilities. Figure 23.7 shows you an overview of the Resource Kit tools.

FIGURE 23.6

More than just utilities come with the Resource Kit.

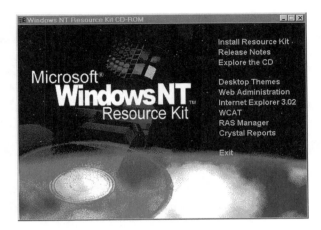

FIGURE 23.7

The Resource Kit has excellent documentation, as do many of the individual utilities.

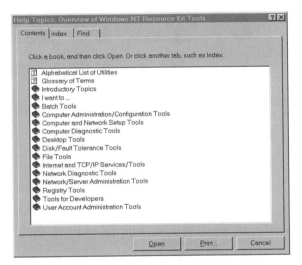

23

Notice the options for the AT command, which is used to schedule events (see Figure 23.8). It is command-line driven, and the syntax is critical. In short, NT shipped with the ability to schedule jobs, but it doesn't come easy; you might have trouble getting the command files you schedule with AT to function correctly. Thankfully, WinAt, the GUI version of AT, ships with the Resource Kit (see Figure 23.9). Of the two choices, I'll take the GUI version, thank you! You merely select when you want the command to run, type in the command, and click OK.

FIGURE 23.8

The AT command and its options.

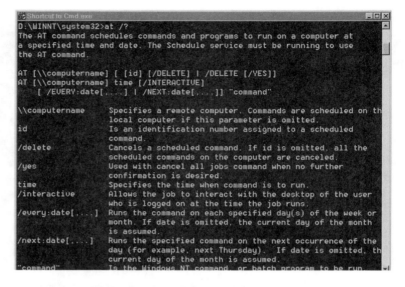

FIGURE 23.9

The WinAt program is much easier to use than the AT command.

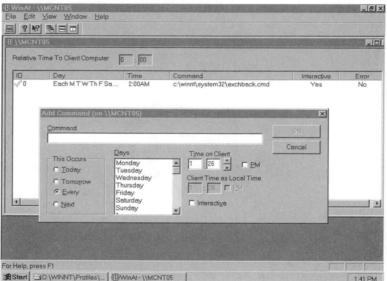

If the scheduler service isn't running, WinAt notices this and asks if you want it started. Also, like many of the other management tools in NT, you can select the computer you want to work with. That means you can schedule jobs on other machines without having to walk all the way over to them.

If you point your newsreader to the Microsoft forums discussed in Hour 24, "Online Resources," you will see literally hundreds of references to the Resource Kit as the solution to the question asked. I could devote an entire book to nothing but Resource Kit utilities and their options, but I hope what you've seen here convinces you. Even though you can buy the Resource Kit by itself, don't. For a bit more money, purchase TechNet; the Resource Kit comes with it.

Summary

Troubleshooting—what we all live for! Completely broken hardware is easy, but intermittently working or flaky hardware is more difficult to pin down because the symptoms can be all over the place. However, nothing compares to the complexity of troubleshooting software. Networking and computers are changing so fast that you need access to as many resources as possible just to stay in one place.

Short of opening a call with Microsoft, which you have to pay for, your first line of defense should be TechNet. With TechNet, you can research a symptom or search for information on how things work. TechNet is the same database used by Microsoft support, so odds are that if you do open a call, it's the first place Microsoft support will look.

It's a tremendous resource to be able to search the technical database, and getting the updates and service packs on CD-ROM is infinitely better than fighting for time on the Internet to download these huge beasts.

The Resource Kit, which comes with TechNet, is filled with many utilities that help fill gaps in the operating system. When monitoring the forums at `msnews.microsoft.com` with your newsreader, you will see the Resource Kit as the answer to many, many questions time after time. The Resource Kit can be purchased separately, but you would do better spending a bit more to buy TechNet, which gives you the Resource Kit, too.

Workshop

Q&A

Q When I have questions, do I have any recourse other than opening a call with Microsoft?

A Absolutely! You can post a message in the forums, you can search Microsoft's Web site, or you can use the querying capabilities of TechNet.

Q How much does TechNet cost?

A A single-user license is $300 for a one-year subscription.

Q What is the Resource Kit?

A The Resource Kit is a collection of utilities, both graphical and command-line based, that fill many holes in the operating system.

Quiz

1. After reading this chapter, you're going to buy _____.

2. You have some money approved for training and support. Which should you purchase: TechNet or the Resource Kit?

3. True or False: When querying, all you can do is put in the keywords you're after. There's no way to fine-tune the queries.

4. True or False: It's not possible to query for words that are near each other in the same topic.

HOUR 24

Online Resources

Thanks to the tremendous explosion of interest in the World Wide Web and Internet connectivity, there's a wealth of information online. Almost all vendors, both software and hardware, now have sites where they post fixes and offer drivers available for download, provide lists of FAQs (frequently asked questions), and supply product information. This Hour you take a look at a few of the available resources; the following topics are covered:

- Search engines
- Newsgroups
- Mailing lists

The World Wide Web

The Web is truly amazing. Anyone and everyone has posted information, covering every topic the mind can imagine; this is both a blessing and a curse. The blessing is that this information is online and easily available; the curse is that there's as much or more garbage online as there is useful information. You can search the Web with search engines like AltaVista or Yahoo!, but often the results of a search are simply overwhelming because of the enormous amount of information available.

Have you ever needed to put in a hard disk and had no idea what jumper settings needed to be changed? Odds are you long ago lost the tiny booklet that came with the drive, showing which pins do what. In lieu of spending hours on hold trying to reach tech support on the phone, you can go to the vendor's Web site and get the drawing immediately. And the Web never sleeps; you won't get a message telling you what hours technical support is available. Everything from patches, drivers, product descriptions, and even free evaluations are there 24 hours a day.

When searching, take a moment to look at the advanced search features. Being able to fine-tune the search gives you more focused results and gets you back into action sooner. For example, at `http://altavista.digital.com/`, if you search on the words `Elvis` and `Memphis`, you get the results shown in Table 24.1. (Note that even changing the letters *M* and *E* to *m* and *e* alters the results!)

TABLE 24.1   SEARCH RESULTS DIFFER WITH SLIGHT CHANGES TO THE QUERY

Name	City	Search Results
Elvis	Memphis	336,780
elvis	Memphis	302,290
elvis	memphis	303,260
+elvis	+memphis	10,784

It's much easier to deal with 10,784 results than over 300,000, but even 10,000 is too many. Nevertheless, you get the idea. Learning to use the full functionality of the search engines can be very helpful. (Each search engine operates a bit differently, but most have a Tips or Hints button you can click to learn about narrowing your search.) In Table 24.1, the first three searches return hits on pages that contain the words *elvis* **or** *memphis*, but the last one shown, `+elvis +memphis`, is actually specifying *elvis* **and** *memphis*.

Of course, you regularly visit `www.microsoft.com` and `www.novell.com`, but you shouldn't limit yourself to official corporate sites. Many sites put up by businesses or individuals have excellent tips, tricks, downloads, and information. For example, John Savill maintains an NT FAQ site at `www.ntfaq.com`, as shown in Figure 24.1.

FIGURE 24.1

Not all the best sites are run by the giants like Microsoft and Novell. This NT FAQ site is an excellent example.

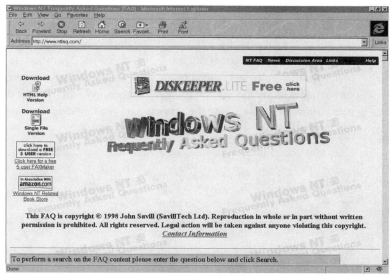

When you get out and start looking on the Web, you will find more networking-related sites than you can possibly keep up with, so happy hunting and learning. It won't be long until you have bookmarks overflowing the screen and leaking out onto the floor!

Microsoft Newsgroups

Newsgroups and support forums can be excellent resources, but, just like the Web, you have to take the good with the bad. If the forum is unmoderated, there's spam and advertising you need to ignore. On a moderated forum or newsgroup, the SysOps, or system operators, keep the advertising and inapplicable posts cleaned out. The idea behind the forums is to keep from reinventing the wheel. Odds are you're not the only one who has ever seen the problem you're currently wrestling with. Posting a question in the correct forum often brings several good answers, but beware: You're just as likely to get an incorrect answer. Even though the person posting the response is trying to help, there's no guarantee he knows what he's talking about.

People post on topics with religious intensity, and often threads that start off on one topic wind up with the individuals vehemently flaming each other. At times, this can be amusing, but it can also be annoying. So consider sitting on your hands a while before making an emotion-filled post!

When someone merely monitors a forum and seldom (if ever) posts, this is called *lurking*. Picking a newsgroup and watching it is an excellent way to keep your fingers on the pulse of what's really going on in the networking world. For example, suppose that Microsoft or Novell comes out with a service pack. You shouldn't rush out, download it, and slap it on your server simply because it's there. Instead, take your time, monitor the forums, and see if the service pack is causing problems. If you don't see message after message talking about how the service pack was installed and now such and such no longer works, then it's probably safe to move ahead.

> One bit of Net etiquette to keep in mind is cross-posting. If you have a question about NT Server and post it in one of the NT forums, you don't need to cross-post it to 50 other unrelated forums.

But enough discussion—time to go look at a list. There are two ways you can get to the newsgroups. The first is with your Web browser. Figure 24.2 shows setting up Netscape to view the messages at msnews.microsoft.com.

FIGURE 24.2

You can use your Web browser to monitor the newsgroups.

If you intend to seriously start monitoring some forums, then you might want to consider a software package called a *newsreader*. The newsreader software has far more functionality because it's designed for just this purpose. Figure 24.3 shows Gravity, a commercial newsreader, pointed to one of the Novell forums. (By now, most sites have a mix of

Novell and NT, and there are client issues that make monitoring a Novell forum important, even if your real interest is in Windows, or vice versa. The end users are going to
need access to both operating systems.) Notice in the middle pane of Figure 24.3 that the
newsreader shows the chain of postings, or the *thread*.

FIGURE 24.3

*A newsreader, such as
Anawave Gravity
shown here, is
designed especially for
reading newsgroups.*

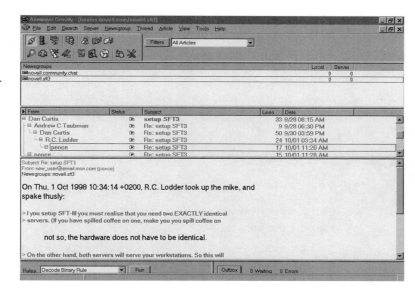

24

Mailing Lists

There are many mailing lists out there, covering every conceivable topic. Mailing lists
send you emails of postings to the list, and they generally have two versions. In the first,
you get each posting to the list as an individual email. In the digest version, you get one
large email containing that day's postings to the list.

One thing to keep in mind about mailing lists is that there's no threading. Message number 1 might be a question, messages number 2, 3, and 4 other questions, and then message 5 might be an answer to the question posed in message 1. Not having the messages
threaded can be a bit confusing.

Also, the volume on some of the lists is incredible, so it's not uncommon to subscribe to
a list and then shortly thereafter unsubscribe! How to find these mailing lists? Use one of
the search engines or post a question in one of the newsgroups!

There are no naming conventions for newsgroups or mailing lists, so you have to search
for them or ask in one of the forums. Msnews.microsoft.com is an excellent place to
begin your online forays; it has more than 700 newsgroups you can subscribe to. Also,
don't forget your hardware and software vendors' Web sites.

Summary

The Internet is truly making a global village out of things. There's practically no topic you can't find information about on the World Wide Web. It's worthwhile to take a few minutes and learn the ins and outs of your favorite search engine to help you focus your searches. You can also use your browser or a newsreader to read and post in the news-groups, and you can start by pointing your newsreader to `msnews.microsoft.com`. Mailing lists are also in abundance and can be found by searching or posting a query. Mailing lists send you emails of the postings as they make it to the list, or you can request the digest version, which sends you only one email containing that day's post-ings. Watch out for the quantity of email you might start to get; the volume can be enor-mous, depending on how many subscribers there are and how active the list is.

Workshop

Q&A

Q Can I use my browser to read the newsgroups at `msnews.microsoft.com`, or do I need a newsreader?

A Your browser will work. For more serious monitoring of the forums, a newsreader has more functionality.

Q What is a mailing list?

A People post questions to a mailing list, and you get the posts and responses as emails. You can subscribe to a mailing list and get either the individual posts or the digest version.

Quiz

For answers to these quiz questions, use what you've learned this Hour to search the Web!

1. Is there a way to trace TCP/IP traffic using NT?

2. How do I remove a hot fix?

3. How do I uncompress a directory?

APPENDIX A

Glossary

1000Base-CX   Extremely fast (1000Mbps) Ethernet, typically strung via copper wire and capable of transmitting a distance of some 75 feet.

1000Base-LX   Extremely fast (1000Mbps) Ethernet, typically strung via fiber-optic cable and capable of transmitting a distance of some 9,000 feet.

1000Base-SX   Extremely fast (1000Mbps) Ethernet, typically strung via fiber cable and capable of transmitting a distance of some 1,500 feet.

1000Base-TX   Extremely fast (1000Mbps) Ethernet, typically strung via copper wire and capable of transmitting a distance of some 330 feet.

100Base-FX   Fast (100Mbps) Ethernet, typically strung via fiber-optic cable and capable of transmitting a distance of some 412 meters.

100BaseT   Fast (100Mbps) Ethernet, supporting various cabling schemes and capable of transmitting a distance of some 205 meters.

10BaseT   Twisted pair Ethernet, capable of transmitting to distances of 328 feet.

10Base2   Coaxial (thin wire) Ethernet, capable of transmitting to distances of 600 feet.

10Base5   Coaxial (thick wire) Ethernet that by default transports data to distances of 1,500 feet.

802.2   An Ethernet frame format (probably the most common), typically used in local area networks.

acceptable use policy (AUP)   Originally established by the National Science Foundation, AUP once forbade use of the Internet for commercial purposes. Today, AUP refers to rules a user must adhere to when using an ISP's services.

access control   Any tool or technique that allows you to selectively grant or deny users access to system resources.

access control list (ACL)   A list that stores information on users and what system resources they're allowed to access.

ACL   *See* **access control list**.

active hub   An active hub is one that has intelligence built into it—for example, to make it error-tolerant. *See also* **hub**.

adapter   A hardware device used to connect devices to a motherboard. In networking context, an Ethernet adapter/card.

adaptive pulse code modulation   A method of encoding voice into digital format over communication lines.

adaptive routing   Routing designed to adapt to the current network load. Adaptive routing diverts data around bottlenecks and congested network areas.

Address Resolution Protocol (ARP)   Maps IP addresses to physical addresses.

administrator   Either a person charged with controlling a network or the supervisory account in Windows NT. (Whoever has Administrator privileges in NT can—but need not necessarily—hold complete control over the network, workgroup, or domain.)

ADSL   *See* **Asymmetric Digital Subscriber Line**.

American National Standards Institute   *See* **ANSI**.

analog system   This term is generally used to describe the telephone system, which uses analog technology to convert voice to electronic signals. Many telephones in modern office systems are *digital*, which means that if you plug your modem into the jack, you risk damage to the modem!

Anonymous FTP   FTP service available to the public that allows anonymous logins. Anyone can access anonymous FTP with the user name anonymous and his or her email address as the password.

A

ANSI   The American National Standards Institute. Check them out at
`http://www.ansi/org`.

answer-only modem   A modem that answers but cannot dial out. (They are useful for preventing users from initiating calls from your system.)

applet   A small Java program that runs in a Web browser environment. Applets add graphics, animation, and dynamic text to otherwise lifeless Web pages.

application gateways   Firewall devices that prevent direct communication between the Internet and an internal, private network. Data flow is controlled by proxies that screen out undesirable information or hosts. *See also* **proxy server**.

application level   Layer 7 of the OSI reference model, the highest layer of the model. The application level defines how applications interact over the network. This is the layer of communications that occurs (and is conspicuous) at the user level. (Example: File Transfer Protocol interfaces with the user at the application level; routing occurs at layer 3, or the network level.)

ARP   *See* **Address Resolution Protocol**.

ARPAnet   Advanced Research Projects Agency Network. This was the original Internet, which, for many years, was controlled by the Department of Defense.

ASCII   American Standard Code for Information Interchange. ASCII is a common standard by which all operating systems treat simple text.

Asymmetric Digital Subscriber Line (ADSL)   A high-speed, digital telephone technology that offers fast downloading (nearly 6MBps) but much slower uploading (about 65KBps). Unfortunately, ADSL is a new technology available only in major metropolitan areas.

asynchronous data transmission   The transmission of data one character at a time.

asynchronous PPP   Run-of-the-mill PPP; the kind generally used by PPP dial-up customers.

asynchronous transfer mode (ATM)   An ATM network is one type of circuit-switched packet network that can transfer information in standard blocks at high speed. (They are not to be confused with automatic teller networks.) ATM packets are called *cells*.

ATM   *See* **asynchronous transfer mode**.

attachment unit interface (AUI)   A 15-pin twisted-pair Ethernet connection or connector.

attribute   The state of a given resource (whether file or directory) and whether that resource is readable, hidden, system, or other.

AUI   *See* **attachment unit interface**.

AUP   *See* **acceptable use policy**.

authenticate   When you authenticate a particular user or host, you are verifying their identity.

authentication   The process of authenticating either a user or host. Such authentication can be simple and applied at the application level (demanding a password), or can be complex (as in challenge-response dialogs between machines, which generally rely on algorithms or encryption at a discrete level of the system).

Authentication Server Protocol   A TCP-based authentication service that can verify the identity of a user. (Please see RFC 931.)

automounting   The practice of automatically mounting network drives at boot or when requested.

back door   A hidden program, left behind by an intruder (or perhaps a disgruntled employee), that allows him or her future access to a victim host. This term is synonymous with *trap door*.

backbone   The fastest and most centralized feed on your network; the heart of your network to which all other systems are connected.

back up   To preserve a file system or files, usually for disaster recovery. Generally, a backup is done to tape, floppy disk, or other, portable media that can be safely stored for later use.

bandwidth   The transmission capacity of your network medium, measured in bits per second.

baseband   Audio and video signals sent over coaxial cable, typically used in cable television transmissions. In particular, the signals are sent without frequency shifting of the wave. (The *base* in 10BaseT refers to this type of signal.)

bastion host   A server that's hardened against attack and can therefore be used outside the firewall as your "face to the world." They are often sacrificial.

biometric access controls   Systems that authenticate users by physical characteristics, such as face, fingerprints, retinal pattern, or voice.

BNC   A coaxial cable or connection used in older Ethernet networks. (BNC connectors look similar to cable television wire connectors.)

bootstrap protocol A network protocol used for remote booting. (Diskless workstations often use a bootstrap protocol to contact a boot server. In response, the boot server sends boot commands.)

border gateway protocol A protocol that facilitates communication between routers serving as gateways.

bottleneck An area of your network that demonstrates sluggish transfer rates, usually casued by network congestion or misconfiguration.

bridge A network hardware device that connects local area networks. Now known as a *switch*.

broadband A very high-speed data transmission system, capable of supporting large transfers of media such as sound, video, and other data. Unlike baseband, broadband can use several different frequencies.

broadcast/broadcasting Any network message sent to all network hosts, or the practice of sending such a message.

bug A hole or weakness in a computer program. *See also* **vulnerability**.

cable modem A modem that negotiates Internet access over cable television networks. (Cable modems provide blazing speeds.)

call back Call-back systems ensure that a trusted host initiated the current connection. The host connects, a brief exchange is had, and the connection is cut; then the server calls back the requesting host.

Carrier Sense Multiple Access with Collision Avoidance (CSMA/CA) A traffic-management technique used by Ethernet. In CSMA/CA, workstations announce to the network that they're about to transmit data.

Carrier Sense Multiple Access with Collision Detection (CSMA/CD) A traffic-management technique used by Ethernet. In CSMA/CD, workstations check the wire for traffic before transmitting data.

Cast-128 An encryption algorithm that uses large keys and can be incorporated into cryptographic applications. (You can learn more by getting RFC 2144.)

CERT *See* **Computer Emergency Response Team**.

certificate authority Trusted third-party clearinghouse that issues security certificates and ensures their authenticity. Probably the most renowned commercial certificate authority is VeriSign, which issues (among other things) certificates for Microsoft-compatible ActiveX components. A *certificate* is used to verify the identity of a server or a user on the network.

certification   Either the end result of a successful security evaluation of a product or system or an academic honor bestowed on those who successfully complete courses in network engineering and support. Two of the most popular are Novell's CNE (Certified NetWare Engineer) and Microsoft's MCSE (Microsoft Certified System Engineer.)

CGI   *See* **common gateway interface**.

Challenge Handshake Authentication Protocol (CHAP)   Protocol (often used with PPP) that challenges users to verify their identity. If the challenge is properly met, the user is authenticated. If not, the user is denied access. See RFC 1344 for further information.

channel   In networking, a communications path.

CHAP   *See* **Challenge Handshake Authentication Protocol**.

circuit   A connection that conducts electrical currents and, by doing so, transmits data. Also refers to a TCP, or "circuit-oriented" connection.

client   Software designed to interact with a specific server application. For example, Web browsers like Netscape Communicator and Internet Explorer are Web clients. They are specifically designed to interact with Web or HTTP servers.

client/server model   A programming model in which a single server can distribute data to many clients (the relationship between a Web server and Web clients or browsers is a good example). Many network applications and protocols are based on the client/server model.

CNE   Certified NetWare Engineer.

COM Port   A serial communications port, sometimes used to connect modems (and even mice).

common carrier   Any government-regulated utility that provides the public with communications (for example, a telephone company).

common gateway interface (CGI)   A standard that specifies programming techniques by which you pass data from Web servers to Web clients. (CGI is language neutral. You can write CGI programs in Perl, C, C++, Python, Visual Basic, BASIC, and shell languages.)

compression   The technique of reducing data size for the purposes of maximizing resource utilization—that is, bandwidth or disk space. (The smaller the data, the less bandwidth or disk space you need for it.)

Computer Emergency Response Team (CERT)   A security organization that acts to disseminate information about security fixes and helps victims of cracker attacks. Find them at `http://www.cert.org`.

copy access   When a user has copy access, it means he or she has privileges to copy a particular file.

cracker   Someone who, with malicious intent, unlawfully breaches the security of computer systems or software. Some folks say *hacker* when they actually mean *cracker*.

CSMA/CA   *See* **Carrier Sense Multiple Access with Collision Avoidance**.

CSMA/CD   *See* **Carrier Sense Multiple Access with Collision Detection**.

DAC   *See* **discretionary access control**.

Data Encryption Standard (DES)   Encryption standard from IBM, developed in 1974 and published in 1977. DES is the U.S. government standard for encrypting non-classified data.

data link level   Layer 2 of the OSI reference model. This level defines the rules for sending and receiving information between network devices.

datagram   A packet or "…a self-contained, independent entity of data carrying sufficient information to be routed from the source to the destination computer without reliance on earlier exchanges between this source and destination computer and the transporting network…" (RFC 1594).

DECnet   An antiquated, proprietary protocol from Digital Equipment Corporation that runs chiefly over proprietary, Ethernet, and X.25 networks.

DES   *See* **Data Encryption Standard**.

DHCP   Dynamic Host Configuration Protocol. A method for allocating IP addresses to hosts "on the fly" instead of assigning them statically. See RFC 1534 and RFC 2132.

digest access authentication   A security extension for HTTP that provides only basic (not encrypted) user authentication. To learn more, see RFC 2069.

digital certificate   Any digital value used in authentication. Digital certificates are typically numeric values, derived from cryptographic processes. (Many values can be used as the basis of a digital certificate, including but not limited to biometric values, such as retinal scans.)

discretionary access control (DAC)   Provides means for a central authority on a computer system or network to either permit or deny access to all users and do so incisively, based on time, date, file, directory, or host.

DNS   *See* **domain name service**.

domain name   A host name or machine name, such as gnss.com. (This is the non-numeric expression of a host's address. Numeric expressions are always in "dot" format, like this: 207.171.0.111.) *See also* **zone**.

domain name service (DNS)   A networked system that translates numeric IP addresses (207.171.0.111) into Internet host names (traderights.pacificnet.net).

DoS   This refers to *denial-of-service*, a condition that results when a user maliciously renders a server inoperable, thereby denying computer service to legitimate users. For example, a user could fill up disk space or TCP connection tables, making it impossible for other users to work.

EFT   Electronic funds transfer.

encryption   The process of scrambling data so it's unreadable by unauthorized parties. In most encryption schemes, you must have a password to reassemble the data into readable form. Encryption is primarily used to enhance privacy or to protect classified, secret, or top-secret information. (For example, many military and satellite transmissions are encrypted to prevent spies or hostile nations from analyzing them.)

Ethernet   A LAN networking technology that connects computers and transmits data between them. Data is packaged into frames and sent via wires.

FDDI   *See* **fiber-optic data distribution interface**.

fiber-optic cable   An extremely fast network cable that transmits data using light rather than electricity. Most commonly used for backbones.

fiber-optic data distribution interface (FDDI)   Fiber-optic cable that transfers data in a ring topology at 100Mbps.

file server   A computer that serves as a centralized source for files.

File Transfer Protocol (FTP)   A protocol used to transfer files from one TCP/IP host to another.

filtering   The process of examining network packets for integrity and security. Filtering is typically an automated process, performed by either routers or software.

firewall   A device that controls access between two networks according to source and destination addresses and ports.

frame   *See* **packet**.

frame relay   Frame relay technology is a public switched network technology. It allows multiple clients to share the same cloud to transmit data from point to point, instead of having a separate point-to-point connection at each site. The providers typically allow clients to transfer information at variable rates. This is a cost-effective way of transferring data over networks because you typically pay for only the resources you use. Unfortunately, you will probably be sharing your frame relay connection with someone else. Standard frame relay connections run at 56Kbps or T1 (1.54Mbps); the actual guaranteed rate is called the CIR, or Committed Information Rate.

FTP   *See* **File Transfer Protocol**.

full duplex transmission   Any transmission in which data is transmitted in both directions simultaneously.

gateway   *See also* **router**. A second definition is a device on a network where two (or more) network protocols are translated into other protocols. Typical examples of such translation include TCP/IP or IPX/SPX to proprietary (mainframe) protocols, such as the Novell or Microsoft SAA gateway.

gigabit   1,073,741,824 bits.

GOPHER   The Internet Gopher Protocol, a protocol for distributing documents over the Net. GOPHER preceded the World Wide Web as an information retrieval tool. (See RFC 1436 for more information.)

granularity   The degree to which something is subdivided. In security, the extent to which you can incisively apply access controls. For example, setting security for a group is less granular than setting security for a user.

group   A value denoting a collection of users. This concept is used in network file permissions. All users belonging to this or that group share similar access privileges.

groupware   Application programs designed to make full use of a network and that often promote collaborative work.

hacker   Someone interested in operating systems, software, security, and the Internet generally. The original (and correct) definition, from the good old days when hackers were the good guys. Also called a *programmer*.

hardware address   The fixed physical address of a network adapter. Hardware addresses are just about always hard-coded into the network adapter. Don't confuse this with the address of a computer; as adapters get swapped out, the computer's network address changes!

hole   *See* **vulnerability**.

host   A computer that offers services to users, especially on a TCP/IP network. Also refers to older mainframe computers.

host table   Any record of matching host names and network addresses. These tables, used to identify the name and location of each host on your network, are consulted before data is transmitted. (Think of a host table as a personal phone book of machine addresses.)

HTML   *See* **hypertext markup language**.

HTTP   *See* **hypertext transfer protocol**.

hub   A hardware device that allows sharing a network segment by repeating signals between ports. (Like the spokes of a wheel, a hub allows many network wires to converge at one point.)

hypertext   A text display format commonly used on Web pages. Hypertext is distinct from regular text because it's interactive. In a hypertext document, when you click on or choose any highlighted word, other associated text appears. This allows powerful cross-referencing and permits users to navigate a whole set of documents pretty easily.

hypertext markup language (HTML)   The formatting commands and rules that define a hypertext document. Most Web pages are written in HTML format.

hypertext transfer protocol (HTTP)   The protocol used to traffic hypertext across the Internet and the underlying protocol of the World Wide Web.

IDEA   *See* **International Data Encryption Algorithm**.

IDENT   *See* **Identification Protocol**.

Identification Protocol (IDENT)   A TCP-based protocol for identifying users. IDENT is a more modern, advanced version of the Authentication Protocol. You can find out more by getting RFC 1413.

IGMP   *See* **Internet Group Management Protocol**.

IMAP3   *See* **Interactive Mail Access Protocol**.

Integrated Services Digital Network (ISDN)   Digital telephone service that offers data transfer rates upward of 128Kbps.

Interactive Mail Access Protocol (IMAP3)   A protocol that allows workstations to access Internet electronic mail from centralized servers. (See RFC 1176 for further information.)

International Data Encryption Algorithm (IDEA)   IDEA is a powerful block-cipher encryption algorithm that operates with a 128-bit key. IDEA encrypts data faster than DES and is far more secure.

Internet   Specifically, the conglomeration of interconnected computer networks connected via fiber, leased lines, and dial up that support TCP/IP. Generally, any computer network that supports TCP/IP and is interconnected, as in "an internet." Usually, a local internet is referred to as an "intranet."

Internet Group Management Protocol (IGMP)   A protocol that controls broadcasts to multiple stations. Part of IP multicasting. *See also* **multicast packet**.

Internet Protocol (IP)   The network layer of TCP/IP; the method of transporting data across the Internet. (See RFC 791.)

Internet Protocol security option.   IP security option used to protect IP datagrams according to U.S. classifications, whether unclassified, classified secret, or top-secret. (See RFC 1038 and RFC 1108.)

Internet Worm   Also called the Morris Worm, a program that attacked the Internet in November 1988. To get a Worm overview, check out RFC 1135.

Internetworking   The practice of using networks that run standard Internet protocols.

InterNIC   The Network Information Center located at `www.internic.net`.

intranet   A private network that uses Internet technologies.

intrusion detection   The practice of using automated systems to detect intrusion attempts. Intrusion detection typically involves intelligent systems or agents.

IP   *See* **Internet Protocol**.

IP address   Numeric Internet address, such as `207.171.0.111`.

IP spoofing   Any procedure in which an attacker assumes another host's IP address to gain unauthorized access to the target.

IPX   Internetwork Packet eXchange. A proprietary data transport protocol from Novell, Inc. that loosely resembles Internet Protocol.

ISDN   *See* **Integrated Services Digital Network**.

ISO   International Standards Organization.

ISP   Internet Service Provider.

Java   A network programming language created by Sun Microsystems that marginally resembles C++. Java is object oriented and is often used to generate graphics and multi-media applications, although it's most well known for its networking power.

JavaScript   A programming language developed by Netscape Communications Corporation. JavaScript runs in and manipulates Web browser environments, particularly Netscape Navigator and Communicator (but also Internet Explorer).

Kerberos   An encryption and authentication system developed at the Massachusetts Institute of Technology, Kerberos is used in network applications and relies on trusted third-party servers for authentication.

Kerberos Network Authentication Service   Third-party, ticket-based authentication scheme that can be easily integrated into network applications. See RFC 1510 for details.

LAN   *See* **local area network**.

LISTSERV   Listserv Distribute Protocol, a protocol used to deliver mass email. (See RFC 1429 for further information.)

local area network (LAN)   LANs are small, Ethernet-based networks.

maximum transmission unit (MTU)   A value that denotes the largest packet that can be transmitted. (Many people adjust this value and often get better performance by either increasing or decreasing it.) Some network problems can be tracked down to MTU issues.

megabyte   1,048,576 bytes. Abbreviated as MB.

MIB   Management Information Base. A collection of SNMP variables for a given network device or group of statistics.

modem   A device that converts (modulates) signals that the computer understands into signals that can be accurately transmitted over phone lines or other media and that can convert the signals back (demodulate) into their original form.

Morris Worm   *See* **Internet Worm**.

MTU   *See* **maximum transmission unit**.

multicast packet   A packet destined for multiple (but not all) stations, possibly on multiple networks. Stations that want to participate in multicasting must join a "multicast group."

multi-homed host   A host that has more than one network interface. Routers and firewalls typically have more than one network interface.

A

NAUN   A Token Ring station's Nearest Addressable Upstream Neighbor; very important to know for troubleshooting purposes.

NE2000   A popular 10MB Ethernet network card, developed by Novell. Many network cards were cloned from this, and it's now a de facto standard.

NetBIOS protocol   A high-speed, lightweight transport protocol commonly used in local area networks, particularly those running LAN Manager, Windows NT, or Windows 95.

netstat   Command that shows the current TCP/IP connections and their source addresses.

NetWare   A popular network operating system from Novell, Inc.

network analyzer   Hardware, software, or both that captures and monitors network traffic. It decodes the traffic into a form that can be read by people.

network file system (NFS)   A system that allows you to transparently import files from remote hosts. These files appear and act as though they were installed on your local machine.

Network Information System (NIS)   A system developed by Sun Microsystems that allows Internet hosts to transfer information after authenticating themselves with a single password. NIS was once called the "Yellow Pages" system.

network interface card (NIC)   An adapter card that lets the computer attach to a network cable. Also known as a NIC.

network level   Layer 3 of the OSI reference model. This level provides the routing information for data, opening and closing paths for the data to travel, and ensuring it reaches its destination.

Network News Transfer Protocol (NNTP)   The protocol that controls the transmission of Usenet news messages.

network operating system (NOS)   An operating system for networks, such as NetWare or Windows NT.

NFS   *See* **network file system**.

NIC   *See* **network interface card**.

NIS   *See* **Network Information System**.

NNTP   *See* **Network News Transfer Protocol**.

NOS *See* **network operating system**.

offline Not available on the network.

one-time password A password generated on-the-fly during a challenge-response exchange. Such passwords are generated by using a predefined algorithm, but are extremely secure because they're good for the current session only.

online Available on the network.

OSI reference model Open Systems Interconnection Reference Model. A seven-layer model of data communications protocols that make up the architecture of a network.

owner The person, user name, or process with privileges to read, write, or otherwise access a given file, directory, or process. The system administrator assigns ownership. However, ownership can also be assigned automatically by the operating system in certain instances.

packet Data sent over a network is broken into manageable chunks called *packets* or *frames*. The size is determined by the protocol used.

packet spoofing The practice of generating packets with forged source addresses for the purposes of cracking; *see also* **IP spoofing**.

Password Authentication Protocol A protocol used to authenticate PPP users.

PCI *See* **peripheral component interface**.

PCM *See* **pulse code modulation**.

penetration testing The process of attacking a host from without to ascertain remote security vulnerabilities. (This process is sometimes called *ice-pick testing*.)

peripheral component interface (PCI) An interface used for expansion slots in PCs and Macintosh computers. PCI slots are where you plug in new adapter cards, including Ethernet adapters, disk controller cards, and video cards, to name a few.

Perl Practical Extraction and Report Language. A programming language commonly used in network programming, text processing, and CGI programming.

petabyte 1,125,899,906,842,620 bytes (abbreviated as PB).

phreaking The process of unlawfully manipulating the telephone system.

physical level Layer 1 of the OSI reference model. This level deals with hardware connections and transmissions and is the only level that involves the physical transfer of data from system to system.

Point-to-Point Protocol (PPP) A communication protocol used between machines that support serial interfaces, such as modems. PPP is commonly use to provide and access dial-up services to Internet service providers.

Point-to-Point Tunneling Protocol (PPTP) A Microsoft-developed specialized form of PPP. Its unique design makes it possible to "encapsulate" or wrap non-TCP/IP protocols within PPP. With this method, PPTP allows two or more LANs to connect using the Internet as a conduit.

POP2 *See* **Post Office Protocol**.

Post Office Protocol (POP2) A protocol that allows workstations to download and upload Internet electronic mail from centralized servers. (See RFC 937 for further information.)

PPP *See* **Point-to-Point Protocol**.

PPP Authentication Protocols Set of protocols that can be used to enhance the security of Point-to-Point Protocol. (See RFC 1334.)

PPP DES The PPP DES Encryption Protocol, which applies the data encryption standard protection to point-to-point links. (This is one method to harden PPP traffic against sniffing.) To learn more, see RFC 1969.

PPTP *See* **Point-to-Point Tunneling Protocol**.

presentation level Layer 6 of the OSI reference model. This level manages the protocols of the operating system, formatting of data for display, encryption, and translation of characters.

protocol A standardized set of rules that govern communication or the way data is transmitted.

protocol analyzer *See* **network analyzer**.

protocol stack A hierarchy of protocols used in data transport, usually arranged in a collection called a *suite* (such as the TCP/IP suite). The actual programs used to implement a protocol stack are colloquially called a "stack," too, such as "the Microsoft TCP/IP stack."

proxy server A server that makes application requests on behalf of a client and relays results back to the client. Often used for a simple firewall; routing domains are typically different. *See also* **application gateway**.

pulse code modulation (PCM) A system of transforming signals from analog to digital. (Many high-speed Internet connections from the telephone company use PCM.)

A

RAID   *See* **redundant array of inexpensive disks**.

RARP   *See* **Reverse Address Resolution Protocol**.

read access   When a user has read access, it means he or she has privileges to read a particular file.

redundant array of inexpensive disks (RAID)   A large number of hard drives connected together that act as one drive. The data is spread out across several disks, and one drive keeps checking information so that if one drive fails, the data can be rebuilt.

Referral WHOIS Protocol (RWHOIS)   A protocol that provides access to the WHOIS registration database, which stores Internet domain name registration information.

repeater   A device that strengthens a signal so it can travel longer distances.

request for comments (RFC)   RFC documents are working notes of the Internet development community. They are often used to propose new standards. A huge depository of RFC documents can be found at http://www.internic.net.

Reverse Address Resolution Protocol (RARP)   A protocol that maps Ethernet addresses to IP addresses.

RFC   *See* **request for comments**.

RIP   *See* **Routing Information Protocol**.

RMON   Remote Monitoring MIB for SNMP. Allows remote monitoring of network devices and segments.

router   A device that routes packets in and out of a network. Many routers are sophisticated and can serve as firewalls.

Routing Information Protocol (RIP)   A protocol that allows Internet hosts to exchange routing information. (See RFC 1058 for more information.)

RSA   RSA (named after its creators—Rivest, Shamir, and Adleman) is a public-key encryption algorithm. RSA is probably the most popular of such algorithms and has been incorporated into many commercial applications, including but not limited to Netscape Navigator, Communicator, and even Lotus Notes. Find out more about RSA at http://www.rsa.com.

RWHOIS   *See* **Referral WHOIS Protocol**.

Secure Sockets Layer (SSL)   A security protocol (created by Netscape Communications Corporation) that allows client/server applications to communicate free of eavesdropping, tampering, or message forgery. SSL is now used for secure electronic commerce. To find out more, see http://home.netscape.com/eng/ssl3/draft302.txt.

secured electronic transaction (SET)   A standard of secure protocols associated with online commerce and credit-card transactions. (Visa and Mastercard are the chief players in developing the SET protocol.) Its purpose is ostensibly to make electronic commerce more secure.

security audit   An examination (often by third parties) of a server's security controls and disaster-recovery mechanisms.

Serial Line Internet Protocol (SLIP)   An Internet protocol designed for connections based on serial communications (for example, telephone connections or COM port/RS232 connections.)

session level   Layer 5 of the OSI reference model. This level handles the coordination of communication between systems, maintains sessions for as long as needed, and handles security, logging, and administrative functions.

SET   *See* **secured electronic transaction**.

sharing   The process of allowing users on other machines to access files and directories on your own. File sharing is a fairly typically activity within local area networks and can sometimes be a security risk.

shielded twisted pair   A network cabling frequently used in IBM Token Ring networks. (STP now supports 100Mbps.)

Simple Mail Transfer Protocol (SMTP)   The Internet's most commonly used electronic mail protocol (see RFC 821).

Simple Network Management Protocol (SNMP)   A protocol that offers centralized management of TCP/IP-based networks (particularly those connected to the Internet).

Simple Network Paging Protocol (SNPP)   A protocol used to transmit wireless messages from the Internet to pagers. (See RFC 1861 for more information.)

Simple Network Time Protocol (SNTP)   A protocol used to negotiate synchronization of your system's clock with clocks on other hosts.

S/Key   One-time password system to secure connections. Because each session uses a different password, sessions that use S/KEY are not vulnerable to packet capture attacks. In other words, even if someone finds out that the password for your current session is "MYSECRET," they don't know the password for the *next* session, "OUTTALUCK." (See RFC 1760 for more information.)

SLIP   *See* **Serial Line Internet Protocol**.

SMB   Server Message Block, the brains behind Microsoft Networking.

SMTP   *See* **Simple Mail Transfer Protocol**.

sniffer   Hardware or software that captures datagrams across a network. It can be used legitimately (by an engineer trying to diagnose network problems) or illegitimately (by a cracker looking for unencrypted passwords). Originally a trade name for Network General's "Sniffer" product, now used generically to mean *network analyzer.*

SNMP   *See* **Simple Network Management Protocol**.

SNMP Security Protocols   Within the SNMP suite, there are a series of security-related protocols. You can find out about them by getting RFC 1352.

SNPP   *See* **Simple Network Paging Protocol**.

SNTP   *See* **Simple Network Time Protocol**.

SOCKS Protocol   Generic circuit proxy protocol that allows for proxy of TCP-based circuits (Socks version 4) and UDP sessions (Socks version 5). (See RFC 1928.)

SONET   Synchronous Optical Network. An extremely high-speed network standard. Compliant networks can transmit data at 2Gbps (gigabits per second) or even faster. (Yeah, you read that right! 2 gigs or better!)

SP3   Network Layer Security Protocol.

SP4   Transport Layer Security Protocol.

spoofing   Any procedure that involves impersonating another user or host to gain unauthorized access to the target.

SSL   *See* **Secure Sockets Layer.**

stack   *See* **protocol stack**.

STP   *See* **shielded twisted pair**.

suite   A term used to describe a collection of similar protocols. It's used primarily when describing TCP- and IP-based protocols (when talking about the "TCP/IP suite").

TCP/IP   Transmission Control Protocol/Internet Protocol. The protocols used by the Internet.

Telnet   A protocol and an application that allows you to control your system from remote locations. During a Telnet session, your machine responds much as it would if you were actually working on its console.

Telnet authentication option   Protocol options for Telnet that add basic security to Telnet-based connections based on rules at the source routing level. (See RFC 1409 for details.)

TEMPEST   Transient Electromagnetic Pulse Surveillance Technology. TEMPEST is the practice and study of capturing or eavesdropping on electromagnetic signals that emanate from any device—in this case, a computer. TEMPEST shielding is any computer security system designed to defeat such eavesdropping.

terabyte   1,099,511,627,776 bytes (abbreviated as TB).

terminator   A small plug that attaches to the end of a segment of coaxial Ethernet cable. This plug provides a resistor to keep the signal within specifications.

TFTP   *See* **Trivial File Transfer Protocol**.

Token Ring   A network that's connected in a ring topology, in which a special "token" is passed from computer to computer. A computer must wait until it receives this token before sending data over the network.

topology   The method or systems by which your network is physically laid out. For example, *Ethernet* and *Token Ring* are both network topologies, as are "star" versus "bus" wiring. The former is a network topology, and the latter is a physical topology.

tracert   A TCP/IP program that records the routers used between your machine and a remote host.

traffic analysis   The study of patterns in communication, instead of the content of the communication. For example, studying when, where, and to whom particular messages are being sent, without actually studying the content of those messages.

transceiver   An essential part of a network interface card (NIC) that connects the network cable to the card. Most 10BaseT cards have them built in, but in some cases, you might have to get a transceiver for an AUI port to 10BaseT.

transport level   Layer 4 of the OSI reference model. This level controls the movement of data between systems, defines the protocols for messages, and does error checking.

trap door   *See* **back door**.

Trivial File Transfer Protocol (TFTP)   An antiquated file transfer protocol now seldom used on the Internet. (TFTP is a lot like FTP without authentication.) Frequently used for "diskless" booting from the network.

Trojan Horse   An application or code that, unbeknown to the user, performs surreptitious and unauthorized tasks that can compromise system security. (Also referred to as a *Trojan*.)

trusted system   An operating system or other system secure enough for use in environments where classified information is warehoused.

A

tunneling   The practice of encapsulating one type of traffic within another type of traffic. For example, if you had only a TCP/IP connection between two sites, you might *tunnel* IPX/SPX traffic within the TCP/IP traffic. Today, tunneling often implies using encryption between two points, thus shielding that data from others who might be surreptitiously sniffing the wire. These types of tunneling procedures encrypt data within packets, making it extremely difficult for outsiders to access such data.

twisted pair   A cable made up of one or more pairs of wires, twisted to improve their electrical performance.

UDP   *See* **User Datagram Protocol**.

UID   See **user ID**.

uninterruptible power supply (UPS)   A backup power supply for when your primary power is cut. They can be small units that keep your PC up for the couple of minutes you need to save your data, or they can be huge units with large batteries that can support your network for several hours.)

UPS   *See* **uninterruptible power supply**.

user   Anyone who uses a computer system or system resources.

User Datagram Protocol (UDP)   A connectionless protocol from the TCP/IP family. (Connectionless protocols transmit data between two hosts, even though those hosts don't currently have an active session. Such protocols are considered "unreliable" because there's no absolute guarantee that the data will arrive as it was intended.)

user ID   In general, any value by which a user is identified, including his or her user name. *See also* **owner** and **user**.

UTP   Unshielded twisted pair. *See also* **10BaseT**.

Vines   A network operating system made by Banyan.

virtual private network (VPN)   VPN technology allows companies with leased lines to form a closed and secure circuit over the Internet between themselves. In this way, such companies ensure that data passed between them and their counterparts is secure (and usually encrypted).

virus   A self-replicating or propagating program (sometimes malicious) that attaches itself to other executables, drivers, or document templates, thus "infecting" the target host or file.

vulnerability   This term refers to any weakness in any system (either hardware or software) that allows intruders to gain unauthorized access or deny service.

WAN   Wide area network.

write access   When a user has write access, it means he or she has privileges to write to a particular file.

yottabyte   1,208,925,819,614,630,000,000,000 bytes.

zettabyte   1,180,591,620,717,410,000,000 bytes.

zone   One level of the DNS hierarchy. *See also* **domain name service**.

APPENDIX **B**

Answers to Quiz Questions

Hour 1

1. False. A dedicated server is used in client/server networks.
2. False. Telnet is used to establish a command-line session with a remote host.
3. D. Two or more networks connected via a router.

Hour 2

1. False. Ethernet is a contention-based system or, in fancy lingo, CSMA/CD.
2. If my math is right, choose D.
3. False. A hub with Fast Ethernet ports and at least one port connected to the legacy 10Base5 network would let you do the rewiring and migration gradually.
4. B.
5. False. A router is used to connect networks.

Hour 3

1. DHCP, or Dynamic Host Configuration Protocol.
2. The `winipcfg` tool for Windows 98 and `ipconfig /all` for NT machines.
3. The first culprit should be your default gateway setting. Because you can access your local resources, it's a pretty safe bet that your IP address and subnet mask are correct. The default gateway comes into play when you try to access hosts that are not on your network, which is what you're trying to do when you attempt to access the corporate network.
4. Broadcast address, or all ones. At this stage, the client doesn't even know its own address, let alone anyone else's, so it has to broadcast.
5. Three bits is from 000 to 111. Because you can't have a network address of all ones or all zeros, you can use only the following: 001, 010, 011, 100, 101, and 110, for a total of six subnets. If you are using 3 bits of the last octet and adding it to the subnet mask, then you have 5 bits available for host IDs. So 2 raised to the 5th power minus 2 gives you the number of available hosts per network: In this case, the answer is 30.

Hour 4

1. False.
2. A.
3. Universal Cable Module (UCM).
4. Null-modem.

Hour 5

1. Binding.
2. NetBEUI and IPX/SPX.
3. False. Only the workgroup name should be the same. The computer name must be unique.

Hour 6

1. False.
2. To key to single logon for all networks is to assign the same password for all your networks.
3. Universal Naming Convention.
4. `\\DESKTOP\WordPro\WP`

B

Hour 7

1. Star.
2. CAT5 UTP cable or Type 1 STP cable.
3. The Ethernet 3-4-5 rule states that there can be no more than five segments within a given network, joined by four repeaters. Out of these five segments, only three can be populated with network nodes.
4. True.

Hour 8

1. False. You need to install Microsoft Services for NDS, too.
2. Novell NetWare Client.
3. Doesn't matter. You can use either the Microsoft client or the Novell client. However, the Novell client has more functionality built in, which you might find more handy to use.

Hour 9

1. Full backup, incremental backup, and differential backup.
2. A differential backup copies only files that have been created or modified since the last full backup was completed. An incremental backup copies only files that have been created or modified since the last full *or* differential backup.
3. True.
4. False.

Hour 10

1. It's possible that the BDCs have not yet synchronized with the PDC, where all changes to the domain database are made. Either wait, or force a synchronization by using Server Manager or the `net accounts /sync` command.

2. This one is a bit of a trick question. The solution is to dual-boot, which would let you boot up into NT and let your son boot up into Windows 9x and play his games. The problem is with the NTFS partition. Only NT can see NTFS, so you won't be able to install Windows 9x. Format the disk using FAT, and install Windows 9x, and then NT.

4. False. You need to promote one of the BDCs to be the PDC, and then shoot the programmers.

5. That would be the single domain model. In the single domain model, there aren't any trust relationships involved!

6. Because there can be only one—and what a great movie!

Hour 11

1. Sandra's effective rights are full control, which she gets from belonging to the `Sysop` group. Full control includes read.

2. No access.

3. False! The *most* restrictive permissions are the ones that apply.

4. You can attach more print devices to the print server, and then enable printer pooling.

5. False. NTFS file permissions override the NTFS folder permissions.

6. True.

Hour 12

1. To establish a connection, both ends must be speaking the same language. You might check the protocol on the problem workstation and see if that protocol is enabled at the RAS server.

2. False. RAS can be set up to allow access to the entire network, and thus route the traffic from the modem onto the network, providing access to any resource on the network.

3. D.

4. Tools include Event Viewer, the RAS Administration program, and Dial-Up Networking Monitor.

Hour 13

1. True.

2. Power User or Administrators.

3. False.

4. Use Network Neighborhood to browse for the directory, right-click on the directory, and then choose Salvage Files from the context menu. Highlight the file for salvage in the dialog box and click Salvage.

B

Hour 14

1. C. WINNT /OX re-creates the three floppy disks that came with the NT CD-ROM.

2. False. The simplest method is to boot from the installation floppy disks and use Setup to remove the NTFS partiton.

3. False. File-level security is available only when using NTFS.

4. Backup domain controller, or BDC, which gets a copy of the database from the PDC.

5. False. You can just go from per server to per seat licensing, not the other way around.

6. The HCL is Microsoft's Hardware Compatibility List. You want to make sure the hardware is compatible before you buy it!

7. False. Running WINNT /B sets up NT without needing floppy disks.

8. True. It's possible to convert FAT to NTFS, but not the other way around without reformatting and thus losing all the existing data. The data would have to be restored from tape.

Hour 15

1. You have to manually demote the original PDC to become a BDC. This process is normally automatic, but because the PDC was not online when you promoted the BDC, naturally the automatic process didn't work.

2. Even though the user did not get disconnected, she can't establish new connections. To have her disconnected when her logon hours expire, you need to check Forcibly Disconnect Remote Users From Server When Logon Hours Expire in the account policy.

3. 14.

4. True. Choose Computer|Shared Directories from the Server Manager menu.

5. Use the Services icon in Control Panel to reach the Services dialog box. From here, you can drill down by using the Startup button and change the service to manual. This means it won't start unless you manually start it.

Hour 16

1. AT and WINAT.

2. By including the /b command-line option when running NTBACKUP.EXE.

3. File Allocation Table.

4. Regedt32.

5. LKGC stands for Last Known Good Configuration, and it is the saved system state (including Registry settings) of the last successful user login. If your Registry is damaged and prevents Windows NT from functioning correctly, you can use LKGC to get back to a previously known "good" state.

Hour 17

1. The solution is to implement two-way trust, so that each domain can access resources in the other domain.

2. The three types of log files are system, security, and application. Audited events are written to the security log file.

3. The maximum size of a log file is 4,194,240KB.

4. True. A volume set can be created on one physical drive.

5. 32.

6. Mirroring and stripe set with parity.

7. False. A stripe set offers no fault tolerance. You need to implement either mirroring or a stripe set with parity.

8. Replication. A WINS server can be set up with a replication partner, so that if the primary fails, the workstations can contact the secondary.

Hour 18

1. Global, scope, and client.

2. True. Scope options do override global options.

3. False. One of the advantages of DHCP is the freedom from having to manually set up each workstation.

4. P-node.

5. 60 minutes.

Hour 19

1. 51 minutes.

2. False. From the master browser, you get a list of backup browsers.

3. False. On NT, you would use the `ipconfig /all` command.

4. The NT Diagnostics program.

5. The `nbtstat -c` command shows the contents of the NetBIOS name cache.

6. False. ARP is used to get the hardware address when you know the protocol, or IP address.

7. Performance Monitor.

Hour 20

1. After the connection to the dial-up server has been established, the Details button in the connection status box (refer back to Figure 20.14) gives the server connection type and protocols the connection has provided.

2. The Internet Connection Wizard.

3. Use `winipcfg`.

4. Use Tracert and specify `www.microsoft.com` as the target name.

5. The answer varies depending on your ISP.

Hour 21

1. You can use either an FTP client or a Web browser.

2. It's the ability to log on to an FTP server using `anonymous` as the user name and your email address as the password.

3. This server supplies weather information for different cities.

4. It's used to store messages you've saved but haven't sent.

Hour 22

1. Two. A primary DNS and a secondary DNS.
2. NAT is short for Network Address Translation. It's an Internet standard protocol that enables a LAN to use one set of IP addresses for internal traffic and a second set of addresses for external traffic.
3. False. Edu is reserved for educational institutions.
4. You can use the Nslookup utility:

   `nslook www.microsoft.com`
5. Proxy cache.

Hour 23

1. TechNet!
2. TechNet. This way you get not only the Resource Kit, but much more, such as the service packs on CD-ROM.
3. False. There are many options you can use to produce a more focused query and, therefore, better results.
4. False. It's possible to query for words that are NEAR each other in the same topic.

Hour 24

For answers to all three questions, take a look on the Web. Hint: You might want to have a look at Figure 24.1 again!

INDEX

Symbols

1X Browser, 382
2GB partitions, 286
3-4-5 Rule (Ethernet), 109-110, 113
9-pin-to-9/25-pin null-modem cable, 63
10Base2, 107
    cables, 22, 108
    coaxial cable, 76
    logical bus, 108
    see also Ethernet
10Base5, 108
10BaseT
    cables, 22-23
        cost, 111
        cross-over, 77
    hubs, 24
    RJ-45 connectors, 109
    upgrading, 109
25-pin-to-25-pin cables, 63-64

32-bit applications, 104
56K modems, 344
100BaseT, 16, 23, 33
    cables, 32
    switches, 29
8250 UART, 59
16450/16550/16650 UART, 59

A

abend (ABnormal ENDing), 7
Acceptable Use Policy (AUP), 423
acceptances of DHCP leases, 50
access rights
    backplanes, 29
    folders, 171, 173
    guests, 69
    Internet, 425

    net use command, 173
    Network Neighborhood, 104
    remote hosts, 387-389
    servers, 195
    share-level security, 92-93, 95, 171-173
    user-level security, 93
    web sites, 429
acknowledgements of DHCP leases, 50
active processes, 327
    channels, 379
    leases, 307
adapters, *see* NICs
Add New Hardware wizard (Backup utility), 139
adding
    NDS service, 117
    NICs, 241
    printers to queues, 132
    protocols, 80-82, 240
    routes, 323
    scope options, 303-304
    services, 240

Address Resolution
 Protocol, *see* ARP
addresses
 IP, 103, 430
 subnet masks, 302
 WINS, 279
 workstations, 53
administration
 RAS, 189-191
 shares, 163, 181
advanced RISC computing
 (ARC path), 292
advanced settings, 84, 123
Alku search engines, 383
alternative newsgroups,
 394, 406
AltaVista search engine, 441
America Online, 359
Ananzi search engine, 383
AND query, 436
anonymous FTP, 385
applets, Java, 404
applications
 gateways, 421
 layers, 36
 log files, 236, 274
 servers, 7
ARC path (advanced RISC
 computing), 292
archiving log files, 276
ARCserve (Cheyene
 Software), 145
ARCserveIT Windows NT
 tool, 259
ARP (Address Resolution
 Protocol), 54, 334
 command, 323-324
 frames, 332
 viewing cache, 47-48, 324
articles (newgroups)
 composing, 399
 follow-ups, 394, 399-400
arts domain names, 414

ASDL (Asymmetric Digital
 Subscriber Line), 344
assigning
 NTFS permissions, 167,
  169-171
 shared folders
  permissions, 164-167
Asymmetric Digital
 Subscriber Line (ADSL),
 344
AT command (Resource
 Kit), 437
AT&T WorldNet Service,
 359
auditing
 directories, 271-273
 files, 271-273, 296
 log off/log on, 271
 policies, 270
 printers, 273
 security, 271
AUP (Acceptable Use
 Policy), 423
authentication of
 BDCs/PDCs, 151
automating
 backups, 143, 261
 Windows NT Backup,
  253-254

B

B-node (broadcast node),
 305
 destinations, 332
 packets, 39, 310
backbones, 30
 collapsed, 29
 networks, 16

backup domain controllers
 (BDCs), 150
 authentication, 151
 backup, 244
 dedicated servers, 151
 domain models, 152-153
 Exchange servers, 151
 installation, 218
 promoting, 243-244
 user accounts, 155-156
Backup Exec Windows NT
 tool, 259
Backup utility
 starting, 138-139
 Task Scheduler, 143-144
 wizards
  Add New Hardware,
   139
  Backup, 139-141
  Restore, 142-143
backups
 automating, 143, 261
 browser computers, 312
 compressing, 141
 designing, 137
 DHCP, 310
 differential, 136-137,
  139, 146
 files, 249-251
 floppy disks, 137
 full, 136-137, 139
 hard drives, 250, 294
 incremental, 137, 146
 JAZ drives, 138
 networks, 140, 145
 Novell NetWare Client,
  202
 PDCs, 244
 permissions, 257
 planning, 136
 Registry, 146, 249, 258

remote drives, 146
scheduling, 143-144
sets, 142
skipped files, 261
tape drives, 137
third-party tools, 259-260
tools
    ARCserve, 145
    Target Server Agent
        (Windows 95/98),
        144
users, 258
verifying, 141
Windows 98, 145
Windows NT, 249-250
    automating, 253-254
    Registry, 254-255, 257
WINS database, 283
WORM drives, 138
ZIP drives, 138
see also disks, duplexing
**bandwidth, increasing,
187-188**
baseband, 21
baud rate, 60
**BDCs (backup domain
controllers), 150**
authentication, 151
backup, 244
dedicated servers, 151
Exchange servers, 151
installation, 218
multiple domain models,
    153
promoting, 243-244
single domain models,
    152-153
user accounts, 155-156
benefits of networks, 9
**bidirectional parallel ports,
60**

bindings
disabling, 241
enabling, 241
protocols, 66-67, 81
security, 84
TCP/IP configuration,
    83-84
bitmaps, 212
bits per second (bps), 337
biz newsgroups, 394
BlackHole, 422
**blocking access to web sites,
429**
"blue screen of death," 7
Boolean queries, 436
boot.ini file, 291, 294, 296
deleting, 220
editing, 292
booting
dual, 157
partitions, 157, 160,
    215-216, 284
bootsec.dos files, 220
**Border Network
Technology, 422**
**BorderWare Firewall
Server, 422**
bps (bits per second), 337
bridges, 32
Ethernet, 25-27
file servers, 26-27
networks, 33
packets, 27
broadband, 21
**broadcast node (b-node),
305**
destinations, 332
packets, 39, 310
**broken trust relationships,
268-269**
browse lists, 311-313

browsers, *see* **Web browsers**
**browsing NetWare 4 with
Network Neighborhood,
128**
built-in user accounts, 154
diagnostic cables, 112
groups, 156
**burned-in MAC addresses,
42**
bus topology, 32
external transceivers, 106
LANs, 106
logical, 108-109
physical, 108
bytecode files (Java), 404

C

**C programming language,
220**
cables
3-4-5 Rule, 109-110, 113
10Base2, 22, 76, 108
10Base5, 20, 108
100BaseT, 23
built-in diagnostics, 112
connectors, 112
cost, 72
cross-over, 101
DCC, 58
Ethernet, 20, 22-23, 77,
    109, 111
IBM, 111
mismatched, 112
modems, 344
networks, 6
null-modem, 62-63
parallel LapLink
    (InterLink), 64-65
populated segments, 109

repeaters, 109
RG-58, 113
signal attenuation, 112
STP, 20, 110
terminators, 112
Token Ring networks, 24,
  110-111, 113
troubleshooting, 101
UTP, 20, 110, 112
caching
ARP, 48
hierarchical, 425, 427
proxy, 424-427, 430
Web server acceleration,
  425, 427-429
call back options, RAS, 191
call waiting, disabling, 341
Canadian domain names,
414
capturing printer ports, 130
Carrier Sense and Multiple
Access/Collision Detection
(CSMA/CD), 17
case-sensitive passwords,
155
Centronics interface, *see*
parallel ports
CERN (European
Laboratory for Particle
Physics), 424
change permissions, 166,
168
Channel Service Unit/Data
Service Unit (CSU/DSU),
411
cheapernets, *see* **10Base2**
networks
Checkpoint, Firewall-l, 422
Cheyenne Software
ARCserve, 145
InnocuLAN, 423

circuit-level gateways, 421
classes
networks, 43, 309
subnet masks, 103
clearing log files, 276
Client for Microsoft
Networks, 79, 89
Client for Novell NetWare,
89, 124
client/server networks, 6
application servers, 7
dedicated server, 6
DHCP, 309
file servers, 7
installation, 79-80
LANs, 8
log on, 80
Multilink, 188
Novell NetWare, 206
  browsing, 128
  configuration, 122
  installation, 118
  network drives, 129
  point and print feature,
    131-132
  printers, 130-131
  properties, 123-126
options, 303
print server, 7
protocols, 194
reservation, 306
coaxial cable, 76
collision domains, 32
Ethernet, 17, 26
hubs, 24
troubleshooting, 28
commands
arp, 323-324
ipconfig/all, 315
nbstat, 320-321
nbtstat -c, 334

net use, 173
NetBIOS, 82
options, 261
ping, 316-317
route, 322
scripting, 371
tracert, 321-322
comments, shares, 95
commercial domain names,
413
comparing
ISPs, 345-346
stripe sets with volume
  sets, 288
compatibility
modems, 366
protocol installation, 66
complete trust relationships,
153
composing articles for
newsgroups, 399
compression
backup, 141
DUN connectoids, 352
headers, 349
modems, 337, 339
CompuServe, 359
computers
accounts, 234-245
descriptions, 88
identification, 88, 240
workgroups, 88
configuration
access control, 93
audit policy, 270
DCC
  guests, 70
  hosts, 68
desktop, 417
DHCP server, 300-301

Dial-Up Networking, 347
    connectoids, 351-354
    Dial-Up Adapter,
        348-349
    modems, 360-362
Event Viewer, 246
file sharing, 92-93
Internet Connection
    Wizard, 358-360
Microsoft Client for
    NetWare Network, 116,
    199
NDS tree, 208
networks
    log on, 87
    printers, 174
newsreaders, 396-398
NICs, 78-79
Novell NetWare
    client, 122, 205-206
    IP Gateway, 202
    protocol preference,
        206
    Workstation Manager,
        202
Performance Monitor, 326
print sharing, 92-93
RAS, 188
    protocols, 187
    screens, 186
scope names, 126
TCP/IP, 83
    advanced settings, 84
    binding, 83-84
    displaying, 369
    gateways, 85
    IP address, 86
    NetBIOS, 84
    WINS, 85-86
user accounts, 227-229
Windows 98, 92
Windows NT DNS Server,
    415

connections
    DCC, 70-71
    Dial-Up Networking, 193
    Ethernet nodes, 113
    hubs, 23
    Internet, 356-357
    IPX/SPX protocol, 83
    ISPs, 343, 366-369
    NetWare
        MS Client Service, 207
        Novell, 208
    NetWare servers, 126-127
    newsgroups, 398
    PPP, 353-354, 361
    printer workstations, 119
    RAS with NT work-
        stations, 195
    shared folders, 172
    SLIP, 361
    user accounts, 231
connectoids (DUN)
    cables, 112
    configuration , 351-354
    creating , 349, 351
    network, log on, 352
    PPP, 352
    RJ-45, 111
    scripts, 354
    SLIP, 352
    software compression, 352
Contextless Login proper-
    ties (Novell NetWare), 124
Control Panel, 242-243, 246
converting
    FAT to NTFS, 158
    partitions to NTFS, 160
cookies, Internet security,
    401-402
Copy option (Novell
    NetWare), 210

copying
    \i386 directorfrom
        CD-ROM, 219
    WINS database, 280
cost
    cables, 72, 77, 111
    Ethernet, 76, 113
    ISDN service, 344
    ISPs, 344-345
    mirroring, 289
    modems, 344
    tape drives, 137
    TechNet, 432, 439
    Token Ring networks, 113
counters, 325
CPUs, NT Server
    requirements, 214
creating
    DUN connectoids, 349,
        351
    scopes, 301-303
    shares, 162
    user accounts, 154,
        229-233
cross-over cables
    (null-modem serial
    cables), 62-63, 77, 101
cross-posting newsgroup
    messages, 394, 444
crossing hubs, 110
CSMA/CD (Carrier Sense
    and Multiple
    Access/Collison Detection),
    17
CSU/DSU (Channel Service
    Unit/Data Service Unit),
    411
Cyberguard Firewall, 422
CyberPatrol, 429
CyperSitter, 429

D

data communications, 337-339

data link layer (layer 2), 37

DCC (Direct Cable Connection)
  access rights, 69
  cables, 58, 72
  computer names, 67
  configuration, 68, 70
  connections, 70-71
  DUN, 72
  file sharing, 68-69
  guests, 73
  hardware requirements, 58-59
  hosts, 57, 73
  installation, 65, 72
  laptop computers, 73
  parallel LapLink cables (InterLink), 64-65
  parallel ports, 58, 61-62
  passwords, 69
  print sharing, 68-69
  serial ports, 58, 61-62
  Windows 95, 73

dedicated connections, 14
  BDCs, 151
  ISPs, 343
  PDCs, 151

Default Capture properties (Novell NetWare), 125

default gateway, 46-47, 54

deinstallation
  modems, 341
  SP3, 226-227
  Windows NT, 220
  see also installation

delete NTFS permissions, 168

deleting
  boot files, 220
  directories, 272
  files, 272
  NICs, 241
  paging files, 220
  protocols, 66, 81, 240
  routes, 323
  scope options, 304
  services, 240
  \winnt (C language), 220

demilitarized zone (DMZ), 421

demoting PDCs to BDCs, 243-244

descriptions of computers, 88

designing backups, 137

desktop configuration, 417

DHCP (Dynamic Host Configuration Protocol), 279
  backups, 308, 310
  broadcasts, 310
  clients, 309
  configuration, 300-301
  installation, 300-301
  IP addresses, 49, 54, 86
  leases, 49-50, 307
  scopes, 301-305
  WINS, 86, 278

Dial-Up Networking (DUN), 195
  configuration, 347-349, 352
  connectoids
    creating , 349, 351-354
    network, log on, 352
    scripts, 354
    software compression, 352

DCC, 72

Dial-Up Adapter, 347-348
  header compression, 349
  log files, 348
  PPP, 348
  file sharing, 355
  installation, 347-348, 370
  Internet Connection Wizard
    configuration, 358-360
    directory services, 364-365
    email services, 362-363
    LDAP, 364-365
    modems, 360-362
    news services, 363-364
  ISPs 356-357
  log files, 348
  NetWare conflicts, 366
  PPP, 348
  print sharing, 355
  proxy servers, 362
  RAS connections, 193
  scripting commands, 371
  status, 192
  troubleshooting, 365-367

dialog boxes, 239

differential backups, 136-137, 139, 146

Direct Cable Connection, *see* DCC

directories
  auditing, 271-273
  deleting, 272
  permissions, 272-273
  properties, 272
  services, 364-365
  shares, 7

disabling
bindings, 241
call waiting, 341
file sharing, 355
print sharing, 355
shares, 95
disconnections
network drives, 100-101
remote, 229
users, 258
Disk Administrator, 290
disks
duplexing, 248
fault tolerance, 291
mirroring, 248, 288-289,
291, 296
partitions, 284
2GB, 286
boot, 157, 160, 215,
284
converting, 160
EISA utilities, 286
extended, 284
FAT, 158
formatting, 157
managing, 285-286
NTFS, 158
numbers, 292-293
primary, 284, 293
system, 157, 215
space, 295
storage, 343
stripe sets, 287, 290-291
volume sets, 288
write performance, 289
displaying
bitmaps, 212
Registry keys, 261
TCP/IP configuration, 369
**DMZ (demilitarized zone),
421**

**DNS (Domain Naming
System) server, 84**
arts, 414
configuration, 84, 415
education, 430
individual, 414
information services, 414
installation, 415
international, 414
Internet, 413-414
managing, 416
merchants, 414
recreational, 414
registration, 414, 430
requirements, 430
Server Search Order, 84
Suffix Search Order, 84
web, 414
domains, 84, 150
accounts, 155
authentication, 151
BDCs, 150-151
collision, 26, 32
computer accounts, 219,
234-235
dedicated servers, 151
Exchange servers, 151
IDs, 240
losing, 150
master, 152
monitoring, 268-270
multiple, 153
PDCs, 150-151
single, 152-153
top-level (TLD), 413
trust relationships,
151-153, 160, 263,
268-269
see also DNS
DOS
FAT, 157
FTP servers, 385
NTFS, 157

downloading
files, 10, 384-386, 406
headers, 398
Netscape Communicator,
380
Novell Client for Windows
95/98, 118
threads, 399
**Dr. Solomon's Anti-Virus
Toolkit, 423**
**Drivers and Patches
(TechNet), 432**
drives
disconnecting, 100
network mapping, 99-100
shares, 94-96, 171
dual-booting, 157
DUN, *see* **Dial-Up
Networking**
duplexing disks, 248
duration of leases, 302
**Dynamic Host
Configuration Protocol,**
see **DHCP**

E

Eagle firewalls, 422
**ECP (Extended Capabilities
Port), 61**
parallel ports
guests, 73
hosts, 73
parallel LapLink cables,
65
UCM, 64-65
editing
boot.ini file, 292
passwords, 229
Registry, 255-257

Registry keys, 260
routes, 323
URLs, 406
educational domain names, 413, 430
effective permissions, 167, 171, 181
EISA utilities partitions, 286
email services
Dial-Up Networking, 362-363
IMAP, 390
Internet requirements, 416
Outlook Express, 390-392
Pegasus Mail, 392
POP, 390
protocols, 389
SMTP, 390
software Web sites, 393
Emergency Repair Disks (ERD), 257
enabling
bindings, 241
JavaScript, 405
shares, 95
stripe sets with parity, 291
encapsulation, NetBEUI, 39
encryption
RAS, 192
troubleshooting, 366
Enhanced Parallel Port (EPP), 61, 64
ERD (Emergency Repair Disks), 257
errors, Token Ring networks, 18
Ethernet, 15-16
3-4-5 Rule, 109-110, 113
10Base2 cable, 22, 107-108
10Base5 cable, 20, 108

10BaseT cable, 22-23, 109
100BaseT cable, 23
bridges, 25-27
cards, 76
collision domains, 17, 24, 26, 28
cost, 113
Fast, 16
Gigabit, 16
hubs, 24
limitations, 16
NICs, 20
nodes, 113
repeaters, 25
star topology, 33
switches, 29
upgrading, 23
European Laboratory for Particle Physics (CERN), 424
Evaluation and Reviewers Guides(TechNet), 432
Event Viewer
configuration, 246
Filter View, 238
Find function, 237-238
log files, 236
applications, 236, 274
archiving, 276
clearing, 276
managing, 276
overwriting, 276
RAS, 191
security, 236, 274
system, 236, 274
troubleshooting, 328
viewing, 274-275, 296
Exchange servers, 151
Excite search engine, 383
execute NTFS permissions, 168

expanding shared folders, 172
expiration dates passwords, 159
Extended Capabilities Port, *see* ECP
extended disk partitions, 284
external modems, 106, 336

F

Fast Ethernet, 16, 23, 33
cables, 32
switches, 29
FAT (File Allocation Table), 156, 221, 261
converting to NTFS, 158
DOS, 157
dual-boot, 157
partitions
booting, 160, 216
disks, 157-158
system, 216
security, 157, 159
Windows NT, 220
fault tolerance, 291
ring networks, 107
stripe sets, 287
volume sets, 288
Windows NT Server, 248
FAX capability, 337
FDDI (fiber distributed data interface), 15
fiber-optic networks, 16
files
auditing, 271-273, 296
backups, 139, 249-251, 261

boot.ini, 291, 294, 296
deleting, 272
downloading, 10, 384-386, 406
hosts, 330
lmhosts, 278, 330, 334
permissions, 167, 169-171, 181, 272-273
properties, 272
read-only, 249
restoring, 136, 142, 252
servers
    bridges, 26-27
    security, 7
    user error, 7
    workstations, 7
sharing, 92-93
    disabling, 355
    hosts, 68-69
    TCP/IP, 355
skipped, 261
temporary, 249
uploading, 10
see also FAT; FTP; NTFS
Filter View (Event Viewer), 238
Find function (Event Viewer), 237-238
finding IP addresses, 334
Finland, domain names, 414
Firewall-l, 422
firewalls, 430
    security, 420-422
    virus protection, 423
    web sites, 422
first octet, IP addresses, 43
flames, 394
flash memory, modems, 337
floppy disk backups, 137
folders
    NTFS, 181,
    permissions, 167, 169-171

read-only, 104
shared, 69, 94-96
    access rights, 171, 173
    connections, 172
    drive letters, 171
    expanding, 172
    net use command, 173
    paths, 171
    permissions, 164-167, 181
    reconnections, 172
follow-ups, articles for newsgroups, 394, 399-400
formatting disk partitions, 157
frame types
    ARP, 332
    IPX/SPX protocols, 82
FTP (File Transfer Protocol), 12, 14
    anonymous, 385
    DOS-based session, 385
    files, 384-386, 406
    Windows 98, 385
full backups, 136-137, 139
full-control permissions, 166, 176
full-duplex mode, 337

G

gateways
    application-level, 421
    circuit-level, 421
    configuration, 85
    DMZ, 421
    packet-filtering, 421
    screening routers, 422
Gigabit Ethernet, 16

global groups, 264
    ISPs, 343
    trust relationships, 265
    user accounts, 156
global scope options, 303
government domain names, 413
groups
    built-in, 156
    global, 156, 264-265
    local, 156, 264-265
    memberships, 230
    permissions, 166, 170
    trust relationships, 264-265
guests
    access rights, 69
    computer names, 67
    DCC, 57, 73
        configuration, 70
        connections, 70-71
    ECP parallel ports, 73
    passwords, 69
    serial ports, 73

H

half-duplex mode, 337
hard drives
    backups, 250, 294
    memory, 220
hard-wiring IP addresses, 54, 299
    limitations, 48
hardware requirements, 221
    DCC, 58-59
    networks, 19
    NT Server, 214-215
    Windows NT Backup, 249

Hardware Compatibility List (HCL), 215
Harris Computer Systems, Cyberguard Firewall, 422
headers
    compression, 349
    downloading, 398
help, *see* **technical support**
HexaBit JUNIOR, 382
hierarchical caching, 425, 427
home directories, 231
hops, 368
hosts, 84
    computer names, 67
    DCC, 57, 73
        configuration, 68
        connections, 70-71
    ECP parallel ports, 73
    files
        name resolution, 330
        sharing, 68-69
    IP addresses, 44, 411
    print sharing, 68-69
    serial ports, 73
hot plugging, 60
HP OpenView OmniBack II web site, 260
HTML (Hypertext Markup Language), 10, 405
HTTP (Hypertext Transfer Protocol), 11, 14, 382
hubs, 24
    collision domains, 24
    connecting, 23
    crossing, 110
hyperlinks, 376-377
Hypertext Markup Language (HTML), 10, 405
Hypertext Transfer Protocol (HTTP), 11, 14, 382

I

\i386 directory, 219
I/O (input/output-performance, 248
IBM, 111
identification (IDs)
    computers, 88
    domains, 240
    workgroups, 88, 240
IIS (Internet Information Server) installation, 218
IMAP (Internet Message Access Protocol), 390
inconsistent MAC addresses, 307
increasing
    hard drive memory, 220
    RAS bandwidth, 187-188
incremental backups, 137, 146
India Search Engine, 383
individual domain names, 414
information services domain names, 414
Info*seek* **search engine, 383**
infrared ports (IrDA), 58, 65, 72
InnocuLAN, 423
installation
    BDCs, 218
    cables, 111
    Client for Microsoft Networks, 79
    DCC, 65, 72
    DHCP server, 300-301
    Dial-Up Networking component, 347-348, 370
    IIS, 218

IPX/SPX, 66
    Microsoft Client for NetWare Network, 116
    modems, 339-341
    NDS service, 117
    networks, 218-219
        adapters, 78
        clients, 79-80
    Novell NetWare Client, 118, 201, 203-204
        print services, 202
        troubleshooting, 133
        Z.E.N. Works, 202
    Novell NT client, 211
    NT Server, 216-218
        FAT, 216
        hardware requirements, 214-215
        licensing modes, 217
        server-based, 222
        standalone servers, 218
    NTFS, 160, 216
    PDCs, 218
    printers, 131-132
    protocols, 66, 81
    RAS, 184-186, 194
    Resource Kit, 436
    SP3, 224-226
    TCP/IP, 104
    TechNet, 433-435
    Windows 98, 105, 145
    Windows NT DNS Server, 415
    WINS, 279-280
    see also deinstallation
Integralis, MIMEsweeper, 423
Integrated Services Digital Network (ISDN), cost, 344
Intel, Virus Protect, 423
interactive Web sites, 405
internal modems, 336

international domain
  names, 414
International Standards
  Organization (ISO), 36
Internet
  access patterns, 425
  AUP, 424
  connections, 356-357
  CSU/DSU, 411
  domain names, 413-414
  email, 416
  Information Server (IIS),
    218
  Message Access Protocol
    (IMAP), 390
  proxy servers, 425-429
  requirements, 411
  routers, 410-411
  security, 401-405
  traffic, 426
  viruses, 422-423
  see also newsgroups; IP
    addresses; ISPs; Telnet
    utility
Internet Connection Wizard
  configuration, 358-360
  Dial-Up Networking, 358
    directory services,
      364-365
    email services,
      362-363
    LDAP , 364-365
    modems, 360-362
    news services, 363-364
Internet Explorer, 374-378
  active channels, 379
  address bar, 375
  content area, 376
  current zone, 376
  function buttons, 375
  History bar, 377
  hyperlinks, 376-377

links bar, 375
pull-down menus, 375
search engines, 378
shortcuts, 378
SSL, 402
status bar, 376
subscriptions, 379
title bar, 375
URLs, 377
Windows NT, 406
Internet Filter web site, 429
InterScan E-Mail Virus
  Wall, 423
IntranetWare Clients for
  Windows 95 v2.2, 133
Iomega web site, 138
IP addresses, 42
  ARP, 324, 334
  configuration, 86
  DHCP, 49, 54
  finding, 334
  first octet, 43
  hard-wiring, 48, 54
  hosts, 44, 411
  length, 53
  Microsoft, 430
  networks, 43-44, 103, 411
  scopes, 302
  spoofing, 430
  static, 299
  subnet masks, 45-46, 103
ipconfig utility, 51, 315-316
IPX/SPX protocol, 40-41
  connections, 83
  frame type, 82
  header compression, 349
  installation, 66
  NetBIOS, 83
  network address, 83
  packets, 82

sockets, 83
source routing, 83
workstations, 53
IrDA ports (infrared ports),
  58, 65, 72
ISDN Integrated Services
  Digital Network), cost, 344
ISO (International
  Standards Organization),
  36
ISPs (Internet Service
  Providers), 359
  comparing, 345-346
  cost, 344-345
  dedicated connections,
    343
  dial-up access numbers,
    342
  disk storage, 343
  global access, 343
  local access, 343, 346
  modem port to user ratio,
    342, 345
  PPP, 342
  SLIP, 342
  speed, 343
  troubleshooting, 366-369
  Web site storage, 343

J

Japan, domain names, 414
Java, 404-405
  applets, 404
  bytecode files, 404
  Virtual Machine (JVM),
    404
JavaScript, 405
JAZ drives, 137-138

K-L

keys in Registry
  displaying, 261
  editing, 260
LANs (local area networks),
  8, 106-107
laptop computers
  DCC, 73
  infrared ports, 58
  Windows 98, 73
Last Known Good
  Configuration (LKGC),
  257, 261
layers in networking
  1 (physical layer), 37
  2 (data link layer), 37
  3 (network layer), 36, 53
  4 (transport layer), 36
  5 (session layer), 36
  6 (presentation layer), 36
  7 (application layer), 36
LDAP (Lightweight
  Directory Access
  Protocol), 364-365
leases (DHCP), 49
  acceptances, 50
  acknowledgements, 50
  active, 307
  duration, 302
  offers, 50
  renewals, 50
  requests, 50
length of passwords,
  227-228
LFN (Long File Name), 258
licensing modes
  per seat, 217, 222
  per server, 217, 222
Lightweight Directory
  Access Protocol, *see*
  LDAP, 364-365

LKGC (Last Known Good
  Configuration), 257, 261
lmhosts file, 278, 330, 334
local access
  accounts, 155
  files, 139
  groups, 156, 264-265
  ISPs, 343, 346
  permissions, 159, 180
  see also NTFS
local area networks (LANs),
  8, 106-107
locating remote hosts, 367
Location Profiles properties
  (Novell NetWare), 126
locked files, backups, 249
lockouts, user accounts,
  228-229
log files (Event Viewer), 236
  applications, 236, 274
  archiving, 276
  clearing, 276
  managing, 276
  overwriting, 276
  recording, 348
  security, 236, 274
  system, 236, 274
  viewing, 274-275, 296
logging options, print
  servers, 178
logical topology, 106-109
login scripts
  Novell NetWare Client,
    206
  user accounts, 231
log off/log on, 271
  clients, 80
  DUN connectoids, 352
  networks, 87, 97
  screens, 361
  single, 104
  user accounts, 232

Long File Name (LFN), 258
losing PDCs, 150
lurking newsgroups, 444

M

M-node (mixed node), 305
MAC addresses, 54
  inconsistent, 307
  NICs, 42
macro viruses, 423
magic cookies, 401-402
mailing lists, 445-446
management document
  printer permission, 175
managing
  log files, 276
  network printers, 176-177
  partitions, 285-286
  trust relationships,
    268-270
  user accounts, 233
  Windows NT DNS Server,
    416
  WINS, 280
  workstations, 119
mapping network drives,
  99-100, 129, 209
master browser computers,
  312
master domain models
  multiple, 153
  single, 152
MAUs (MSAUs), 31
Maximum Transfer Unit
  (MTU), 348
member servers, 222
memberships in groups, 230

memory
  flash, 337
  hard drive, 220
  NT Server requirements,
    214
merchant domain names,
414
Microsoft
  Client for NetWare
    Networks, 116-117,
    126-127, 134
  IP address, 430
  Knowledge Base
    (TechNet), 432
  newsgroups, 443
    browsers, 446
    cross-posting, 444
    lurking, 444
    moderated, 443
    newsreader, 444
  Novell Directory Services,
    117
  web site, 442
military domain names, 413
Milky Networks
  Corporation, BlackHole,
  422
MIMEsweeper, 423
mirroring, 288-289
  cost, 289
  disks, 248, 296
  troubleshooting, 291
misc newsgroups, 394
mismatched cables, 112
mixed node (M-node), 305
modems
  56K, 344
  bits per second (bps), 337
  cable, 344
  compatibility, 366

  cost, 344
  data communications
    protocols, 337-339
  deinstallation, 341
  Dial-Up Networking,
    360-362
  duplex modes, 337
  external, 336
  FAX capability, 337
  flash memory, 337
  installation, 339-341
  internal, 336
  Multilink, 187-188, 194
  RAS, 194
  standards, 337
moderated newsgroups,
394, 443
monitoring
  counters, 325
  wire activity, 334
Montana Pathfinder search
engine, 383
MS Client Service for
NetWare, 198
  configuration, 199
  connections, 207
  NDS, 199
MSAU (Multistation Access
Unit), 31
MTU (Maximum Transfer
Unit), 348
multi-node networks, 105
Multilink, 194
  clients, 188
  PPP connections, 353-354
  RAS, 187-188
multiple domain models,
153
Multistation Access Unit
(MSAU), 31

N

name resolution, 328
  hosts file, 330
  lmhosts file, 330
  NetWare, 133
  newsgroups, 394
  protocols, 126
  shares, 92
  UNC, 92, 99
  user accounts, 155
  Web sites, 382
  WINS, 278
  workstation, 305
NAT (Network Address
Translation), 412-413, 430
nbstat command, 320-321,
334
NCBS (NetBIOS Command
Blocks), 82
NCP (NetWare Core
Protocol), 123
NCSA Mosaic, 381
NDPS (Novell Distributed
Print Services), 118
NDS (Novell Directory
Service), 117, 199, 208
NEAR operator queries,
436
net use command, 173
NetBEUI (NetBIOS
Extended User Interface),
40
  broadcast packets, 39
  encapsulation, 39
  Protected mode, 82
  redirectors, 82
  sessions, 82

NetBIOS
  Command Blocks
    (NCBS), 82
  configuration, 84
  Extended User Interface,
    see NetBEUI
  IPX/SPX protocol, 83
**The Netherlands, domain
  names, 414**
NetNanny web site, 429
Netscape, 379-381
  newsreaders, 396
  SSL, 402
NetWare, 200
  Administrator
    (NWAdmin), 199
  backups, 202
  clients, 205-206
    configuration, 122
    installation, 118
  connections, 208
  Copy option, 210
  Core Protocol (NCP), 123
  Dial-Up Networking, 366
  installation, 201-204
  IP Gateway, 202
  login, 206
  Map Network Drive
    option, 209
  MS Client Service, 198
    configuration, 199
    connections, 207
    NDS, 199
  naming conventions, 133
  Network Neighborhood,
    128
  protocol preference, 206
  Salvage Files option, 209
  servers, 126-127
  Workstation Manager, 202
  Z.E.N Works, 202

**Network Address
  Translation (NAT),
  412-413, 430**
**Network Associates, Inc.,
  423**
Network dialog box
  opening, 239
  Services tab, 246
Network Monitor, 330-332
Network Neighborhood
  accessing, 104
  browse lists, 311-313
  NetWare 4, 128
  viewing, 98, 333
networks
  backbone, 16, 29
  backups, 137, 140
  benefits, 9
  bridges, 33
  cables, 6, 101
  client/server
    application server, 7
    dedicated server, 6
    file server, 7
    installation, 79-80
    print server, 7
  domains, 150-151
  drives
    disconnecting, 100-101
    mapping, 99-100, 129
    Windows NT Backup,
      258
  Ethernet, 15
    10Base2, 107-108
    10Base5, 108
    10BaseT, 109
    collisions, 17
    limitations, 16
  FDDI, 15-16
  hardware, 19
  hubs, 110

  installation, 218-219
  IP addresses, 83, 103, 411
    classes, 43
    first octet, 43
    hosts, 44
  layers
    ARP, 47-48
    IPX/SPX, 40-41
    default gateway, 46-47
    DHCP, 48-50
    IP addresses, 42-45
    routing, 36, 53
    TCP/IP, 41
    utilities, 50-52
  log on, 87, 97
  organizations domain
    names, 413
  peer-to-peer, 6, 14
    backups, 145
    workgroups, 88
  printers, 176-177
    configuration, 174
    pooling, 178
    scheduling, 179
  protocols, 6, 81
  routers, 30
  security, 419
    firewalls , 420-422
    proxy servers, 419-420
    viruses , 422-423
  software, 19
  switches, 27-30
    backplane, 29-30
  Token Ring, 15, 17-18
    cables, 24
    STP, 18
  Token Ring, 110
    cables, 113
    cost, 113
    errors, 18

MSAUs, 31
UTP, 18
workgroups, 149
see also Ethernet; NICs
newsgroups, 393, 443-445
  alternative, 394, 406
  articles, 394
    composing, 399
    follow-ups, 399-400
  browsers, 446
  business, 394
  computer, 394
  connections, 398
  cross-posting, 394, 444
  Dial-Up Networking,
    363-364
  discussion, 395
  flames, 394
  headers, 398
  lurking, 444
  Microsoft, 443-445
  miscellaneous, 394
  moderated, 394, 443
  naming conventions, 394
  news, 394
  newsreaders, 395-396,
    444-445
    configuration, 396-398
    Netscape
      Communicator, 396
  posting, 395
  reading, 398
  recreational, 394
  science, 395
  shouting, 395
  smileys, 395
  social issues, 395
  spamming, 363
  subscribing, 395
  threads, 395, 399, 445
  unsubscribing, 395
  see also Internet

**NICs (network interface
  cards), 19, 89, 218**
  adding, 241
  configuration, 78-79
  deleting, 241
  Ethernet, 20
  installation, 78
  MAC addresses, 42
  Plug-and-Play compliant,
    78
  protocols, 67
  Token Ring networks, 20
  UTP, 20
**no access permissions, 165,
  175**
non-browser computers, 312
NOT query, 436
notebook computers, 72
**notification options, print
  servers, 178**
**NovaNet 7 Windows NT
  tool, 260**
Novell NetWare Client, 200
  backups, 202
  browsing, 128
  clients, 206
  configuration, 122,
    205-206
  connections, 208
  Copy option, 210
  Directory Service (NDS),
    117, 199, 208
  Distributed Print Services
    (NDPS), 118
  installation, 118, 201,
    203-204, 211
    print services, 202
    troubleshooting, 133
  IP Gateway, 202
  login, 206
  mapping drives, 129, 209

printers
  adding to queues, 132
  capturing ports, 130
  point and print,
    131-132
  uncapturing ports, 131
  properties, 123-126
  protocol preferences, 206
  Salvage Files option, 209
  servers connections,
    126-127
  web site, 442
  Windows 95/98, 133
    downloading, 118
    Target Server Agent,
      144
  Workstation Manager, 202
  Z.E.N. Works, 202
nslookup utility, 416
**NTFS (NT File System),
  156, 216, 221, 259**
  auditing, 271
  converting from FAT, 158
  deinstallation, 220
  disk partitions, 157-158
  DOS, 157
  dual-boot, 157
  installation, 160
  partitions, 160
  permissions, 180-181
    assigning, 167,
      169-171
    change permission, 168
    delete, 168
    execute, 168
    files, 167, 169-171
    folders, 167, 169-171
    read-only, 168
    security, 157-159
    shared folders
      permissions, 171

standard, 168-169, 181
take ownership, 168
write, 168
Windows NT
**null-modem serial cables
(cross-over cables), 62-63,
77, 101**
**NWAdmin (NetWare
Administrator), 199**

O

offers, DHCP leases, 50
**offline reading of
newsgroups, 398**
**one-way trust relationships,
265-267, 296**
**online reading of
newsgroups, 398**
**online technical support,
439**
**Ontrack Computer Systems
Inc., Dr. Solomon's
Anti-Virus Toolkit, 423**
opening
resources, 236
Network dialog box, 239
options
scopes, 303-305
Windows NT Backup, 261
OR query, 436
**organizational domain
names, 413**
**OSI (Open Systems
Interconnection) model**
application layer, 36
data link layer, 37
network layer, 36, 53
physical layer, 37
presentation layer, 36

session layer, 36
transport layer, 36
Outlook Express, 390-392
**overriding permissions, 171,
181**
overwriting log files, 276
**Ownership
Information(TechNet), 432**

P

P-node (peer node), 305
packet bursts, 123
Packet Internet Groper,
see **ping utility**
packets, 31, 33, 82
filtering, 421
MTU, 348
rebuilding, 25
transmitting, 27
paging files, 220
**parallel LapLink cables
(InterLink), 64-65**
parallel ports, 60
bidirectional, 60
DCC, 58, 72
ECP, 64-65, 73
EPP (Enhanced), 61, 64
Extended Capabilities
(ECP), 61
speed, 61-62
unidirectional, 60
**Parallel Technologies web
sites, 65**
parameters
ipconfig/all command, 315
tracert command, 322
partitions
2GB, 286
boot, 157, 160, 215, 284

converting, 160
EISA utilities, 286
extended, 284
FAT, 158
formatting, 157
managing, 285-286
NTFS, 158
numbers, 292-293
primary, 284, 293
system, 157, 215
passwords
case sensitive, 155
editing, 229
expiration dates, 159
guests, 69
length, 227-228
maximum length, 160
one-way trust
relationships, 266
RAS, 192
restrictions, 228
shares, 95, 104
troubleshooting, 366
unique, 228, 246
user accounts, 155, 230
paths
shared folders, 171
user accounts, 231
**Personal Computer
Memory Card
International Association
(PCMCIA), 370**
**PDCs (primary domain
controllers), 160, 221**
authentication, 151
BDCs, 244
dedicated servers, 151
demoting, 243-244
domain models, 152-153
Exchange servers, 151
installation, 218
losing, 150

trust relationships, 267
user accounts, 155-156
peer node (P-node), scope options, 305
peer-to-peer networks, 6, 14
  backups, 145
  clients, 79-80
  configuration, 92
  LANs, 8
  workgroups, 88
Pegasus Mail, 392
per seat/server licensing modes, 217, 222
performance
  I/O (input/output), 248
  monitoring, 324-326
  tape drives, 138
permissions
  directories, 272-273
  effective, 167, 171, 181
  FAT, 159
  files, 169, 272-273
  folders, 169, 181
  groups, 166, 170
  local, 159
  NTFS, 158-159, 180-181
    assigning, 167, 169-171
    change permission, 168
    delete, 168
    execute, 168
    files, 181
    folders, 181
    read-only, 168
    standard, 181
    take ownership, 168
    write, 168
  overriding, 171, 181
  printers, 175, 273
    full control, 176
    manage document, 175
    no access, 175

RAS, 188, 190
Scheduler service, 258
shared folders, 171, 181
  assigning, 164-167
  change, 166
  full control, 166
  no access, 165
  read, 165
standard, 168-169
users, 166, 170
Windows NT Backup, 257
persistant cookies, 401
phrase queries, 436
physical bus, 160, 108
  10Base2, 108
  10Base5, 108
physical layer (layer 1), 37
physical security, 159
ping utility, 51-52, 102, 104, 316-317, 333, 367-368
pinouts, 63-64
plain old telephone service (POTS), 344
planning backups, 136
Plug-and-Play (PnP) compliant, 59, 78
plug-ins, 374
point and print feature, 131-132, 211
Point-to-Point Protocol (PPP), 342, 370
  connectoids, 352, 361
  Dial-Up Adapter, 348
  multilink connections, 353-354
  RAS, 184
policies for user accounts, 227-229
pool folders, print servers, 178
pooling printers, 178, 181

POP (Post Office Protocol), 390
populated cable segments, 109
ports
  infrared, 65
  parallel, 58, 60
    bidirectional, 60
    Extended Capabilities (ECP), 61
    unidirectional, 60
  printer
    capturing, 130
    uncapturing, 131
  RAS, 191
  serial, 58
    hot plugging, 60
    UART, 59-60
Post Office Protocol (POP), 390
posting to newsgroups, 395, 400
potential brower computers, 312
POTS (plain old telephone service), 344
PPP (Point-to-Point Protocol), 342, 370
  connectoids, 352, 361
  Dial-Up Adapter, 348
  multilink connections, 353-354
  RAS, 184
presentation layer (layer 6), 36
primary disk partitions, 284, 293
primary domain controllers (PDCs), 150, 160, 221
  authentication, 151
  BDCs, 244
  dedicated servers, 151

demoting, 243-244
domain models, 152-153
Exchange servers, 151
installation, 218
losing, 150
trust relationships, 267
user accounts, 155-156
primary hard drives, 248
print servers, 7, 174, 202
logging options, 178
notification options, 178
pool folders, 178
properties, 177-178
security, 7
user error, 7
workstations, 7
print sharing, 92-93
disabling, 355
hosts, 68-69
TCP/IP, 355
printers, 174
adding to queues, 132
auditing, 273
capturing, 130
document spooling, 179
installation, 131-132
networks
configuration, 174
managing, 176-177
scheduling, 179
Novell NetWare, 131-132
permissions, 273
full control, 176
manage document, 175
no access, 175
pooling, 178, 181
sharing, 96-97, 181
uncapturing, 131
workstations, 119
Prodigy Internet, 359

profiles of user accounts, 231
promoting BDCs to PDCs, 243-244
properties
directories, 272
files, 272
Novell NetWare clients
Advanced Login, 123
Advanced Settings, 123
Client, 124
Contextless Login, 124
Default Capture, 125
Location Profiles, 126
Protocol Preferences, 126
Service Location, 126
print servers, 177-178
TCP/IP, 314
Protocol Preferences properties (Novell NetWare), 126
protocols
adding, 80-82, 240
binding, 66, 81
deleting, 66, 81, 240
email, 389
installation, 66, 81
LDAP, 371
modems, 338-339
name resolution, 126
networks, 6, 81
Novell NetWare, 206
PPP, 184
RAS
clients, 194
configuration, 187
SLIP, 184
Windows NT, 219
workstations, 101
see also specific protocols

proxy servers, 425-427
caching, 430
hierarchical, 427
Web server
acceleration, 427-429
Dial-Up Networking, 362
security, 419-420
WWW, 424
purchasing TechNet, 432
push/pull replication partners (WINS), 280

Q-R

queries, 436, 440
queues, printers, 132
RAID (redundant array of inexpensive disks), *see* disks, mirroring; stripe set with parity
Raptor Systems, Eagle, 422
RAS (Remote Access Service), 58, 183
administration, 189-191
bandwidth, 187-188
call back options, 191
clients, 194
Dial-Up Networking, 193
encryption, 192
Event Viewer, 191
installation, 184-186, 194
modems, 187-188
NT Workstation, 184, 195
passwords, 192
permissions, 188, 190
PPP, 184
protocols, 187
routers, 194
screens, 186

servers, 195
Service Pack 3, 186
SLIP, 184
status, 190, 192, 195
user accounts, 233
read-only
backups, 249
folders, 104, 165
NTFS permissions, 168
shares, 95, 165
reading newsgroups, 398
rebuilding packets, 25
rec newsgroups, 394
receptacles, 111
reconnections, shared
folders, 172
recording log files, 348
recreational domain names,
414
redirectors, 82
reducing Internet traffic,
426
redundant array of
inexpensive disks (RAID),
see **disks, mirroring; stripe**
set with parity
registration, domain names,
414, 430
Registry
backups, 146, 254-255,
258
editing, 255-257
keys
displaying, 261
editing, 260
LKGC, 257
remote computers, 249
restoring, 146, 255, 257
Windows NT, 257
reinstallation, Service Pack
3, 186, 246

reloading remote name
cache, 321
Remote Access Service,
see **RAS**
remote hosts
accessing, 387-389
backups, 146, 249, 258
disconnections, 229
locating, 367
name cache, 321
testing, 368
renewals of DHCP leases, 50
repeaters
cables, 109
Ethernet, 25
replication, push/pull
partners, 280
requests for DHCP leases,
50
reservation, clients, 306
Resource Kit, 440
AT command syntax, 437
installation, 436
TechNet, 432
utilities, 436
resources
Network Neighborhood,
333
open, 236
restarting Windows, 101
Restore Wizard (Backup
utility), 142-143
restoring
files, 136, 142, 252
Registry files, 146, 257
Windows NT, 255
restrictions, passwords, 228
reverse-proxy cache, 430
RG-58 cable, 108, 113
Ring In/Ring Out (RI/RO)
receptacle, 111

ring topology networks, 107
RJ-45 connectors
10BaseT cables, 109
UTP cables, 111
route tables, 323
routers, 30, 32
command, 322
hops, 368
Internet, 410-411
packets, 31
RAS, 194
scope options, 304
screening, 422
running DCC with DUN, 72

S

Salvage Files option (Novell
NetWare), 209
scheduling
backups, 143-144
networks, 179
sci newsgroups, 395
scopes, 85, 309
creating, 301-303
IP addresses, 302
leases
active, 307
duration, 302
names, 126
options, 309-310
adding, 303-304
broadcast node, 305
deleting, 304
mixed node, 305
peer node, 305
routers, 304
subnet masks, 302

screens
  log on, 361
  RAS configuration, 186
  routers, 422
scripts
  commands, 371
  DUN connectoids, 354
SCSI controllers, 292
Seagate Software
  Backup Exec Desktop 98,
    144
  web site, 259
search engines, 378, 383,
  441-442
  see also Web sites
secondary hard drives, 248
secondary servers, 279
Secure HTTP (S-HTTP),
  403
Secure Sockets Layer (SSL),
  402-403
security, 159
  access control, 92
  application servers, 7
  auditing, 271
  binding, 84
  FAT, 157
  file servers, 7
  gateways
    application-level, 421
    circuit-level, 421
    packet-filtering, 421
    screening routers, 422
  Internet
    cookies, 401-402
    Java, 404-405
    shopping, 402-403
  log files, 236, 274
  networks, 419
    firewalls, 420-422
    proxy servers, 419-420

NTFS, 157-158
passwords
  case sensitive, 155
  expiration dates, 159
  guests, 69
  maximum length, 160
  user accounts, 155
permissions, 158-159
physical, 159
print servers, 7
RAS, 191-192
share-level, 93-95
viruses, 422-423
Serial Line Internet
  Protocol (SLIP), 184, 342,
  352, 361, 370
serial ports
  baud rates, 60
  DCC, 58
  guests, 73
  hosts, 73
  hot plugging, 60
  null-modem, 62-63
  speed, 61-62
  UART, 59-60
  USB, 59
Server Manager, 319-320
  domains, 234-235
  shares, 235
server-based installation,
  222
servers
  bindings, 241
  member, 222
  NetWare, 126-127
  NICs, 241
  print
    logging options, 178
    notification options,
     178
    properties, 177-178
    spool folders, 178

protocols, 240
proxy, 424
RAS, 195
services
  adding, 240
  deleting, 240
  starting, 243
standalone, 218
statistics, 334
Service List Protocol (SLP),
  126
Service Location properties
  (Novell NetWare), 126
Service Pack 3, 223, 432
  deinstallation, 226-227
  installation, 224-226
  reinstallation, 186, 246
Services option
  adding, 240
  Control Panel, 242-243,
    246
  deleting, 240
  Network dialog box, 246
  starting, 243
sessions
  layer 5, 36
  NetBEUI, 82
Setup files, RAS
  installation, 185
shares, 7
  access rights, 95, 171, 173
  administrative, 163, 181
  comments, 95
  connections, 172
  creating, 162
  disabling, 95
  drives, 94-96, 171
  enabling, 95
  expanding, 172
  files, 92-93
  folders, 69, 94-96

naming conventions, 92
network drives, 99-100
paths, 171
permissions, 171, 181
    assigning, 164-167
    change, 166
    full control, 166
    no access, 165
    read, 165
printers, 92-93, 96-97,
    174, 181
reconnections, 172
resources, 103
security, 95
Server Manager, 235
violation errors, 104
Windows 98, 92
**shielded twisted pair cable
(STP), 18, 20, 110**
**shopping on the Internet,
security, 402-403**
shortcuts
    Internet Explorer, 378
    telnet utility, 406
shouting, newsgroups, 395
**signal attenuation, cables,
112**
**Simple Mail Transfer
Protocol (SMTP), 390, 423**
**Simple Network
Management Protocol
(SNMP), 120**
**single domain models,
152-153**
skipped files, 261
**SLIP (Serial Line Internet
Protocol), 184, 342, 352,
361, 370**
**SLP (Service List Protocol),
126**
smileys, 395

**SMTP (Simple Mail
Transfer Protocol), 390,
423**
**SNMP (Simple Network
Management Protocol),
120**
soc newsgroups, 395
**sockets, IPX/SPX protocol,
83**
software
    compression, 352
    networks, 19
source routing, 83
**SP3 (Service Packs), 223,
432**
    deinstallation, 226-227
    installation, 224-226
    reinstallation, 186, 246
spamming, newsgroups, 363
speed
    ISPs, 343
    modems, 337
    ports, 61-62
spoofing IP addresses, 430
**spooling documents to
printers, 179**
**SSL (Secure Sockets Layer),
402-403**
standalone servers, 218
standards, modems, 337
star topology, 32, 106
starting
    Backup utility, 138-139
    Network Monitor, 330-331
    Outlook Express, 390
    services, 243
    Windows NT Backup, 249
static IP addresses, 299
status
    RAS, 190-192, 195
    servers, 334
    stripe set with parity, 290

storage
    email, 343
    Web sites, 343
**STP (shielded twisted pair)
cable, 18, 20, 110**
stripe set with parity
    disks, 287
    enabling, 291
    fault tolerance, 287
    status, 290
    volume sets, 288
subnet masks, 54, 302
    classes, 103
    IP addresses, 45-46
subscribing
    Internet Explorer, 379
    newsgroups, 395
    TechNet, 432
support, *see* **technical
support; troubleshooting;
utilities**
SurfWatch web site, 429
Swiss Search engine, 383
switches, 27-30
    backbone, 29
    backplane, 29-30
    Ethernet, 29
    Fast Ethernet, 29
    winnt.exe files, 219
**Symantec Norton AntiVirus,
423**
system
    log files, 236, 274
    partitions, 157, 215-216

T

**take ownership NTFS
permissions, 168**
talk newsgroups, 395

tape drives, 137
  backups, 138
  cost, 137
  Windows NT Backup, 249
Target Server Agent (Novell), 144
Task Manager, 327
Task Scheduler, 143-144
TCP/IP, 41-42, 46-47, 50
  advanced settings, 84
  ARP, 47-48, 334
  binding, 83-84
  Client for Microsoft Networks, 89
  configuration, 83, 369
  default gateway, 46-47
  DHCP, 49-50
  DNS, 84
  file sharing, 355
  gateways, 85
  installation, 104
  IP addresses, 42, 86
    classes, 43
    first octet, 43
    networks, 43-44
    subnet masks, 45-46
  NetBIOS, 84
  PING utility, 102
  print sharing, 355
  properties, 314
  utilities, 52
    ipconfig, 51
    ping, 51-52
    winipcfg, 50
  WINS, 85-86
TechNet, 440
  cost, 432, 439
  Drivers and Patches, 432
  Evaluation and Reviewers Guides, 432
  installation, 433-435

  Microsoft Knowledge Base, 432
  Ownership Information, 432
  queries, 436
  Resource Kit, 432
  Service Packs, 432
  subscribing, 432
  Technical Information, 432
  Training Materials, 432
  web sites, 432
  White Papers, 432
Technical Information (TechNet), 432
technical support
  online, 439
  Resource Kit, 436
  see also troubleshooting
TechnoFIND search engine, 384
Telnet utility, 11-12, 14
  remote hosts, 387-389
  shortcuts, 406
temporary backup files, 249
terminators, cables, 112
testing remote hosts, 368
Thailand domain names, 414
thicknets (10Base5 networks), 108
thinnets (10Base 2 networks), 107
  cables, 22, 108
  coaxial cable, 76
  logical bus, 108
  see also Ethernet
threads
  downloading, 399
  mailing lists, 445

  newsgroups, 395
  newsreaders, 445
Time-To-Live (TTL), 426
TLDs (top-level domains), 413-414
Token Ring network, 15, 17, 110
  cables, 24, 113
    IBM, 111
    STP, 110
    UTP, 110
  cost, 113
  errors, 18
  MSAUs, 31
  NICs, 20
  physical topology, 113
  UTP, 18
top-level domains (TLDs), 413-414
topologies
  bus, 106
  logical, 106
  physical, 106
  ring, 107
  star, 106-107
tracert utility, 321-322, 334, 368
traffic on the Internet, reducing, 426
Training Materials(TechNet), 432
transceivers
  10Base5 networks, 108
  external, 106
transmitting packets, 27
transport layer (layer 4), 36
Trend Micro Devices, InterScan E-Mail Virus Wall, 423

troubleshooting

active process, 327

cables, 62, 112

collision domains, 28

Dial-Up Networking, 365-366

dialers, 367

encryption, 366

event logs, 328

files, 296

ISP connections, 366-369

mirror failures, 291

modems, 366

network cables, 101

Novell NetWare Client, 133

NTFS installation, 160

passwords, 366

printers, 181

RAS

  encryption, 192

  Event Viewer, 191

  passwords, 192

sharing violation errors, 104

tasks, 327

user accounts, 160, 366

Windows 98, 101

see also utilities

trust relationships, 263

broken, 268-269

domains, 151-153, 160

groups, 264-265

managing, 268-270

one-way, 265-267, 296

PDCs, 267

two-way, 267, 296

TTL (Time-To-Live), 426

two-way trust relationships, 267, 296

U

UART (Universal Asynchronous Receiver Transmitter), 59-60

UCM (Universal Cable Module), 64-65

UNC (Universal Naming Convention), 92, 99, 104

uncapturing printer ports, 131

unidirectional parallel ports, 60

uniform resource locators (URLs), 11, 14

editing, 406

Internet Explorer, 377

unique passwords, 228, 246

United States domain names, 414

Universal Asynchronous Receiver Transmitter (UART), 59-60

Universal Cable Module (UCM), 64-65

Universal Naming Convention (UNC), 92, 99, 104

Universal Serial Bus (USB), 59

unshielded twisted pair cable (UTP), 110

NICs, 20

Token Ring networks, 18

RJ-45 connectors, 111-112

unsubscribing from newsgroups, 395

upgrading

Ethernet, 23, 109

WINS, 281

uploading files, 10

URLs (uniform resource locators), 11, 14

editing, 406

Internet Explorer, 377

USB (Universal Serial Bus), 59

Usenet, *see* **newsgroups**

user accounts, 154

BDCs, 155-156

built-in, 154

connections, 231

creating, 154, 229-233

disconnection, 258

domain, 155

errors, 7

groups, 156

home directories, 231

local, 155

lockouts, 228-229

login scripts, 231-232

managing, 233

naming conventions, 155, 366

passwords, 227-228, 230

  case sensitive, 155

  editing, 229

  maximum length, 160

  restrictions, 228

  unique, 228

paths, 231

PDCs, 155-156

permissions, 166, 170

policies, 227-229

profiles, 231

RAS server, 233

remote, 229

security, 155

Server Manager, 235

troubleshooting, 160, 366

User Manager, 155
audit policy, 270
group memberships, 230
user accounts
creating, 229-233
disconnections, 229
home directories, 231
lockouts, 228-229
login scripts, 231-232
managing, 233
passwords, 227-228
paths, 231
profiles, 231
RAS server, 233
utilities, 52
arp command, 323-324
Event Viewer, 328
ipconfig, 315-316
nbstat command, 320-321
nslookup, 416
NT Diagnostic, 318
Performance Monitor,
324-326
PING, 102, 104, 333,
367-368
ping command, 316-317
Resource Kit, 436
route command, 322
Server Manager, 319-320
Task Manager, 327
TCP/IP, 50-52
Telnet, 11-12, 14,
387-389, 406
tracert, 321-322, 334, 368
winipcfg, 314, 369
see also troubleshooting
**UTP (unshielded twisted
pair) cable, 110**
NICs, 20
Token Ring networks, 18
RJ-45 connectors, 111-112

V

V.x protocols, 338-339
verifying backups, 141
viewing
ARP frames, 332
log files, 274-275, 296
Network Neighborhood,
98, 333
open resources, 236
WINS database, 282-283
**virtual serial COM ports
(infrared ports), 58, 65, 72**
viruses, 423
volume sets, 288

W

**WANs (wide area
networks), 8, 14, 31**
**Warp Nine Engineering web
site, 65**
Web browsers, 10, 14
1X Browser, 382
HexaBit JUNIOR, 382
Internet Explorer, 374-378
NCSA Mosaic, 381
Netscape Communicator,
379-381
newsgroups, 446
WebSurfer for Windows
95, 382
Wildcat! Navigator, 382
Web sites
Agent, 396
blocking access, 429
CyberPatrol, 429
CyberSitter, 429
domain names, 414
email software, 393

firewalls, 422
Gravity, 396
HP OpenView OmniBack
II, 260
interactive, 405
Internet Filter, 429
Iomega, 138
mailing lists, 446
Microsoft, 442
naming conventions, 382
NetNanny, 429
newsreaders, 396
NovaNet, 260
Novell, 442
Parallel Technologies, 65
proxy servers, 424
Seagate Software, 259
search engines, 383,
441-442
security, 402-403
servers, 10, 14, 425-429
storage, 343
SurfWatch, 429
TechNet, 432
Virtual Access, 396
virus protection, 423
Warp Nine Engineering,
65
WebScanX, 423
WebShield, 423
**WebSurfer for Windows 95,
382**
White Papers(TechNet), 432
**wide area networks
(WANs), 8, 14, 31**
wildcard queries, 436
Wildcat! Navigator, 382
**WINAT Command
Scheduler, 254**

Windows 95/98
Backup utility, 138, 145-146
DCC, 73
DUN scripting commands, 371
FAT16/32, 259
FTP servers, 385
IntranetWare Clients for Windows 95 v2.2, 133
laptop computers, 73
networks, 105
Novell client, 133
Outlook Express, 390
peer-to-peer networks, 92
point and print, 211
restarting, 101
shares, 92, 103
Windows for Workgroups, 150
Windows Internet Name Service, *see* **WINS**
Windows NT Backups
automating, 253-254
command-line options, 261
files, 250-252
hard drives, 250
hardware requirements, 249
LFN (Long File Name), 258
locked files, 249
permissions, 257
read-only files, 249
Registry, 254-255, 257
remote network drives, 258
Scheduler service, 258
skipped files, 261
starting, 249

tape drives, 249
temporary files, 249
Windows NT Server
ARCserveIT tool, 259
AT Scheduler, 253
Backup Exec tool, 259
boot disk, 294
Diagnostic, 318
DNS Server, 415-416
FAT partitions, 220, 259
fault tolerance, 248
HP OpenView OmniBack II tool, 260
installation
BDCs, 218
FAT, 216
hardware requirements, 214-215
NTFS, 216
PDCs, 218
icensing modes, 217
standalone servers, 218
Internet Explorer, 406
member servers, 222
NovaNet 7 tool, 260
NTFS, 220, 259
protocols, 219
RAS connections, 195
Resource Kit, 254
restarting, 101
Welcome screen, 212
Windows NT Workstation, 184, 195
winipcfg utility, 50, 314, 369
winnt.exe files, 219
WINS (Windows Internet Name Service), 277, 295
addresses, 279
configuration, 85-86
database, 282-283

DHCP server, 86, 278
installation, 279-280
Manager, 280
name resolution, 278
replication, 280
secondary servers, 279
updating, 281
workstations, 305
wire activity, 334
wizards
Backup utility
Add New Hardware, 139
Backup, 139-141
Restore, 142-143
Internet Connection, 358-360
word queries, 436
workgroups, 149
identification, 88
IDs, 240
models, 160
scopes, 85
workstations
addresses, 53
application servers, 7
file servers, 7
lease renewals, 50
managing, 119
name resolution, 305
print servers, 7
printer connections, 119
protocols, 101
RAS connections, 195
World Wide Web (WWW), *see* **web sites**
WORM drives, 137-138
write NTFS permissions, 168
write performance, 289
WWW (World Wide Web), *see* **web sites**

X-Z

X.500 directories, 117
Yahoo! search engine, 383,
 441
ZIP drives, 137-138